Readings in Western Civilization

𝔊 **Vere dignum**

University of Chicago Readings in Western Civilization
John W. Boyer and Julius Kirshner, General Editors

University of Chicago
Readings in Western Civilization

John W. Boyer and Julius Kirshner, General Editors

1
The Greek
Polis

**Edited by Arthur W. H. Adkins
and Peter White**

The University of Chicago Press

Chicago and London

Eric Cochrane, 1928–1985

ἀθάνατος μνήμη
Immortal memory

DF222
G74

Arthur W. H. Adkins is the Edward Olson Professor in the departments of Classical Languages and Literatures, New Testament and Early Christian Literature, and Philosophy, and in the College, and he is Chairman of the Committee on the Ancient Mediterranean World.

Peter White is associate professor in the departments of Classical Languages and Literatures and the Committee on the Ancient Mediterranean World and in the College.

The University of Chicago Press, Chicago 60637
The University of Chicago Press, Ltd., London
© 1986 by The University of Chicago
All rights reserved. Published 1986
Printed in the United States of America
95 94 93 92 91 90 89 88 87 86   5 4 3 2 1

Library of Congress Cataloging-in-Publication Data
Main entry under title:

University of Chicago readings in Western civilization.

  Includes bibliographies and indexes.
  Contents: v. 1. The Greek polis / edited by Arthur
W.H. Adkins and Peter White—   —v. 4. Medieval
Europe / edited by Julius Kirshner and Karl F. Morrison.
    1. Civilization, Occidental—History—Sources.
2. Europe—Civilization—Sources. I. Boyer, John W.
II. Kirshner, Julius. III. Title: Readings in Western
civilization.
CB245.U64   1986   940   85-16328
ISBN 0-226-06934-6 (v. 1)
ISBN 0-226-06935-4 (pbk.: v. 1)

Contents

Series Editors' Foreword

This series is the result of almost four decades of teaching the History of Western Civilization course at the College of the University of Chicago. The course was founded in its present form in the late 1940s by a group of young historians at Chicago, including William H. McNeill, Christian Mackauer, and Sylvia Thrupp, and has been sustained during the past twenty-five years by the distinguished teaching of Eric Cochrane, Hanna H. Gray, Charles M. Gray, and Karl J. Weintraub. In the beginning it served as a counterpoint to the antihistorical and positivistic thrust of the general education curriculum in the social sciences in the Hutchins College. Western Civilization has since been incorporated as a year-long course into different parts of the College program, from the first to the last year. It now forms part of the general intercivilizational requirement for sophomores and juniors. It is still taught, as it has been almost constantly since its inception, in discussion groups ranging from twenty to thirty students.

Although both the readings and the instructors of the course have changed over the years, its purpose has remained the same. It seeks not to provide students with morsels of Western culture, nor to nourish their moral and aesthetic sensitivities, and much less to attract recruits for the history profession. Its purpose instead is to raise a whole set of complex conceptual questions regarding the nature of time and change and the intended and unintended consequences of human action and consciousness. Students in this course learn to analyze past events and ideas by rigorously examining a variety of texts. This is in contrast to parallel courses in the social sciences, which teach students to deploy synchronic and quantitative techniques in analyzing society, usually without reference to historical context or process.

Ours is a history course that aims not at imparting relevant facts or exotic ideas but at providing students with the critical tools by which to analyze texts produced in the distant or near past. It also serves a related purpose: to familiarize students with major epochs of that Western historical tradition to which most of them, albeit at times unknowingly, are heirs. The major curricular vehicle of the course is the *Readings in Western Civilization*, a nine-volume series of primary sources in translation, beginning with Periclean Athens and concluding with Europe in the twentieth century. The series is not meant to be a comprehensive survey of Western history. Rather, in each volume, we provide a large number of documents on specific themes in the belief that depth, not breadth, is the surest antidote to superficiality. The very extensiveness of the documentation in each volume allows for a variety of approaches to the same theme. At the same time the concentrated focus of individual volumes makes it possible for them to serve as source readings in more advanced and specialized courses.

Many people contributed to the publication of these volumes. The enthusiastic collaboration and labors of the members of the Western Civilization staff made it possible for these *Readings* to be published. We thank Barbara Boyer for providing superb editorial direction to the project and Mary Van Steenbergh for her dedication in creating beautifully text-edited manuscripts. Steven Wheatley's advice in procuring funding for this project was invaluable. Members of the University of Chicago Press have given their unstinting support and guidance. We also appreciate the confidence and support accorded by Donald N. Levine, the Dean of the College at the University of Chicago. Above all, we are deeply grateful for the extraordinary dedication, energy, and erudition which our late colleague and former chairperson of the course, Eric Cochrane, contributed to the *Readings in in Western Civilization*.

We are grateful to the National Endowment for the Humanities for providing generous funding for the preparation and publication of the volumes.

John W. Boyer and Julius Kirshner

General Introduction

The *polis*, or city-state, was the characteristic political form in Greece when the Greeks learned to write in the late eighth century B.C., and for the next four hundred years it remained the environment in which most Western literature was produced. The polis was an autonomous community; in formal terms it usually consisted of one or more magistrates or executives, a council, which was both advisory and deliberative, and a citizen assembly. But definitions varied greatly from one community to another. The three parts of the government could be differently balanced, and qualifications for participation in each could be fixed broadly or narrowly. Actual city-states ranged from hereditary monarchies and tyrannies at one extreme to radical democracies at the other. Fifth-century Athens counted as one of the latter because all significant power rested with the citizen assembly, and there was no property qualification for citizenship. But even Athens did not confer citizenship on all within its borders. It had a large slave population and a class of permanent residents (called *metics*) who did not have Athenian parents and were thereby barred from citizenship.

Geographically, the polis consisted of a political and religious center and a tract of countryside. The center was usually a fortified town (though the Spartans did not protect themselves with walls). The countryside contained much of the community's economic base: farms, vineyards, olive groves, grazing lands, and quarries or mines, depending on the region. Often it included outlying villages whose political functions had been wholly integrated with the central government. Athens was a large city-state, covering the entire promontory of Attica, an area of almost a thousand square miles. Its territory, both the town and the country districts, was carved into more than a hundred geographical and administrative subdivisions called *demes*.

The contemporaries who described and pondered the political experience of Athens have made it incomparably better known to us than any

1

other polis. Documents about Athens or by Athenians make up at least
two-thirds of this volume. The documents have not been arranged in topical categories, however, because in most cases they pose more than single
issues. Narrowly focused texts, such as letters, diplomatic papers, and
topical essays, are practically nonexistent for the fifth century. Not even
political speeches are extant until the next century. What we find instead
is a rich tradition of poetry, most recently enlarged by the addition of
drama, and a newly formed but ambitious prose literature consisting of
history, forensic oratory, and philosophical investigations into the cos-
mos, society, and human ethics.

The documents in this volume fall into four unequal groups. The first
two documents, in the opinion of fifth-century Greeks, provided memories of what Hellenic society was like toward the close of the heroic age,
some eight centuries earlier. The second group (documents 3–6) consists
of short pieces and fragments by poets from four different cities of mainland Greece. Earlier than all the prose writers, and predemocratic if not
positively antidemocratic in spirit, they speak openly of values that continued to motivate political behavior long after theorists and reformers
attempted to make a science of government. The great majority of documents (7–18) portray aspects of the polis, and chiefly of Athens, during
the fifth and fourth centuries B.C. (The *History* of Thucydides is too long
to be included here, but at Chicago it is the primary text in the light of
which all others are read.) The documents have most to say about theories and the practical functioning of government and about the impact
of constitutions on human nature; about citizenship in relation to issues,
such as status, wealth, and individualism, that complicate it; about the
meaning of justice and law; about education and its close orientation to
civic purposes; and about the all-powerful role of oratory in public life.
One selection (document 10) gives a rare look at the position of women
in Greek society. Other important aspects of the polis (slavery, economy,
and religion, for example) are poorly documented in this volume; that is
because, in general, these subjects cannot be illustrated with appropriate,
connected readings. The last two documents are chronologically the latest
and make a kind of epilogue; they describe philosophies of action developed for an environment in which the polis had ceased to be the most
important form of political organization.

Notes and Explanations

Money

Four denominations are mentioned in the readings. The basic unit of currency was a silver coin, the drachma; it is impossible to convert this or

any other denomination into modern money equivalents, but a drachma was a day's wage for a laborer. A drachma was worth six obols (three obols being the daily stipend for jury service at Athens). One hundred drachmas made a mina, and six thousand made a talent.

Dating

Where possible, dates are converted to a specific year B.C. But many events in Athenian history are dated only by archon-years; that is, they are synchronized with the series of magistrates after whom the years were named. An archon's term ran roughly from midsummer of one of our years to midsummer of the next. Archon-years therefore have to be converted to split dates, like 423/422 B.C.

Court Procedure

Many documents in this volume are connected in some way with the Athenian judicial system, which was organized very differently from any current system. In the first place, Athenians distinguished between public and private cases rather than between criminal and civil cases. Public cases were usually prosecuted, not by officials like our public prosecutors, but by ordinary citizens who brought suit on their own initiative. In certain kinds of cases the successful prosecutor collected a substantial reward, and some prosecutions were motivated by the desire to do harm to enemies. Both the prosecutor and the defendant had to speak and handle the presentation of evidence in person. There were not yet professionals who conducted legal business for the layman, though there were speech-writers, who could be hired to write a speech for prosecutor or defendant to deliver. Under the democratic regime, magistrates at Athens gradually lost the power to render verdicts on cases brought to their attention. They continued to conduct preliminary proceedings, but by the fourth century all cases of any significance were submitted to a jury trial. There were several different courts, to which cases were routed according to their nature. The jury panels in all courts were huge by modern standards, consisting of from two hundred to two thousand or more jurors, who reached their verdict by simple majority vote.

Suggestions for Background Reading

W. M. McNeill's *History of Western Civilization: A Handbook* (rev. ed.; Chicago, 1986) was written as a background to the whole of the Western Civilization program at the University of Chicago.

Narrative histories of Greece down to the death of Alexander include

A History of Greece, by J. B. Bury and Russell Meiggs (4th ed.; New York, 1975), and *A History of Greece to 322 B.C.*, by N. G. L. Hammond (Oxford, 1959). The third part of the third volume of the *Cambridge Ancient History*, edited by J. Boardman and N. G. L. Hammond (Cambridge, Eng., 1982), is concerned with the expansion of the Greek world between the eighth and the sixth centuries B.C. *The Lyric Age of Greece*, by A. R. Burn (London, 1960), covers a similar period of time. The scope of M. I. Finley's *Early Greece: The Bronze and Archaic Ages* (New York, 1970) is from roughly 3000 B.C. to 500 B.C. W. W. Tarn's *Hellenistic Civilization* (3d ed., revised by the author and G. T. Griffiths; London, 1966), *The Hellenistic Age: Aspects of Hellenistic Civilization* (2d ed.; Cambridge, Eng., 1925), by J. B. Bury, E. A. Barber, E. Bevan, and W. W. Tarn, and A. R. Burn's *Alexander the Great and the Hellenistic Empire* (2d ed.; London, 1963) will serve as an introduction to the Hellenistic world.

The following books are concerned with particular topics or employ methods that may prove useful in discussing the documents. M. I. Finley's *The World of Odysseus* (rev. ed.; New York, 1978) analyzes the world of the Homeric poems from the point of view of a social anthropologist. I. Linforth's *Solon the Athenian* (Berkeley, 1919) employs a close analysis of the surviving poems to reconstruct the life of Solon and the history of his times. G. B. Grundy's *The Great Persian War and Its Preliminaries: A Study of the Evidence, Literary and Topographical* (London, 1901) and *Thucydides and the History of His Age* (2d ed.; Oxford, 1948) are the earliest works in English that systematically discuss events in Greek history in the context of topographical, economic, and technical constraints upon the agents. *Moral Values and Political Behaviour in Ancient Greece*, by A. W. H. Adkins (London and Toronto, 1972), discusses the values of the period down to the end of the fifth century B.C. Discussions of ancient economics are to be found in C. G. Starr, *The Economic and Social Growth of Early Greece, 800–500 B.C.* (New York, 1977), and in M. M. Austin and P. Vidal-Naquet, *Economic and Social History of Ancient Greece: An Introduction* (Berkeley, 1977). M. I. Finley discusses Aristotle and economic analysis in a paper in *Studies in Ancient Society*, edited by M. I. Finley (London, 1974). C. Hignett, *A History of the Athenian Constitution to the End of the Fifth Century B.C.*, furnishes a detailed discussion of the Athenian constitution. F. M. Cornford's *Thucydides Mythistoricus* (London, 1965) skeptically examines Thucydides' claim to scientific objectivity as a historian. V. Ehrenberg's *The People of Aristophanes* (Oxford, 1943) sets Aristophanes' characters in a social and historical context. W. R. Connor's *The New Politicians of Fifth-Century Athens* (Princeton, 1971) closely studies the emergence of "leaders of the people" in the developed Athenian democracy.

As introductions to the philosophical texts included here, the following works should prove useful. P. Shorey, *What Plato Said* (Chicago, 1933), and A. E. Taylor, *Plato: The Man and His Work* (7th ed.; London, 1960), expound Platonic doctrines with close attention to the texts. W. D. Ross, *Aristotle* (5th ed., rev.; London, 1956), performs a similar service for Aristotle. A. A. Long's *Hellenistic Philosophy: Stoics, Epicureans, and Sceptics* (New York, 1974) and J. M. Rist's *Stoic Philosophy* (London, 1969) and *Epicurus: An Introduction* (Cambridge, Eng., 1972) well exemplify the recent upsurge of interest in Hellenistic philosophy.

Homer

"Homer," as we imagine him today, is almost an abstraction: he is the culmination of a centuries-old tradition of oral poetry in Greece. His predecessors, and perhaps "Homer" himself, were master singers who composed as they performed, without the aid of writing, creating their tales by improvisation and memory from a store of traditional stories, scenes, and narrative formulas. We cannot certainly distinguish what is newly told from what is retold at any point in the Homeric poems, much less decide whether the same man was responsible for both the *Iliad* and the *Odyssey*. We think that the Homeric poet or poets lived and sang toward the end of the eighth century B.C. To Greeks of the fifth century, however, Homer was a distinct individual: a blind bard who recited his works at festivals and other leisure gatherings as he traveled up and down the islands of the eastern Aegean and the adjacent mainland. They realized from his own comments that he must have lived long after the period in which his epics were set. They also believed that he lived at least three or four centuries before themselves.

Greeks believed that the heroic society described by Homer flourished at a time corresponding to the thirteenth or early twelfth century in our chronology. Excavations have revealed the remains of a civilization that dates to that time and that shows both striking similarities and striking inconsistencies with the civilization that Homer depicts. Greek tradition and archeology alike indicate that this civilization (which we call "My-cenaean," after one of its principal sites) was overthrown by invaders in the twelfth century. The Homeric poems are therefore epics about a society that had vanished. In most cases it is uncertain whether the details we read are memories of the Mycenaean age, or reflections of post-Mycenaean institutions, or pure imaginings of the poet. But for Greeks of the fifth century these questions hardly arose. It was assumed simply that

6

Homer showed them their society as it had existed in olden times. For the purposes of this volume, it is best to try to cultivate their perspective and to consider how the communities described in the *Iliad* and the *Odyssey* compare with the classical polis.

---

1. Homer, *Odyssey*, Book 2: The Assembly at Ithaca

Now when the young Dawn showed again with her rosy fingers,
the dear son of Odysseus stirred from where he was sleeping,
and put on his clothes, and slung a sharp sword over his shoulder.
Underneath his shining feet he bound the fair sandals
and went on his way from the chamber, like a god in presence.
He gave the word now to his clear-voiced heralds to summon
by proclamation to assembly the flowing-haired Achaians,
and the heralds made their cry, and the men were assembled swiftly.
Now when they were all assembled in one place together,
he went on his way to assembly, in his hands holding a bronze spear,
not all alone, but a pair of light-footed dogs went with him.
Athene drifted an enchantment of grace upon him,
and all the people had their eyes on him as he came forward.
He sat in his father's seat, and the elders made way before him.
The first now to speak to them was the hero Aigyptios,
who was bent over with age, and had seen things beyond number.
His own dear son, Antiphos the spearman, had gone off
with godlike Odysseus to Ilion, land of good horses,
in the hollow ships, and now the wild Cyclops had killed him
deep in his cave, and this was the last man he had eaten.
He had three other sons. One of them, Eurynomos,
went with the suitors; the other two kept the estates of their fathers.
Even so, he could not forget the lost one. He grieved and mourned
      for him,
and it was in tears for him, now, that he stood forth and addressed them:
"Hear me now, men of Ithaka, and the word I give you.
Never has there been an assembly of us or any session
since great Odysseus went away in the hollow vessels.
Now who has gathered us, in this way? What need has befallen
which of the younger men, or one of us who are older?
Has he been hearing some message about the return of the army

From *The Odyssey of Homer: A Modern Translation*, translated by Richmond Lattimore. © 1965, 1967, by Richard Lattimore. Reprinted by permission of Harper & Row, Publishers, Inc.

which, having heard it first, he could now explain to us?
Or has he some other public matter to set forth and argue?
I think he is a good man and useful. So may Zeus grant him
good accomplishment for whatever it is his mind desires."
   He spoke, and the dear son of Odysseus was glad for the omen,
nor did he remain seated long, his heart was for speaking,
and he stood in the middle of the assembly. The herald Peisenor,
a man of deep discretion, put into his hands the scepter.
First, in answer to the old man, he spoke and addressed him:
"Old sir, the man is not far, but here; you yourself shall know him.
It is I who assembled the people. To me this grief comes closest.
Not that I heard some message about the return of the army,
which, having heard it first, I could now explain to you;
nor have I some other public matter to set forth and argue,
but my own need, the evil that has befallen my household.
There are two evils. I have lost a noble father, one who
was king once over you here, and was kind to you like a father;
and now here is a greater evil, one which presently
will break up the whole house and destroy all my livelihood.
For my mother, against her will, is beset by suitors,
own sons to the men who are greatest hereabouts. These
shrink from making the journey to the house of her father
Ikarios, so that he might take bride gifts for his daughter
and bestow her on the one he wished, who came as his favorite;
rather, all their days, they come and loiter in our house
and sacrifice our oxen and our sheep and our fat goats
and make a holiday feast of it and drink the bright wine
recklessly. Most of our substance is wasted. We have no man here
such as Odysseus was, to drive this curse from the household.
We ourselves are not the men to do it; we must be
weaklings in such a case, not men well seasoned in battle.
I would defend myself if the power were in me. No longer
are the things endurable that have been done, and beyond all decency
my house has been destroyed. Even you must be scandalized
and ashamed before the neighboring men about us, the people
who live around our land; fear also the gods' anger,
lest they, astonished by evil actions, turn against you.
I supplicate you, by Zeus the Olympian and by Themis
who breaks up the assemblies of men and calls them in session:
let be, my friends, and leave me alone with my bitter sorrow
to waste away; unless my noble father Odysseus
at some time in anger did evil to the strong-greaved Achaians,

for which angry with me in revenge you do me evil
in setting these on me. But for me it would be far better
for you to eat away my treasures and eat my cattle.
If you were to eat them, there might be a recompense someday,
for we could go through all the settlement, with claims made public
asking for our goods again, until it was all regiven.
But now you are heaping me with troubles I cannot deal with."
      So he spoke in anger, and dashed to the ground the scepter
in a stormburst of tears; and pity held all the people.
Now all the rest were stricken to silence, none was so hardy
as to answer, angry word against word, the speech of Telemachos.
It was Antinoös alone spoke to him in answer:
      "High-spoken intemperate Telemachos, what accusations
you have made to our shame, trying to turn opinion against us!
And yet you have no cause to blame the Achaian suitors,
but it is your own dear mother, and she is greatly resourceful.
And now it is the third year, and will be the fourth year presently,
since she has been denying the desires of the Achaians.
For she holds out hope to all, and makes promises to each man,
sending us messages, but her mind has other intentions.
And here is another stratagem of her heart's devising.
She set up a great loom in her palace, and set to weaving
a web of threads long and fine. Then she said to us:
'Young men, my suitors now that the great Odysseus has perished,
wait, though you are eager to marry me, until I finish
this web, so that my weaving will not be useless and wasted.
This is a shroud for the hero Laertes, for when the destructive
doom of death which lays men low shall take him, lest any
Achaian woman in this neighborhood hold it against me
that a man of many conquests lies with no sheet to wind him.'
So she spoke, and the proud heart in us was persuaded.
Thereafter in the daytime she would weave at her great loom,
but in the night she would have torches set by, and undo it.
So for three years she was secret in her design, convincing
the Achaians, but when the fourth year came with the seasons returning,
one of her women, who knew the whole of the story, told us,
and we found her in the act of undoing her glorious weaving.
So, against her will and by force, she had to finish it.
Now the suitors answer you thus, so that you yourself
may know it in your mind, and all the Achaians may know it:
send your mother back, and instruct her to be married
to any man her father desires and who pleases her also.

But if she continues to torment the sons of the Achaians,
since she is so dowered with the wisdom bestowed by Athene,
to be expert in beautiful work, to have good character
and cleverness, such as we are not told of, even of the ancient
queens, the fair-tressed Achaian women of times before us,
Tyro and Alkmene and Mykene, wearer of garlands;
for none of these knew thoughts so wise as those Penelope
knew; yet in this single matter she did not think rightly;
so long, I say, will your livelihood and possessions be eaten
away, as long as she keeps this purpose, one which the very
gods, I think, put into her heart. She is winning a great name
for herself, but for you she is causing much loss of substance.
We will not go back to our own estates, nor will we go elsewhere
until she marries whichever Achaian man she fancies."
      Then the thoughtful Telemachos said to him in answer:
"Antinoös, I cannot thrust the mother who bore me,
who raised me, out of the house against her will. My father,
alive or dead, is elsewhere in the world. It will be hard
to pay back Ikarios, if willingly I dismiss my mother.
I will suffer some evil from her father, and the spirit will give me
more yet, for my mother will call down her furies upon me
as she goes out of the house, and I shall have the people's
resentment. I will not be the one to say that word to her.
But as for you, if your feeling is scandalized by my answer,
go away from my palace and do your feasting elsewhere,
eating up your own possessions, taking turns, household by household.
But if you decide it is more profitable and better
to go on, eating up one man's livelihood, without payment,
then spoil my house. I will cry out to the gods everlasting
in the hope that Zeus might somehow grant a reversal of fortunes.
Then you may perish in this house with no payment given."
      So spoke Telemachos, and for his sake Zeus of the wide brows
sent forth two eagles, soaring high from the peak of the mountain.
These for a while sailed on the stream of the wind together,
wing and wing, close together, wings spread wide. But when
they were over the middle of the vociferous assembly,
they turned on each other suddenly in a thick shudder
of wings, and swooped over the heads of all, with eyes glaring
and deadly, and tore each other by neck and cheek with their talons,
then sped away to the right across the houses and city.
Then all were astounded at the birds, when their eyes saw them,
and they pondered in their hearts over what might come of it,

and Halitherses, Mastor's son, an aged warrior,
spoke to them. He was far beyond the men of his generation
in understanding the meaning of birds and reading their portents.
Now, in kind intention toward all, he spoke and addressed them:
"Hear me now, men of Ithaka, what I have to tell you;
but what I say will be mostly a warning to the suitors,
for a great disaster is wheeling down on them. Surely Odysseus
will not be long away from his family, but now, already,
is somewhere close by, working out the death and destruction
of all these men, and it will be an evil for many others
of us who inhabit sunny Ithaka. So, well beforehand,
let us think how we can make them stop, or better let them
stop themselves. It will soon be better for them if they do so.
I who foretell this am not untried, I know what I am saying.
Concerning him, I say that everything was accomplished
in the way I said it would be at the time the Argives took ship
for Ilion, and with them went resourceful Odysseus.
I said that after much suffering, with all his companions
lost, in the twentieth year, not recognized by any,
he would come home. And now all this is being accomplished."
    Then in turn Eurymachos, son of Polybos, answered:
"Old sir, better go home and prophesy to your children,
for fear they may suffer some evil to come. In these things
I can give a much better interpretation than you can.
Many are the birds who under the sun's rays wander
the sky; not all of them mean anything; Odysseus
is dead, far away, and how I wish that you had died with him
also. Then you would not be announcing all these predictions,
nor would you so stir up Telemachos, who is now angry,
looking for the gift for your own household, which he might give you.
But I will tell you straight out, and it will be a thing accomplished:
if you, who know much and have known it long, stir up a younger
man, and by talking him round with words encourage his anger,
then first of all, it will be the worse for him; he will not
on account of all these sayings be able to accomplish anything;
and on you, old sir, we shall lay a penalty, and it will grieve your
mind as you pay it, and that for you will be a great sorrow.
I myself, before you all, will advise Telemachos.
Let him urge his mother to go back to her father's,
and they shall appoint the marriage and arrange for the wedding presents
in great amount, as ought to go with a beloved daughter.
For I think the sons of the Achaians will not give over

their harsh courtship, for in any case we fear no one,
and surely not Telemachos, for all he is so eloquent.
Nor do we care for any prophecy, which you, old sir,
may tell us, which will not happen, and will make you even more hated;
and his possessions will wretchedly be eaten away, there will not
be compensation, ever, while she makes the Achaians put off
marriage with her, while we, awaiting this, all our days
quarrel for the sake of her excellence, nor ever go after
others, whom any one of us might properly marry."
      Then the thoughtful Telemachos said to him in answer:
"Eurymachos, and all you others who are haughty suitors,
I no longer entreat you in these matters, nor speak about them,
since by now the gods know about this, as do all the Achaians.
But come now, grant me a swift ship, and twenty companions
who can convey me on a course from one place to another.
For I am going to Sparta and going to sandy Pylos
to ask about the homecoming of my father, who is long absent,
on the chance of some mortal man telling me, or of hearing a Rumor
sent by Zeus. She more than others spreads news among people.
Then if I hear my father is alive and on his way home,
then, hard pressed though I be, I will still hold out for another
year. But if I hear he has died and lives no longer,
then I will make my way home to the beloved land of my fathers,
and pile up a tomb in his honor, and there make sacrifices
in great amount, as is fitting. And give my mother to a husband."
      So he spoke, and sat down again, and among them rose up
Mentor, who once had been the companion of stately Odysseus,
and Odysseus, going on the ships, had turned over the household
to the old man, to keep it well, and so all should obey him.
He in kind intention now spoke forth and addressed them:
"Hear me now, men of Ithaka, what I have to tell you.
No longer now let one who is a sceptered king be eager
to be gentle and kind, be one whose thought is schooled in justice,
but let him always rather be harsh, and act severely,
seeing the way no one of the people he was lord over
remembers godlike Odysseus, and he was kind, like a father.
Now it is not so much the proud suitors I resent
for doing their violent acts by their minds' evil devising;
for they lay their heads on the line when violently they eat up
the house of Odysseus, who, they say to themselves, will not come back;
but now I hold it against you other people, how you all

sit there in silence, and never with an assault of words try
to check the suitors, though they are so few, and you so many."
    Then Leokritos, son of Euenor, spoke forth against him:
"Mentor, reckless in words, wild in your wits, what a thing
you have said, urging them to stop us. It would be difficult
even with more men than these to fight us over our feasting.
For even if Odysseus of Ithaka himself were to
come back, and find the haughty suitors feasting in his house,
and be urgent in his mind to drive them out of his palace,
his wife would have no joy of his coming, though she longs for it
greatly, but rather he would meet an unworthy destiny
if he fought against too many. You have spoken to no purpose.
Come then, all people disperse now, each to his own holdings,
and Mentor and Halitherses will push forward this man's journey,
since these from the first have been his friends, as friends of his father.
But, I think, he will sit still for a long time, waiting for messages
here in Ithaka, and will never accomplish this voyage."
    So he spoke, and suddenly broke up the assembly,
and the people scattered and went their ways, each to his own house,
while the suitors went away into the house of godlike Odysseus.
    But Telemachos, walking along the sea beach away from the others,
washed his hands in the gray salt water and prayed to Athene:
"Hear me, you who came yesterday, a god, into our house
and urged me on to go by ship out over the misty
face of the sea, to ask about the homecoming of my father
who is so long absent: now all this is delayed by the Achaians
and particularly the suitors in their evil overconfidence."
    So he spoke in prayer, and from nearby Athene came to him
likening herself to Mentor in voice and appearance.
Now she spoke aloud to him and addressed him in winged words:
"Telemachos, you are to be no thoughtless man, no coward
if truly the strong force of your father is instilled in you;
such a man he was for accomplishing word and action.
Your journey then will be no vain thing nor go unaccomplished.
But if you are not the seed begotten of him and Penelope,
I have no hope that you will accomplish all that you strive for.
For few are the children who turn out to be equals of their fathers,
and the greater number are worse; few are better than their father is.
But since you are to be no thoughtless man, no coward,
and the mind of Odysseus has not altogether given out in you,
there is some hope that you can bring all these things to fulfillment.

So now, let be the purpose and the planning of these senseless
suitors, since they are neither thoughtful men nor just men,
and have not realized the death and black fatality
that stands close by, so that on a day they all must perish.
And that journey for which you are so urgent will not be long now,
such a companion am I to you, as of your father.
I will fit you out a fast ship, I myself will go with you.
But now you must go back to the house, and join the suitors,
and get ready provisions for the journey, pack all in containers,
have wine in handled jars, and barley meal, men's marrow,
in thick leather bags, and I, going round the town, will assemble
volunteer companions to go with you. There are ships in plenty
here in seagirt Ithaka, both old and new ones,
and I will look them over for you to find out the best one,
and soon we shall stow our gear and put out onto the wide sea."
     So spoke Athene, daughter of Zeus, nor did Telemachos
delay long after he had heard the voice of the goddess,
but went on his way to the house, the heart troubled within him.
He came upon the haughty suitors, there in his palace,
skinning goats and singeing fatted swine in the courtyard.
Antinoös, with a smile, came straight up to Telemachos,
and took him by the hand and spoke and named him, saying:
"High-spoken intemperate Telemachos, now let no other
evil be considered in your heart, neither action
nor word, but eat and drink with me, as you did in past time.
The Achaians will see to it that all these things are accomplished,
the ship, and chosen companions, so that you may the more quickly
reach sacred Pylos, after news about your proud father."
     Then the thoughtful Telemachos said to him in answer:
"Antinoös, there is no way for me to dine with you
against my will, and take my ease, when you are so insolent.
Is it not enough, you suitors, that in time past you ruined
my great and good possessions, when I was still in my childhood?
But now, when I am grown big, and by listening to others
can learn the truth, and the anger is steaming up inside me,
I will endeavor to visit evil destructions upon you,
either by going to Pylos, or remaining here in the district.
But I will go; that journey I speak of will not be made void;
but as a passenger; for I control no ship, not any
companions; this, I think, was the way you wished to have it."
     He spoke, and lightly drew away his hand from Antinoös'
hand, but the suitors about the house prepared their dinner,

and in their conversation they insulted him and mocked him,
and thus would go the word of one of the arrogant young men:
"Surely now Telemachos is devising our murder.
Either he will bring some supporters from sandy Pylos,
or even from Sparta, now he is so terribly eager;
or perhaps his purpose is to go to Ephyre, that rich
corn land, so that thence he can bring back poisonous medicines
and put them into our wine bowl, and so destroy all of us."
    And thus would speak another one of these arrogant young men:
"Who knows whether, when he goes in a hollow ship, he also
might perish straying far from his people, as did Odysseus?
Were this to happen, he would lighten all our work for us.
Then we could divide up his possessions, and give the house
to this man's mother to keep, and to the man who marries her."
    So they spoke, but he went down into his father's high-roofed
and wide storeroom, where gold and bronze were lying piled up,
and abundant clothing in the bins, and fragrant olive oil,
and in it jars of wine, sweet to drink, aged,
were standing, keeping the unmixed divine drink inside them,
lined up in order close to the wall, for the day when Odysseus
might come home even after laboring through many hardships.
To close it there were double doors that fitted together
with two halves, and there by night and day was a woman
in charge who, with intelligent care, watched over all this,
Eurykleia the daughter of Ops the son of Peisenor.
Now Telemachos called her to the room, and spoke to her:
"Dear nurse, come, draw me some sweet wine in the handled
jars, choicest of all you have in your keeping, next after
what you are saving for the ill-fated man, the day when Zeus-sprung
Odysseus might come home, escaping death and its spirits.
Fill me twelve in all and fit them all with covers.
And pour me barley into bags stitched strongly, of leather.
Let me have twenty measures of the choice milled barley. You be
the only one that knows this. Let all be gathered together,
for I will pick it up in the evening, after my mother
climbs to her upper chamber and is ready for sleeping.
For I am going into Sparta and to sandy Pylos,
to ask after my dear father's homecoming, if I might hear something."
    So he spoke, and the dear nurse Eurykleia cried out,
and bitterly lamenting she addressed him in winged words:
"Why, my beloved child, has this intention come into
your mind? Why do you wish to wander over much country,

you, an only and loved son? Illustrious Odysseus
has perished far from his country in some outlandish region.
And these men will devise evils against you, on your returning,
so you shall die by guile, and they divide all that is yours.
No, but stay here and guard your possessions. It is not right
for you to wander and suffer hardships on the barren wide sea."
    Then the thoughtful Telemachos said to her in answer:
"Do not fear, nurse. This plan was not made without a god's will.
But swear to tell my beloved mother nothing about this
until the eleventh day has come or the twelfth hereafter,
or until she misses me herself or hears I am absent,
so that she may not ruin her lovely skin with weeping."
    So he spoke, and the old woman swore to the gods a great oath,
and after she had sworn to it and completed the oath taking,
she drew the wine in the handled jars at once thereafter
and poured his barley into bags stitched strongly of leather,
but Telemachos went back into the house and joined the suitors.
    Now the gray-eyed goddess Athene thought what to do next.
In the likeness of Telemachos she went all through the city
and, standing beside each man as she came to him, told them
all to assemble beside the fast ship in the evening.
Then she asked Noëmon, the glorious son of Phronios,
for a fast ship. And he with good will promised it to her.
    And the sun set, and all the journeying ways were darkened.
Now she drew the fast ship down to the sea, and in her
stowed all the running gear that strong-benched vessels carry.
She set it at the edge of the harbor, and around her the good companions
thronged and were assembled and the goddess urged on each man.
    Now the gray-eyed goddess Athene thought what to do next.
She went on her way, into the house of godlike Odysseus,
and there she drifted a sweet slumber over the suitors,
and struck them as they drank, and knocked the goblets out of
their hands, and they went to sleep in the city, nor did any one
sit long, after sleep was fallen upon his eyelids.
Afterward gray-eyed Athene spoke to Telemachos
when she had called him out from the well-established palace,
likening herself to Mentor in voice and appearance:
"Telemachos, already now your strong-greaved companions
are sitting at the oars, and waiting for you to set forth.
So let us go, and not delay our voyaging longer."
    So spoke Pallas Athene, and she led the way swiftly,
and the man followed behind her walking in the god's footsteps.

But when they had come down to the sea, and where the ship was,
they found the flowing-haired companions there by the seashore.
Now the hallowed prince, Telemachos, spoke his word to them:
"Here, friends, let us carry the provisions. They are all ready
and stacked in the hall. But my mother has been told nothing of this,
nor the rest of the serving women. Only one knows the story."
    So he spoke and led the way, and the rest went with him.
They all carried the provisions down, and stowed them in the strong-
        benched
vessel, in the way the dear son of Odysseus directed them.
Telemachos went aboard the ship, but Athene went first
and took her place in the stern of the ship, and close beside her
Telemachos took his place. The men cast off the stern cables
and themselves also went aboard and sat to the oarlocks.
The goddess gray-eyed Athene sent them a favoring stern wind,
strong Zephyros, who murmured over the wine-blue water.
Telemachos then gave the sign and urged his companions
to lay hold of the tackle, and they listened to his urging
and, raising the mast pole made of fir, they set it upright
in the hollow hole in the box, and made it fast with forestays,
and with halyards strongly twisted of leather pulled up the white sails.
The wind blew into the middle of the sail, and at the cutwater
a blue wave rose and sang strongly as the ship went onward.
She ran swiftly, cutting across the swell her pathway.
When they had made fast the running gear all along the black ship,
then they set up mixing bowls, filling them brimful
with wine, and poured to the gods immortal and everlasting
beyond all other gods they poured to Zeus' grey-eyed daughter.
All night long and into the dawn she ran on her journey.

2. Homer, *Iliad* 18.474–617: The Shield of Achilles

He cast on the fire bronze which is weariless, and tin with it
and valuable gold, and silver, and thereafter set forth
upon its standard the great anvil, and gripped in one hand
the ponderous hammer, while in the other he grasped the pincers.
    First of all he forged a shield that was huge and heavy,
elaborating it about, and threw around it a shining
triple rim that glittered, and the shield strap was cast of silver.

From *The Iliad of Homer*, translated by Richard Lattimore. Chicago: University of Chicago Press, 1951. © 1951 by The University of Chicago.

There were five folds composing the shield itself, and upon it
he elaborated many things in his skill and craftsmanship.
    He made the earth upon it, and the sky, and the sea's water,
and the tireless sun, and the moon waxing into her fullness,
and on it all the constellations that festoon the heavens,
the Pleiades and the Hyades and the strength of Orion
and the Bear, whom men give also the name of the Wagon,
who turns about in a fixed place and looks at Orion
and she alone is never plunged in the wash of the Ocean.
    On it he wrought in all their beauty two cities of mortal
men. And there were marriages in one, and festivals.
They were leading the brides along the city from their maiden chambers
under the flaring of torches, and the loud bride song was arising.
The young men followed the circles of the dance, and among them
the flutes and lyres kept up their clamour as in the meantime
the women standing each at the door of her court admired them.
The people were assembled in the market place, where a quarrel
had arisen, and two men were disputing over the blood price
for a man who had been killed. One man promised full restitution
in a public statement, but the other refused and would accept nothing.
Both then made for an arbitrator, to have a decision;
and people were speaking up on either side, to help both men.
But the heralds kept the people in hand, as meanwhile the elders
were in session on benches of polished stone in the sacred circle
and held in their hands the staves of the heralds who lift their voices.
The two men rushed before these, and took turns speaking their cases,
and between them lay on the ground two talents of gold, to be given
to that judge who in this case spoke the straightest opinion.
    But around the other city were lying two forces of armed men
shining in their war gear. For one side counsel was divided
whether to storm and sack, or share between both sides the property
and all the possessions the lovely citadel held hard within it.
But the city's people were not giving way, and armed for an ambush.
Their beloved wives and their little children stood on the rampart
to hold it, and with them the men with age upon them, but meanwhile
the others went out. And Ares led them, and Pallas Athene.
These were gold, both, and golden raiment upon them, and they were
beautiful and huge in their armour, being divinities,
and conspicuous from afar, but the people around them were smaller.
These, when they were come to the place that was set for their ambush,
in a river, where there was a watering place for all animals,
there they sat down in place shrouding themselves in the bright bronze.

But apart from these were sitting two men to watch for the rest of them
and waiting until they could see the sheep and the shambling cattle,
who appeared presently, and two herdsmen went along with them
playing happily on pipes, and took no thought of the treachery.
Those others saw them, and made a rush, and quickly thereafter
cut off on both sides the herds of cattle and the beautiful
flocks of shining sheep, and killed the shepherds upon them.
But the other army, as soon as they heard the uproar arising
from the cattle, as they sat in their councils, suddenly mounted
behind their light-foot horses, and went after, and soon overtook them.
These stood their ground and fought a battle by the banks of the river,
and they were making casts at each other with their spears bronze-headed;
and Hate was there with Confusion among them, and Death the
        destructive;
she was holding a live man with a new wound, and another
one unhurt, and dragged a dead man by the feet through the carnage.
The clothing upon her shoulders showed strong red with the men's blood.
All closed together like living men and fought with each other
and dragged away from each other the corpses of those who had fallen.
    He made upon it a soft field, the pride of the tilled land,
wide and triple-ploughed, with many ploughmen upon it
who wheeled their teams at the turn and drove them in either direction.
And as these making their turn would reach the end-strip of the field,
a man would come up to them at this point and hand them a flagon
of honey-sweet wine, and they would turn again to the furrows
in their haste to come again to the end-strip of the deep field.
The earth darkened behind them and looked like earth that has been
        ploughed
though it was gold. Such was the wonder of the shield's forging.
    He made on it the precinct of a king, where the labourers
were reaping, with the sharp reaping hooks in their hands. Of the cut
        swathes
some fell along the lines of reaping, one after another,
while the sheaf-binders caught up others and tied them with bind-ropes.
There were three sheaf-binders who stood by, and behind them
were children picking up the cut swathes, and filled their arms with them
and carried and gave them always; and by them the king in silence
and holding his staff stood near the line of the reapers, happily.
And apart and under a tree the heralds made a feast ready
and trimmed a great ox they had slaughtered. Meanwhile the women
scattered, for the workmen to eat, abundant white barley.
    He made on it a great vineyard heavy with clusters,

lovely and in gold, but the grapes upon it were darkened
and the vines themselves stood out through poles of silver. About them
he made a field-ditch of dark metal, and drove all around this
a fence of tin; and there was only one path to the vineyard,
and along it ran the grape-bearers for the vineyard's stripping.
Young girls and young men, in all their light-hearted innocence,
carried the kind, sweet fruit away in their woven baskets,
and in their midst a youth with a singing lyre played charmingly
upon it for them, and sang the beautiful song for Linos
in a light voice, and they followed him, and with singing and whistling
and light dance-steps of their feet kept time to the music.

    He made upon it a herd of horn-straight oxen. The cattle
were wrought of gold and of tin, and thronged in speed and with lowing
out of the dung of the farmyard to a pasturing place by a sounding
river, and beside the moving field of a reed bed.
The herdsmen were of gold who went along with the cattle,
four of them, and nine dogs shifting their feet followed them.
But among the foremost of the cattle two formidable lions
had caught hold of a bellowing bull, and he with loud lowings
was dragged away, as the dogs and the young men went in pursuit of him.
But the two lions, breaking open the hide of the great ox,
gulped the black blood and the inward guts, as meanwhile the herdsmen
were in the act of setting and urging the quick dogs on them.
But they, before they could get their teeth in, turned back from the lions,
but would come and take their stand very close, and bayed, and kept
      clear.

    And the renowned smith of the strong arms made on it a meadow
large and in a lovely valley for the glimmering sheepflocks,
with dwelling places upon it, and covered shelters, and sheepfolds.

    And the renowned smith of the strong arms made elaborate on it
a dancing floor, like that which once in the wide spaces of Knosos
Daidalos built for Ariadne of the lovely tresses.
And there were young men on it and young girls, sought for their beauty
with gifts of oxen, dancing, and holding hands at the wrist. These
wore, the maidens long light robes, but the men wore tunics
of finespun work and shining softly, touched with olive oil.
And the girls wore fair garlands on their heads, while the young men
carried golden knives that hung from sword-belts of silver.
At whiles on their understanding feet they would run very lightly,
as when a potter crouching makes trial of his wheel, holding
it close in his hands, to see if it will run smooth. At another
time they would form rows, and run, rows crossing each other.

And around the lovely chorus of dancers stood a great multitude
happily watching, while among the dancers two acrobats
led the measures of song and dance revolving among them.
    He made on it the great strength of the Ocean River
which ran around the uttermost rim of the shield's strong structure.
    Then after he had wrought this shield, which was huge and heavy,
he wrought for him a corselet brighter than fire in its shining,
and wrought him a helmet, massive and fitting close to his temples,
lovely and intricate work, and laid a gold top-ridge along it,
and out of pliable tin wrought him leg-armour. Thereafter
when the renowned smith of the strong arms had finished the armour
he lifted it and laid it before the mother of Achilleus.
And she like a hawk came sweeping down from the snows of Olympos
and carried with her the shining armour, the gift of Hephaistos.

Tyrtaeus, Solon, Theognis

Tyrtaeus, Solon, and "Theognis" all wrote poems in the elegiac meter. In early Greece the elegiac meter was used for a variety of purposes, important among which were formal public exhortation and advice. These uses are exemplified by the poems printed here.

Tyrtaeus of Sparta is preeminently the poet of the Second Messenian War, which is commonly dated ca. 640–620 B.C. Later tradition held that Tyrtaeus was an Athenian and even that he was a lame Athenian schoolmaster of little intelligence, lent to the Spartans by the Athenians when the Spartans asked for help in the war. In fact, there is no reason to doubt that Tyrtaeus was a Spartan. His poems continued to be held in high esteem: a fourth-century Attic orator informs us that they were still performed in his day before the Spartan army went into battle. The Spartans decisively won the Second Messenian War and subjugated and helotized the Messenians, their western neighbors. The poems express not only the values and behavior expected of the Spartan hoplite (heavy-armed infantryman) but those of hoplites everywhere in Greece.

Solon of Athens is the first Athenian poet of whom we know anything. (At this time poetry—or verse—was the medium for memorable public utterance, so that any public figure who wished his views to be remembered had to turn to poetry.) It was not as a poet but as a statesman, lawgiver, and moralist that Solon was primarily remembered by Athenians; but his surviving work sometimes attains to poetry and rarely falls short of effective rhetoric. Solon was archon at Athens in 594/593 B.C., and was later given full powers as a *nomothetes* to revise the Athenian laws and constitution. Aristotle in his *Constitution of Athens* (document 16 of this volume) seems to have little contemporary evidence for the social, economic, and political crisis of Solon's day apart from the poems themselves. It is important to observe that Solon is not describing the crisis or his solution but is engaging in political rhetoric.

Theognis undoubtedly existed. He proudly proclaims his existence in his poetry, and he undoubtedly wrote some of the 1,400 verses ascribed to him, but they are best regarded as an anthology of short poems by different hands, united by their generally oligarchic attitudes. The earliest poems may be from the seventh century, the latest from the fifth. Some of the most interesting of the Theognid poems reflect the problems of values caused by the rise in Megara—and elsewhere in Greece—of a group of people who were prosperous but not of the old landed aristocracy. In earlier Greece wealth consisted in land and in the movable and immovable goods and chattels on the land. The possessors of the land, and they alone, could afford to equip themselves with the full armor the community needed for its defense. They were perceived, by themselves and others, as possessing the qualities most needed by the community and so were termed *agathoi* or *esthloi*, the most powerful terms available for the commendation of men and women. Since land was inherited, the *agathoi* of any generation were the children of the *agathoi* of the preceding generation and the parents of the *agathoi* of the next. In marrying a wealthy bride, the *agathos* married a wife of good pedigree; thus the noble families were kept sharply distinct from their inferiors. In Theognis' Megara, all this was changed, and the poet's attitude to the change is in no doubt.

3. Two Poems by Tyrtaeus

Tyrtaeus 10W: Exhortation to the Young Hoplite

Beautiful-and-honorable [*kalon*] it is for a brave [*agathos*] warrior[1] to die, fallen among the foremost fighters, in battle for his native land; but to leave his polis and rich fields and beg—that is most painful of all, as he wanders with his dear mother and aged father, his small children and wedded wife. Detested he will be in the eyes of all those to whom he comes, constrained by need and hateful poverty. He shames his birth and belies his glorious appearance; dishonor and misery are his companions. If no account is

Translated by Arthur W. H. Adkins from the Greek text of Tyrtaeus' poems in M. L. West, *Iambi et Elegi Graeci ante Alexandrum Cantati*, vol. 2 (Oxford: Clarendon Press, 1972).

1. In Greek, *aner* denotes an adult male who possesses the qualities most admired by society, while *anthropos* denotes the other members of the human race. I have rendered *aner* by "warrior."

taken of a warrior who is a wanderer, if there is no respect for him or his family in the future, then let us fight with all our hearts for this land and die for our children, no longer hesitating to risk our lives. Young men, stand firm beside each other and fight. Do not begin shameful flight or fear. Rather create a mighty, valorous spirit in your breasts, and do not show love for your lives when you are fighting with warriors. Do not flee, abandoning the older men, whose knees are no longer nimble. For shameful-and-ugly [aischron] it is for an older warrior to fall among the foremost fighters and lie out ahead of the young men—a man whose hair is already white and his beard gray—as he breathes out his valorous spirit in the dust, holding his bloody genitals in his own hands, his body laid bare. Shameful-and-ugly [aischra] is this to the eyes, and a cause of resentment to look upon. But to the young men all is seemly, while the glorious flower of lovely youth is theirs. To men the young man is admirable to look upon, and to women lovable while he lives, and beautiful-and-honorable when he lies among the foremost fighters. So let a man take a firm stance and stand fast, with both feet planted upon the ground, biting his lip with his teeth.

Tyrtaeus 11W: The Hoplite's Handbook

But since you are of the race of unconquered Heracles, be of good cheer. Zeus is not yet turning his neck away from you. Do not fear the mass of warriors, and do not flee. Let a warrior hold his shield directly against the foremost fighters, reckoning his life to be his enemy and the black spirits of death to be as dear as the rays of the sun. For you know well the destructive deeds of Ares [the war god] who causes many tears. You are well acquainted with the temper of grievous war, young men; you have been in the company of those who fled and those who pursued and have reached satiation with both. For those who remain by their comrades' sides and have the courage to go into the melee and among the foremost fighters—they die in smaller numbers and preserve the people behind them; but of warriors who have fled in terror all the valor [arete] is gone. No one could ever complete the tally of all the woes [kaka] which come upon a warrior if he suffers what is shameful [aischra]. Pleasant it is to cleave the back of a fleeing warrior from behind in fierce battle; but shameful-and-ugly [aischros] is a corpse lying in the dust with the point of a spear driven through its back from behind. No; rather let a man take a firm stance and stand fast, with both feet planted upon the ground, biting his lip with his teeth, having hidden his thighs and calves below and his chest and shoulders with the belly of his broad shield. In his right hand let him brandish his mighty spear and make his crest wave terribly over his head. By doing mighty deeds let him teach himself to fight. Let him not stand beyond the range of the missiles, for he has a shield. Rather let him go near and slay his warrior foe, wounding him at close quarters with long spear or sword. Having set foot by foot and thrust shield against shield, and having drawn near, crest to crest, helmet to helmet, and chest to chest, let him fight with a warrior, grasping either the hilt of his sword or a long spear. And you, you light-armed, crouching on this side and on that beneath the shield, have at them with great handstones and with polished spears as you cast your javelins at them, standing close to the men in full armor.

4. Two Poems by Solon

Solon 4W: *Eunomia* and *Dusnomia*

Solon 4W is a poem of political rhetoric whose effect depends in part on characteristics of the Greek language that cannot be fully rendered in another language. Frequently a word or a phrase can be interpreted in more than one way, for Solon intended his audience to receive more than one message. The Greek original of the whole of the second paragraph is laden with ambiguities. The English inevitably impoverishes the original and renders nonsequiturs more apparent.

At three points there is a lacuna of at least one line in the Greek text.

Our polis will never perish as a result of the apportionment of Zeus and the intentions of the blessed immortal gods; for such a great-hearted guardian, daughter of a mighty father, Pallas Athena, holds her hands in protection over it. But the citizens themselves, persuaded by wealth, are willing to destroy a mighty polis by their follies, and the mind of the leaders of the people is unjust. For the leaders it is prepared that they should suffer many griefs as a result of their great hubris. For they do not know how to restrain the excesses sprung from satiety or how to discipline in peaceful quiet the present merriments of the feast. . . . They grow wealthy, relying on unjust deeds. . . . Sparing neither sacred nor public property, they steal by snatching, one from one source, one from another, nor do they reverence the august abode where justice is set, she who in silence knows what is happening, and what has occurred in the past, and in time at all events comes to exact requital.

This is now coming upon the whole polis as an inescapable wound, and it comes swiftly to grievous slavery, which stirs up civic strife among the

Translated by Arthur W. H. Adkins from the Greek text of Solon's poems in M. L. West, *Iambi et Elegi Graeci ante Alexandrum Cantati*, vol. 2 (Oxford, Clarendon Press, 1972).

people and sleeping [civil?] war, which destroys the lovely prime of many. For by the action of enemies a much-beloved polis is swiftly brought to hardship in meetings by those who wrong their friends. These woes go to and fro in the land; and, of the poor, many arrive at another land, sold and bound in unseemly fetters. . . . Thus a woe of the people comes home to each individual, and the courtyard gates are no longer willing to shut it out, but it leaps over the high fence and finds a man nonetheless, even if he is in flight in a corner of his chamber.

These things my heart bids me tell the Athenians: that *dusnomia*[1] causes very many woes to a polis. *Eunomia* shows forth everything orderly and appropriate and often puts shackles on the unjust; she makes the rough smooth, ends the insolence of satiety, dims hubris, and dries up the growing blossoms of infatuation, straightens crooked judgments, and tames proud deeds; she ends the deeds of civil conflict, ends the wrath of grievous strife, and all things among mankind are appropriate and prudent under her rule.

Solon 13W: Prosperity, Justice, and the Hazards of Life

Pierian Muses, glorious children of Memory and Olympian Zeus, listen to me as I call upon you in prayer. Grant that I may always enjoy prosperity from the immortal gods and a good reputation from all men. Grant that I may be so sweet to my friends and bitter to my enemies as to be revered by the one and feared by the other. I desire to have riches, but I do not wish to possess them unjustly: punishment assuredly comes later. The wealth that the gods give abides with a man steadfastly, from lowest base to summit; but that which men gain by insolent aggression does not come in a seemly manner. Constrained by unjust deeds, it accompanies a man reluctantly and swiftly is blended with ruinous folly, which grows from small beginnings like those of fire. Trivial it is at first, but its end is painful, for the works of insolence do not remain long with mortals. No; Zeus watches over the end of all things. All of a sudden, just as the clouds are quickly scattered by a spring gale, which stirs up the depths of the billowing un-

---

1. *Eunomia* and *dusnomia* cannot be neatly rendered. *Nomos*, at least in somewhat later Greek, can mean "law," and the words have been supposed to characterize states of affairs in which the laws are good and bad, respectively, or states of affairs in which the laws are obeyed or disobeyed. But *eunomia* and *dusnomia* are derived from the root *nem*, "to apportion," and can readily mean, respectively, states of affairs in which everything is shared out well or badly: a sense that is not irrelevant to Solon's political program. None of the possible senses need be excluded: the words were as imprecise in Solon's day as they appear to us. They are political slogans and, like many political slogans since, combine a high emotive charge with a vague denotation.

harvested sea, ravages the handsome farmsteads of men over the wheat-bearing land, and comes to lofty heaven, the abode of the gods, and makes the sky clear to look upon once more, and the beautiful might of the sun shines over the rich earth, but not a cloud is to be seen any longer—such is the requital of Zeus. He is not swift to anger on each occasion, like a mortal man; but it is always true that it does not escape his notice forever who has a wicked heart. Requital is made manifest in the end, at all events: but one man pays the penalty straightway, another later; and those who themselves escape, and the doom of the gods does not come to strike them—nevertheless it comes later; and, though they are not responsible, the children of the wrongdoers or the family later pay for the deeds of their fathers. We mortals, the highborn and the base alike, think in this way: each one supposes that he is faring well until he meets with suffering; then he grieves in his turn; but until then we gape and take pleasure in feather-brained hopes. Whoever is burdened by grievous diseases has it in mind that he will be healthy. Another man who is a coward thinks he is a brave warrior, and the man whose form is graceless thinks he is handsome. Anyone who is penniless, and constrained by the tasks of poverty, expects nevertheless to get many possessions. Men quest eagerly in different directions. One roams over the fishy sea in ships, borne by grievous winds, not grudging the risk to his life in his longing to bring home gain. Someone else, one of those whose concern is with the crooked plough, cuts the earth with its many trees, toiling for hire throughout the year. Another, skilled in the tasks of Athena and Hephaestus of many crafts, gains his livelihood with his hands. Another who has been taught the gifts of the Olympian Muses understands the measure of lovely wisdom. Apollo, the lord who sends his arrows afar, makes another man a prophet, with whom the gods consort. He discerns a woe coming upon a man from far away; but neither an omen nor sacrifices will ward off a man's lot. Others are doctors, performing the task of Paeon with his many drugs, and their work too has no sure end. Often from a small pain develops great suffering that no one could relieve by giving soothing drugs; but a doctor touches with his hands another man, one racked by hurtful and grievous diseases, and straightway makes him healthy. Their appointed lot brings harm and benefit upon mortals, and the gifts of the immortal gods are not to be escaped. There is risk in everything that one does, and no one knows where he will make his landfall when his enterprise is at its beginning. One man, trying to act effectively, fails to foresee something and falls into great and grim ruination, but to another man, one who is acting ineffectively, a god gives good fortune in everything and escape from his folly. There is no visible limit of riches set for men; for those of us who now have the most abundant livelihood strive to double it; who could satisfy all of them? The immortals furnish gains for mortals, but gains change hands when out of them appear folly and ruin, which Zeus sends to restore the balance.

5. Three Poems by Theognis

Theognis 53–68W: Social Upheaval

Cyrnus, this polis is still a polis, but its people are different. Formerly they knew nothing of legal decisions or laws but wore goatskins around their flanks—wore them to shreds—and grazed like deer outside this polis. And now they are *agathoi*,[1] son of Polypaüs; and those who were formerly *esthloi* are now *deiloi*. Who could bear to look upon this? . . . They cheat one another as they laugh at one another, since they do not know the distinctive marks of *kakoi* or of *agathoi*. Son of Polypaüs, befriend none of these citizens from your heart for any purpose. No; feign friendship so far as words are concerned, but share no serious business whatsoever with them. Else you will come to know the mind of wretched men, how there is no trustworthiness in their deeds, but they love deceits and trickeries and fine-spun plots, like men who are already lost.

Theognis 173–78W: Poverty and the *Agathos*

It is poverty that overwhelms an *agathos* man most of all, Cyrnus, more than grizzled old age or constant fever. In fleeing poverty, Cyrnus, one should hurl oneself even into the deep-yawning sea and down precipitous cliffs. For a man overwhelmed by poverty can neither say nor do anything: his tongue is fast bound.

Theognis 183–92W: Breeding, Good and Bad

Well bred [of good *genos*], Cyrnus, are the rams, donkeys, and horses we seek out. A man wants them to mate from *agathoi*. But an *agathos* man feels no care at marrying the *kake* daughter of a *kakos* father if the father

---

Translated by Arthur W. H. Adkins from the Greek text of the *Theognidea* in M. L. West, *Iambi et Elegi Graeci ante Alexandrum Cantati*, vol. 1 (Oxford: Clarendon Press, 1971).

1. *Agathoi* is the plural of *agathos, kake* the feminine singular of *kakos*. *Esthlos* is synonymous with *agathos*; *deilos* is synonymous with *kakos*. *Esthla* and *kaka* are the neuter plural forms of *esthlos* and *kakos*.

gives him much property, nor does a woman refuse to be the wife of a *kakos* man but wants a rich husband rather than an *agathos* one. It is property that they prize: an *esthlos* man has married the child of a *kakos* one, a *kakos* the child of an *agathos*. Wealth has thrown lineage [*genos*] into confusion. So do not be surprised, son of Polypaüs, that the lineage [*genos*] of the citizens is being dimmed: *esthla* are being mingled with *kaka*.

Pindar

Pindar (522–442 or 518–438 B.C.) was from Thebes, a city ruled by
oligarchs and perpetually at odds with Athens, its neighbor to the south.
Thebes was also in bad odor among Greeks generally for having collabo-
rated with the invading Persians in 480 B.C. But Pindar himself was wel-
comed all over the Greek-speaking world. Towns and wealthy individuals
from Sicily to Rhodes and Cyrene engaged him to write choral works for
festivals and other grand occasions. Pindar composed both the music and
the words and trained the choruses who sang and danced his pieces (it is
to dance movements that the words "turn," "counterturn," and "stand"
in the poem refer). The only part of his output that has been preserved
complete are the four books of songs he wrote for victors in athletic
contests.

6. Pindar, *Sixth Nemean Ode*

Pindar wrote the *Sixth Nemean* ode for a young aristocrat (Alkimidas)
who had won the boys' wrestling contest in the biennial competition at
Nemea, in the northeast corner of the Peloponnese. The Nemean games,
along with those at Olympia, Delphi, and the Isthmus of Corinth (all of
which Pindar contrives to mention in the poem), made up the great Pan-
hellenic festivals. All Greeks, and only Greeks, were eligible to compete.
The events pitted individuals against one another; there were no team
sports. The games provided one of the rare occasions, apart from war,
that brought Greeks from different places into organized contact with one

From *Pindar's Victory Songs*, translated by Frank J. Nisetich. Baltimore: Johns Hopkins
University Press, 1980.

another. An athlete's victory was perceived as his city's victory, and cities honored their champions extravagantly.

Although physical culture was important to all Greeks, only rich families could afford the level of training that produced contenders at the great games. And only the rich could commission praise-singers like Pindar. Victory poems therefore express ideas not just of the poet but of that segment of society that purchased his services. The poem for Alkimidas illustrates ideas about family, failure, and glory that Greek aristocrats brought to sport, and it gives us a glimpse of families who in the middle of the fifth century exerted themselves in the belief that their excellence ran back to the seed of heroes and of gods.

Turn 1

There is one race of men,
  one race of gods.
    Yet from one mother
      we both take our breath.
    The difference
   is in the allotment
of all power,
        for the one is nothing
while the bronze sky exists forever,
a sure abode.
      And yet, somehow,
we resemble the immortals,
   whether in greatness of mind
    or nature, though we know not
   to what measure
day by day and in the watches of the night
    fate has written that we should run.

Counterturn 1

And now Alkimidas
  gives clear proof
   that the power
    born in the blood
   is like
  the fruit-bearing fields
that now, in alternation,
          yield mankind
yearly sustenance from the ground
and now, again, resting
        withhold their strength.

See, he comes
   from Nemea's joyful contest,
     a boy contender, pursuing
    the career that Zeus
has allotted him: he has shown himself
   a hunter destined for success in wrestling,

Stand 1   treading in the footprints of his father's father,
Praxidamas—
              for he, victorious at Olympia,
first brought the Aiakidai garlands from Alpheos;
and having won the crown five times at Isthmos
and three times at Nemea,
              he put an end
to the obscurity of Sokleidas, his father,
who proved to be
             greatest of the sons of Hagesimachos

Turn 2   because of his own three sons,
   winners of prizes, who reached ˙
     the peaks of triumph
       and had their share of toil.
     But, with divine favor,
   the contest
in the heart of Greece
           has declared
no other house a steward of more
crowns for boxing.
           I hope, with this boast,
to hit the target squarely,
   like an archer:
     come, Muse, direct
   upon this clan
the glorious breath of song—
     for when men have passed out of our midst

Counterturn 2 poems and legends
   convey their noble deeds,
    and these are not lacking
      to the Bassidai, a race
    renowned of old,
   who sail in ships laden

with their own triumphal songs
                              and can provide
the plowmen of the Pierides
with many a hymn
                    by their proud achievements.
For in the sacred ground
  of Pytho, Kallias too—
    a scion of this family—
having bound his fists
in leather thongs, found
      favor with golden-distaffed

Stand 2   Leto's children,
                        and shined by Kastalia at evening
in the Graces' attendance.
                        The bridge
of the unwearying sea[1] honored Kreontidas once
in the biennial celebrations of the men thereabouts,
when bulls are slain in Poseidon's sanctuary;
                              and once
he decked his brow in the lion's leafage[2]
beside the shadowy primeval mountains of Phleious.

Turn 3   There are broad approaches
        from every direction
          that bards may take
            to adorn this island—
          for the Aiakidai,
        by the display
of their great deeds,
                      have bequeathed to it
a glorious heritage, and their name
flies far over earth
                  and across the sea:
even into the midst
  of the Ethiopians
    it made its way, when Memnon
    failed to return:

1. The "bridge" is the Isthmus of Corinth, where the Isthmian Games were held.
2. The wreath of wild celery, which was the prize for the games at Nemea, where Heracles had slain the Nemean lion.

Achilleus had fallen upon them
heavily, stepping from his chariot

Counterturn 3   the day he caught
the son of gleaming Dawn
on the point
of his raging spear.
Men of old have also
made these matters
into a high road of song,
and I myself, intent
upon my theme, follow them here.
But the wave rolling
nearest the ship's keel
is always a man's first concern.
I come,
a messenger gladly embracing
my double burden,
proclaiming that you,
Alkimidas, have provided this

Stand 3   twenty-fifth triumph for your glorious clan,
from the games called sacred.
Near the holy grove
of Kronos' son a sudden lot deprived
both you, my child, and Polytimidas
of two Olympic garlands.
And I would add that Melesias
steered your hands and drove your strength,
a charioteer
equal in speed to a dolphin flashing through the sea.

Herodotus

Herodotus must have been born sometime in the 480s, and he probably
died in the 420s. His parents were well-to-do citizens of Halicarnassus,
which is situated on one of the peninsulas jutting out into the Aegean
from the coast of what is now southwest Turkey. He grew up in a region
where the circle of Greek culture intersected the Oriental world of non-
Greeks, or "barbarians," as the Greeks spoke of them. Although Halicarnassus was a Greek town, its population included an indigenous Carian
element. Some members of Herodotus' own family had Carian rather
than Greek names. When the tyrant who governed Halicarnassus survived an uprising against him and consolidated his power, Herodotus
left home; exile was to be the common experience of Greek historians.
Herodotus moved from place to place, making his longest stopovers in
Samos, north of Halicarnassus; in the city of Athens, where he is said to
have received a rich prize for a public reading of his history; and in
the colony of Thurii, which Athens founded on the Gulf of Tarentum in
southern Italy in 443 B.C. He also returned briefly to his birthplace after
the tyranny was finally overthrown. But his travels took him a long way
beyond the Greek-speaking world. He implies in his history that he went
as far north on the Black Sea as the Dnieper River, as far east as
Babylon, and, down the Nile, as far south as Aswan.

The travels are woven into his history in the form of ethnographies.
The last three books give a straightforward account of Xerxes' ill-fated
attack on Greece in 480 B.C. The first six books contain a series of lei-
surely background narratives: Herodotus describes the peoples who had
already been swallowed up by the Persian empire, and he recapitulates
the history of the principal Greek states that were allied against Persia.
The early books especially, with their loops leading from one digression
into another, illustrate Herodotus' eclectic turn of mind. They are filled

with echoes of Greek poetry, philosophy, and science: Herodotus seems to have soaked up every intellectual influence of his day. What he has read often colors the way he writes history. It was he, for example, who introduced the convention by which historical figures are made to utter speeches containing details the historian could not possibly have known; in this he was probably inspired by the set speeches he found in Homer.

The following excerpts are about constitutions, which Herodotus considered one of the strongest forces molding human behavior. The first two passages describe revolutions in the form of government at Athens during the sixth century B.C. The last purports to summarize a discussion about government that occurred in Persia late in the same century.

7. Three Selections from Herodotus' *History*

Herodotus, *History* 1.59–63: The Installation of the Pisistratid Tyranny

Pisistratus' three attempts to secure power cover the years from about 560 to 540 B.C. Aristotle provides a more connected but less nearly contemporary account of the same events in the *Constitution of Athens* (document 16), chapters 13 and following.

1.59   On inquiring into the condition of these two nations, Croesus found that one, the Athenian, was in a state of grievous oppression and disunity under Pisistratus, the son of Hippocrates, who was at that time tyrant of Athens. Hippocrates, when he was a private citizen, is said to have gone once upon a time to Olympia to see the games, when a wonderful prodigy happened to him. As he was sacrificing, the cauldrons which stood near, full of water and of the flesh of the victims, began to boil without the help of fire, and continued till the water overflowed the pot. Chilon the Lacedaemonian, who happened to be there and to witness the prodigy, advised Hippocrates, if he were unmarried, never to take into his house a wife who could bear him a child; if he already had one, to divorce her; if he had a son, to disown him. Chilon's advice did not at all please Hippocrates, who disregarded it, and some time after became the father of Pisistratus. This Pisistratus, at a time when there was civil contention in Attica between the party of the Sea-coast headed by Megacles the son of Alcmaeon,

From *The History of Herodotus*, translated by George Rawlinson. New York: D. Appleton & Co., 1861. Translation revised by Peter White.

and that of the Plain headed by Lycurgus, son of Aristolaides, formed the project of making himself tyrant, and with this view created a third party. Gathering together a band of partisans, and giving himself out for the protector of the Highlanders, he contrived the following stratagem. He wounded himself and his mules, and then drove his chariot into the market-place, professing to have just escaped an attack of his enemies, who had attempted his life as he was on his way into the country. He besought the people to assign him a guard to protect his person, reminding them of the glory which he had gained when he led the attack upon the Megarians, and took the town of Nisaea, at the same time performing many other exploits. The Athenians, deceived by his story, appointed him a band of citizens to serve as a guard, who were to carry clubs instead of spears, and to accompany him wherever he went. Thus strengthened, Pisistratus broke into revolt and seized the citadel. In this way he acquired the sovereignty of Athens, which he continued to hold without disturbing the previously existing offices or altering any of the laws. He administered the state according to the established usages, and his arrangements were fine and good.

1.60   However, after a little time, the partisans of Megacles and those of Lycurgus agreed to forget their differences, and united to drive him out. So Pisistratus, having by the means described first made himself master of Athens, lost his power again before it had time to take root. No sooner, however, was he departed than the factions which had driven him out quarrelled anew, and at last Megacles, beset with strife, sent a herald to Pisistratus, with an offer to re-establish him on the throne if he would marry his daughter. Pisistratus consented, and on these terms an agreement was concluded between the two, after which they proceeded to devise the mode of his restoration. And here the device on which they hit was the silliest to be found in all history, more especially considering that the Greeks have been from very ancient times distinguished from the barbarians by superior sagacity and freedom from foolish simpleness, and remembering that the persons on whom this trick was played were not only Greeks but Athenians, who have the credit of surpassing all other Greeks in cleverness. There was in the Paeanian district a woman named Phya, whose height only fell short of four cubits by three fingers' breadth, and who was besides comely to look upon. This woman they clothed in complete armour, and, instructing her as to the pose which she was to maintain in order to carry off her part, they placed her in a chariot and drove to the city. Heralds had been sent forward to precede her, and to make proclamation to this effect: "Citizens of Athens, receive again Pisistratus with friendly minds. Athena, who honours him above all men, herself conducts him back to her own citadel." This they proclaimed in all directions, and immediately the rumour spread throughout the country districts that

Athena was bringing back her favourite. The people of the city also, fully persuaded that the woman was the veritable goddess, venerated her, and received Pisistratus back.

1.61 Pisistratus, having thus recovered the sovereignty, married, according to agreement, the daughter of Megacles. But since he already had a family of grown up sons, and the Alcmaeonids were supposed to be under a curse, he did not have relations with her in the normal way, as he did not want children by his new wife. She at first kept this matter to herself, but after a time, either her mother questioned her, or it may be that she told it of her own accord. At any rate, she informed her mother, and so it reached her father's ears. Megacles, indignant at receiving an affront from such a quarter, in his anger instantly made up his differences with the opposite faction, on which Pisistratus, aware of what was planning against him, took himself out of the country. Arriving at Eretria, he held a council with his children to decide what was to be done. The opinion of Hippias prevailed, and it was agreed to aim at regaining the sovereignty. The first step was to obtain advances of money from such states as were under obligation to them. By these means they collected large sums from several countries, especially from the Thebans, who gave them far more than any of the rest. To be brief, time passed, and all was at length ready for their return. A band of Argive mercenaries arrived from the Peloponnese, and a certain Naxian named Lygdamis, who volunteered his services, was particularly zealous in the cause, supplying both men and money.

1.62 In the eleventh year of their exile the family of Pisistratus set sail from Eretria on their return home. They occupied the coast of Attica at Marathon, where they encamped, and partisans from the capital and others from the country districts, who loved tyranny better than freedom, streamed out to join them. At Athens, while Pisistratus was obtaining funds, and even after he landed at Marathon, no one paid any attention to his proceedings. When, however, it became known that he had left Marathon, and was marching upon the city, the whole force of the state was levied and led against the returning exiles. Meantime the army of Pisistratus, which had advanced from Marathon, met their adversaries near the temple of the Pallenian Athena and pitched camp opposite them. Here a certain prophet, Amphilytus by name, an Acarnanian, moved by a divine impulse, came into the presence of Pisistratus, and approaching him uttered this prophecy in the hexameter measure:

"Now has the cast been made, the net is outspread in the water,
Through the moonshiny night the tunnies will enter the meshes."

1.63 Such was the prophecy uttered under divine inspiration. Pisistratus, apprehending its meaning, declared that he accepted the oracle, and instantly led on his army. The Athenians from the city had just finished their midday meal, after which they had dispersed, some to dice, others to sleep, when Pisistratus with his troops fell upon them and put them to rout. As soon as the flight began, Pisistratus thought of a very clever scheme to prevent the Athenians from regrouping and to keep them disunited. He mounted his sons on horseback and sent them on in front to overtake the fugitives. As they caught up with them, they delivered Pisistratus' message, which was not to worry, and to go back to their own homes. The Athenians took the advice, and Pisistratus became for the third time master of Athens.

Herodotus, *History* 5.62–73: The Overthrow of the Pisistratids and the Organization of the Cleisthenic Democracy

When Pisistratus died in 527 B.C., the tyranny passed to his sons, Hippias, Thessalus, and Hipparchus. Hipparchus was assassinated in 514, and the ouster described in the following passage was accomplished four years afterwards.

5.62   Having thus related the dream which Hipparchus saw, and traced the descent of the Gephyreans, the family to which his murderers belonged, I must proceed with the matter of which I was intending to speak, and tell how the Athenians were freed from their tyrants. Upon the death of Hipparchus, Hippias, who was tyrant, grew harsh towards the Athenians. The Alcmaeonids, an Athenian family which had been banished by the Pisistratids, joined the other exiles, and endeavoured to procure their own return and to free Athens by force. They seized and fortified Leipsydrium above Paeonia, and tried to gain their object by arms; but great disasters befell them, and their purpose remained unaccomplished. Then, since they were willing to use any method against the Pisistratids, they contracted with the Amphictyons to build the temple which now stands at Delphi, but which in those days did not exist. Being men of great wealth and members of an ancient and distinguished family, they proceeded to build the temple much more magnificently than the plan obliged them. Besides other improvements, instead of the coarse stone of which the temple was to have been constructed according to the contract, they made the facings of Parian marble.

5.63   These same men, if we may believe the Athenians, during their stay at Delphi persuaded the Pythian priestess by a bribe to tell the Spartans, whenever any of them came officially or privately to consult the oracle, that they must free Athens. So the Lacedaemonians, when they found no answer ever returned to them but this, sent at last Anchimolius, the son of Aster—a man of note among their citizens—at the head of an army against Athens, with orders to drive out the Pisistratids, although they were bound to them by the closest ties of friendship. For they esteemed the things of heaven more highly than the things of men. The troops went by sea and were conveyed in transports. Anchimolius brought them to an anchorage at Phalerum, and there the men disembarked. But the Pisistratids, who had previous knowledge of their intentions, had sent to Thessaly, which was allied with Athens, with a request for aid. The Thessalians, in reply to their entreaties, sent them by a public vote 1000 horsemen, under the command of their king, Cineas of Conia. When this help came, the Pisistratids laid their plan accordingly: they cleared the whole plain about Phalerum so as to make it fit for the movements of cavalry, and then charged the enemy's camp with their horse, which fell with such fury upon the Lacedaemonians as to kill many, including Anchimolius the general, and to drive the remainder to their ships. Such was the fate of the first army sent from Lacedaemon, and the tomb of Anchimolius may be seen to this day in Attica; it is at Alopecae, near the temple of Heracles in Cynosarges.

5.64   Afterwards, the Lacedaemonians despatched a larger force against Athens, which they put under the command of Cleomenes, son of Anaxandridas, one of their kings. These troops were not sent by sea, but marched by the mainland. When they came into Attica, their first encounter was with the Thessalian horse, which they shortly put to flight, killing above forty men; the remainder retreated without more ado to Thessaly. Cleomenes proceeded to the city, and, with the aid of such of the Athenians as wished for freedom, besieged the tyrants, who had shut themselves up within the Pelargic wall.

5.65   There would have been small chance of the Pisistratids falling into the hands of the Spartans. The Spartans did not intend to maintain a siege, and the Pisistratids were well provisioned beforehand with stores both of meat and drink. It is likely that after a few days' blockade the Lacedaemonians would have gone back to Sparta, had not an event occurred most unlucky for the besieged, and most advantageous for the besiegers. The children of the Pisistratids were made prisoners, as they were being removed out of the country. By this calamity all their plans were upset, and as the ransom of their children they consented to the demands of the Athenians, and agreed within five days' time to quit Attica. Accordingly they soon afterwards left the country, and withdrew to Sigeum on the Scamander, after reigning thirty-six years over the Athenians. By descent they were Pylians, of the family of the Neleids, to which Codrus and Melanthus likewise belonged, who in former times arrived as immigrants and became

kings of Athens. And hence it was that Hippocrates came to think of calling his son Pisistratus: he named him after the Pisistratus who was a son of
Nestor. Such then was the mode in which the Athenians got rid of their
tyrants. What they did and suffered worthy of note from the time when
they gained their freedom until the revolt of Ionia from King Darius, and
the coming of Aristagoras to Athens with a request that the Athenians
would lend the Ionians aid, I shall now proceed to relate.

5.66   The power of Athens had been great before, but now that the tyrants were gone it became greater than ever. Two men in Athens were pre-
eminent: Cleisthenes, an Alcmaeonid, who is said to have persuaded the
Pythian priestess, and Isagoras, the son of Tisander, who belonged to an
eminent house. His ancestry I am not able to trace further, but his kinsmen
offer sacrifice to Carian Jupiter. These two men strove together for the mastery; and Cleisthenes, finding himself the weaker, allied himself with the
common people. Afterwards he divided the Athenians into ten tribes instead of four, and changed the old names of the tribes, which used to be
called after the sons of Ion (Geleon, Aegicores, Argades, and Hoples).
Cleisthenes invented designations based on the names of heroes, who were
all from Attica except for Ajax. Although he was a foreigner, he was included as a neighbour and ally.

5.67   I believe that in acting thus Cleisthenes was imitating his maternal grandfather, Cleisthenes the tyrant of Sicyon. This Cleisthenes, when
he was at war with Argos, put an end to the contests of the rhapsodists at
Sicyon, because in the Homeric poems Argos and the Argives were so constantly the theme of song. He also conceived the wish to drive Adrastus,
the son of Talaus, out of his country, seeing that he was an Argive hero. For
Adrastus had a shrine at Sicyon, which still stands in the marketplace of
the town. Cleisthenes therefore went to Delphi, and asked the oracle if he
might expel Adrastus. To this the Pythian priestess is reported to have
answered: "Adrastus is the Sicyonians' king, but you are only a stone-
thrower." So when the god would not grant his request, he went home and
began to think how he might contrive to make Adrastus withdraw of his
own accord. After a while he hit upon a plan which he thought would suc-
ceed. He sent envoys to Thebes in Boeotia, and informed the Thebans that
he wished to bring Melanippus the son of Astacus to Sicyon. The Thebans
consented, and Cleisthenes carried Melanippus back with him, assigned
him a precinct within the government-house, and built him a shrine there in
the safest and strongest part. I must explain that Melanippus was brought
in because he was Adrastus' great enemy, having slain both his brother
Mecistes and his son-in-law Tydeus. Cleisthenes, after assigning the precinct to Melanippus, took away Adrastus' sacrifices and festivals and transferred them to his adversary. Hitherto the Sicyonians had paid extraordi-

nary honours to Adrastus, because the country had belonged to Polybus, and Adrastus was Polybus' daughter's son, so that when Polybus died without sons, he left Adrastus his kingdom. Besides other ceremonies, the Sicyonians used to honour Adrastus with tragic choruses, which they assigned to him rather than Dionysus, on account of his calamities. Cleisthenes now gave the choruses to Dionysus, transferring to Melanippus the rest of the sacred rites.

5.68 Such were his doings in the matter of Adrastus. With respect to the Dorian tribes, not wanting the Sicyonians to have the same tribes as the Argives, he changed all the old names for new ones. Here he took special occasion to mock the Sicyonians, for he drew his new names from the words "pig" and "ass," adding the usual tribe endings; only in the case of his own tribe he did nothing of the sort, but gave them a name drawn from his own kingly office. For he called his own tribe the Rulers, while the others he named Pig-folk, or Ass-folk, or Swine-folk. The Sicyonians kept these names, not only during the reign of Cleisthenes, but for sixty years after his death. Then, however, they decided to change to the well-known names of Hyllaeans, Pamphylians, and Dymanatae, taking at the same time, as a fourth name, the title of Aegialeans, from Aegialeus the son of Adrastus.

5.69 This was what the Sicyonian Cleisthenes had done. The Athenian, who was his grandson on his mother's side and had been named after him, resolved, from contempt (as I believe) of the Ionians, that his tribes should not be the same as theirs. And so he followed the pattern set by his namesake of Sicyon. Having brought entirely over to his own side the common people of Athens, whom he had before disdained, he gave all the tribes new names, and made the number greater than formerly. Instead of the four tribe-leaders he established ten; he likewise placed ten demes in each of the tribes; and he was, now that the common people took his part, very much more powerful than his adversaries.

5.70 Isagoras in his turn lost ground, and countered by calling in Cleomenes the Lacedaemonian, who had been on close terms with him since the siege of the Pisistratids; in fact Cleomenes is accused of having been intimate with Isagoras's wife. At this time the first thing that he did was to send a herald and demand that Cleisthenes and a large number of Athenians besides, whom he called "the Accursed," should leave Athens. This message he sent at the suggestion of Isagoras: for in the affair referred to, the Alcmaeonids and their partisans bore the taint of a slaying with which he and his friends were not connected.

5.71 The way in which the Accursed at Athens got their name was this. There was a certain Athenian called Cylon, a victor at the Olympic games, who aspired to the sovereignty, and aided by a group of companions, he made an attempt to seize the citadel. But the attack failed, and Cylon became a suppliant at the statue of Athena. At this point the heads of the naucraries, who in those days were the officials in charge, induced the fugitives to leave by a promise to spare their lives. Nevertheless they were all slain, and the blame was laid on the Alcmaeonids. All this happened before the time of Pisistratus.

5.72   When the message of Cleomenes arrived, requiring Cleisthenes and the Accursed to be expelled, Cleisthenes departed of his own accord. Cleomenes, however, came to Athens with a small band of followers nevertheless, and on his arrival he sent into banishment seven hundred Athenian families, which were pointed out to him by Isagoras. Succeeding here, he next endeavoured to dissolve the council, and to put the government into the hands of three hundred partisans of Isagoras. But the council resisted, and refused to obey his orders, whereupon Cleomenes, Isagoras, and their followers took possession of the citadel. Here they were attacked by the rest of the Athenians, who took the side of the council, and were besieged for the space of two days. On the third day the Lacedaemonians among them were allowed to leave the country under a truce. And so the word which came to Cleomenes received its fulfilment. For when he first went up into the citadel, meaning to seize it, he entered the sanctuary of the goddess in order to question her. But before he got through the doorway, the priestess arose from her throne and said: "Stranger from Lacedaemon, turn back and do not enter the holy place. It is not lawful for a Dorian to set foot here." He answered, "But I am not a Dorian, but an Achaean." Disregarding the warning, Cleomenes made his attempt, and so he was forced to retire, together with his Lacedaemonians. The rest were cast into prison by the Athenians, and condemned to die, among them Timasitheus the Delphian, of whose prowess and courage I have great things which I could tell.

5.73   So these men died in prison. The Athenians directly afterwards recalled Cleisthenes and the seven hundred families which Cleomenes had driven out. They also sent envoys to Sardis to make an alliance with the Persians, for they knew that war would follow with Cleomenes and the Lacedaemonians. When the ambassadors reached Sardis and delivered their message, Artaphernes, son of Hystaspes, who was at that time governor of the place, inquired who they were, and in what part of the world they dwelt, that they wanted to become allies of the Persians. When he had received his answer, he said brusquely that if the Athenians chose to give earth and water to King Darius, he would conclude an alliance with them; but if not, they must go home again. The envoys, acting on their own authority, accepted the terms because they were anxious to form the alliance. But on their return to Athens, they incurred strong censure.

Herodotus, *History* 3.80–84: The Debate in Persia about Constitutions

The line of legitimate Persian kings was broken when Cyrus' son Cambyses died (522 B.C.) and a palace official of the Magian tribe seized power. Seven Persian noblemen formed a conspiracy and eliminated the usurper. Herodotus reports that they then held the following discussion, though he anticipates some resistance to the idea that sixth-century Persians would have talked so much like contemporary sophists.

3.80   When five days were gone, and the hubbub had settled down, the conspirators met together to consult about the situation. At this meeting speeches were made to which many of the Greeks give no credence, but they were made nevertheless. Otanes recommended that the management of public affairs should be entrusted to the whole nation. "To me," he said, "it seems advisable that we should no longer have a single man to rule over us—the rule of one is neither good nor pleasant. You cannot have forgotten the excesses to which Cambyses went, and the excesses of the Magi you have yourselves experienced. How indeed is it possible that monarchy should be a well-adjusted thing, when it allows a man to do as he likes without being answerable? Give even the best of men this power, and it would upset his accustomed way of thinking. His manifold good things puff him up with pride, while envy is so natural to humankind that it cannot but arise in him. But pride and envy together include all wickedness, both leading on to deeds of savage violence. A ruler ought to be devoid of envy since he possesses all that the heart can desire, but the contrary is seen in his conduct towards the citizens. He is jealous of the most virtuous among his subjects, and wishes their death; while he takes delight in the meanest and basest, being ever ready to listen to the tales of slanderers. A king, besides, is beyond all other men intractable. Pay him court in moderation, and he is angry because you do not show him more profound respect—show him profound respect, and he is offended again, because (as he says) you fawn on him. But the worst of all is, that he sets aside the laws of the land, violates women, and puts men to death without trial. Majority rule, on the other hand, has in the first place the fairest of names, *isonomy*; and further it is free from all those outrages which a king commits. There, places are given by lot, the magistrate is answerable for what he does, and all measures are brought before the people. I vote, therefore, that we do away with monarchy, and raise the people to power. For in majority rule there is every advantage."

3.81   Such were the sentiments of Otanes. Megabyzus spoke next, and advised the setting up of an oligarchy: "In all that Otanes has said to per-

The Debate in Persia about Constitutions 45

suade you to put down monarchy," he observed, "I fully concur; but his recommendation that we should give power to the people seems to me not the best advice. For there is nothing so void of understanding, nothing so full of wantonness as the unwieldy rabble. It is unthinkable that men who are trying to escape the licence of a tyrant should submit to the licence of an undisciplined mob. The tyrant, in all his doings, at least knows what he is about, but a mob is altogether devoid of knowledge; for how should there be any knowledge in a rabble, which is untaught, and has no natural sense of what is right and fit? It rushes wildly into state affairs with all the fury of a stream swollen in the winter, and confuses everything. Let the enemies of the Persians be ruled by democracies; but let us choose out from the citizens a certain number of the worthiest, and put the government into their hands. For thus we ourselves shall be among the governors, and the policies of the best men are likely to turn out best."

3.82 This was the advice which Megabyzus gave, and after him Darius came forward, and spoke as follows: "All that Megabyzus said against democracy was well said, I think; but about oligarchy he did not speak advisedly; for take these three forms of government, democracy, oligarchy, and monarchy, and let them each be at their best, I maintain that monarchy far surpasses the other two. What government can possibly be better than that of the very best man in the whole state? The counsels of such a man are like himself, and so he governs the mass of the people blamelessly; while at the same time his measures against evil-doers are kept more secret than in other states. Contrariwise, in oligarchies, where men vie with each other in the service of the commonwealth, fierce enmities are apt to arise between man and man, each wishing to be leader, and to carry his own measures; whence comes open strife, then bloodshed, then monarchy follows; and this too shows how far that rule surpasses all others. Again, in a democracy, it is impossible for there not to be malpractices: these malpractices, however, do not lead to enmities, but to close friendships, which are formed among those engaged in them, who must stick together to carry on their villainies. And so things go on until a man stands forth as champion of the people, and puts down the evil-doers. He is admired by the people for his services, and from being admired soon comes to be appointed king; so that here too it is plain that monarchy is the best government. Lastly, to sum up all in a word, from whom, I ask, was it that we got the freedom which we enjoy?—did the people give it to us, or an oligarchy, or a monarch? As a single man recovered our freedom for us, my recommendation is that we keep to the rule of one. Even apart from this, we ought not to change the laws of our forefathers when they work fairly; for to do so would not be good."

3.83 Such were the three opinions brought forward at this meeting; the four other Persians voted in favour of the last. Otanes, who wished to give his countrymen a democracy, when he found the decision against him, arose a second time, and spoke thus before the assembly: "Brother conspirators, it is plain that the king who is to be chosen will be one of ourselves, whether we make the choice by casting lots, or let the people choose, or use some other method. Now, as I have neither a mind to rule nor to be ruled, I shall not enter the lists with you in this matter. I withdraw, however, on one condition—none of you shall claim to exercise rule over me or my descendants forever." The six agreed to these terms, and Otanes withdrew and stood apart from the contest. And still to this day the family of Otanes continues to be the only free family in Persia. They submit to the king only so far as they themselves choose, while keeping the laws of the land.

3.84   After this the six took counsel together, as to the fairest way of setting up a king: and first, with respect to Otanes, they resolved, that if any of their own number got the kingdom, Otanes and his descendants should receive year by year, as a mark of special honour, a Median robe, and all the other gifts which are accounted most honourable in Persia. And these they resolved to give him, because he was the man who first planned the outbreak, and who brought the seven together. These privileges, therefore, were assigned specially to Otanes, but the rest they were all to share. Each was to be free to enter the palace unannounced whenever he pleased, unless the king was sleeping with his wife; and the king was to be bound to marry into no family excepting those of the conspirators. Concerning the appointment of a king, the resolve to which they came was this: they would ride out together next morning into the skirts of the city, and he whose horse first neighed after the sun was up should have the kingdom.

The Old Oligarch

Both the author and the date of this odd tract are unknown. It is preserved under the name of Xenophon (ca. 430–355 B.C.) along with other
works by him. But it is written in a style unlike his, and it seems to describe what Athens was like during the early years of the Peloponnesian
War, when Xenophon was only a child. For lack of a better designation,
the author is commonly nicknamed "The Old Oligarch," on the basis of
his expressed political sentiments. By his own testimony he appears to be
a citizen of Athens, identified in some way with the aristocracy, and perhaps currently residing abroad.

His essay is the earliest example of a genre that came into vogue as
sophists of the fifth century stimulated discussion about the nature and
ideal design of the state. *Politeia* at this period does not mean "constitution" in the modern sense (none of the old city-states of mainland Greece
had a written constitution) but "civic character"—customs and public
attitudes as well as laws and institutions. Unlike Aristotle's longer work
of the same name (document 16), this tract is a disputation rather than a
description. The author announces a thesis and proceeds to prove it, considering first the internal organization of the city and then Athens in relation to other states. His approach is not particularly theoretical. He is less
interested in government structures than in the means by which a particular class can dominate them. His practical orientation gives him a good
eye for detail; within the space of a few pages he tells more about life
in Athens than any writer except Aristophanes.

The author's dispassionate tone makes it difficult to be sure of the
effect he hopes to achieve with his argument. We must try to imagine the
probable reactions both of oligarchs and of democrats. The suggestions
of the last paragraph are particularly artful. There is a play on two senses
of *oligoi*, "few" and "oligarchs," and on two uses of the verb *atiman*,

"to dishonor" and "to deprive of civic status" (in the translation of the paragraph, "deprive of civic status" represents *atiman* throughout, to emphasize that the same Greek word is being used). In effect, our author is telling his readers that the oligarchs, and they alone of the citizens of Athens, are unjustly deprived of status and that unjust deprivation of status should make one angry. He also maintains that the oligarchs, being few, are unable to attack the democracy with success. Until this paragraph is reached, a democratic reader might suppose that our author is accepting democratic arguments for the appropriateness of democratic rule (there is no need to suppose that the arguments used are original with the author), and, after reading the last paragraph, he might be convinced that the oligarchs were harmless. True, any perceptive democratic reader would not need to be informed that to deprive an *agathos* of status is an insult that demands effective action to regain it, and to claim that he can do nothing is to compound the insult. But the author's skill in handling language would render it difficult to prosecute him as a dangerous enemy of the democracy, even though his last paragraph, as the culmination of all that has preceded it, is an incitement to any oligarch to express his anger in violent action.

---

8. The Old Oligarch, *The Constitution of Athens*

About the political system of the Athenians, that they actually chose such a system—I don't congratulate them for it. For in so choosing they have chosen that people of no account do better than people of merit. I certainly don't congratulate them for that. But since it pleased them to do so, I will demonstrate how well they protect their system and successfully pursue the rest of their policies, though wrong policies in the eyes of other Greeks.

First I'll say this—it's fair enough that the poor and the general populace amount to more there than the well-born and the rich, for this reason: because the general populace operates the ships and bestows power on the city. Steersmen and stroke-callers and unit captains and prow-men and shipwrights—these are the ones who bestow power on the city, much more than heavy-armed infantrymen, well-born people, and people of substance. Since that's the way it is, it seems to be right for everybody to have a share in public office, both elective and by lot, and right to let any citizen speak who wants to.

Such offices as bring safety if they are in meritorious hands—and danger to the whole people if they aren't—the general populace feels no need

Translated by Charles M. Gray.

to participate in. That is, it doesn't think it has to participate through lottery in generalships or cavalry commanderships. For the populace recognizes that there is more advantage in not exercising those offices itself but for those to exercise them who are most able to. But the populace seeks to exercise those offices that pay wages or bring profit to one's household.

A fact that some people find amazing—that they generally allot more to the no-good, the poor, and the vulgar than to the meritorious—is actually a manifest means to preserve their democracy. For if the poor and vulgar and ne'er-do-well thrive and grow numerous, they build up the democracy. But if the rich and the meritorious thrive, the vulgar strengthen that which is opposite to themselves, and for every country that which is best is antithetical to democracy. For among the best people there is the least unrestraint and injustice, the most precise concern for things of value; but in the populace there is the most ignorance, disorder, and vice. For poverty has a strong tendency to lead them into shameful ways, along with the lack of education and the ignorance that lack of money causes for some people.

Someone might say that they ought not to let everybody speak in turn or to give counsel but only the ablest and best men. Yet even in this they are very well-advised—when they let even the worthless ones speak. For if the meritorious did the speaking and counseling, it would be good for those like themselves but not good for the vulgar. As it is, when a worthless man who wants to can get up and speak, he will find his way to what is good for him and for those like him.

One might ask, "How can such a man know what's good for himself and the general populace?" But the people know that the ignorance and worthlessness and friendly intentions of this man are more beneficial than the virtue and wisdom and unfriendly intentions of the person of merit. A city doing things this way wouldn't, of course, be very *good*, but the democracy would be best preserved by such ways. For the populace does not want to be a slave in a city with good laws[1] but to be free and to rule, and being under bad law makes little difference to it. For from what *you* do not consider a regime of good law the populace takes strength and is free. If you are looking for good law, the first thing you will envisage is the able setting the laws. Then the meritorious will put checks on the worthless, and the people of merit will do the counseling about the city and will not permit crazy people to be members of the Council or to speak or participate in the Assembly. Now the immediate result of these good things would be that the populace would fall into slavery.

---

1. "With good laws" and similar expressions used here are an insufficient translation of the word *eunomia*, which in its various forms characterizes the state as "well-ordered generally," "law-abiding," and more.

Moreover, unrestraint on the part of slaves and resident aliens is very prevalent with the Athenians, and it isn't permitted to beat them there, nor will a slave stand aside for you. I'll explain what's behind the local practice: if it were lawful for a free person to beat a slave, resident alien, or freedman, lots of Athenians mistaken for slaves would get beaten. For the populace there is no better in its clothing than slaves and resident aliens, and its appearance is no better.

If someone is amazed at this too, that they let slaves live it up there and in some cases to lead lives of great splendor: this too they would seem to do on considered opinion. For where there is naval power it is necessary for slaves to work for money, so that . . .[2] And where there are rich slaves there is no longer any advantage in my slave's being afraid of you. (In Sparta, by contrast, my slave *is* afraid of you.) If your slave is afraid of me, he will even venture to give his own money so as to avoid any risk to himself.

Therefore we have effected social equality[3] even for slaves in relation to the free and for resident aliens in relation to citizens, since the city needs resident aliens, owing to the abundance of crafts and to the fleet. Therefore we have quite reasonably given social equality [*isegoria*] to resident aliens too.

The populace there has deposed from favor those who give serious attention to physical training and fine arts, considering all that to be valueless, since it knows itself to be incapable of practicing such things. As for equipping choruses and gymnasiums and warships, they know that the rich equip choruses, while the populace is part of them, and that the rich equip the gymnasiums and the warships, while the populace have gymnasiums and ships provided for them. Therefore the populace thinks it appropriate to receive money for singing and running and dancing and sailing in the ships, so that it gets the money and the rich get poorer. In the lawcourts, too, justice is of no more concern to them than what is advantageous for themselves.

About the allies and the fact that when the people sail out [to the allied cities] they bring malicious prosecutions and generally hate the better sort of people: knowing that the ruler is necessarily hated by the ruled, and that, if the rich and powerful are strong in the cities, the rule of the Athenian populace will be short-lived, therefore they get the better sort sentenced to deprivation of their civic privileges, and they take away their money and drive them out and kill them, and they build up the no-account. But the meritorious Athenians protect the meritorious people in the allied

---

2. Text corrupt for the rest of this sentence.

3. *Isegoria* strictly means "equal right to speak" but was generalized to "equal rights." By definition, slaves' legal and political rights are not equal to free people's; we would assign the equality here to the "social" sphere.

cities, knowing that it is always good for them to preserve the best people in the cities.

One might say that it would be Athens' strength if the allies were able to bring in money. To the vulgar, however, it seems better for each individual Athenian to have the allies' money and for the latter to have no more than they need to live and, being incapable of plotting, to work for a living.

The Athenian populace is also thought ill-advised in this, that they compel the allies to sail to Athens for lawsuits. But they by contrast reckon up all the advantages that the Athenian populace gets from this too: First, receiving year-round jurors' fees from the sums deposited with the court. Then, sitting at home, without any sailing of ships, they manage the allied cities, protect those of the popular party, and destroy those opposed to it in the lawcourts. But if each of the allies held lawsuits at home, since they are disaffected from the Athenians they would destroy those of their number who were friendliest to the Athenian populace.

In addition to these points, the Athenian populace profits in the following ways from lawsuits for the allies being at Athens. First, the 1 percent tax collected in the Piraeus yields more for the city; if someone's got flats to rent, he'll do better; so, too, if someone has a team of horses or a slave for hire. Another item: the court-summoners do better through allies coming to stay a while.

Furthermore, if the allies didn't come for lawsuits, they would pay honor only to those of the Athenians who sail out to the allied states—generals, commanders of triremes, and ambassadors. But as it is, each one of the allies has been forced to flatter the populace of Athens, knowing that one who comes to Athens must get a favorable or unfavorable judgment from the populace, not anybody else, as Athenian law requires. And he is forced to ask for favor in the lawcourts and to clasp the hands of people going in. So in this way the allies are more the slaves of the Athenian populace.

In addition, through having possessions beyond their own borders, and through offices extending beyond those borders, they and their attendants have learned rowing without noticing it. For it is necessary for a person who sails frequently to take hold of an oar—both the man himself and his servant—and also to learn nautical terms. And good steersmen come to be through experience of sailing and through practice. Some have practiced piloting a sailing vessel, some a cargo ship, and from there some go on to triremes. And the multitude can row as soon as it gets on a ship, since it has practiced all its life.

Their infantry, which is considered the Athenians' least strong point, has been set up that way on purpose. They figure they are inferior to and fewer than their enemies—but compared to their allies, who pay tribute, they are strongest even on land, and they think the infantry is good enough if they're superior to their allies.

Besides, something like this has by good luck been their situation: in the case of a land-based empire, it is possible for small cities to join forces and fight together. But in the case of a sea-based empire consisting of islanders, it is not possible for cities to join in a single force. For the sea is in between them, and their rulers dominate the sea. And if the islanders manage to join as one force in a single island, they will be destroyed by hunger.

Insofar as there are cities on the mainland ruled by the Athenians, the big ones are dominated by means of fear and the small ones entirely by means of need. For there is no city that does not need to import or export to some degree. It can't do so if it's not obedient to the rulers of the sea.

For another thing, it is possible for the rulers of the sea to do what land powers sometimes can: to devastate territory belonging to more potent states. For it is possible to sail to a place where there are no, or few, enemy forces, and, if they attack, one can get on one's ship and sail away. And someone operating this way has fewer problems than someone conducting a relief operation by land.

Furthermore, sea-rulers can sail away from their own country as far as you like, but land-rulers can't go many days' journey away from their own territory. For marches are slow, and one going on foot can't have food for very long. And one going by land must either go through friendly country or else fight and win; but one who is sailing can disembark where he is more powerful, and, where he is not, he does not have to disembark in that country but can sail along until he reaches a friendly country or those weaker than himself.

Moreover, those who are most powerful by land have difficulty enduring the crop diseases that are sent by Zeus, but those powerful by sea endure them easily. For not every country is diseased at once, so that for sea-rulers food comes from a healthy place.

If I need to mention even minor matters, by virtue of domination of the sea they have in the first place discovered all sorts of good cheer through mingling with various foreigners. Whatever is sweet in Sicily or in Italy, in Cyprus, Egypt, or Lydia, in Pontus or the Peloponnese or anywhere else— all these are gathered in one place through domination of the sea.

And by hearing every way of speaking, they have picked out this expression from one, that from another. The Greeks tend to have distinctive dialects, ways of life, and fashions in dress, but the Athenians employ mixed modes, taken from all the Greeks and the barbarians.

As for sacrifices and rituals, festivals and temples: knowing that it is not possible for every poor man to sacrifice and feast and establish sacred places and have a great and beautiful city to live in, the commoners have discovered how to manage these things. Thus the city sacrifices many victims under public auspices. And it's the populace that feasts and receives shares of the sacrificed animals.

Some of the rich have private gymnasiums and baths and bathhouses, but the populace builds for itself plenty of its own wrestling arenas, bathhouses, baths. And the crowd manages to benefit more from these than the happy few.

They alone are able to possess the wealth of the Greeks and the barbarians. For if some city is rich in shipbuilding wood, where will it dispose of it if it can't persuade the rulers of the sea? And if some city is rich in iron or bronze or flax, where will it dispose of it if it doesn't persuade the sea-ruler? From precisely these things I get my ships: wood, iron, bronze, flax, beeswax, each from a different place.

Besides, those opposed to us aren't allowed to take things elsewhere, or else they don't use the sea. And I, producing nothing from the earth, possess all these things by way of the sea. But no other city has two of them. Wood and flax don't exist in the same place, but where there is a lot of flax, the country is flat and unwooded. Bronze and iron don't come from the same city, nor do any other two or three of the products come from one city, but one here and one there.

Moreover, alongside every mainland there is either a projecting coast or an offshore island or some strait, so that it is possible for the masters of the sea to anchor there and harry the people inhabiting the mainland.

One thing they lack. For if the Athenians ruled the sea from an island base, they could do evil if they wanted to and suffer none, so long as they ruled the sea and could avoid having their own country ravaged and having to face enemies there. But as it is, the farmers and the rich Athenians are apt to fawn on the enemy, while the general populace, since it knows they won't burn or wreck anything of its, lives without fear and does not fawn on them.

Another fear besides they'd be rid of if they inhabited an island: the city would never be betrayed by the upper-class minority, the gates be opened and the enemy burst in on them. For how could this happen if they lived on an island? No one would conspire against the populace if they lived on an island. For now if people organize conspiracies they do so because they place hope in the enemy, whom they might bring in by land. But if they inhabited an island, they would not have to fear this either.

Since, then, they didn't have the luck to inhabit an island originally, here's what they do now: they put their property on the islands for safekeeping and trust to their dominance of the sea, and they disregard the Attic countryside's getting cut to pieces, knowing that if they take pity on it they will be deprived of other, greater goods.

Furthermore, it is necessary for oligarchic cities to stand by alliances and oaths. And if they don't abide by contracts, and you are wronged by someone, one has the names of the few who made the agreement. But whatever the general populace agrees to, it can blame on the individual who spoke or moved the question, while it can deny to the other party that it was present or is satisfied with things that the others know were settled in full democratic assembly. And if it doesn't please the populace that such agreements should exist, it finds a thousand pretexts for not doing what it doesn't want to. If any bad comes from what the populace has advised, it alleges that a few people actively opposed to the scheme have ruined it. But if good comes from it, they put all the "blame" on themselves.

Furthermore, they don't permit the general populace to be made the butt of comedies and to be ill-spoken of, in order that they may hear no evil about themselves. But they encourage comedies about individuals, if someone wants to lampoon one, knowing well that the object of comedy is rarely the populace or the majority, but a rich or highly born or powerful person—whereas few of the poor and vulgar are made fun of in comedies, and not even those unless it is for being busybodies and trying to get more than the common people have, so it's no grief to them when such types are the butt of comedy.

So this is what I say: the Athenian populace knows which of the citizens are meritorious and which are good-for-nothing, and, knowing this, they love those who are well disposed and useful to themselves, even if they are good-for-nothing, and they hate the people of quality very much. For they don't think the virtue of the latter does them any good, but bad. And some are the opposite of this: though actually belonging to the populace, they are not "popular" by nature.

But I forgive the populace their democracy. For it is pardonable for any man to help himself. But anyone who does not belong to the populace and has chosen to live in a democratic city rather than an oligarchic one is prepared to do injustice and has recognized that it is more possible for someone bad to go unnoticed in a democratic city than in an oligarchic one. Certainly I don't commend the way the Athenian political system is. But since it pleases them to be democratic, they seem to me to do a good job of preserving their democracy by arranging things as I have shown.

Moreover, I notice that some people criticize the Athenians about this, because sometimes it's impossible for a person who sits there a whole year to get his business done with the Council or the popular Assembly. And this is the case at Athens for no other reason than that, owing to the abundance of business, they can't send everybody off with his taken care of. How could they, when, to start with, they have to have festivals in quantity like no other Greek city (and during the festivals it is less possible for anyone to do city business); and then to judge civil suits, and criminal cases, and investigations of official conduct, in quantity such as all other people put together don't have to judge; and the council has to deliberate about many things concerning war, many things concerning pecuniary ways and means, many concerning legislation, many concerning problems that arise at any given time with regard to the city, and many that affect the allies; and has to receive tribute and to give attention to dockyards and temples? So why is it any wonder, when there is so much business, that it is impossible to get through everybody's?

Some say that if a person comes to the council or popular assembly with money, he gets his business done. I agree that a lot gets done with money at Athens and that still more would get done if still more people gave money; yet this I know for sure, that the city hasn't the capacity to deal with all who want something, not even if someone were to give them gold and silver in any imaginable amount.

It is also necessary to judge these things: whether someone has failed to repair his ship or has built on public land. And further: to adjudicate every year matters involving chorus-sponsors at the Dionysia, the Thargelia, the Panathenaea, the Promethia, and the Hephaestia. Also, every year four hundred commanders of triremes are installed, and it's necessary to adjudicate about this for any who wish it. In addition, they have to scrutinize officials and adjudicate in that area, and to investigate orphans and install jailkeepers. These things come up every year.

Then from time to time it's necessary to judge military offenses, and any other sudden wrongdoing that occurs, and cases of unaccustomed outrage and impiety. I omit many things altogether, but the main things have been discussed, except for assessments of tribute. That takes place for the most part every four years.

Now then, mustn't one suppose that all these things have to be judged? Let anyone say what should not be. And if you must agree that they all have to be judged, that necessarily means throughout the year—as things are now, they sit in judgment during the whole year and still can't do enough to put a stop to wrongdoing, owing to the sheer number of people.

Well then, somebody will say that the judging is necessary but that fewer people are needed to do the judging. Now, that would have to mean (unless the number of courts were reduced) that there would be few people in each court, so that it would be easy to prepare oneself to face a few jurors and to bribe the whole court, and the chance of a just judgment would be much less.

In addition, you've got to consider that the Athenians have to have festivals, during which it's impossible to judge cases. And festivals they have—twice as many as other people. For the sake of argument, however, I'll assume they have the same number as the city that has fewest.

Now, these things being as they are, I say it would be impossible for Athens to do business differently than she does, except as one might add or subtract small details. But to make major changes so as not to take something away from the democracy would be impossible. One could of course find many ways to make the political system *better*. But it is not easy to do an adequate job of discovering how they could conduct their political business better *so as also* to permit democracy to exist (except for what I just said—adding or subtracting small details).

In this respect also the Athenians do not seem to *me* well advised: that they side with the worst people in cities torn by civil dissension. But they do this on considered opinion. For if they sided with the best people they would side with those who don't see things the way they do. In no city is the best element kindly disposed to the populace, but the worst element in every city is friendly toward it. For similar people have a friendly attitude toward similar people. Thus the Athenians opt for what befits them. Whenever they have sided with the best people, it hasn't benefited them. On the contrary, the populace in Boeotia was enslaved in a short time. Likewise when they sided with the best people in Miletus—in a short time they revolted and massacred the common people. Likewise when they took the Spartans' side against the Messenians—in a short time the Spartans subdued the Messenians and made war on the Athenians.

One might suppose that no one has been unjustly deprived of civic status in Athens. I say that there are people who have been unjustly deprived of it. However, they are merely a few men. But it takes more than a few to attack the democracy at Athens, since this too is a fact of life: men who are justly deprived of their civic status do not take the matter to heart; those who are unjustly deprived of it do so. Now, how could anyone suppose that the many are unjustly deprived of status at Athens, where the common people hold the magistracies? It is for failing to rule justly or to speak and act justly that people are deprived of their civic status at Athens. Anyone who considers these matters must draw the conclusion that there is no danger from those who are deprived of their civic status at Athens.

Aristophanes

Aristophanes was an Athenian. He seems to have been born in the 440s and to have lived for about sixty years. He began writing comedies for his city's dramatic festivals during his twenties, if not before, and over the forty years of his career he averaged about a play a year. We have eleven. Cleon, the politician he attacks in this and other comedies, tried using the courts to intimidate him on more than one occasion, but without success. Otherwise, very little is known about Aristophanes' life. *The Wasps* was produced early in 422, several months before Cleon was killed in battle and Athens and Sparta signed a truce that closed a decade of fighting.

Though Aristophanes came up with some inspired plots for his plays, plot was a fairly late improvement in the history of Greek comedy. The first performances were loosely structured scenes of song and dance, and even Aristophanes' plays follow dramatic conventions that modern readers find bizarre. Three scenes in *The Wasps* are variations of scenes that were typical in Old Comedy: the formal debate between father and son that comes a third of the way through the play, the long address that the chorus directs to the audience two-thirds of the way through, and the orgiastic party that ends the play. As for the subject matter, Aristophanes' characters and situations are caricatures rather than imitations of reality. The problem is to judge at what point his presentation of Athenian justice begins to touch the underlying truth.

The texts of ancient plays, unlike modern ones, did not include descriptions of the set or stage directions by the playwright. In the version that follows, all such material has been added by the translator. It should be regarded simply as his best guess about the way in which Aristophanes' play should be acted.

9. Aristophanes, *The Wasps*

Characters of the Play

SOSIAS ⎤
XANTHIAS ⎦ *Slaves of Phobokleon*
PHOBOKLEON, *son of Philokleon*
PHILOKLEON, *an elderly Athenian juror*
FIRST KORYPHAIOS
SECOND KORYPHAIOS
CHORUS *of elderly Athenian Jurors (WASPS)*
FIRST LITTLE BOY
SECOND LITTLE BOY
FLEAHOUND, *a dog*
CHOWHOUND, *a dog*
A FLUTE-GIRL
A BANQUET GUEST
MYRTIA, *proprietress of a bakery*
CHAIREPHON
THE MAN WHO LOOKS LIKE EURIPIDES
A WITNESS
SLAVES
ASSORTED KITCHEN UTENSILS
PUPPIES
OUTRAGED GUESTS AND SMALL TRADESMEN
THREE SONS OF KARKINOS

Scene: A street in Athens. In the background, center, the house of Philokleon and Phobokleon, a two-storied dwelling with a front door, a side door, and a second-story window. A huge net covers the entire façade, draped so that the doors are free. Over the front door, a wreath. Phobokleon is asleep on the flat roof. On guard before the house, armed with long iron spits, are the two slaves, Sosias and Xanthias. They are very weary. Xanthias, in fact, is asleep. The time is shortly before dawn.

Translated by Douglass Parker in *Aristophanes: Three Comedies: The Birds, The Clouds, The Wasps*, edited by William Arrowsmith; translated by Arrowsmith and Douglass Parker. Ann Arbor: University of Michigan Press, 1969. All notes to this text are by the translator, except for note 16, which was added by the volume editors.

SOSIAS
Shaking Xanthias.
   Xanthias!
No answer. He shakes again.
      What the hell do you think you're doing?

XANTHIAS
I'm studyin'. How to Relieve the Watch. One easy
lesson.
He goes back to sleep.

SOSIAS
     You're aching for trouble. Have you forgotten
what we're guarding? A MONSTER!

XANTHIAS
           Scares me so much
I'm afraid to stay awake.
Back to sleep again.

SOSIAS
        Okay, it's your neck. . . .
Go ahead, see if I care. . . . Why should I care?
I can hardly keep *my* eyes open.
He snuggles down.
          Delicious!
He goes to sleep; then, after a moment or two
of silence, begins to thrash around wildly, kick-
ing Xanthias awake.

XANTHIAS
Now what? Have you gone crazy? Or did you join
those holy-rolling Asiatic Korybants?[1]

SOSIAS
          Neither.
But it *was* a divine visitation. *And* from Asia.
Bacchos descended and filled me with his presence.
He produces a wine bottle and drinks. Xanthias,
after a look, produces his bottle and drinks.

---

1. Priests of the goddess Kybele, whose rites were distinguished by wild dancing.

XANTHIAS
A fellow-worshipper! The real afflatus—Phrygian
liquid sleep. One thing about Oriental religion—
it's *restful*.

He drinks again.

Except, it made me dream just now—
incredible!

SOSIAS
Me, too. A highly abnormal nightmare. . . .
You tell yours first.

XANTHIAS
I seemed to see an eagle
swoop down, massive and vast, upon the city,
clench in his claws a brazen buckler, bear it
aloft to heaven—
and turn into Kleonymos, and throw
the shield away.

SOSIAS
Say what you want about Kleonymos,
he's a wonderful riddle.

XANTHIAS
How so?

SOSIAS
It can win you a drink:
"What animal defends itself by shedding *its armor?"*

XANTHIAS
That dream—what an omen!

SOSIAS
Don't worry. It can't mean anything
disastrous.

XANTHIAS
Kleonymos can't mean anything *but*.
—It's your turn; you tell your dream.

SOSIAS

                                   Mine's a big one.
It concerns the whole hull of the Ship of State.

XANTHIAS

Then get a move on, man, and lay the keel.

SOSIAS

I'd no sooner gone to sleep than I dreamed about sheep,
all members of the Assembly, meeting on the Pnyx. *Dressed* sheep—
they all were carrying canes and wearing cloaks.
Up front, I saw a greedy, rapacious whale
haranguing these poor sheep in a booming bellow,
the bloated blatting of a swollen sow.

XANTHIAS

                                  Pew!

SOSIAS

What's wrong?

XANTHIAS

                          You can stop right there. Whales, sows—
your nightmare stinks of rotten leather; it reeks
of that tanner Kleon.[2]

SOSIAS

                          Then this filthy whale
took up a bag and filled it with lumps of fat.

XANTHIAS

Oh, god, it *is* Kleon! He's sacking Greece!

SOSIAS

Squatting on the ground beside the whale
I saw Theoros. He had a crow's head. At least,
that's what *I* said it was. But Alkibiades—he was
in my dream—*he* said Theoros was a sapsucker.[3]
Alkibiades isn't much on birds.

---

2. The demagogue owned a leather factory, and Aristophanes never forgot it.
3. There is a play here in the Greek on Alkibiades' lisp, which substituted *l* for *r*, so that Theoros

XANTHIAS

                              Maybe not.
He *is* a pretty good judge of character, though.

SOSIAS

But isn't that mysterious, Theoros turning into a crow?

XANTHIAS

No mystery at all. Best thing that could happen.

SOSIAS

                                              How?

XANTHIAS

How? He's a man, then suddenly he becomes a crow—
the interpretation's obvious. Your dream means that Theoros
will soar away from us—

SOSIAS

                    And what?

XANTHIAS

                              —and CROAK!
He ducks as Sosias, disgusted, swings wildly,
then picks up the two iron spits and chases him
around the stage.

SOSIAS

Stop, you subtle soothsayer! Come here, you two-bit
prophet—I want to give you your pay: two spits!

XANTHIAS

Hold it! Let me tell the audience the plot.
The chase stops. He turns to the audience.
                    First, Gentlemen, a few preliminary remarks.
Don't look for anything too high-brow from us;
or for any slapstick smuggled out of Megara.
We haven't got those two slaves chucking chestnuts
out of a basket to keep the audience happy,

---

has the head of a *kolax*, "flatterer," rather than a *korax*, "raven." Rogers' *raven-cwaven* alternation is
the nearest English. Better to forget the lisp.

or Herakles to be swindled out of his supper again.
As for the aesthetic bit—that's out. We won't
bring on Euripides to get another working over.
Now Kleon's illustrious, thanks to luck[4]—no matter,
we won't chop him up into hash *again*: No Politics.
We merely have a little plot with a moral—
not too refined and dainty for *you*, of course,
but rather more intelligent than smutty farce.
So look—

Pointing at Phobokleon.

                that's our master there—asleep
topside—the big fellow—the one up on the roof.
He's locked his father indoors, and set us two
on sentry duty so the old man can't go out.
The father's sick with a baffling, unnatural disease,
so strange that none of you would ever guess it
unless I told you . . .

Listening to some imaginary voice from the audience.

                    You don't believe me? Try it!

Listening again and pointing.

      There's Pronapes' son Amynias.—You say the old man's
sick with *dice*-addiction?

SOSIAS

                  Dice-addiction!
He's judging from his own disease.—Dead wrong, Amynias!

XANTHIAS

Not quite.—Take fifty per cent, Amynias. Addiction
is half of the affliction.

*Jerking a thumb at Sosias, who is beckoning
to someone in the audience.*

                Sosias is telling Derkylos
the old man's addicted to *drink*.

SOSIAS

                  I certainly am not!
That's a gentleman's disease. What would *he* know about it?

---

4. By virtue of his victory over the Spartans at Sphakteria in the summer of 425.

XANTHIAS
Pointing again.

You have a theory, Nikostratos? He's a *sacrifice*-addict—
a religious fanatic? No. Oh, then you say
he's a *hospitality*-addict?

SOSIAS

You mean like Philoxenos, the Perfect
Host? Perfect to a fault—he's a bugger. NO!

XANTHIAS
To the audience in toto.

These feeble guesses are futile—you'll never find out.
If you really want to know, then quiet down,
and I'll tell you the master's disease in just a minute.
He pauses and waits for silence.

He's a JURY-addict! Most violent case on record.
He's wild to render verdicts, and bawls like a baby
if ever he misses a seat on the very first bench.
He doesn't get any sleep at night, not a wink.
Or, if he closes his eyes a speck, he's in Court—
all night his mind goes flapping around the water-clock.
You know those pebbles that the Jurors drop into the urns
marked *Guilty* and *Not Guilty*, to record their votes on the verdict?
Well, he's squeezed *his* pebble so often and so hard
that when he wakes up, he has three fingers stuck together,
like someone putting incense on the festival altar.
And worse. Let him see the name of a fathead faggot
scrawled on a wall—"*I letch for Demos; he's a doll*"—
and he scratches beside it, "*I itch for the Jury; it's a jewel.*"
Once his rooster didn't crow till sundown. Know
what he said? "That cock's corrupt! The officials under investigation
bribed him to wake me up too late for Court!"
Now he shouts for his shoes right after supper;
he's over there *way* before dawn, and goes to sleep
clutching a courtroom column just like a barnacle.
And nasty—watch him in action! When he takes his tablet
to fix the penalty, he always draws the Long Line:[5]

5. Athenian juries, in certain cases, established the penalty—or rather chose between one proposed by the defendant and one proposed by the plaintiff. The choice of the individual juror was indicated by a line drawn by a stylus on a wax tablet: short for minimum, long for maximum.

everyone gets the maximum sentence from him!
Then off for home like a bee—or a *bumble*-bee—
wax just plastered underneath his fingernails.
He's petrified that he might run out of those pebbles
he uses for voting; so he keeps a *beach* in the house.
In sum, he's insane; the more we reason with him,
the more he judges everybody else. Absolutely
hopeless. Incurable.

So now we've locked him up
with bolts, and watch to be sure he doesn't go out.
The son, you see, takes his daddy's disease quite hard.
First, he tried the Word Cure. Gently he wheedled
and pleaded the old man to put away his cloak
and stay home.

Didn't work. So next, the Water Cure.
Dunked him and dosed him.

No dice.

Then Applied Religion.
Made him a Korybant.

Tambourine and all, his daddy
banged his way into court for more drumhead justice.
Finally, as a last recourse, he turned to Pure Prayer.
One night he grabbed the old man, sailed over to Aigina,
and bedded him down for the cure in Asklepios' temple . . .
and up he popped at dawn by the jury-box gate!
Since then, we never let him out of the house.
At first, he kept sneaking out the pipes and drains
and running away. And so we plugged up all
the holes with hunks of rag, and sealed them tight.
He reacted rather like a jackdaw—kept banging pegs
in the wall, running down, and hopping off.
At last we took these nets and draped them around
all over the house—and *now* we keep him in.
One more thing about the old man—he's a KLEON-addict!
—I mean it! That's his name, in fact: PHILOKLEON!
His son takes the opposite tack. In this and everything.
He *hates* Kleon. And that's *his* name: PHOBOKLEON!
He's sort of a snooty, snorty, holier-than-thou-er . . .

PHOBOKLEON

Awake.

Xanthias! Sosias! You asleep?

XANTHIAS

Oh-oh!

SOSIAS

What's up?

XANTHIAS
Phobokleon.

PHOBOKLEON
Pointing at the side door.
One of you get over here right away!
Xanthias obeys.
Father's gone and got into the stove. He squeaked in
somehow, and now he's skittering around like a mouse.
—*You* see that he doesn't slip out the bathtub drain.
Sosias runs to the house.
—*You* keep leaning on that door.

XANTHIAS
Yessir! Yessir!
*Silence. Then the trapdoor on the chimney is
slowly raised from within.*

PHOBOKLEON
Almighty Poseidon, what's that creaking in the chimney?
*Philokleon's head begins to emerge cautiously
from the chimney.*
Hey, who are you?

PHILOKLEON
I'm smoke, and I'm issuing forth.

PHOBOKLEON
Smoke? That's nice. What wood are you from?

PHILOKLEON
I'm peach wood.[6]

*He starts to clamber out. Phobokleon shoves
him back.*

---

6. In Greek, *sykinou,* "fig-wood," with the consequent play on *sykophantēs,* "informer."

PHOBOKLEON
Impeacher-wood? Too acrid. Back you go!
He shoves Philokleon all the way back into the
chimney and slams the trapdoor over the opening,
then lifts a large log over it.
Peace to your ashes. I'm putting the damper down—
with a log on top. Think up another one.
He drops the log on the chimney with a crash.
I don't have troubles enough—now I'll be famous—
son of a smudgepot, a smokestack for my family tree!
The front door shakes violently.

SOSIAS
Somebody at the door.

PHOBOKLEON
Push hard! Squeeze tightly!
Show what you're made of!
The slaves strain against the front door.
I'll be down and help you.
Watch out—keep an eye on that door bar. You know what he's like.
He'll probably chew the nut right off the bolt.
He disappears into the house.

PHILOKLEON
From behind the locked front door.
What are you up to? Damn you, let me out to judge!
Do you want Drakontides to be *acquitted?*

SOSIAS
Would that bother you?

PHILOKLEON
BOTHER? The oracle at Delphoi warned me once:

"Thy first acquittal bringeth thy final summons!"

SOSIAS
Apollo preserve us from prophecies like that one!
Phobokleon emerges from the side door and puts
his shoulder to the front door.

PHILOKLEON
Please let me out—I'll bust!

PHOBOKLEON

The answer is NO!

PHILOKLEON

Then I'll—I'll gnaw the net through with my teeth!

PHOBOKLEON

You don't *have* any teeth.

PHILOKLEON

Consarn it all!

How can I kill you? How? Give me my sword!

Or—quick! Bring me a tablet—I'll *sentence* you!

PHOBOKLEON

I'm afraid the old man's plotting something desperate.

PHILOKLEON

Me? I wouldn't think of it.

I only want

to bring the donkey out and sell him. That's all.

It's market day, you know.

PHOBOKLEON

Oh, come, now. *I*

can sell the donkey.

PHILOKLEON

Not as good as *I* can!

PHOBOKLEON

Better, by god!

PHILOKLEON

Will you *please* let the donkey out?

SOSIAS

He's a slippery old cuss. And talk about excuses!

Just to get out of the house!

PHOBOKLEON

And what good did it do?

All that angling and not a single bite.

> Still, I'd better go in and get that donkey;
> we can't have Papa popping out again.

He unbars the door, enters the house, and leads out
the donkey. Philokleon is hanging underneath it,
as Odysseus hung under the Kyklops' ram, face up,
but has miscalculated a little; his head is directly
under the donkey's rear. The donkey appreciates
this not at all, and hee-haws piteously.

> Packass, why all the tears? Don't you *want* to be sold?
> Get a move on!

The donkey stands stock-still and bawls louder.

> Why all the noise? Are you carrying
> an Odysseus—something like that?

SOSIAS
Peeking under the donkey and espying Philokleon.

> By god, he *is!*
> One of those snuck under him right back here!

PHOBOKLEON
What's that? Let me see.

> —There he is, all right. What *is* this?
> Pardon me, sir, but who might you be?

PHILOKLEON

> Nobody.

PHOBOKLEON
Nobody? Hmmm. From what country?

PHILOKLEON

> Ithaka. Son of
> Skedaddle.

PHOBOKLEON

> A likely story. Well, Nobody, no bloody
> fun for you!

To Sosias.

> Drag him out of there! Hurry!

As Philokleon's head emerges from between the
donkey's rear legs.

> That old dunghill—of all the places to hide!
> what do I tell my friends?

"Oh, that old foal
is my father. He's the biggest man in the Borough."

PHILOKLEON
Clinging to the donkey and fending off Sosias.
You let me alone, or there's going to be a fight!

PHOBOKLEON
You'll have to fight us both—what's so important?

PHILOKLEON
I'll lose my ass!
He is dragged out.

PHOBOKLEON
You're rotten—all tricks and no scruples.

PHILOKLEON
Rotten? Me? You're badly mistaken, son.
Why, a man like me's just at his tastiest—well hung,
right in my prime. Wait till you see the stake
I'm going to leave you.

PHOBOKLEON
Take that ass and shove it—
and yourself—back in the house!

PHILOKLEON
As he and the donkey are forced back in.
Help!
Colleagues! Jurors! Kleon! Somebody!
HALP!

PHOBOKLEON
Slamming the door shut after Philokleon.
Shout to your heart's content—this door stays locked!
—Sosias, pile lots of rocks against the door—
then stick the pin back into the bar again,
and shove the beam against *that*. Then both of you
find that bowl—the huge one—and roll it up.
And please show a little speed!
*The slaves obey in a flurry of action. Suddenly
Sosias, near the house, gives a jump.*

SOSIAS
Ouch! They got me!

Rubbing his head, as the others turn to him
incredulously.

Honestly—some plaster hit me!
Where'd it come from?

XANTHIAS
There's probably a mouse up there. *It* hit you.

SOSIAS
Looking up.

A mouse?

Up where?
Philokleon's head appears at the edge of the roof.
That's no mouse.
But I see something
that tunneled under the tiles.
To Phobokleon.
You'd better hurry
and sell this house, Boss—it's got *Jurors!*

PHOBOKLEON
Seeing his father.

Again?
Why do these things happen to me? Now he's a sparrow,
all set to fly away! Where did I put that net?
He grabs a long-handled net and waggles
it at Philokleon.
Shoo! Back in there! Shoo!
Philokleon's head disappears. Phobokleon looks
around hopelessly.
I swear to god,
I'd rather be up north with the army, and freeze
myself blue, blockading Skione, than try
to keep this idiot father of mine at home.

SOSIAS
Well, I guess we've scared him off for good.
All the holes are plugged—he can't sneak out.
What about a nap?
Phobokleon frowns at him.

Not a *long* one—

He produces his bottle again.

just a—

just a drop?

PHOBOKLEON

Are you crazy? Father's friends are coming—
the other Jurors! In just a minute or two,
they'll be along to summon him.

SOSIAS

A minute or two?
It won't be light for an hour!

PHOBOKLEON

I know. They must
have got up late today. They usually stagger by
this street just at midnight, carrying lamps.
They summon father by mumbling and moaning those ancient,
sticky-sweet, Asiatic songs by Phrynichos.

SOSIAS

So?
It's just a bunch of old men—what's the worry?
If they make any ruckus, we can throw a few rocks.
That'll shake them up.

PHOBOKLEON

This is *not* "just a bunch of old men,"
you cretin! These are authentic Athenian Jurors,
choked with pride, crammed with spleen and venom.
Shake *them* up, anger *them*—and you'll discover
You've annoyed a nest of maddened wasps.
A sting,
keen and sharp, projects from each one's loins.
When they're aroused, they spring with wild cries
and sting, and jump, and judge like fiery sparks.

He returns to the roof.

SOSIAS

I say don't worry. Give me my rocks, and I
can eradicate any wasps' nest—jurors or not.

*In spite of Phobokleon's injunctions, he and the two
slaves go to sleep almost immediately—and, as will
appear, quite soundly. A short pause, and the
Chorus of* Wasps—*that is, of Old Men who sit on
juries—staggers on. They are divided into two
Semichoruses, each led by a Koryphaios and a little
boy with a lamp. They wear tattered cloaks and, in
the place of the normal comic phalluses, enlarged
representations of wasps' stings. Their chief characteristic is age: they are impossibly old and crabbed,
and walk bent, scanning the ground, in a painful
shuffle that contrasts sharply with the exhortations of
the First Koryphaios.*

FIRST KORYPHAIOS
Forward, boys—brisk's the word!
*To one dodderer who is not moving appreciably
slower than the rest.*

Hey, Komias, you're dragging!
Once you whipped us along. Now look at you—rotten leather.
Charinades here makes better time!
To the Second Koryphaios.

Hey, there, Strymodoros!
Euergides—did he make it? Did Chabes come in from Phlya?

SECOND KORYPHAIOS
They're all here—the last of the Boys of the Old Brigade.
He stops, lost in reminiscence.

Byzantion—how long ago? Why, it's nearly fifty years!
And what a wild bunch we were! Remember that baker's wife?
You and I, we went halves. We slipped off watch and split her
breadboard up for kindling. Mad?—Those were the days!

FIRST KORYPHAIOS
Fine, fine—but let's hurry to Court!

Put some muscle in it!
Laches gets it today! He's up for survey. They say
he's loaded—got pots of money—squeezed Sicily dry.
And the Boss—Kleon—was mighty insistent yesterday:
"Be EARLY!" he said. "Bring a triple ration of ANGER!" he said.
"Whatever you do, CONVICT that criminal!"—That's what he said.
So we'd better rush and be there, boys, before it gets light.

SECOND KORYPHAIOS
Yes, move along, but look sharp—that's what the lamps are for.
Watch out for pebbles—we can't have Jurors taking the rap!

SECOND LITTLE BOY
To the Second Koryphaios.
Daddy, Daddy, there's mud ahead—right there! Watch out!

SECOND KORYPHAIOS
Stopping and peering.
Dratted lamp—can't see. Take a twig and push up the wick.

SECOND LITTLE BOY
No, Daddy—I can push it up better with this. See?
He inserts his finger into the lamp.

SECOND KORYPHAIOS
Oh, you've got a head on *you*—waggle the wick with your finger—
and slosh all the oil—that expensive, hard-to-get oil—

                                                              you IDIOT!
It's no skin off *your* nose when I have to pay those prices!
He hits the Second Little Boy.
There, that'll teach you!

SECOND LITTLE BOY   .
                    Any more lessons like that, Daddy,
and we'll blow out our lamps and go home. See how you like it alone—
you'll stumble and fumble and muck around like ducks in the dark.

SECOND KORYPHAIOS
I punish bigger and better men than you, sonny,
every . . .
He slips.
                    Oops! the mud! I'm up to my knees in GUCK!
And look at all that snuff on the wicks—sure sign of a cloudburst
in three-four days. Oh, it's good for the crops—what's left of them.
Nothing like oceans of rain and a good, stiff, chilly North wind.

FIRST KORYPHAIOS
Well, here's Philokleon's house. Wonder what happened to him?
I don't see him waiting around to join the group. That's odd.
Never had to rout him out before. He was always first—
head of the line, singing the old songs. He's mad for music. . . .
That's an idea: we can . . .

Suddenly to the Chorus, which is about
to plod right by.

HALT!

The Chorus halts.

. . . *sing* him out to work.

—Places, men! Strike up a song; make it a good one!
Let's bring our crony out as fast as he can crawl!

FIRST SEMICHORUS

Singly.

> Where's the old man? Why doesn't he come
> to the door? Or at least say hello?
> Do you suppose he lost his shoes?
> That's sad. He could stub a toe.
> Sprain an ankle. Strain a vein.
> Rupture himself—you never know.

Tutti.

> He's the nastiest man on the jury—
> malign, marblehearted, and mean!
> Though others may yield to defendants' appeals,
> he thinks that acquittal's obscene!

SECOND SEMICHORUS

Singly

> What discomposed him? Yesterday's
> false Friend of Democracy.
> Our bogus Secret Agent in Samos?[7]
> The defendant we let go FREE?
> It infected our colleague. Fever. Colic.
> Mercy is bad for his allergy.

Tutti, to the house.

> Recover your health in the jury—
> we're serving a traitor from Thrace.[8]
> He's fat and he's flush and the pickings are plush!
> Come down and we'll set you a place!

A pause. Silence
from the house.

FIRST KORYPHAIOS
All right, boy, let's move along.

---

7. A reference to the unsuccessful revolt of that island from enforced Athenian democracy in 440.

8. The Thracian cities Amphipolis and Eion were betrayed by their inhabitants to the Spartan general Brasidas in 424.

The First Little Boy steps to the center of the
stage, then stops.

Come on, start up.

The First Little Boy starts up, not the procession,
but a double duet with the Koryphaioi, molto con
espressione, *in which the Boys parody the impossi-*
bly pathetic youngsters whom Euripides would occa-
sionally deprive of their mothers (as in the Alcestis*)*
or feed to the Minotaur (as in the lost Theseus*).*

FIRST LITTLE BOY

O Father, gentle Father,
I beg of thee a boon.

FIRST KORYPHAIOS

Name me the toy; I'll buy it,
O best-belovèd Son.

FIRST LITTLE BOY

Not toys. I faint with famine;
a Fig to make me whole?

FIRST KORYPHAIOS

A fig's too damned expensive,
you glutton! Go to hell!

FIRST LITTLE BOY

We'll refuse to light your way!

FIRST KORYPHAIOS

I struggle every day,
buying wood, and grain, and meat
for the three of us to eat
from my petty jury pay,
you miserable pigs—
Oh! Woe!

And you want Figs!

SECOND LITTLE BOY

O Father dear, a query:
Suppose they should decree
No Court Today—where, Father,
would that leave you and me?

SECOND KORYPHAIOS

> We wouldn't have the money
> to buy the food we want—
> before we could afford it,
> we could ford the Hellespont!

SECOND LITTLE BOY

> Poor Mother, why was I
> born into this world to di-
> et on wrangles and disputes,
> bitter writs and sour suits?
> Oh, the fruitless mimicry
> of my foodless little sack!
> Alas! Alas!
> >   My life's a lack!

*The Little Boys dissolve into sobs, and the Chorus
seems about to follow suit. The threatened inunda-
tion is staved off, however, by the appearance of
Philokleon at the window, behind the net.
Quaveringly he breaks into song, a song which
bears a rather horrid resemblance to the monody of
a shackled Euripidean heroine—Andromeda, say, or
Danae.*

PHILOKLEON

> Aye weary do I waste at this aperture
> lusting to list to your overture,
> but heark for no hymns from me, Belovèd—
> I cannot sing.
> >   Whence, oh whence my deliverance?
> They fence me pent 'neath dire surveillance
> In durance vile, the while I burn,
> yearning, to burst my bonds and sojourn
> joined with you for some sweet spell . . .
> in Court, and raise all kinds hell.

The music changes.

> O Zeus who launchest the lightning,
> metamorphose me to smoke.
> Infuse me with Proxenides' bluster,[9]
> or the Flabber-Gas of Aeschines, son of Bloat,

9. This man and Aischines were two well-known boasters, the Athenian equivalent for "hot air" being "smoke." (Which lies at the bottom of the translation "smudgepot" in line 151 above.)

and float me away on a tissue of lies.
Lord, shed sudden grace on Thy servant,
the slave of his convictions.
Cast me on a blast of unleavened levin,
roast me in the ash, catch me to heaven,
and waft me to rest in tartar-sauce . . .
or, better, Sovereign,
make me the rock on which they count
the verdict. Thanks. Amen.

FIRST SEMICHORUS

A point of information,
strictly *entre nous*—
Who shut you up? Who threw the bolt?
Who, dammit, who?

PHILOKLEON
It was my son—Phobokleon. But shhh! Don't shout—that's him
right there in front, asleep. So please, not so loud.

FIRST SEMICHORUS

What's behind this outrage?
Where do his motives lie?
We trust he adduced some flimsy excuse—
Why, dammit, why?

PHILOKLEON
He refuses to let me judge, or court any trouble. He claims
he intends to lap me in luxury at home. And I say no.

FIRST SEMICHORUS

That Fibberkleon's elusive!
Obviously evasive!
He means to muzzle a patriot
who dares to expose the truth about
the way our Navy's going to pot.
The evidence—conclusive:
your son's a SUBVERSIVE!

FIRST KORYPHAIOS
No time to waste. You need a novel synthesis, a striking
scheme to spring yourself without disturbing your offspring.

PHILOKLEON
Easy to say—but what? *You* try—I'm ready for anything.
I'm wild to stroll along the docket, just me and my ballot.

FIRST KORYPHAIOS
You require scope. Scoop out a hole somewhere and slip through,
muffled in rags, like Odysseus at Troy.

PHILOKLEON
                            Odysseus I tried
already. Not that hole. Besides, they've sealed the place—
no niche big enough for a gnat. Think of something else.

FIRST KORYPHAIOS
Remember our Navy days? When we took Naxos—and you took off
without leave? You stuck some stolen spits in the wall and *ran* down.

PHILOKLEON
Oh, I remember, but how does that help? I'm forty years older.
There's no resemblance.

              THEN I was mighty—muscular—sly—
              a matchless master at poaching.
              All unperceived I could steal away . . .
              besides, nobody was watching.
              NOW I'm besieged by a whole damned army
              loaded with ordnance, vigilant, vast.
              Those two at the door are waiting to skewer me
              like a common domestic pest.

        AND the spits that I'd have to make do with
        are the ones they'll run me through with!

SECOND SEMICHORUS
              But now it's NOW, and it's morning!
              This is an emergency!
                  Speed your planning! Improve the shining
                  hour, honey-bee!

PHILOKLEON
I'm afraid there's only one way open—to gnaw through the net.
—Pardon me, Artemis, goddess of traps! Don't be nettled.

SECOND SEMICHORUS
As Philokleon begins to chew the strands.

> The man who squares his jaw is
> the man who never succumbs.
> Attack that mesh—forward, gnash!
> Courage! Grind those gums!

PHILOKLEON
Well, it's done. I chewed it through.
The Chorus breaks into a cheer.

> Stop that shouting!
> Please proceed with caution—you'll wake up Phobokleon!

SECOND SEMICHORUS
> Suspend your apprehension;
> leave him to our discretion.
> He'll cease his sacrilegious abuse
> with his heart in his mouth!
> With his heart in his shoes
> he'll run for his life—and probably lose!
> We'll stop his profanation
> of Demeter's legislation! [10]

SECOND KORYPHAIOS
Now for a rope. Secure one end to the window, the other to you.
Then let yourself down. Slowly. Be brave; remember the motto:
Trust in Zeus, and take short views.

PHILOKLEON
Busy with the rope.

> A teeny question:
> If they should hook me on this line, and haul me back in—what then?

SECOND KORYPHAIOS
We'll call on our Courage, that old oaken Courage, and drive them away!
They won't pen *you* up again—no sir! We'll think of something.

PHILOKLEON
*Clambering into a rope seat and dangling just
below the window.*

> All right. I place my life in your hands. If anything happens,
> take me up, and mourn me, and bury me under the Bar.

---

10. One would expect the Chorus to say "Demeter's mysteries." The confusion is, of course,

SECOND KORYPHAIOS
Nothing is going to happen!
                              Of course, you might invoke
your ancestral gods before you slide. Why take chances?

PHILOKLEON
Dangling in prayer.
          Lord of Lawsuits, Patron of Plaintiffs, Lykos my Master,[11]
          whose eternal delights—even as mine—are the screams and wails
                    of convicted defendants; whose shrine is set,
                    the better to feast thine ears, at Court;
                    who choose, alone of the gods, to sit
                    on the losing side by the mourner's seat—
                    save thy neighbor, preserve him intact,
                    and nevermore, from this day hence,
          will I piss on thy precinct or fart on thy fence.
*He descends slowly on the rope, as quietly as he
can. But his prayer has awakened Phobokleon.*

PHOBOKLEON
From the roof, to Sosias.
          Hey, wake up!
Both slaves wake.

SOSIAS
                         What's wrong?

PHOBOKLEON
                              A voice is whirring around,
          I think. The old man didn't slip out another hole?

SOSIAS
Looking up.
          God, no! He's tied himself to a rope and sliding down!

PHOBOKLEON
Looking straight down and seeing his father.
          Again, you old cesspool? What do you think you're doing?
          Get back up there!

Aristophanes' way of indicating to what extent religion and politics have been confused by these litigious old men. At least, this is the usual explanation.

11. Son of the legendary King Pandion of Athens; his statue, in the form of a wolf (*lykos*) was set, we are told, before each court.

*Sosias pulls the blockade from the front door and
runs in. Xanthias, still fuddled, stands confused until
Phobokleon addresses him.*

—Don't just stand there—

climb up outside

and hit him with the wreath!

XANTHIAS

What wreath?

PHOBOKLEON

The Thanksgiving wreath—

over the front door, stupid! If we deck his bow, maybe
he'll back his stern inside. But whatever you do, do it FAST!
*He disappears into the house. Xanthias grabs the
wreath from over the door and clambers up the net,
hand over hand. When he comes even with Philokleon, he flails at him with the wreath. During the
next speech, Sosias and Phobokleon appear at the
window and haul the rope in slowly, and Xanthias
keeps pace with the rising Philokleon, beating away.*

PHILOKLEON

Sorely beset, to the audience.

A word to all this year's prospective plaintiffs—

HALP!

Hey, informers—Jekyll! Leech! You, Finque!
And all you parasites—Skimpole! Grafton!
Come on, fellows, you need me! Don't let them haul me back!
A little aid?

A little succor?

Last Chance—

*Just as Phobokleon and Sosias pull him through the
window.*

HAAALP!

*Xanthias follows him in, still flailing, and the four
disappear inside the house. The Chorus bursts into
action.*

FIRST KORYPHAIOS

Throwing off his cloak.

The Wasps are ruffled! Our nest's been disturbed! No Delay!
Let's churn up our Double-Distilled, Triple-Action ANGER!

The members of the Chorus throw off their cloaks,
exposing their stings, which they raise to the ready.
The Little Boys collect the cloaks.

ENTIRE CHORUS
>   Raise the Sting and hold it high, Boys!
>   Show them how we stand,
>   fierce to cut and thrust for Justice,
>   feared throughout the land!

FIRST KORYPHAIOS
To the Little Boys.
>   Drop those cloaks! Run and shout the news to Kleon!
The Little Boys drop the cloaks and exit at a run.

ENTIRE CHORUS
>   Fight and smite the foe of Athens!
>   Hit with all your hate!
>   Show your Fury! Save the Jury—
>   Bulwark of the State!

A locomotive cheer:

>   AËRATE HIM!
>   PERFORATE HIM!
>   THAT'S THE WAY TO WIN!
>   OPEN UP HIS HEART AND LET THE
>   SUN
>   SHINE
>   IN!

Phobokleon emerges from the house, followed by
Xanthias, Sosias, and, in the clutches of the two
slaves, Philokleon.

PHOBOKLEON
Gentlemen, gentlemen, please! Stop shouting and hear my case.

FIRST KORYPHAIOS
We'll shout if we want to! As loud as we want to!
>   —Won't we, men?

PHOBOKLEON
It won't make a bit of difference. I refuse to let him go.

FIRST KORYPHAIOS
What's that? You WON'T? You refuse to obey the Voice of the People?

PHOBOKLEON
Precisely.

FIRST KORYPHAIOS
      Patent, plain, and obvious DICTATORSHIP!
To the audience.
    O Athens, Pearl of Attica!
                      O Theoros, Peer of Debasement!
    O all you spongers,
              scroungers,
                      moochers,
                              chiselers,
                                        fatcats—
in short, Everybody in Charge—
                      DID YOU HEAR WHAT HE SAID?

SOSIAS
Holy Herakles, they DO have stings! Don't you see them, Boss?

PHOBOKLEON
That's what finished Philippos, the sophist—they ran him through
three suits in one afternoon. Completely gouged. Sad case.

FIRST KORYPHAIOS
And that's the way we'll finish YOU off!
To the Chorus, who complies with his orders.
                COMPANY, TEN-*SHUN!*
  RIGHT-*FACE!*
          CLOSE-*RANKS!*
                DRESS UP THAT LINE!
All right, men, let's put some spleen into it. Be Nasty!
Pointing at Phobokleon.
    There's our objective! Make sure that he knows, in future, what sort
    of a swarm he roused!
             PRESENT . . . *STINGS!*
The Stings, which have been sagging slightly, are
snapped to the ready again.
                    READY, AIM . . .

SOSIAS
God, this is awful—we're really going to FIGHT? *THEM?*
It scares me green just to see those prongs!

FIRST KORYPHAIOS
To Sosias.

Release that man!
I warn you, the time will come when you'll envy turtles their shells!
He waggles his Sting wickedly. Sosias tries to bolt,
but is cuffed by Phobokleon, and continues, reluc-
tantly, to hold Philokleon.

PHILOKLEON
Colleagues! Jurors! Talesmen! Angry Wasps!
COME ON!
To the First Semichorus.

Mount a savage sortie there and spear them in the rear!
To the Second Semichorus.

A frontal attack—lance their fingers! Stab their eyes!
Phobokleon leaves Philokleon with the slaves, runs
to the front door, opens it, and yells inside.

PHOBOKLEON
Hey, Midas! Phrygian! Help—come here! You, too, Greedy!
The three slaves trundle forth. Phobokleon
points at Philokleon.

Grab that man! And don't let go of him for anybody—
because if you do, it's solitary confinement! Bread and water!
To the Chorus, as the three slaves fill in around
Xanthias and Sosias.

Keep up your blather—I know what it means. Look at my father!
He hurries into the house. The First Koryphaios
continues to work on Sosias.

FIRST KORYPHAIOS
Let him go—unless you relish the prospect of being a scabbard!

SOSIAS
A *s-scabbard?*

FIRST KORYPHAIOS
Or maybe a quiver.

SOSIAS
A-quiver? God, I AM!
He attempts to bolt again, but is prevented by

Xanthias and the other slaves. Philokleon tries
another prayer.

PHILOKLEON

O Twi-formed Kekrops, founder of Athens, hero-headed,
snake-shanked—Juror above, defendant below—
are you going to let an Old Athenian like me be mauled
by these FOREIGNERS? My foreigners? The ones I whipped
and whopped and taught to weep five quarts to the gallon—

                                               HUH?

SECOND KORYPHAIOS

The proof is plain—old age is nothing but a skein of agony.
What miserable evidence—two slaves mauling their poor old master!
Have they forgotten the love he covered them with in the old days?
The sheepskin jackets? The lambskin vests? The dogskin caps?
The care he showered on their feet each winter? No, their feet
didn't freeze; their hearts did. Look in their eyes: no gratitude,
no respect for anything old—not even old shoes.

PHILOKLEON
To Sosias.

Hear that? I'm kind, I'm considerate—

                                    NOW will you let me go,
you dirty sonofabitch? Don't you remember all those skins?
Or yours—when I caught you stealing grapes, and took you out
to the olive-tree, and flayed you like a Man—forgot that?
I took the hide off clean—slaveskin all over the place.
You were *famous*—the Talk of the Town for weeks! But gratitude? Respect?
Not YOU!
With a nervous glance at the door.

                        Hurry up! He'll be back in a minute—LET ME GO!
Only Sosias is tempted, and the old man struggles
fruitlessly. The Chorus advances slowly toward the
slaves, who retreat, dragging Philokleon with them.

FIRST KORYPHAIOS
To Xanthias and Sosias, who are in the forefront of
the group.

You can't delay your day of reckoning much longer, you two!
Then you'll know what manner of men WE are! Our hearts
are written on our faces—full of gall, and spleen, and law!
The Chorus presses on. The slaves and Philokleon
back toward the front door. Just as they reach it, the

door bursts open and Phobokleon bursts out, carry-
ing a club and a lighted torch. He gives the club to
Xanthias.

PHOBOKLEON
Hit them, Xanthias! Beat the Wasps away from the house!

XANTHIAS
I am, I AM!

PHOBOKLEON
Shoving the torch into Sosias' reluctant hands.
Smudge them out, Sosias! Smoke them off!

XANTHIAS
Swinging his club.
GIT! GO TO HELL!

PHOBOKLEON
Pushing Sosias.
SCAT! GET OUT OF HERE!

SOSIAS
Eyes closed, torch held stiffly before him.

Shoo—please?

PHOBOKLEON
That's it, Xanthias! Club them, boy!
To the nearly catatonic Sosias.
—Pour on the smoke!
The Wasps, merely very old men, are easily routed
and retreat without much resistance to the side of
the stage. The attack ceases. Phobokleon releases
Sosias, who opens his eyes, takes in the situation,
and swaggers over to the Chorus.

SOSIAS
Scared off, huh? Could have told you—you didn't have a chance.
The First Koryphaios brandishes his sting. Sosias
races back to his own group.

PHOBOKLEON
Even *you* couldn't have driven them off so easily, Sosias,
if they'd been trained on different songs. Take the awful stuff

that Philokles writes. Why, they could strangle you with a single chord.

ENTIRE CHORUS

To the same tune as the fight song, but without the
final locomotive.

> Now the Poor can see their Peril,
> feel its slippery grip,
> know its stealthy aggrandizement
> DREAD DICTATORSHIP!

SECOND KORYPHAIOS

Pointing at Phobokleon.

> There's Exhibit A: the arrogant Autocrat himself!

ENTIRE CHORUS

> See him keep us from our City's
> Laws so flagrantly!
> No excuses can confuse us.
> *He* wants TYRANNY!

PHOBOKLEON

To the Chorus.

> Is there any way to stop these fights, and that awful screeching?
> Can't we hold a parley and come to some compromise?

SECOND KORYPHAIOS

> Parley? Compromise? With YOU—an Enemy of the People?
> Just look at you: the Compleat Pro-Spartan Aristocrat.
> Those crazy tassels on your clothes spell Lunatic Fringe. And that messy
> beard declares you're a hero-worshipping mimic of Brasidas.[12]
> Parley with a Spartan-lover? To put it Laconically,
>   NO!

PHOBOKLEON

> I'm tempted to let Father go. I can't fight a war every morning.

SECOND KORYPHAIOS

> You think you have troubles now? This is just the appetizers! (Please
> excuse our table-talk.) You don't hurt at all—not yet.
> Just wait for the main course, down in Court, when the Public Counsel
> carves you to bits with these charges. *Plus* a new one: SUBVERSIVE!

---

12. Because of his recent and threatening victories in Thrace, the Spartan general was a name for
the popular party to beat the conservatives with in 422.

PHOBOKLEON
Will you kindly get the hell out of here? Or is there a law
that says we have to stand here trading blows all day?

SECOND KORYPHAIOS
Leave? Desert my duty? Not while I'm alive! Me leave
a man unguarded who wants to bring DICTATORSHIP back?

PHOBOKLEON
"Dictatorship" and "Subversive"—that covers every case
you judge, large or small. Everything you do, in fact:
the universe in two nouns. It's the same way all over town.
I hadn't heard the *word* "Dictator" for fifty years
in Athens, and suddenly it's cheaper than smelt. It clutters up
the Market-place, chokes the shops—you trip on it.
Example. You don't want sardines for supper; what you want
is a nice, fat, juicy sea-bass. So down to the Mart you go,
and BUY a nice, fat, juicy sea-bass. And the man next door,
—who, incidentally, just happens to sell sardines—starts up:
"Sea-bass, huh? That's real rich food—expensive, too.
TOO expensive for a real Athenian democrat. Hey, Mac—
why the bass? You want to bring DICTATORSHIP back?"
Or say you're having herring for lunch, and you want an onion,
a pretty, round onion, to keep it company. Have you ever
tried to buy that onion? You do, and the woman next door—
you know, the one who sells scallions—takes a squint, and:
                                                    "You think
that Athens pays taxes so you can have fancy food? Hey, Mac—
why the onion? You want to bring DICTATORSHIP back?"

SOSIAS
Boy, are you right—you can't even get out of line in a whorehouse!
Yesterday noon I told this girl to climb on top
and you'd think I'd tried to start a revolution!
                                        "SUBVERSIVE!
There's only one way to do this," she says, "and that's flat!
You're trying to raise up Hippias' DICTATORSHIP!"
                                        I ask you!

PHOBOKLEON
I know. That's what goes in Court. It's music to *them*.
Take my case. All I want to do is keep Father away

from this early-to-Court-and-early-to-lie-and-do-the-defendant-
one-in-the-eye mode of existence; I want him to lead
a pleasant, luxurious, gentleman's life, like Morychos.
And what do they charge me with? Committing some heinous crime:
I'm a SUBVERSIVE; I'm plotting to restore DICTATORSHIP.

PHILOKLEON
By god, they're right, too! Can't you understand me, Son?
I don't WANT all this pie in the sky and pigeon's milk,
not me, not if I have to be barred, debarred, and disbarred
from the only life I know. And live like Morychos—why?
I'm not one of your goormays; I don't like eels, or rayfish.
What *I* like's a little lawsuit, chopped up fine
and stewed in its own juice. We call it a case-erole.

PHOBOKLEON
Habit, Father, sheer habit. A conditioned obsession—a deep one.
And yet, if you'll just keep quiet and listen to what I say,
I think that I can change your mind. I'll demonstrate
that your entire way of life is a Grand Mistake.

PHILOKLEON
I'm mistaken to JUDGE?

PHOBOKLEON
                    Worse. You're a butt, a laughingstock,
all unconscious, to men you nearly enshrine. In a word,
you're a SLAVE, and don't know it.

PHILOKLEON
                    Don't talk any slavery to ME—
I rule the WORLD!

PHOBOKLEON
                    Correction: you serve. Your rule's an illusion.
—All right, prove me wrong.
                    You "reap the fruits of Hellas"—
Demonstrate. Show us a fruit or two. Produce your profit.

PHILOKLEON
Will I ever!
Pointing to the Chorus.
                    I'll make a speech and let them arbitrate.

PHOBOKLEON
And so will I.
To the slaves.
           All right, everyone, let him go.
The slaves obey and enter the house. Philokleon,
free, yells after them.

PHILOKLEON
And bring me a sword!
To Phobokleon.
           By god, if I lose a debate with YOU,
I'll stick a sword in the ground, point up, and fall on it,
face down, the way Ajax did when he lost to Odysseus.
Sosias returns with a sword, gives it to Phobokleon,
and re-enters the house.

PHOBOKLEON
Handing the sword to Philokleon.
                          Pardon me,
but there's one little thing—the Oath.

PHILOKLEON
                    What Oath?

PHOBOKLEON
                          You should know more
about it than I do. The Oath where you specify the penalty you'll pay
if you fail to abide by the—how do you say it?—the disposition
of this debate.

PHILOKLEON
            Oh, *that* Oath.
Sonorously.
                 I pledge myself to abide
by the just, impartial decision of this just, impartial Board
of Arbitration. If I should fail to do so, this be my punishment:
May I never, whenever the toasts go round, touch a drop—of my pay.

ENTIRE CHORUS
Arranged in judging position, it sings to Philokleon.
          Defend the Old School's Honor!
            Let none her Glory dim!
        Be fresh in word and manner . . .

PHOBOKLEON

Breaking in on the Chorus, which holds on grimly to
the "-er," he calls toward the house.

    Bring me out a tablet and a stylus—and be quick about it!
Noticing the Chorus' held note.

    A fine exhibition he'll make, with a song like *that* to inspire him.

ENTIRE CHORUS

Continuing the song, with a baleful wave at
Phobokleon.

            . . . but don't be fresh like *him*!
      The verdict on your Great Debate
      can overrule and abrogate
      our Way of Life! The stakes are great.
        If you incur the loss—
              he's Boss!

PHOBOKLEON

Seated at a table, he receives the tablet and stylus
from Xanthias.

    That's fine. He'll talk at random; I'll write at memorandum.

PHILOKLEON

Nervously, to the Chorus.

    You were saying—what happens to us if he wins the debate?

ENTIRE CHORUS

      We'll be reviled and called effete!
      We'll be repealed as obsolete!
      They'll only use us to complete
        the files in some parade—
          unpaid!

FIRST KORYPHAIOS

To Philokleon.

    And so, old friend, you who intend to debate and defend,
    from stern to stem, the range of our rule, the utter extent
    of our kingdom—courage! Extend your tongue to its utmost—
                           and utter!

PHILOKLEON

    I spring from the post to establish our claim as Best of Breed.
    No Crowned or Sceptred Potentate can surpass our power.
                            We're kings.

The proof is plain: what creature on earth can match the delight,
the luxury, power, respect, and glory that falls to the lot
of that little old man, the simple Athenian Juror?

                                        None!

Example. I rise from my bed in the morning to find them waiting,
the Men of Importance and Size (some of them *six feet tall!*),
waiting for me, by the Bench. No sooner do I go inside
than a tender hand steals into mine, still warm from tapping
the Treasury. And then they beg, and bow, and wheedle, and whine.
"Father," they say (they call me Father), "pity me, Father.
You must have been a Quartermaster, or held a Public Trust.
You know what it is to feather your nest. Pity me, Father."
Do you think that a Very Important Person like that would know
that I was alive, if I hadn't acquitted him once before?

PHOBOKLEON
Yes, I'd better put that down. Let's see—

                                        Beggars.

He writes the one word. Philokleon glares at him.

PHILOKLEON
Well, sir, I'm all begged up, my bad temper's wiped off clean;
I've made my promises of mercy—so I take my seat and proceed
to forget every one. It's not that I shut my ears to the pleas;
I listen to them all. Every rhetorical trick in the book
is unfolded, and, as for kinds of flattery—well, if I haven't
heard it in Court, it doesn't exist.

                              I'll be specific:

First, The Paupers. They plead—or scream—that they're poor, and so
Not Guilty. They heap their disasters so deep I almost believe them—
they sound as poor as I am.

                              Next the Story-Tellers, with Fairy-Tales,
or little quips from Aesop, or else, on occasion, a Joke.
If I shake with laughter, the theory runs, I'll shed my anger.
I don't.

                    When this fails, and we sit like rocks, they summon The Kids
(as they're called)—the little girls and boys, dragged up by the hand.
They bend them down and make them bleat—and me, I listen.
Then the father, trembling with grief or fear (or maybe religion)
entreats me, as though he were praying to a god, to spare his children—
by acquitting *him* on the charge of embezzling public funds.
"If you delight to hear the bleat of a poor little lamb,"
says he, "be moved by the plea of this little lost sheep—my son."

Of course, if our taste is for pig-meat, he begs us to pity his daughter.[13]
(And in this case, I admit, we unscrewed our anger a bit.)
Well, now, I ask you: doesn't this show our position, and power—
a contempt for wealth which makes mere money something to laugh at?

PHOBOKLEON
I'll get that down. Point Two: *The money is something to laugh at.*
—But as Ruler of Hellas (you said it, I didn't), just how do you profit?

PHILOKLEON
How? Why, son, we have Sex, the Drama, Music, Money . . .
You name it!
                First, we're the body that examines prospective citizens,
puts handsome boys to a probing to see just how they'll fit in
to the life of the City. We're thorough.
                                Or the Arts: Suppose an actor—
say Oiagros—is accused. He knows his plea had better consist
of that beautiful soliloquy from the *Niobe*, recited for us alone;
unless he'd rather be convicted.
                                And Music? Ever see a flute-player
when he's won a case? Notice sometime. He waits around,
reed at the ready, till Court's adjourned, to pipe a march
when the Jury retires.
                        Next, Money: A man dies with only a daughter,
but designates a son-in-law and heir in his will, all signed and sealed.
What do we do in Probate? We break that will to bits,
and assign those bits, *and* the daughter, to the highest . . . well,
    beseecher.
It's safe and easy, since nobody audits *our* books—No Other
Public Office Can Make That Statement.

PHOBOKLEON
                                True. Congratulations—
on *that* alone. But the poor heiress! That's downright immoral—
breaking a young girl's will and tampering with her entailment.

PHILOKLEON
But better is Respect: When the Senate and Assembly have trouble
    impeaching,
they pass a decree and remand the rascals to us for trial.
And then it's Pure Pie—Praise from the Greats of Athenian politics—

---

13. The usual pun on *choiros* ("pig" and "female genitalia") that is so thoroughly employed in *Acharnians* 764 ff.

that clever young lawyer Euathlos, or maybe the famous athlete
(he holds the record for the shield-put) Flee-onymos.[14] They cover us
   with Love,
and say they'll "Uphold the Humble" and "Sweat for the Salt of the
   Earth."
What's more, no speaker can *ever* ram a motion through Assembly
without *our* votes. So Court adjourns early—short day, full pay.
Why, even *Kleon* respects us. He barks and flattens the rest,
but doesn't even snap at our heels. He's Our Defender, in fact:
He throws his arms around us and shoos the flies away—

Violently to Phobokleon.

a damned sight more than you ever did for your own father!
Or take Theoros. He's *Important* . . .
                                        You know Theoros?

A negative silence from Phobokleon.

Why, everyone knows Theoros! *He's* like Euphemios—
that *Big!*
              You *do* know Euphemios?

Another negative silence.

                                        Well, take Theoros—
Know what he does? He takes a sponge and shines our shoes!
A man like that! Yes, sir!
                          Well, take a good long look.
Those are the profits you pen me away from. Count those Blessings;
then figure out how to convince me that I'm a SLAVE or a SERVANT!

PHOBOKLEON

Aside.

Talk till you're sick—and you will be. I'll show you up, soon enough.
You and your Holy Assizes! Ass-holes of Athens, that's you.
And your mighty Orbit of Influence—the ring you leave in the bathtub.

PHILOKLEON

But I almost completely forgot my greatest joy as a Juror:
I get my pay and go home at night, and they all see me coming,
and give me a big hello—just because of that money. My daughter
washes me off, and massages my feet, and calls me "Popsy,"
bends down for a kiss—and fishes the money right out of my mouth.
And the little woman talks sweetly for once, and serves me cake,

---

14. The Greek gives *Kolakonymos*, a punning compound of *kolax* (flatterer) and Kleonymos. Since Kleonymos was also a notorious coward (remember Xanthias' dream about the eagle), Flee-onymos seemed a permissible liberty.

that puffy sweet cake, and sits beside me. "Go on and eat,"
she says, "there's more—eat it all." Then my star's at its brightest.
I don't have to worry about supper, and keep looking over at you
and that grumbling, grousing steward, who lives in terror that he might
have to make me another cake.

                           I have no worries *at all*,
thanks to my Bulwark, my Armor against the Slings and Arrows
and so forth. Refuse me a drink if you choose, I always have with me
my faithful donkey full of wine—

He drags from the folds of his cloak an enormous
wine-jar with two huge handles.

                                 and I pour him myself.
And he opens his jaws, and brays at your bowls—

He drinks deeply from the jar, which gurgles loudly,
then sets it down.

                                      and farts like an army!
This is my job, my Empire—the Greatest Empire on earth!

He takes another drink.

       On earth?—

                  Why isn't my Empire just as good as Zeus's?

                What they say about Zeus,
                        they say about Me!
                When we kick up a fuss
                        in fixing a fee,
              the passers-by rush
                        and shout out, "Hey!
                        Thunder in the Jury—
                        Zeus Almighty!"

Faster yet; almost swelling into a god.
                When I brandish the lightning
                        and throw it,
              the rich men are frightened,
                        and show it—
              they blubber! They shit, and
                        don't know it!
                        And they're so mighty,
                        so hoity-toity!

Assuming a statuesque pose, pointing an imperious
finger at Phobokleon, and going as fast as he can.
                What's more, YOU'RE *scared*—
                    you, too!

YOU fear me! By GOD
    you DO!
But I'M not afraid
    of YOU!
Completely overcome by his divine role.
            Puny, petty
            MORTALITY!

ENTIRE CHORUS
    A more persuasive lecture
        these ears have never heard.
    Such clarity! Such structure! . . .

PHILOKLEON
Relaxing into a strut, he interrupts the Chorus.
    Yup. He must have thought he'd clip my vines by default;
    he certainly knows well enough that *I* don't lose debates.

ENTIRE CHORUS
            . . . Such Wizardry of the Word!
    His speech sustained my self-esteem
    and summoned me, in dream, to seem
    Grand Juror in the Court Supreme,
            to hear the Happy Isles'
                retrials!
Phobokleon rises.

PHILOKLEON
    Look at him shift his ground and fidget—no self-control!
    —Before tonight, I'll make you look like a flogged dog, boy!

ENTIRE CHORUS
To Phobokleon.
            No vain Chicane, no sly Finesse
            can shake the Faith that I profess!
            I only guarantee success
                to one Device, i.e.—
                be ME!

SECOND KORYPHAIOS
Wherefore, unless you really have something to say, my advice
to you is this: It's time to look around for a millstone,
sharp, fresh-hewn. Perhaps *it* can crush the edge of my temper.

PHOBOKLEON

Taking his place and addressing the Chorus.
      To cure a disease so long engrained in the Body Politic
demands far more than the rude and feeble wit of a mere
Comic Poet. I begin, therefore, with a prayer from Homer:
Scion of Kronos, Zeus our father . . .

PHILOKLEON
                        Don't "father" me!
You show me how I'm a SLAVE, right quick, or I'll murder you!
God, what a thought! Murderers don't get fed at the Feasts!

PHOBOKLEON
Very well, *Daddy*, smooth your brow a little and listen.
First, some simple arithmetic.—No, not with pebbles;
use your fingers.
                  Figure up the total of all the tribute
that Athens receives from the Federated States, and add to this
the direct taxes *plus* all those little one-per-cents,
court-costs, confiscations, mine-franchises, rents,
sales-tax, licenses, duties, tariffs, wharfage *and* tonnage,
and we get a sum of . . . roughly, twenty thousand talents.
Now deduct from this the annual pay of all the Jurors,
six thousand of you—at least, that's all we have for the moment—
giving us a total salary (let's see: six thousand Jurors,
three obols a day, eighteen days a month, times ten,
divide by six, divide by a hundred, divide by sixty)—
yearly, the Jurors cost Athens one hundred and fifty talents.

PHILOKLEON
Out of twenty thousand? We don't even get *ten per cent?*

PHOBOKLEON
Why, no. Not at all.

PHILOKLEON
                But where does the rest of the money go?

PHOBOKLEON
Where? To the men with the mottoes, who will always "Uphold the
    Herd"
and "Sweat for the Salt of the Earth." So now you're held up and
    sweated,

and it's all your doing. *You* let them slather you in slogans, and *you*
elected them. To rule, of course, *you*. But not only you:
They petrify the Federated States with other slogans—e.g.,
"PAY THE TRIBUTE OR I ROLL THE THUNDER AND
    COLLAPSE THE CITY!"—
and proceed to squeeze fat bribes (fifty talents at a crash) for
    themselves;
while you, you're content to nibble the edges of your Empire's garbage.
The impression this makes on our Allies is not too hard to imagine.
They see you, the scum of Athens, weazening away on a diet
of ballot-box scraps, topped off, for dessert, with a succulent nothing,
and conclude, quite naturally, that you're as important as a fiddler's
    franchise.
So, without more ado, they turn to your leaders—and the stream begins.
They literally lave them in luxury: pillows, and dishes of fish,
honey, sesame, flagons of wine, firkins of cheeses,
cups and goblets, garlands and chaplets, clothing and carpets,
Health, Wealth, Long Life, Prosperity, and Such.
                                        While you—
the Ruler, the Founder, the Grand Panjandrum who shaped this Empire
with the strokes of your oar, on Land and Sea—from your vast domain
you derive not even one head of garlic to season your smelts!

PHILOKLEON
Well, that's true enough. I had to send out to a friend for three cloves
last night . . . but *this* is SLAVERY? Get to the point—you're killing me!

PHOBOKLEON
I submit this as Slavery in its most acute form: when men like those,
ringed by their toadies and jackals, can roll in public gold,
but you are, perforce, overjoyed if they dribble you three little obols!
What a fine reward for the toil and agony that won our wars!
Not precisely a reward, of course: you *work*. By the numbers, where
and when they tell you. And that's what sticks in my gorge,
when a fancy young pansy like Chaireas' brat (not even a citizen!)
waggles up to you, legs well apart, with that fairy air,
and orders you to be in Court early tomorrow:
                                        "If a *single* one
comes after they blow the signal, he simply *won't* get *paid!*"
But Time doesn't matter to *him*; he's a Public Prosecutor and draws,
come early, come late, *six* obols. Plus supplementary bribes from
    defendants.

These he splits with Defendant's Counsel—an intimate of his circle.
Then these strange bedfellows arrange the case, decide the outcome,
rough out a script, and fall to.

You'd think they were handling a saw.
One pushes, one pulls—and, right in the middle, there's you. Watching.
For your pay, as it happens; so the whole sordid mess slips by you.

PHILOKLEON
That's what they do? To *me?* Do you mean it? Son, you're rocking
the bottom of my being—tugging at my reason—what ARE you doing?

PHOBOKLEON
Consider this rationally. You, and everyone else, could be *Rich*—
if you didn't let these Friends of the People keep you caged.
You *do* rule the world, or most of the world, from the Black Sea to
     Sardinia,
and what's your Profit?

Your pitiful pay, doled out in dabs—
the exact amounts to keep you teetering on the edge of starvation.
They mean you to stay poor, don't you see? Their motive is obvious:
Hunger knows no friend but its Feeder.

And so, whenever
your Tamers are threatened, they cluck their tongues, and flick your
     leash,
and you leap, ravening, on their enemies and tear them to bits.
But if these men *did* have the public welfare at heart,
it would be child's play to attain. Just take a look at the books:
At present, one thousand cities are paying tribute to Athens.
Assign them each the board of only twenty Athenians—
and twenty thousand citizens would swim in savory stew,
and wreaths, and crowns, and cream, and Grade-A Milk and Honey,
tasting their fitting prize for saving Hellas at Marathon.
But, as things are now, you act like migrant olive-pickers:
no matter where he leads you, you follow the man with the obols.

PHILOKLEON
What's come over me *now?* I can feel my hand getting numb . . .
and the sword—can't hold it any longer. I'm soft as a grape.

PHOBOKLEON
Whenever you frighten your Masters, they say you can have Euboia,[15]

15. Perikles, in 445, planted Athenian colonists on this grain-fertile island, and promise of the
same became a pie-in-the-sky maneuver for the demagogues who came after him.

and fifty bushels of wheat apiece—
$\qquad\qquad\qquad\qquad$ and you never get any.
No, I'm wrong: not too long ago, they gave you five bushels:
But you barely got *that*, of course—they accused you of being an
$\quad$ alien—
they trickled it out by the quart—and it wasn't wheat—
$\qquad\qquad\qquad\qquad\qquad\qquad$ it was barley.

$\qquad$ Which is why I've kept you from the Courtroom premises.
$\qquad$ You can't subsist on hollow promises,
$\qquad$ on imitation ersatz substitutes,
$\qquad$ steamed in scorn by chauvinist chefs.
$\qquad$ You need Nourishment; I'm frantic to feed you;
$\qquad$ Unlimited Menu—with a single proviso:
$\qquad$ the larder and cellar are stuffed and unlatched,
$\qquad$ so absolutely no more three-obol drafts
$\qquad\qquad$ of the Milk of the City Cashier.

SECOND KORYPHAIOS
Who said, *Don't judge till you've heard both sides*—remember?
$\quad$ Regardless,
he had something there.
The Chorus huddles, then the First Koryphaios turns
to Phobokleon.

FIRST KORYPHAIOS
$\qquad\qquad$ This Body's thoroughly considered decision,
Sir, is that YOU WIN, by considerably more than a mile.
In token whereof, we unstring our rods of anger and office
and dip them to you.
$\qquad\qquad$ —By the Numbers, Men: One, Two,
$\qquad\qquad\qquad\qquad$ DROOP!
The Stings, which have been at the ready, fall at the
command.

SECOND KORYPHAIOS
Now a word to you, dear friend of our youth, comrade in our creed:

SECOND SEMICHORUS
Picking up the cue and singing to Philokleon.
$\qquad\qquad$ Give in to his Logic, yield to his Proofs,
$\qquad\qquad$ give in to his object—stop being obtuse!
$\qquad$ I wish *I* had a relative to tell me what to do

so clearly and precisely, but the Lucky Man is YOU!

At your elbow there's a god;
　　he's giving you a hand.
Take his favors. Don't be awed—
　　accept them while you can!

PHOBOKLEON

I promise all comforts prescribed for his years:
gruel for his gums; chiffon; warm furs
to keep out the cold; a whore to indulge
in comprehensive below-the-belt massage.
But look—not a word; not even a wheeze:
I don't expect thanks, but I'm not exactly pleased.

FIRST SEMICHORUS

Singing to Phobokleon.

He's come to his senses, returned to himself,
　　he's come to repentance—he's going to get well!
He rues his rash litigiousness, his passion for so long.
Be patient, please. He's just found out his every act was wrong!

For the future, you're his norm:
　　he'll heed your eloquence;
he'll change his life, revise, reform—
　　he *may* acquire some sense!

PHILOKLEON

OH, WOE, WOE, WOE, etcetera!

PHOBOKLEON

At last!—What's all the shouting for?

PHILOKLEON

In a Euripidean transport of grief.

Press not on me these paltry promises!
Lost are my loved ones! Reft am I left!
No more to tread those precious premises,
to hang on the Herald's accents soft:
"WE LACK ONE VOTE! WE'RE ONE VOTE SHORT!
WHO IS IT? DON'T NOBODY LEAVE THIS COURT!
STAND UP!"—and proudly to rise alone
and stride to the urns and cast the last stone!
—PRESS ON, O SOUL! ALL SPEED, O SOUL!

MAKE HASTE, O—

        (Where'd I put that soul?)

—HITHER, SHADOWY ONE!

             —And Kleon

better not let me catch him stealing

        down in Court!

        He better not!

        He . . .

The reversal is too much. He stands mute, confused,
bewildered.

PHOBOKLEON
Enough of this, Father. For heaven's sake, give in!

PHILOKLEON
I'll give in, boy. Anything you ask. Except—
don't ask me to renounce that *one* thing . . .

PHOBOKLEON

                What one thing?

PHILOKLEON
My jury career. Before I give in on *that*,
they'll render the final verdict on me in Hades.

PHOBOKLEON
I know it's your greatest delight, and I won't stop you.
But don't go down to Court any more. What you need
is a change of venue. So stay right here, in the privacy
of your own home, and judge the servants.

PHILOKLEON

               Judge the Servants,
boy? On what charge?

PHOBOKLEON

        The charge doesn't change; just the Court.
For example, a simple misdemeanor: The maid "forgets"
to lock the door—she *says*. *We* prove Intent;
it's an open and shut case. So what do you do? You stick her—
with a smallish fine. One drachma. You've done it a thousand
times in Court. And this is Law at Leisure,
tailored to suit you, the easy, *rational* way.

If the day dawns bright, be a Solar Solon. Just move
the Court out into the sun. But suppose it snows.
Why freeze? There's Fireside Fining! Or, if it rains,
bring in your verdict—bring it inside, and be comfortable!
And sleep till noon, if you want; *then* open the session.
No official can turn you away for coming late
to your private jury box!

PHILOKLEON

       Now, *that* sounds nice.

PHOBOKLEON

But that's not all—no, *Sir!*
         Remember those endless
speeches when you were starving, eating your heart out
for a big, fat bite of Defendant, done to a turn?
Well, that's all over. Mix Litigation with your Lunch!

PHILOKLEON

Can I judge my best if I'm chomping on my food?

PHOBOKLEON

Better than your best! Your efficiency will double—triple!
It's a proven fact: in order to digest the evidence,
a jury needs to RUMINATE!

PHILOKLEON

       You're getting there, Son.
I'm wavering. But there's one little point you haven't mentioned.
Who's going to pay me?

PHOBOKLEON

     I'll pay you.

PHILOKLEON

         Well, that's just grand.
I'll draw all my pay to myself. Won't have to share it.
I've been burned on that.
      The other day Lysistratos,
that practical joker, drew a drachma, the pay
for him and me, and got it changed at the fish-market.
Three obols for him, three for me. So I popped mine in
my mouth to take home, and—ugh! That taste! That smell!

I spat them out. He'd given me three mackerel scales![16]
That jokester! I started to haul him to Court, of course.

PHOBOKLEON
What was his reaction to that?

PHILOKLEON
                    Him? Oh, he said
that I had the belly of a billy-goat. "You're pretty quick
at digesting good, hard cash." That's what he said.

PHOBOKLEON
But no more of that for *you!* Another advantage
of the New Home Jury System!

PHILOKLEON
                    And no small one, either.
He ponders briefly.
Son, you've won your case; you can sign me up!
Let's get to the judging!

PHOBOKLEON
                    Wait right here. Don't move.
I'll bring out all the necessary equipment.
He enters the house.

PHILOKLEON
I can't believe my eyes. I heard a prophecy
once which said it was only a matter of time
before every Athenian judged cases right at home,
and built a little courthouse on his front porch,
right next to the shrine to Hekate. And it's coming true!

PHOBOKLEON
*Returning at the head of a column of slaves who
carry various improbable objects, he waves expan-
sively at them.*
                    And here we are. What do you say to *that?*
My original estimate has been greatly amplified.
For example, this.
He holds up an enormous jug.

16. The obol was in fact a small silver-grey coin, smaller than a fingernail.

PHILOKLEON
What's that?

PHOBOKLEON
A chamber pot.
Put the case that you're passing judgment and need
to pass water. This hangs right at hand. That prong
should hold it nicely.

PHILOKLEON
Son, that shows some sense!
And it's mighty thoughtful, too. Just the thing
for an old sea-dog like me. I'll have safe harbor
for a floating kidney.

PHOBOKLEON
Bringing a brazier and a bowl.
And here's a fire, and a bowl
of lentil soup. If you're hungry, warm it and eat.

PHILOKLEON
Now, that's ingenious! With colic or fever, I'll stay in,
and eat my soup, and still collect my fee!
Phobokleon advances with a rooster in a cage.
But why the rooster?

PHOBOKLEON
We provide for every contingency:
You know how defendants' speeches make you doze—
well, this cock crows you awake in time for conviction!

PHILOKLEON
All this is wonderful, son, but I miss one thing.

PHOBOKLEON
Name it.

PHILOKLEON
Do you think you could have them bring me
the shrine to the Juror's Protector—Lykos? I'd like it.

PHOBOKLEON
Caught flat-footed.
Why, certainly. It's—it's here already.

PHILOKLEON
Peering around.

Where?

PHOBOKLEON
*Desperate, then suddenly pointing at the huge
chamber pot.*
Here's the hero.

PHILOKLEON

That's Lykos?

PHOBOKLEON

Certainly.
You pour libations at a shrine, don't you? Well?

PHILOKLEON
Dubiously, to the chamber pot.
Master, please pardon me—but you were pretty hard
to recognize.

PHOBOKLEON

I don't see why. He seems as big
as Kleonymos.

PHILOKLEON
Looking inside the chamber pot.

You're right—another hollow hero.

PHOBOKLEON
The quicker you sit down, the quicker I'll call
the first case.

PHILOKLEON
Taking a seat.

Son, I was sitting before you were born.
Call away!

PHOBOKLEON
In a worried aside.

Let's see. What case to introduce first?
Just who in this house has done anything wrong?

Oh, well—

Raising his voice to an official bellow:
     CALL THRATTA, THE MAID, FOR BURNING UP—

PHILOKLEON

                                    Hold it, son!
You'll be the death of me! Imagine calling a case
in a Court without a Bar!

PHOBOKLEON
                    A Bar?

PHILOKLEON
                              That fence
between the jury and everyone else. Why, that's
the holiest thing in Court. You want bad luck?

PHOBOKLEON
We don't *have* a Bar.

PHILOKLEON
                         Well, I'll run inside and get one.
I can rustle one up right away—need a Bar. Watch!
He dashes into the house.

PHOBOKLEON
What next, I wonder? Habit's an awful thing.
*Xanthias runs out of the house, yelling over his
shoulder.*

XANTHIAS
Go to hell!
Muttering.
             Try to feed a dog like that!

PHOBOKLEON
What's the matter?

XANTHIAS
                 What else *could* be the matter?
That grabby dog Chowhound,[17] of course! Jumped into the pantry,

---

17. In Greek, *Labēs*, "Grab"—a pun on the general Laches, as the plaintiff (here "Fleahound")
is *Kyōn* "Dog"—a pun on Kleon.

clamped onto a rich Sicilian cheese and gulped
the whole thing down!

PHOBOKLEON

That's *it!*

XANTHIAS

What's *what?*

PHOBOKLEON

The *crime*—
the first case I'll introduce to father for judgment.
You stay here and prosecute.

XANTHIAS

Not on your life,
not me!
But the other dog there says *he'll* prosecute,
if someone files a charge.

PHOBOKLEON

Excellent! Fine!
Go bring them both out here.

XANTHIAS

Just as you say, Sir.
He exits into the house. After a short pause, Phi-
lokleon emerges from the house, carrying a section
of fence.

PHOBOKLEON
What in the world is *that?*

PHILOKLEON

The pigpen. Our Bar.

PHOBOKLEON
You mean the pen for the pigs we sacrifice to Hestia?

PHILOKLEON
Yup.

PHOBOKLEON
But that's sacrilege!

PHILOKLEON
Not sacrilege—sacri*fice*.
Lets the defendant know where he stands. Be fair,
that's what I say.
But bring on that first case—
I've got that old conviction-itch.

PHOBOKLEON
One moment.
We need the docket and the indictments.
He enters the house.

PHILOKLEON
I tell you, boy,
you're grinding me down. Delays, delays, delays—
you're killing me!
He shows the wax tablet he uses to pass sentence.
I only want to plow
a nice long furrow in my little field here.

PHOBOKLEON
Returning with some scrolls.
Here we are.

PHILOKLEON
Then call that first case!

PHOBOKLEON
Pretending to peruse the scrolls.
Let's see;
who's first . . .

PHILOKLEON
Tarnation!

PHOBOKLEON
What's wrong?

PHILOKLEON
I forgot the urns—
the Jury's ballot boxes! Makes me sick!
He rises.

PHOBOKLEON
Hey, there! Where are you going?

PHILOKLEON

> To get the *urns!*

PHOBOKLEON

Sit down; I saw to that. We'll use these pots.
He places two small pots on the table.

PHILOKLEON

That's pretty—real pretty. We've got everything,
all we need. Except—
> where's the water-clock?
*He rises. Phobokleon pushes him down and points at
the chamber pot again.*

PHOBOKLEON

> There.

PHILOKLEON

That? A water-clock?

PHOBOKLEON

> What else could it be?

PHILOKLEON
Dubiously.
> Er—sure.
He shrugs and surveys the scene happily.
Well, nothing's missing. You know the Court like a native.

PHOBOKLEON
Calling into the house.
> Bring out the myrtle, the incense, the holy fire!
> And hurry! Court can't be convened before
> we invoke the gods and beg them for their blessings.
Slaves from the house bring the desired articles.

FIRST KORYPHAIOS
To Philokleon and Phobokleon.
> From war and trouble
> you've made a noble
> metamorphosis.
> And so, to your vows
> we add our prayers
> for your success.

To the Chorus.

Now let holy silence
preface our petitions.

ENTIRE CHORUS

Pythian God
Apollo, heed
our hymn and bless our word.
Attune the plan
of this young man
to *our* existence, Lord.
And may it bring
our wandering
to rest in clear accord.
Hail, Paian—Healer!

PHOBOKLEON

Mighty Apollo, God of the Ways, Watcher at the Gate,
receive this rite, newly minted, fresh for my father.
Soften and supple the stiff, the unbending oak in his soul;
honey and mellow his temper's tartness, the must of his heart.
Sweeten him, Lord, to the human race,
prone to pity, tending to tears,
tears for the suppliant,
tears for the victim—
none for the plaintiff—
his bitterness bottled,
his anger unnettled.

ENTIRE CHORUS

The canons you
set forth, so new,
provide for us a key.
Our descant prayers
we raise to yours
in perfect harmony.
This note of grace
from youth to age
is no set cadency.
Hail, Paian—Healer!

*The prayer over, the Chorus retires to the wings and
Xanthias brings from the house two dogs, Chow-*

hound (the defendant) and Fleahound (the plaintiff).
Phobokleon, who acts the parts of various court offi-
cials during the succeeding scene, addresses the
Jury—Philokleon—now in the manner of a herald.

PHOBOKLEON
OYEZ! ALL JURORS IN THEIR SEATS! POSITIVELY NO
   ADMITTANCE TO THE BOX AFTER THE COMMENCEMENT
   OF DEBATE!

PHILOKLEON
Settling himself.
   Who's the defendant?

PHOBOKLEON
Pointing at Chowhound.
                He is.

PHILOKLEON
                   Oh, what I've got
in store for him—Unanimous Conviction!

PHOBOKLEON
                  ATTENTION!
THE INDICTMENT: THE CASE OF FLEAHOUND, OF
   KYDATHENEA,
VS. CHOWHOUND, OF AIXONE! THE CHARGE: UNLAWFUL
POSSESSION AND SELFISH DESTRUCTION OF ONE SICILIAN
CHEESE! PROPOSED PENALTY: IMPOUNDMENT, THIRTY
LEASHES, AND PERMANENT CONFINEMENT IN A WOODEN
   COLLAR!

PHILOKLEON
A stock penalty. They're getting soft. When *I*
pass sentence on him, by god, he'll die like a dog!

PHOBOKLEON
THE DEFENDANT CHOWHOUND WILL ADVANCE TO THE
   BAR OF JUSTICE!

PHILOKLEON
As the terrified dog shambles up to the railing in
front of him.

Criminal Type. I can spot them every time:
Pointy ears, eyes set close together, weak chin,
wet nose . . .

Chowhound gives a dog's yawn.

There! See that? He's showing his teeth!
Trying to Intimidate the Jury, eh? I'll fix him!
—But where's the plaintiff? Where's this Fleahound fellow?

FLEAHOUND
GRRRRROWF!

PHOBOKLEON
Weakly.

He's here. Another Chowhound, that's what he is.

PHILOKLEON
Now, wait. You must admit he's a powerful barker . . .

PHOBOKLEON
. . . and licker of pots. And boots.
—ORDER IN THE COURT!
PLAINTIFF, MOUNT THE STAND AND BRING YOUR CHARGE!

*Fleahound mounts a bench. Philokleon turns to the
brazier where the soup is heating, and pours out a
bowlful.*

PHILOKLEON
This seems a good time to sustain my judgment with soup.

FLEAHOUND
*In a roar, the volume varying, seemingly at random,
from very loud to much louder.*

Gentlemen of the JURY! You have already HEARD the writ
I WROTE, and there's no point in reading IT again!
That mealy-mouthed MONGREL there is ACCUSED
of High CRIMES and MISDEMEANORS—i.e., he cheated
ME! and all the yo-heave-HO boys in our NAVY!
Just what did this PUTRID pooch do? He BOLTED away
into a corner, a DARK corner! And there
he GUZZLED up a WHOLE CHEESE—
SICILICED it to bits!

PHILOKLEON
Yup. True enough. That stinker belched just now,

and I nearly got choked by the smell of cheese! GUILTY—
out of his own mouth.

FLEAHOUND

And *I* DIDN'T get a BITE!
Look here—WHO'S going to help you OUT—WHO'S
going to look AFTER you, if people start to STOP
kicking in—I MEAN, throwing a SCRAP
or two to ME, your faithful HOUND—Your BODYGUARD?

PHILOKLEON

Indignant.

And he didn't give any to *me*, the Body Politic!
Oh, but he's a sly one—sharp—he bites—
just like this—ouch!—soup. Dammit, it's hot!

PHOBOKLEON

Father, for heaven's sake! You can't condemn him
before you've heard both sides!

PHILOKLEON

Oh, come, now—look
at the facts. The case is clear.
With a wave at Fleahound.

It barks for itself.

FLEAHOUND

You CAN'T acquit him—of ALL the dogs in the WORLD,
that man's the SELFISHEST greedyguts there IS!
Know what he DID to that Sicilian HOARD?
He sailed AROUND the plate—

he STRIPPED the rind
of all the CHOICEST sections, and wolfed it DOWN!
All that was LEFT was the HOLES!

PHILOKLEON

Holding up a flap of his motheaten cloak.

And I got those.

FLEAHOUND

One more REASON to PUNISH him . . .

PHOBOKLEON

. . . is because
one trough isn't big enough to feed two thieves?

FLEAHOUND
. . . is THIS—to serve your FAITHFUL HOUND! Don't let
my BARKING go in vain! If he goes FREE,
I'LL NEVER BARK *AGAIN!*

PHILOKLEON
                              Bravo! Bravo!
Fleahound bows and steps down.
          Now *that's* an accusation—crimes and more crimes!
Pointing to Chowhound.
                                                      That man's

          solid larceny!
To the rooster.
                    You agree, old cock?
                                        By god,

          he winked!
                    —Bailiff! Where's the Bailiff?

PHOBOKLEON
                                        I'm here.

PHILOKLEON
Well, pass me the pot!

PHOBOKLEON
                    Get it yourself. I'm also
          Herald, and it's time for me to call the witnesses.
Philokleon rises and avails himself
of the chamber pot.
          I CALL THE WITNESSES FOR THE DEFENDANT CHOWHOUND.
As he summons them, a host of kitchen implements
emerge from the house and take up positions before
him.
          BOWL!
                    GRINDER!
                              CHEESE-GRATER!
                                        GRILL!
                                                  STEW-POT!
          AND ALL THE OTHER UTENSILS UNDER SUBPOENA!
          —Haven't you finished pissing yet?
                                        BE SEATED!

PHILOKLEON
Don't need to, son—but I know someone who *will:*

He leers savagely at Chowhound, who cringes.
>Oh, am I going to scare the shit out of him!

PHOBOKLEON
Don't be such a compulsive grouch. Whenever
you see a defendant, it's always dog-eat-dog.
—THE DEFENDANT WILL MOUNT THE STAND AND MAKE
>HIS PLEA!

Chowhound, in terror, climbs on the bench and
trembles, unable to utter a sound.
>Well, say something! Speak *up*, dog! Make your plea!

PHILOKLEON
I don't think there's a single thing he *can* say.

PHOBOKLEON
No, you're wrong. I know the trouble—he's sick.
I saw it happen to old Thoukydides once
when he was on trial:
>Litigation Lockjaw.
It comes on suddenly. No immediate cure.
To Chowhound.
>All right, down, out of my way.
>I'll defend you.

Chowhound leaves the bench; Phobokleon mounts it
and addresses Philokleon.
>Gentlemen of the Jury:
>Give a dog a bad name,
and his defense in a Court of Law becomes difficult.
But I shall make the attempt—make it because
he is A Good Dog, and chases away the wolves.

PHILOKLEON
He's a thief, too—and worse than that, a SUBVERSIVE!

PHOBOKLEON
I object. Of all today's dogs, this is Best in Show.
The perfect type to tend a huge and brainless
flock of sheep.

PHILOKLEON
>What profit is that?—HE EATS
THE CHEESE!

PHOBOKLEON
What profit? List his points: he fights
your battles, guards your premises—what profit?

PHILOKLEON
                                        HE EATS
THE CHEESE!

PHOBOKLEON
              Oh, yes, the cheese.
                              So he steals a little—
and why? Because he's rough and tough—and that's
the thing we need, in a dog or a general.
                              Pardon
his lack of polish; he never studied the harp.

PHILOKLEON
Holding up a scroll.
I wish he'd never learned to write. Or hide things.
He buried that cheese somewhere in his Statement to the Court.

PHOBOKLEON
Stepping down.
Please try to be fair and hear my witness out.
—CHEESE-GRATER, MOUNT THE STAND!
                              Now then, speak up.
When Chowhound is alleged to have seized the Sicilian cheese,
you held the post of steward?
The Cheese-Grater nods.
                              Now then, answer clearly:
Did you portion out your receipts to these soldiers here?
*He gestures at the other utensils. The Cheese-Grater
nods. Phobokleon addresses Philokleon.*
—He affirms that the soldiers received the regular grate.

PHILOKLEON
I say he's lying—his story's full of holes!

PHOBOKLEON
Oh, Sir, I implore your compassion. Pity the underprivileged.
Behold the luckless Chowhound! His only sustenance
the scrapings of tables, the heads of fish!

Chowhound fidgets madly.
                                              Condemned
to a restless existence—a rover with no place for his head!
With a wave at Fleahound.
         Compare this sleek, well-kenneled cur. What profit?
         His profit. A watchdog—an *inside* watchdog, who snarls
         for his cut when anyone enters. And gets it—or bites.

PHILOKLEON
But what's bitten ME? I'm sick—I'm going all soft
inside! I can feel it slithering, winding over me—
the Juror's fatal disease—*Creeping Persuasion!*

PHOBOKLEON
Gentlemen of the Jury, O Father, heed now my entreaty.
Harden not your hearts, but melt it in mercy!
Deign not to demolish this dog!
                                    —Where are the children?
*Xanthias herds a group of crying puppies out of
the house.*
         MOUNT THE STAND, O POOR, O PITIFUL PUPS!
*The puppies climb the bench beside Phobokleon,
who cuddles them.*
         You sorry, stricken whelps of a helpless hero,
         Whine!
                 Whimper!
                          Weep!
                              Beseech the Court
         to melt in Simple Humanity for your miserable sire!
*The air is rent with hideous doggy howls. Philokleon
is reduced to tears.*

PHILOKLEON
Stop! I can't stand it! Step down! STEP DOWN!

PHOBOKLEON
                                              I shall
step down, though I know that Juror's Trap, that Quasi-Legal
Fiction. You let the defendant think he's won
by shouting "Step Down!" and down he steps, breaks off
his defense—whereupon you convict him. Nevertheless,
I shall step down . . .

PHILOKLEON
Recovering his spleen at the last moment.

. . . STRAIGHT

TO

HELL!

Disgustedly throwing down his soup-bowl.

This eating—
It's no good, that's all. Just now I melted every grain
of Sense I own in tears—and why? Because
I was full of hot soup, that's why!

PHOBOKLEON

You mean he's *convicted?*

PHILOKLEON
It's difficult to tell at this point. The votes aren't in.

PHOBOKLEON
Father, dear Father, turn to Finer Things!
To kindness, and justice! Take this pebble and close
your eyes for the painful task, the work of a moment.
Speed to the Second Urn and *acquit* him, Father!

PHILOKLEON
No, son, those Finer Things aren't for me. Pardon
my lack of polish; I never studied the harp.
He starts for the table with the voting urns.
Phobokleon intercepts him and grabs his arm.

PHOBOKLEON
I'll take you over, Father; I know a shortcut.
He leads Philokleon to the table by a route which
includes a number of dizzy twirls, so that when his
father arrives before the table, he is quite confused.

PHILOKLEON
Pointing to the Second Urn. The markers of the
Urns, if any, are turned away from him.
Is this the First Urn—the one for "GUILTY"?

PHOBOKLEON

That's it.

PHILOKLEON
Dropping his voting-pebble in the Second Urn.
    Then there's my vote!

PHOBOKLEON
Aside.
                   He took the bait! In spite
    of himself, he voted to acquit!
                        —I'll tally the votes.

PHILOKLEON
Impatiently.
    Well, what's the verdict?

PHOBOKLEON
                   Time will tell. Be patient.
*He empties out the Urns, one after the other, very
deliberately.*
    —THE DEFENDANT CHOWHOUND IS FOUND TO BE
       NOT GUILTY!
Philokleon falls senseless to the ground.
    Father, Father, what's wrong?
                     Oh, *dear!*
                          WATER!
*Xanthias dashes up with a jug of water and empties
it over Philokleon.*
    Excelsior, Father!

PHILOKLEON
Struggling up feebly on one elbow.
                   Don't play tricks on me, Son.
    Was he really, truly acquitted?

PHOBOKLEON
                   I swear it.

PHILOKLEON
Falling back.
                          I'm extinct.

PHOBOKLEON
    Don't brood—put it out of your mind. Here now, stand up.
He helps Philokleon rise and supports him.

PHILOKLEON

But how can I live with what I've done? How
can I bear that dreadful load on my conscience? How?
I ACQUITTED A DEFENDANT! What evil fate will befall me?

Raising his arms to heaven.

O gods on high, adored and honored, absolve your
servant, a sinner in spite of himself! My nature
is not so heinous as to plot a deed like that!

PHOBOKLEON

Of course it isn't. Away with these worries, Father.
Place yourself in my hands. My sole concern
will be your care and comfort. The two of us
will go *everywhere* together, sampling all
the sophisticated, genteel joys that Athenian society
offers—dinners, banquets, parties, and the theater.
The balance of your days will pass in utter bliss,
and never again will you play the demagogues' dupe.
Let's go inside.

PHILOKLEON

A broken man.

All right, Son, if you say so.
*They enter the house, Philokleon guided tenderly by
his son, followed by the puppies, the utensils, the
dogs, and the slaves.*

FIRST KORYPHAIOS

Hail and farewell, friends!
May fortune attend your
every venture!

Turning to the audience.

Meanwhile, to you Numberless Millions,
I offer a message of caution:
PROTECT YOUR GOOD NAME.
The ensuing remarks contain
pith and profit in plenty;
and any self-respecting
audience, caring at all
to avoid the general
appellation of IGNORAMUS

—and worse—really must
be improved thereby.
        Verbum sap., say I.
Stepping forward.
People of Athens, prove your vaunted taste for Truth
and attend the Complaint which the Poet brings against the spectators.
WANTON INJURY, WITHOUT PROVOCATION, AGAINST A
    BENEFACTOR—
so runs the charge brought by Our Bard.
                        He was ever your Savior,
from his first, incognito essays at the stage—when he took a leaf
from the book of that supple, sage ventriloquist-prophet EURYKLES,
and cast his very self and voice into others' mouths[18]
to pour forth a purest stream of comedy, funny and ribald—
down to the day when he threw off the mask and ran his own risks,
charioteer for his own, his private stable of Muses.
Through all that time your safety and comfort was his only concern.
And then, when you raised him, and prized and praised him as none
    before him,
did conceit inflate and balloon his brain? Perhaps he perverted
his talents and titles, scouring the schools for talented perverts
(like certain comedians who shall be nameless)?
                        The answer is NO!
What's more, if a thwarted pederast pressed him to slander a boy-love
back into bed, he refused. His Muses are public servants,
not private pimps; his sense of fitness knows Right from Wrong.

—Next, his aims are high. When he took to the stage, he attacked no
    MEN,
but with Herakles' courage and rage he loaded his Chorus for
    MONSTER
and marched on the mighty, assailing all manner of Gogs, Magogs,
and Demagogues. From his first performance, he dared to measure his
    strength
with that rankest of reptiles, the Brown-Tailed, Saw-Toothed
    KLEONOSAURUS REX.
Its eyes flashed fire with a whorehouse glare, while in its hair
in a writhing mass, a hundred heads of lousy leeches
circled and weaved—and kissed its foul ass. It screamed in the voice

18. Those of Philonides and Kallistratos, who produced Aristophanes' first plays.

of a roaring river in labor, and bore the stink of a seal,
the greasy balls of a female troll, the rump of a camel.
But before this sight, did our dauntless poet take fright—or a bribe?
No, friends, not a bit. For you he warred then—for you he wars now.

Again, last year he turned his sights on those vampire demons
of chills and fever who stole by night to strangle fathers
and suck the breath from fathers' fathers; who then lay down
in their beds to plot and paste together a cruel collage
of suit and summons, writ and witness, against the harmless.
He attacked these informers with such success that many leaped,
scared out of their wits and beds, to complain to the courts that they,
as alien goblins, were suffering torture commonly reserved
for full-fledged citizens.
                            In short, you'd found a Champion to cleanse
and purge your city of evil—
                            Wherefore (and here's the core
of the Complaint) last year, when your Savior sowed New Ideas by the
    sackful,
your heads were so hard that you ruined his crop. Nothing came up.
You betrayed him, and gave, in your idiot folly, LAST PRIZE to *THE
    CLOUDS!*—
to the best of all comedies ever performed (a firmstanding fact,
which Our Author repeatedly urges the god Dionysos to witness).
This award confers dishonor on YOU, for slow-witted dullness.
ARISTOPHANES suffers no slur from those with a *right* to opinions:
he wrecked his hopes—
                            but only because he was passing his rivals.
                    Hence, for the future,
                    you witless wonders,
                    when poets you find
                    with freshness of mind
                    who exhibit intentions
                    toward novel invention
                    of thought or expression,
                    cherish them, nourish them,
                    cull their conceptions
                    and carefully place
                    them in chests with sachets—
                    and through the next year
                    the clothes that you wear

>　　will give off an air
>　　of ineluctable savoir-faire.

FIRST SEMICHORUS
>　Long ago—
>　　　We were mighty in the dance,
>　　　we were mighty at advance,
>　and our mightiness resided in the sting we bear;
>　　　but our power didn't last,
>　　　and our lustihood is past,
>　and whiter than the swan fade the flowers of our hair.

>　　From these remnants we must recover
>　　some spark, some trace of youthful vigor.
>　　　　And my old age
>　　　　is more than a match
>　　　—at least, in my estimation—
>　　for the pansy poses, girlish curls,
>　　and happy homosexual whirls
>　　of the younger de-generation!

FIRST KORYPHAIOS
And now, to you in the audience who swell with confusion, curiosity
pricked by these spiky stings, intellects squeezed by our wasp waists,
a palliative explanation: the cause of our costume in a very few words,
words carefully chosen so as not to puzzle the dullards among you.
We, then, whom you behold so sharply appointed, are *Attic*
(and thence contentious)—the only authentic race of Attica,
tracing our lineage to those sprung from the soil by spontaneous
　　generation.
For virulent virility, we remain unmatched. At Pest Removal,
the City has not known our peer in sheer belligerence, as witness
the coming of the Persians.
>　　　　　　　Their aim was simple—to drive us from
>　our hives.

And they put the entire City to the torch to supply the smoke.
Straightway, forth we swarmed, our bravery bolstered with gall.
We took our stand with shield and spear in single combat,
and ground our jaws with ire as they blotted out the sun with arrows.
But the owl of omen flew over our ranks before the attack,
and when evening blotted the sun in truth, the Persians bolted,

routed. We raced behind and riddled their Oriental rears,
while their jaws and brows ballooned, harpooned by our Sting.
                                                    Wherefore,
since men are known by their attributes, throughout barbarian lands
we are famed as the manliest race alive: the ATTIC WASP.

SECOND SEMICHORUS
        Then it was—
                I inspired so much dread
                that I never was afraid;
        when I sailed against the foe I made him kneel or flee;
                for my mind was free and clear
                of these new civilian fears:
        "Can I make a good rebuttal?"
                                "Who'll inform on me?"

                The only conviction that ever we bore
                assigned the verdict to the fastest oar.
                        And that we plied;
                        but now must plead
                        Guilty in the First Degree
                to pillaging the Persians' power
                of gold, and thus providing for
                our young delinquents' larceny.

SECOND KORYPHAIOS
Observe us, and you will find complete correlation between
our habits, manners, ways of life, and those of Wasps.
Imprimis: The world holds no other creature which, when ruffled,
can hope to approach us in presence of rancor or absence of temper.
And all our other activities are equally nasty and waspish.
Clumped together in swarms we sit in our *hives*, you might say—
the Archon's Court, the Eleven's Court, the converted Odeion—
and render judgment.
                        We're packed in solidly, squeezed against
the walls, bent double right down to the ground, not able to move.
Compare the wasp-grubs, sealed in cells.
                                        We're industrious, too.
To win subsistence by stinging *everyone* without distinction
is Very Hard Work—and that's the way we earn our living.
There, too, comes trouble: we have our drones, who laze among us

but have no stings, and yet, in their pointless existence, devour
the fruit of our labors without a hint of motion or effort,
not even a bit of bitterness.
                              But our greatest vexation is to view
our salary swilled by a NON-VETERAN slacker, whose hand never
   knew
oar, nor lance, nor blister upraised in his Country's defense.
Hence, my decision:
                       In future, no citizen without a sting
may draw the Juror's three obols. Briefly:
                                        No prick, no pay.

*The Chorus retires. Philokleon stumps from the
house in vexation, clutching his threadbare cloak
with the tenacity of a drowning man. He is followed
by the equally tenacious Phobokleon, who carries a
new cloak of Persian make, very shaggy, which he is
intent upon exchanging for his father's old one.*

PHILOKLEON

Pressing his cloak desperately to his bosom.
         If you take me out of this cloak, it'll be feet first!
         We were in the service together—it saved my life!
         There we were, shoulder to shoulder, standing off
         the first attack of the winter—I might have frozen!

PHOBOKLEON
I don't think you appreciate nice treatment, Father.

PHILOKLEON
Why should I? Just costs me money.
                                   Take eating—
I filled up on herring yesterday, and so it cost me
three obols—a whole day's pay—to get *this* cloak cleaned!

PHOBOKLEON
I'm afraid you don't have much choice.
                              You know the agreement.
You've made me your legal guardian, once and for all.

PHILOKLEON

Sulkily.

Oh, all right. What do you want me to do?

PHOBOKLEON
Simple. Take off that worn, sleazy old cloak,
and put on this bright, spanking new robe here.
Be the smart, natty man of the world you really are.
He removes the old cloak from his father, who,
though resigned, is none too co-operative. The pro-
cess is thus rendered rather more difficult than it
should be.

PHILOKLEON
Emerging at length from his cloak.
What's the point in having children, anyway?
I fathered him, and now he smothers me.

PHOBOKLEON
Proffering the robe.
Less chatter and more action—put this on!

PHILOKLEON
Son, will you tell me what the hell this *is?*

PHOBOKLEON
It's Persian—they call it a burnoose.

PHILOKLEON
                              Burn whose?

PHOBOKLEON
Or else an astrakhan.

PHILOKLEON
                    I thought it was a scatter rug.

PHOBOKLEON
Understandable—you've never been to Sardis
on one of those embassies. If you had, you'd know
what it is.
            But now you don't.

PHILOKLEON
                    You're right enough there—

It looks to me like Morychos' overcoat—

                                        with Morychos
still inside it.

PHOBOKLEON
              It's *Persian*, I tell you—woven
in Ekbatan. It's an *astrakhan!*

PHILOKLEON
                         ASS-trakhan?
Those tricky Persians'll fleece anything that walks.

PHOBOKLEON
Oh, stop it, father. This is a Persian burnoose,
woven in Ekbatan at absolutely ruinous expense.
One of these consumes sixty pounds of wool.

PHILOKLEON
Hungriest looking cloak I ever saw.

PHOBOKLEON
PLEASE STAND STILL AND PUT THIS ON!

PHILOKLEON
Accepting reluctantly and sniffing.

                                        Pew!—
         You're right, it's astrakhan.
He starts to slip it on.
                         Burnoose, too—
         God, it's hot in there!
He takes it off.

PHOBOKLEON
                    PUT THAT THING ON!

PHILOKLEON
I won't. Son, if you feel like this, why not
stick me in the oven right away? It's quicker.

PHOBOKLEON
Very well, *I'll* put it on you.

He envelops Philokleon in the shaggy robe, then notices the old cloak lying on the ground. All his frustration emerges in a violent kick at it, accompanied by an address.

Get out of here!

PHILOKLEON
Faintly, from the depths.
Anyway, keep a fork handy.

PHOBOKLEON
Why a fork?

PHILOKLEON
To fish me out of here before I melt.

PHOBOKLEON
Surveying.
Let's see—what next? Those shoes are a disgrace.
Here, take them off. Put on these Spartan slippers.

PHILOKLEON
Spartan slippers?
That's enemy produce—contraband!
They're hostile. They'll corrupt my sole.
I refuse.

PHOBOKLEON
Kneeling to fit the first slipper on.
Come on, father—quick march, off to Sparta.
Put your foot in it.

PHILOKLEON
What you're doing is a disgrace—
Making me step on Spartan soil. I feel
as though half of me were deserting to the enemy.

PHOBOKLEON
And the other foot.

PHILOKLEON
Nope—not that one. The big toe
hates Spartans—gets inflamed every time I turn south.

PHOBOKLEON
Sorry, this is the way things are.

PHILOKLEON
Now completely covered, except for his head, from
which he wipes the sweat.
                        Nothing
is worse than growing old—can't do this,
can't do that. Now I can't even catch cold.

PHOBOKLEON
Will you let me get this slipper on?
                              There we are.
Now, walk as though you had money. You know, a little
insolence, a little lecherousness. Wiggle a little!

PHILOKLEON
Rich, eh?
He tries a tentative strut.
                Like this? Watch me walk, and tell me
which rich man you think I look like.
He swaggers.

PHOBOKLEON
                            Hmmm.
Hard to say. Rather like a pimple with a bandage on.

PHILOKLEON
What's that, son? Like a pimp? But *which* rich man?
Doesn't matter—I know just the thing—
a bump, and a grind, and a couple of shakes of the tail.

PHOBOKLEON
Fine, just fine. Now, then, to Conversation.
Will you be able to hold your own in weighty
discourse with clever, witty, learned men?

PHILOKLEON
Nobody better.

PHOBOKLEON
Doubtfully.
                        Well, what would you say? Do you have
an anecdote, maybe?

PHILOKLEON
                    I've got millions.

PHOBOKLEON
                                        For example?

PHILOKLEON
Well, first there's how they snared the ogress Lamia
and she farted loose; and then there's the one about Little
Kardopion, taking his mother by the . . .

PHOBOKLEON
                                        No!
Not that! No fairy tales! You'll have to be realistic:
Everyday stories about everyday human beings—
domestic anecdotes—things around the house.

PHILOKLEON
Things around the house? Oh, I get you now.
Like this:
          Once upon a time a cat and a mouse . . .

PHOBOKLEON
OF ALL THE GAUCHE, UNLETTERED IDIOTS!—and I quote
(Theogenes said it to another collector of crap!):
Are you going to talk about cats and mice in *Society?*

PHILOKLEON
Sulkily.
What *am* I supposed to tell them?

PHOBOKLEON
                              Important things—
stories that confer some dignity, fix some *fashion*
on you as narrator. For instance, tell them how
you were Athens' representative at a festival—you,
and Androkles, and Kleisthenes.

PHILOKLEON
                         Kleisthenes? I thought you said
no fairy tales. And anyway, I never represented
Athens—except at Paros. Got two obols a day
for that—the same as all the other privates.

PHOBOKLEON

Er—yes. Well, no matter: You've been to Olympia.
Remember? Ah, what a story! You saw Ephoudion,
old and grizzled as he was, hold his own against
young Askondas, wrestling catch-as-catch-can.
Ah, that was a battle, now! Age against youth—
the stag at bay! Tell them of Ephoudion's might—
how, for all his gray hairs, his chest was a brass-bound
barrel, his hands were hammers, his sides were steel,
his breast was bronze, his—

PHILOKLEON

                                        Stop it, son—that's foolish.
He couldn't fight—he couldn't even move.

PHOBOKLEON

Deflated.

Well, that's the clever set's conversation.
                                        We'd better
try something else. Let's have a suggestion from you.
Now, if you're drinking and making society small talk,
what would you tell your hosts was the most manly deed
you performed in those far-off days of your youth?

PHILOKLEON

                                             Most manly?
Most grown-up? Oh, sure—I stole Ergasion's vine-poles.

PHOBOKLEON

Vine-poles? No, no, NO! Didn't you ever
chase a boar, or at least a rabbit, or run
in a relay? What's your most heroic accomplishment?

PHILOKLEON

Heroic? I took a dare once—you know Phaÿllos?

PHOBOKLEON

The Olympic runner?

PHILOKLEON

                              That's the one. I took after him—
And I caught him. A close race. Beat him by just two votes—
libel suit. But I was in condition, then.

PHOBOKLEON
Enough!
   Let's accomplish what we can. Lie down,
and learn to be convivial, fit for civilized intercourse.

PHILOKLEON
All ears.
  How do I lie down for *that?* Hurry up!

PHOBOKLEON
          With grace.

PHILOKLEON
Hurling himself onto his back, and assuming,
roughly, the fetal position.
  This what you want?

PHOBOKLEON
      Definitely, irrevocably, NO.

PHILOKLEON
Well, then, *how?*

PHOBOKLEON
Manfully.
      First, extend the knees.
  That's it.
     Now, slide the body in supple, liquid curves—
the ones they teach in school—over the tapestries.
Philokleon looks dubiously at his astrakhan. He
becomes more and more confused as Phobokleon
sweeps on.
  Take up a piece of plate and praise it to the skies.
  Inspect the ceiling. Marvel at the richly woven
  hangings in the hall.
As if to a Waiter.
       Water for our hands—over here!
  Bring in the tables! And now we dine.
He mimes eating.
         And now
  the finger-bowls.
He mimes washing.

                    And now we pour libations.
He mimes pouring and drinking.

    PHILOKLEON
That's a dream of a dinner, son—and just as filling.

    PHOBOKLEON
Not to be stopped.
    The flute-girl gives us a note. Our fellow-guests
    are here—Theoros, Aischines, Phanos, and Kleon,
    and there's somebody else right by him. Who is it?
He squints and cranes, imitated by Philokleon, who
is still confused.
                                     Oh,
    it's Akestor's son.—When you're in *this* sort of company,
    father, you have to know your drinking songs.

    PHILOKLEON
Oh, I do.

    PHOBOKLEON
    When the man before you sings a line,
    do you know how to top it?

    PHILOKLEON
                      Perfectly.

    PHOBOKLEON
                        Really?

    PHILOKLEON
I'm even better than the yodelers up in the hills.

    PHOBOKLEON
Well, we'll soon find out. Now, I'll be Kleon,
and I'll start off the "Harmodios." You try to top it.
Sings.
        Never again will Athens find . . .

    PHILOKLEON
Sings.
        . . . a thief like you; *you've stolen her blind.*

PHOBOKLEON
You can't sing *that!* They'd howl you into your grave!
I can hear Kleon now:
"I'LL EXTERMINATE YOU!
EXTIRPATE YOU! EXCISE YOU FROM THE COUNTRY!"

PHILOKLEON
Excellent! Let him threaten—I'll sing another:

O Captain! my Captain! you've sold the bloody sail,
and hocked the mast, and pawned the poop, and traded the after-rail.
The Ship of State is still afloat, but trembles on the brink:
Sit down! Stop throwing your weight around! Do you want the boat
  to SINK?

PHOBOKLEON
Adequate, adequate.
                    But there's Theoros now, lying
at Kleon's feet. He strokes his hand, and sings:

> *"Admetos friended Herakles:*
> *his profit was exceeding.*
> *So learn from stories such as these:*
> *be friends with men of breeding."*

Do you have a song for that?

PHILOKLEON
                    A *lyric*, no less:
> *I'll never be ready*
> *to play the toady*
> *or wear the shackle*
> *of the two-faced jackal.*

PHOBOKLEON
Now then, after him, Aischines takes it up.
He's a man of colossal culture, mighty in music—
by his own admission. His song, of course, concerns *him:*

> *"Up North, in a song-competition,*
> *I tied with a woman musician.*

> *What money we grossed!*
> *We're Thessaly's toast. . . ."*

PHILOKLEON

> *We boasted it into submission.*

PHOBOKLEON

Well, you *do* understand the way to sing. That's something.
So, now for dinner at Philoktemon's. Which means we'd better
take food.
Turning to the house.
                    Hey, boy!
Sosias appears at the door.
                              Pack lunch for the two of us.
Sosias retires into the house.

PHILOKLEON

                                        Lunch?

PHOBOKLEON

Certainly. Philoktemon never serves *food*—it's a *party*!
For once, we're going to get drunk.

PHILOKLEON

                              No, son—not that!
Nothing good ever came out of bottles. Just trouble—
Breaking and Entering, Theft, Assault and Battery—
then the morning after, the hangover, those fines to pay . . .
Your wine's a mocker, and mighty expensive, too.

PHOBOKLEON

But not in Society, Father; not with Gentlemen!
Finesse is the word in these circles. You make a gaffe—
a lawsuit? No, it's a simple social lapse,
quickly soothed and smoothed by the intercession of friends;
Conversation leads to Reconciliation.
Or *you* release the tension, with a funny fable
from Aesop, or a Sybaris-story [19]—a people-fable.

---

19. A conventionalized anecdote, purporting to have taken place in the city of Sybaris in southern
Italy. These Sybaritic fables used human characters rather than animals, as in the fables of Aesop.

Learn one at the banquet. Then, if something goes wrong,
you tell it, convert the crisis into a joke,
and your accuser will laugh urbanely, release you,
and return to the happy eddy of High Society.

PHILOKLEON
That so? I'd better learn a lot of those fables.
Crime without Punishment. What'll they think of next?

PHOBOKLEON
So it's off to Society! Way for Men of Fashion!
Father and son set off eagerly and exit right, fol-
lowed shortly from the house by Sosias, who carries
a heavy lunchbasket.

FIRST SEMICHORUS [20]
I thought I was The Champion,
at dining-out The Best.
I never dreamed that mincing fop,
AMYNIAS, could wrest
away my Prize for Guestmanship;
he somehow didn't seem equipped,
        because he doesn't EAT,
        not Amynias.

His manners were disgraceful.
Leogoras, the glutton,
invited him to gorge himself
from muffins down to mutton,
and you know what that shittard *did?*
He came—but *wouldn't eat!* Instead,
        he fiddled with a quince—
        that Amynias!

He differed from his goodly host—
the fundamental gaffe!
But now he's done a sharp reverse
and made me eat my laugh.
He went upon an embassy

---

20. This ode, a very crabbed bit of Greek on which no two commentators seem to agree, has been expanded to show how it may have meant *something.*

to check on things in Thessaly
                    and carried off my crown,
                    did Amynias!

Up North, he didn't grace the Rich
and Mighty with his presence;
he ate and drank exclusively
with greasy, stinking peasants
who served him NOTHING!
                              What a coup!
I take my napkin off to you,
                    you greasy, stinking, starveling
                    Slob, Amynias!

FIRST KORYPHAIOS
Is Automenes in the audience?
                              Congratulations, sir—
you've been chosen FATHER OF THE YEAR!
                              Take a bow, sir!—
Three fine sons, unsurpassed in their service to ART!
We all know and love Son #1, Arignotos the Harper—
a harper's harper, I might say—unmatched in music.
And Son #2, Automenes Jr., the eminent Actor—
well, gentlemen, words fail me—what indescribable skill!
But it's Son #3, Ariphrades, who staggers the senses—
what an endowment of Natural Talent! Would you believe it,
gentlemen, that slip of a boy, completely untaught (his father
swears he never took a lesson in his life), devised,
by his own unaided wits, a method of Oral Expression
which enables him daily to visit the tightest spots in the city
and come off top dog through the use of his golden tongue?
                              Best Wishes,
Automenes, Father of Three:
                    a HARPER,
                              an ACTOR,
                                        a PERVERT!

SECOND SEMICHORUS[21]

*   *   *

21. We have lost the antistrophe and the beginning of the speech here given to the Second
Koryphaios.

SECOND KORYPHAIOS
To rectify the record:
                    Rumor has it that I, the author,
have kissed and made up with Kleon. It alleges that he scratched and
    badgered
until I buried the hatchet.
                    A canard. Here are the facts:
I found I was fighting alone.
                    When the Tanner dragged me to court,
I expected popular support from the folks who flocked to the case.
And what did I get? Laughs.
                    He peeled my skin off in strips;
I howled—and the spectators roared.
                    Dimly, I saw that my backing
was only a comedian's claque, political voyeurs assembled
to see me prodded until I produced some tasty billingsgate.
Faced with such odds, I changed my tactics—played the ape,
flattered Kleon a bit.
                    But what does he think today,
now that this docile doormat is pulling the rug from under him?

*Sosias, battered, bloody, bruised, and torn, reels in
from the right, watched with amazement and con-
sternation by the Chorus. With a great deal of agony, he manages to stagger to center stage, where
he suddenly straightens up, advances, and speaks in
a relatively untortured tone.*

SOSIAS
I should like to take the present opportunity
to congratulate all you turtles, wherever you are.
Oh, happy creatures cradled in horny carapaces,
triply serene in solid siding on your ribs,
what a consummate genius was yours, to roof
your backs with tile, shelter from blows!—Whereas,
I'M BLACK AND BLUE! MY RIBS ARE CLUBBED ALL TO
    HELL!

FIRST KORYPHAIOS
What's the trouble, boy? (Since common usage
decrees that "boy" refers to one who suffers
beatings, be he old or young.[22])—But what's the trouble?

---

22. A pun on *pais* "boy" and *paiein* "beat" underlies this Euripidean sententiousness.

SOSIAS

The trouble's that old disaster Philokleon—what else?
Nobody could possibly get that drunk; but *he* managed.
He beat the cream of Athenian alcoholism—easy!
What a party! Every local lush, lecher,
loud-mouth, pervert, bully-ragger—they were all there:
Hippyllos, Antiphon, Lykon, Lysistratos, Theophrastos,
that slimy dancer Phrynichos and his pansy friends.
But Philokleon won the Degeneracy Prize hands down,
going away. And quickly, too. He filled himself up
and went completely wild, treating us all
to an exhibition of kicks, jumps, brays, farts—
an ass at a banquet of barley. Then he beat the hell
out of me: "BOY!" he'd shout—WHOP!

"BOY!"

WHOP!

Then Lysistratos saw him, and sharpened up his tongue:
"Hey, old man," he said, "what are you? A new way
to spice up leftovers? No, you look more like a jackass
loose in the pea-patch." But Philokleon brayed right back.
He compared Lysistratos—now, let me get this straight—
to a locust—who'd lost—the fig leaves—off his old overcoat—
". . . just like that playwright Sthenelos sheared of his props!"
No one knew what he meant, but they clapped like mad—
except Theophrastos. He's a wit. He sneered.
The old man charged right up. "What call have *you* got,"
he bawled, "to be so snotty and hoity-toity?
You suck the socks of every rich man in town!"
Then he got sort of insulting. He went right down
the guest-list, calling names like a mule-skinner,
all the time babbling these . . . *fables*, he called them. Just words—
no plot, no point, no place in the conversation.
Finally, when he's absolutely stinking, he leaves,
reels off for home—and clobbers everyone he meets
with his torch. And what's even worse than that . . .

Shouts, thumps, and crashes from offstage right.

Oh-oh!

That's him—I know that stagger by ear. Goodbye.
Beatings are one thing I do very well without.

*He limps quickly and painfully into the house. After
a short pause, a curious procession enters from the
right. It is led by Philokleon, raving drunk—a condition in which he remains for the rest of the play.*

*He carries a torch in one hand and clutches at a
stark naked flute-girl, whom he has stolen from the
party, with the other. They are followed, at a very
slight distance, by an irate band of banquet-guests,
small tradesmen, etc., whom Philokleon has managed to outrage in one way or another during the
course of the evening. He keeps this group at bay by
brandishing his torch at it occasionally.*

PHILOKLEON
Singing a drunken variation on a wedding march.
>   Take up the torch! Hic!
>   Here comesh the bride!
>   Some-body behind me
>   will have his hide fried!
>   Here comesh the bride!
>   Hold high the torch! Hic!

He waves the torch at the followers.
>   Haul your asses out of here
>   or I'll scorch you in the crotch! Hic!

*He makes a sudden lunge. The crowd shrinks back.
He turns. The crowd presses nervously toward him.
One guest from the banquet advances.*

GUEST
You're not going to get away with this! You'll pay!
Tomorrow! And being a minor is no damn excuse!
Breaking and Entering! Theft! Assault and Battery!
We'll all come down together and SUBPOENA you!

PHILOKLEON
>   A real SUBPOENA—for ME?
>   Gee!

Shaking his torch.
>   Thash ancient history—
>   don't let me
>   hear any more
>   about COURTS!

He jabs at the crowd with the torch.
>   Parry!
>   Thrust!

He moves back and squeezes the flute-girl
experimentally.

      Here's the stuff!

He squeezes again.

      Moshtes' and beshtes'—

He gives a third, magnificent squeeze, and addresses
the heavens.

      SCREW JUSTICE!!!

Turning to the crowd again.

      Git! Where's that lawyer?

The guest who brought the accusation hurriedly
buries himself in the crowd.

      Everybody out of here!

He swings the torch wildly. The crowd stampedes
back the way it has come and exits. Philokleon
watches with alcoholic satisfaction, then turns to the
flute-girl and motions her to the front door. He gazes
at the upper window.

  All right, honey-bee, first thing to do is get in.
  You mount—upsy daisy!

He looks at the window again.

      'Shtoo high—need a rope.

Shows his phallus.

  Here'sh one—grab this.

       Careful—that rope'sh pretty rotten—
  but a little friction—hic!—won't hurt it any.
  C'mon, you little cockchafer, chafe away!

The flute-girl shakes her head.

  Now look, is this gratitude? You know those guests
  were just about to make you open up and play
  that Lesbian lay—but I put the snatch on you.
  You could do's mush for me. Or lend me a hand—

The flute-girl is unmoved. He tries the sulks.

  But hell, you won't—won't even try. I know you:
  you're juss a tease—you'll make thish come unshcrewed.
  Thash what you did to everyone elsh.—Look,
  I'll tell you what. You be nice t'me *now*—
  real nice—you know—and when that son of mine dies,
  I'll buy your contract, all legal—and you can be
  my concubine. How's that, you queen of a quim? All right?

Don't worry; I've got money, but it's all in trusht—
I'm not of age: can't touch an obol—just yet.
How's about it?

The flute-girl smiles, nods, and sidles up to him. He
puts an arm around her, suddenly withdraws it, then
replaces it cautiously, looking around warily.

                   We'll have to be careful—I'm WATCHED!
It's that moss-backed son—won't let me out of his sight.
Oooh, he's mean! And stingy?—Did you ever eat *half*
of a caraway seed? That's what he serves *me!*
Anyway, he's afraid I'll get corrupted or something.
I'm an only father, you know.

                     —Oh-oh! Here he comes,
fast. I get the feeling we're the target.
Here! Quick—hold this torch and make like a statue.
He needs a hazing, and I'm just the boy to do it.
I'll use the trick he tried on me before
my initiation. Be a brother to your son, as the saying goes.

He hands the torch to the flute-girl, who freezes into
an appropriate attitude. He then adjusts his mantle
and assumes an innocent expression just in time to
greet Phobokleon as he rushes in from the right.

PHOBOKLEON
Angry both at the theft of a flute-girl and at the
failure of a theory of father-raising.

        There you are, you Senile Delinquent! You old
Bandersnatch! The Great Lover himself—too limp
for Rigor Mortis! You won't get away with this!

PHILOKLEON
Hungry, son? Do you want a nice fried lawsuit
with plenty of sauce?

PHOBOKLEON
               This is terrible, Father!
Fun's fun—but you can't steal the flutist from a feast!

PHILOKLEON
Flutist? What flutist? You're babbling, boy. Looks like
you fell right off your pedestal and cracked your head.

PHOBOKLEON
Pointing at the flute-girl.
> You know perfectly well what flutist—THAT ONE!

PHILOKLEON
> That's no flutist, son. It's a public fixture.

PHOBOKLEON
> A fixture?

PHILOKLEON
> A torch. They burn them to the gods.
He knocks Phobokleon's hands away from the girl.
> Be reverent, son.

PHOBOKLEON
> A *torch?*

PHILOKLEON
> Yup. New model—
> see the handy-dandy slit? Fits anywhere.

PHOBOKLEON
> What are these?

PHILOKLEON
> Additional handles—reduce fatigue.

PHOBOKLEON
> What's this black patch in the middle?

PHILOKLEON
> That patch? Pitch.
> Get one of these torches hot and out it comes.

PHOBOKLEON
> What's this back here? An ass if I ever saw one!

PHILOKLEON
> That's a knot in the wood. Interesting formation.

PHOBOKLEON
> A knot? What are you talking about?

To the flute-girl.

—Come here, you!

He starts to drag her off right.

PHILOKLEON
Grabbing the flute-girl and tugging.
    Hey, son, what are you up to?

PHOBOKLEON
                    More than you are.
I'm taking this girl away from you and back
to the banquet. Face facts, Father: You're worn out,
used up, rotten. *You* can't do a thing!

PHILOKLEON
    Now, wait a minute. You listen to me!
Phobokleon, surprised, stops.
                    Once
I represented Athens at the Olympics,
and there I saw Ephoudion, old and grizzled,
fight young Askondas and hold his own—and more!
That old fellow lifted up his fist—like this—
He raises his right hand high.
    and brought it down hard—like this—
*He strikes Phobokleon a terrific blow on top of the
head, and knocks him down.*
                    and felled the whelp—
    like that!
*He quickly ushers the flute-girl into the house,
shouting over his shoulder.*
    Watch out—next time you get a black eye!

PHOBOKLEON
Staggering to his feet as his father returns.
    By god—he finally learned the Olympia bit!
*Myrtia, a proprietress of a bakery-shop, enters hold-
ing an empty breadbasket in one hand and dragging
Chairephon, a tall, cadaverous man who is to be her
witness, by the other. She has to keep chivvying
Chairephon, who is rather unhappy about the whole
affair.*

MYRTIA
To Chairephon.
>Come ON! Stand right here, please!
>>>HERE, idiot!
>There he is! There's the man who ruined me!
Phobokleon starts suddenly, and looks wonderingly
at Philokleon.
>He beat me up with his torch,
She brandishes the basket.
>>>and knocked *this* over—
>squashed the bread—ten obols—and the cover—four more.

PHOBOKLEON
Aside, to Philokleon.
>Do you see what you've done—you and your wine?
>All the troubles and lawsuits back again!

PHILOKLEON
>Why, no, son. All we need is an anecdote—
>Conversation leads to Reconciliation.
>You just watch me reconcile this old bag here.

MYRTIA
>Oh, you'll pay, you will! You won't get off so easy!
>No, sir, no one can ruin the stock of Myrtia,
>daughter and successor of Ankylion and Sostrate—
>an old, established firm—and not suffer!

PHILOKLEON
>Listen to me, woman. I want to tell you
>a pretty little fable.

MYRTIA
>>Not me, you don't!

PHILOKLEON
>Aesop was coming home from dinner one evening
>when he was barked at by a shaggy, drunken bitch.
He moves closer to Myrtia. She recoils.
>And Aesop said,
Yelling in Myrtia's ear.
>>"YOU BITCH, YOU BITCH, YOU BITCH!

It'd be a good idea for you to trade
that nasty tongue in on some grain—YOU BITCH!"

MYRTIA
Slander, too? Well! I don't know what your name is,
but I'll summon you before the Board of Trade
to face the charge of Damaging Merchandise. And here's—
Tugging at Chairephon.
and here's my witness—
Tugging again, this time with success.
                              (come ON!)
                                   Chairephon!

PHILOKLEON
You don't mean that. Here's another; see how it strikes you.
The poet Lasos was competing with Simonides once.
Know what he said? He said: "I couldn't care less."

MYRTIA
Oh, he did, did he!

PHILOKLEON
                    And here's old Chairephon. Hi, there!
Chairephon cowers behind Myrtia.
          Pasty-Face is a witness for Rose-Red here—
He indicates Myrtia, who is crimson with fury.
          that's quite a match. You look like Ino, hanging
          by the feet. Of Euripides. Begging him not to cast her
          in one of his plays.
Myrtia grabs Chairephon and stalks off without a
word. Philokleon, beatific, watches them leave, then
turns back to the house. Phobokleon continues
watching for a moment.

PHOBOKLEON
                    Here comes somebody else.
          Looks like another subpoena; he's brought his witness.
Beaten and bruised, there enters haltingly a Man
who looks like Euripides. He is followed by a Wit-
ness, who carries stylus and tablet.

THE MAN WHO LOOKS LIKE EURIPIDES
AGONY! MALAISE! ALACKADAISY!

Grisard, attend:

I'll criminate thee with ATROCITY!

PHOBOKLEON

Atrocity? Oh, no!

See here, Sir—set whatever penalty you wish,
and I'll pay it for him, and thank you in the bargain.

PHILOKLEON
It's my place, son. I'm overjoyed to make restitution.
He's right—I admit Assault and Battery.
To the Man Who Looks Like Euripides, sweetly.

—Sir,

please step over here.
The Man Who Looks Like Euripides complies,
groaning. The Witness follows.

I desire to be your friend

in perpetuity. Can't we settle this out of Court?
Will you allow me to fix the amount of the fine
I'll have to pay, or would *you* prefer to set it?

THE MAN WHO LOOKS LIKE EURIPIDES
Pronounce the escheat. Fain would I eschew
dispute and suit.

—OOOO!

PHILOKLEON

A man of Sybaris

fell out of a chariot once and smashed his skull
to smithereens; he was no horseman. A friend of his
came up and said, "The cobbler should stick to his last."
In your case, friend, it means you should hobble off fast
to the Free Clinic.
He knocks the tablet out of the Witness's hands,
breaking it. Phobokleon buries his head in his
hands.

PHOBOKLEON

If you have one virtue, it's consistency.

THE MAN WHO LOOKS LIKE EURIPIDES
To his Witness, who stands stupidly holding
his stylus.

  Impress in mind's inmost recess these insults!
He starts to leave.

PHILOKLEON
Don't run off. Listen: In Sybaris once, a woman
smashed a hedgehog.[23]

THE MAN WHO LOOKS LIKE EURIPIDES
To his Witness.

        Attest that witless thrust!

PHILOKLEON
Just what the hedgehog did—it called a witness.
And the woman of Sybaris said, "You'd show more sense,
if you forgot this witness-business entirely,
and ran as quick as you could to buy a bandage."

THE MAN WHO LOOKS LIKE EURIPIDES
Indulge thy raging, till thou'rt led to judging!
OUCH!
He limps off, groaning, followed by the Witness. As
Philokleon watches in satisfaction, Phobokleon
sneaks softly behind him.

PHOBOKLEON
In a low voice which is not heard by Philokleon.
    You simply can't stay here any longer.
I'll just lift you up and . . .
He scoops the old man up in his arms.

PHILOKLEON

       What are you doing?

PHOBOKLEON

          Me?

I'm carrying you inside. If I leave you here,
every witness in town will be used up in half an hour.
He strides for the door, lugging his father.

---

 23. In Greek, *echinos*, not only the animal, but a vase, and one associated with courtroom practice. But the straight translation seems to have the required degree of insanity, so I have let it stand.

PHILOKLEON
Once Aesop was accused . . .

PHOBOKLEON
                              I couldn't care less!

PHILOKLEON
. . . by the people of Delphi. They said he'd stolen a vase
that belonged to Apollo. But he told them the story
about the beetle.
                  Once upon a time, a beetle . . .

PHOBOKLEON
Reaching the door at last.
          I'll put an end to you *and* your beetles, by God!
*The house-door closes behind them. Philokleon can
still be heard babbling his fable.*

FIRST SEMICHORUS
                    I envy Philokleon's luck,
                        so happily arranged.
                His rough, and rude, and often crude
                        mode of life has changed.
[Crashes and yells from the house.]
                    He's learned the theory, has it pat;
                        now comes the execution.
                He turns to Ease and Luxuries—
                        a Total Revolution!
*[The flute-girl appears at the upper window,
screams, and disappears.]*
                    But will he really wish to shift
                        from Habit's well-worn routes?
                Dame Nature's hard to disregard—
                        will he join in New Pursuits?
*[The door of the house bursts open, and out flies the
flute-girl, chased by Philokleon. He pursues her
around the stage.]*
                    Others change, for New Ideas
                        accomplish more than kicks.
                With a gentle jog, the Oldest Dog
                        will gladly learn New Tricks!
*[Phobokleon and the slaves (Xanthias excepted)
hurry from the house and chase Philokleon. The*

flute-girl escapes, but back into the house. Pho-
bokleon and the slaves catch Philokleon and
re-enter, carrying him.]

SECOND SEMICHORUS
All men of sensibility
will join me, I feel sure,
as now I raise a song of praise
to the Author of this cure.
[More crashes and yells from the house.]
All Hail to Philokleon's son!
Exalt him to the skies!
Did ever lad so love his dad?
Was ever boy so wise?
[The flute-girl, screaming again, appears at the
upper window. She is in the clutches of Philokleon,
who is in turn being beaten by Phobokleon with the
torch. The tableau disappears suddenly.]
What manners! What demeanor! What
behavior in a boy!
What soft address! What gentleness!
It made me melt with joy!
[The door bursts open, and the trio emerges: The
flute-girl, chased by Philokleon, chased by Pho-
bokleon with the torch.]
And in debate, this paragon
inspired his parent's notions
to Things Above, by Filial Love—
the noblest of emotions!

ENTIRE CHORUS
ALL HAIL, PHOBOKLEON!
[Philokleon catches the flute-girl. Phobokleon trips
and drops the torch. Philokleon scoops it up, throws
the flute-girl over his shoulder, and beats his howl-
ing son before him into the house.]

Xanthias emerges from the house, shaking his head.

XANTHIAS
Dionysos, what a mess! Some god's been playing stagehand,
meddling with the set. The house is an absolute snarl.

It's the old man. After all these years, he took
a drink, and heard one note from the flute—and bang!
the combination sent him right out of his head.

    To his feet.
He's mad, but now he's mad for dancing. Been at it
all night long. No end in sight. Except his.
By now, he's worked through all those antique dances
that Thespis taught his choruses a century ago,
and claims he's ready for the Modern School. Performers
in tragedies today, like Phrynichos and all his ilk,
are feeble old fogies, he says: they can't match *him!*
He's even threatened to come out here in a while
and show the young men up by dancing them down
at all their own steps. Talk about the light fantastic!

He sits down, leaning against the door.

PHILOKLEON
*From behind the door, declaiming Euripidean
fustian.*

    Who couches before the courtyard portals?
The door rattles. Xanthias jumps away.

XANTHIAS
To the audience.

    You're about to witness an outbreak of plague.
He runs off.

PHILOKLEON
    Ho, there! Unshoot the bolts!

*The door bursts open, and Philokleon jigs forth. He
is rehearsing the violent movements of a grotesquely
acrobatic dance. After him, sad and defeated, comes
Phobokleon.*

            'Tis time!
    The gambado commences!

PHOBOKLEON
Wearily.

            And sanity ends.

PHILOKLEON
    Let's see. How does Phrynichos do it?

Suiting action to words, as far as possible.
> He begins with a flourish, a sudden convulsive
> contortion of the ribs! A blare from the nostrils!
> A ruffle and scrunch of splintered vertebrae!

PHOBOKLEON
> How are you treating it? Hellebore? Hemlock?

PHILOKLEON
> He coils in a crouch like an angry cock . . .

PHOBOKLEON
> If that doesn't work, we could stone you, of course.

PHILOKLEON
> . . . then lashes a kick that scrapes the stars!

PHOBOKLEON
> And his ass gapes wide to the spectators' stares.

PHILOKLEON
> You'd better watch out for yourself!

*He revolves and jumps more and more wildly. Pho-
bokleon moves out of the way.*

> And now
> the final pirouette, the supple, unsocketed
> whizzing and whirring of a dislocated femur!

*He spins and kicks more frantically, coming to a
stop before Phobokleon.*

> Pretty good, huh?

PHOBOKLEON
> Positively NO! Utter Delirium!

PHILOKLEON

Paying no attention, he advances to the audience.

> An Announcement:
> To All Performers from the Tragic Stage
> Who Make Any Pretense to Excellence in the Dance, I Fling
> a Blanket Challenge: COME UP AND COMPETE WITH *ME!*

Silence.

> —Anybody? Nobody?

PHOBOKLEON

Here comes one—but that's all.

A small dancer, dressed as a crab, scurries on stage.

PHILOKLEON

What happened to *him?*

PHOBOKLEON

Heredity. He's the son of Karkinos [24]
the dancer—you know what a crusty old crab *he* is.

PHILOKLEON

That's no competition. A downbeat or two from me,
and he's done. Cooked. Dished. He'll make a nice mouthful,
the way he makes hash of the rhythm.

A second crab-clad dancer scurries up.

PHOBOKLEON

I wouldn't have your luck.
What bait are you using? You caught another crab—
his brother.

PHILOKLEON

I didn't mean for this to be a dinner-dance.
I wanted a ballet.

PHOBOKLEON

Looking off.

You've got a buffet—three crabs.

PHILOKLEON

Three?

PHOBOKLEON

Well, here comes another son of Karkinos.

A very tiny crab-dancer scurries on.

PHILOKLEON

What's this creeping thing? A trivet? A spider?

24. A tragic poet, upon the literal meaning of whose name ("the crab") the entire following dance scene is based.

PHOBOKLEON

That's the youngest—the shrimp of the family. They all
act, but he writes. That makes it a real tragedy.

PHILOKLEON

O Karkinos, how you must jump for joy at your offspring!
And the whole bunch of little bounders has dropped on *us!*

To Phobokleon.

I must enter the lists. To celebrate my victory in the dance,
fix something for my opponents. A sauce. Use plenty of capers.
And now to see crabbed youth compete with age.

He moves to the center of the stage to
begin the dance.

FIRST KORYPHAIOS

To the Chorus.

All right, men, let's pull back a little and give them room.
We don't want to be in the way when they try those whip-top spins.

The Chorus forms a large semicircle, in which the
Sons of Karkinos begin their wild dance.
Philokleon waits.

ENTIRE CHORUS

To the Sons of Karkinos.

Aloft! ye crustacean lords of gyration,
eccentrically tracing your dizzy descent from the
undulant loins of the God of the Ocean!
O Arthropod paladins, sires of Circuity!
Scuttle and pound on the sterile salt strand!
Scurry and stamp! O ye kinsmen to shrimp!

In wild revolution, in whirligig tension,
enjumble and fumble the force of a tragedy!
Mount to the climax with pouncing distortion,
then bound to the sky to confound the peripety!
Flick with your kick the shriek of a claque,
engulfing the plays in brainless applause.

To Philokleon as he spins into the dance.

In giddy glissade, let vertigo reign! Embellish the eddy
and spiral your shins to the stars!

To the Sons of Karkinos, as Philokleon spins among
them.

                                  Be bobbins, and reel to make ready
    your master's turbinate triumph! Oh, wheel to the liege of the sea—
    who scuds and unsettles those lords of the stage, his children three!
At this point the dancing contest turns into a rout.
Philokleon, spinning and kicking, attacks in turn the
three crabs and pursues them in a mad circle. The
Chorus addresses the maelstrom plaintively.
    Please lead us off. You can keep up the dance if you must, but *hurry!*
    It's not that innovations annoy us, but we *do* have a worry:
    We admit that many actors have had the chance to dismiss
    the Chorus by using a final dance—
                                 BUT NEVER A DANCE LIKE *THIS!*
Still gyrating and jumping, Philokleon pursues the
three Sons of Karkinos off-stage; the Chorus and
cast follow, dancing just as madly as their leaders.

Lysias

Lysias (ca. 440–380) lived most of his life in Athens but was not an Athenian. His father was a Syracusan who had settled in Athens and owned a prosperous business there. But residency did not confer citizenship, and so he and his family held only the in-between status of *metics*—foreigners with limited rights and obligations as permanent residents. By joining the new colony of Thurii in southern Italy, Lysias and his brother did acquire citizenship rights there. He lived in Thurii for a decade or so but was driven out with the rest of the pro-Athenian element after the destruction of the Athenian army and navy at Syracuse in 413. The two brothers went back to Athens where they again established a comfortable existence. Lysias gained a reputation as a public speaker and, for a short time, taught rhetoric. But in 403 the oligarchic regime that was forced on Athens at the end of the Peloponnesian War seized most of the family's assets and murdered Lysias' brother. Lysias escaped, helped finance the revolution that restored democratic rule in Athens, and was rewarded for his services with a grant of citizenship. But the grant was promptly overturned on a technicality. From that time on, having no other assets to support him, Lysias earned his living by writing speeches for less adroit speakers involved in legal proceedings in the courts or the assembly. He is said to have written over two hundred speeches, more than double the number produced by any other speech-writer of his time. About two dozen authentic speeches have been preserved.

10. Lysias, *On the Killing of Eratosthenes*

On the Killing of Eratosthenes was written for a man (Euphiletus) who had killed his wife's lover (Eratosthenes). Under Athenian law, a husband did have the right, as Euphiletus maintains, to kill an adulterer taken in the act. But this is the only case in which an injured husband is known to have exacted that penalty; ordinarily he settled for the grisly humiliation of the adulterer or for payment of a stipulated sum of money. What happened to Euphiletus shows the risk of the more violent proceeding. The dead man's relatives brought a charge of murder on the grounds that Eratosthenes was entrapped and was not taken in the act of adultery. If Euphiletus lost the case, he in his turn was liable to the death penalty. We do not know how the trial turned out or what happened to Euphiletus' wife. Under the law, he was obliged to divorce her.

Apart from illustrating Athenian trial procedure, the speech gives some impression of the domestic economy of a family that was not well-to-do. It shows what sort of property they owned and how work routines were divided between husband and wife. And it tells a great deal about the position of women in Athenian society.

I would give a great deal, members of the jury, to find you, as judges of this case, taking the same attitude towards me as you would adopt towards your own behaviour in similar circumstances. I am sure that if you felt about others in the same way as you did about yourselves, not one of you would fail to be angered by these deeds, and all of you would consider the punishment a small one for those guilty of such conduct.

Moreover, the same opinion would be found prevailing not only among you, but everywhere throughout Greece. This is the one crime for which, under any government, democratic or exclusive, equal satisfaction is granted to the meanest against the mightiest, so that the least of them receives the same justice as the most exalted. Such is the detestation, members of the jury, in which this outrage is held by all mankind.

Concerning the severity of the penalty, therefore, you are, I imagine, all of the same opinion: not one of you is so easy-going as to believe that those guilty of such great offences should obtain pardon, or are deserving of a light penalty. What I have to prove, I take it, is just this: that Eratosthenes seduced my wife, and that in corrupting her he brought shame upon my

From *The Murder of Herodes and Other Trials from the Athenian Law Courts*, by Kathleen Freeman. London: Macdonald & Co. Ltd., 1946.

children and outrage upon me, by entering my home; that there was no other enmity between him and me except this; and that I did not commit this act for the sake of money, in order to rise from poverty to wealth, nor for any other advantage except the satisfaction allowed by law.

I shall expound my case to you in full from the beginning, omitting nothing and telling the truth. In this alone lies my salvation, I imagine—if I can explain to you everything that happened.

Members of the jury: when I decided to marry and had brought a wife home, at first my attitude towards her was this: I did not wish to annoy her, but neither was she to have too much of her own way. I watched her as well as I could, and kept an eye on her as was proper. But later, after my child had been born, I came to trust her, and I handed all my possessions over to her, believing that this was the greatest possible proof of affection.

Well, members of the jury, in the beginning she was the best of women. She was a clever housewife, economical and exact in her management of everything. But then, my mother died; and her death has proved to be the source of all my troubles, because it was when my wife went to the funeral that this man Eratosthenes saw her; and as time went on, he was able to seduce her. He kept a look out for our maid who goes to market; and approaching her with his suggestions, he succeeded in corrupting her mistress.

Now first of all, gentlemen, I must explain that I have a small house which is divided into two—the men's quarters and the women's—each having the same space, the women upstairs and the men downstairs.

After the birth of my child, his mother nursed him; but I did not want her to run the risk of going downstairs every time she had to give him a bath, so I myself took over the upper storey, and let the women have the ground floor. And so it came about that by this time it was quite customary for my wife often to go downstairs and sleep with the child, so that she could give him the breast and stop him from crying.

This went on for a long while, and I had not the slightest suspicion. On the contrary, I was in such a fool's paradise that I believed my wife to be the chastest woman in all the city.

Time passed, gentlemen. One day, when I had come home unexpectedly from the country, after dinner, the child began crying and complaining. Actually it was the maid who was pinching him on purpose to make him behave so, because—as I found out later—this man was in the house.

Well, I told my wife to go and feed the child, to stop his crying. But at first she refused, pretending that she was so glad to see me back after my long absence. At last I began to get annoyed, and I insisted on her going.

"Oh, yes!" she said. "To leave *you* alone with the maid up here! You mauled her about before, when you were drunk!"

I laughed. She got up, went out, closed the door—pretending that it was a joke—and locked it. As for me, I thought no harm of all this, and I had not the slightest suspicion. I went to sleep, glad to do so after my journey from the country.

Towards morning, she returned and unlocked the door.

I asked her why the doors had been creaking during the night. She explained that the lamp beside the baby had gone out, and that she had then gone to get a light from the neighbours.

I said no more. I thought it really was so. But it did seem to me, members of the jury, that she had done up her face with cosmetics, in spite of the fact that her brother had died only a month before. Still, even so, I said nothing about it. I just went off, without a word.

After this, members of the jury, an interval elapsed, during which my injuries had progressed, leaving me far behind. Then, one day, I was approached by an old hag. She had been sent by a woman—Eratosthenes' previous mistress, as I found out later. This woman, furious because he no longer came to see her as before, had been on the look-out until she had discovered the reason. The old crone, therefore, had come and was lying in wait for me near my house.

"Euphiletus," she said, "please don't think that my approaching you is in any way due to a wish to interfere. The fact is, the man who is wronging you and your wife is an enemy of ours. Now if you catch the woman who does your shopping and works for you, and put her through an examination, you will discover all. The culprit," she added, "is Eratosthenes from Oea. Your wife is not the only one he has seduced—there are plenty of others. It's his profession."

With these words, members of the jury, she went off.

At once I was overwhelmed. Everything rushed into my mind, and I was filled with suspicion. I reflected how I had been locked into the bedroom. I remembered how on that night the middle and outer doors had creaked, a thing that had never happened before; and how I had had the idea that my wife's face was rouged. All these things rushed into my mind, and I was filled with suspicion.

I went back home, and told the servant to come with me to market. I took her instead to the house of one of my friends; and there I informed her that I had discovered all that was going on in my house.

"As for you," I said, "two courses are open to you: either to be flogged and sent to the tread-mill, and never be released from a life of utter misery; or to confess the whole truth and suffer no punishment, but win pardon from me for your wrong-doing. Tell me no lies. Speak the whole truth."

At first she tried denial, and told me that I could do as I pleased—she knew nothing. But when I named Eratosthenes to her face, and said that he was the man who had been visiting my wife, she was dumbfounded, thinking that I had found out everything exactly. And then at last, falling at my feet and exacting a promise from me that no harm should be done to her, she denounced the villain. She described how he had first approached her after the funeral, and then how in the end she had passed the message on, and in course of time my wife had been over-persuaded. She explained the way in which he had contrived to get into the house, and how when I was in the country my wife had gone to a religious service with this man's mother, and everything else that had happened. She recounted it all exactly.

When she had told all, I said:

"See to it that nobody gets to know of this; otherwise the promise I made you will not hold good. And furthermore, I expect you to show me this actually happening. I have no use for words. I want the *fact* to be exhibited, if it really is so."

She agreed to do this.

Four or five days then elapsed, as I shall prove to you by important evidence. But before I do so, I wish to narrate the events of the last day.

I had a friend and relative named Sostratus. He was coming home from the country after sunset when I met him. I knew that as he had got back so late, he would not find any of his own people at home; so I asked him to dine with me. We went home to my place, and going upstairs to the upper storey, we had dinner there. When he felt restored, he went off; and I went to bed.

Then, members of the jury, Eratosthenes made his entry; and the maid wakened me and told me that he was in the house.

I told her to watch the door; and going downstairs, I slipped out noiselessly.

I went to the houses of one man after another. Some I found at home; others, I was told, were out of town. So collecting as many as I could of those who were there, I went back. We procured torches from the shop near by, and entered my house. The door had been left open by arrangement with the maid.

We forced the bedroom door. The first of us to enter saw him still lying beside my wife. Those who followed saw him standing naked on the bed.

I knocked him down, members of the jury, with one blow. I then twisted his hands behind his back and tied them. And then I asked him why he was committing this crime against me, of breaking into my house.

He answered that he admitted his guilt; but he begged and besought me not to kill him—to accept a money-payment instead.

But I replied:

"It is not I who shall be killing you, but the law of the State, which you, in transgressing, have valued less highly than your own pleasures. You have preferred to commit this great crime against my wife and my children, rather than to obey the law and be of decent behaviour."

Thus, members of the jury, this man met the fate which the laws prescribe for wrong-doers of his kind.

Eratosthenes was not seized in the street and carried off, nor had he taken refuge at the altar, as the prosecution alleges. The facts do not admit of it: he was struck in the bedroom, he fell at once, and I bound his hands behind his back. There were so many present that he could not possibly escape through their midst, since he had neither steel nor wood nor any other weapon with which he could have defended himself against all those who had entered the room.

No, members of the jury: you know as well as I do how wrong-doers will not admit that their adversaries are speaking the truth, and attempt by lies and trickery of other kinds to excite the anger of the hearers against those whose acts are in accordance with Justice.

(*To the Clerk of the Court*):

Read the Law.

(*The Law of Solon is read, that an adulterer may be put to death by the man who catches him.*)

He made no denial, members of the jury. He admitted his guilt, and begged and implored that he should not be put to death, offering to pay compensation. But I would not accept his estimate. I preferred to accord a higher authority to the law of the State, and I took that satisfaction which you, because you thought it the most just, have decreed for those who commit such offences.

Witnesses to the preceding, kindly step up.

(*The witnesses come to the front of the Court, and the Clerk reads their depositions. When the Clerk has finished reading, and the witnesses have agreed that the depositions are correct, the defendant again addresses the Clerk*):

Now please read this further law from the pillar of the Court of the Areopagus:

(*The Clerk reads another version of Solon's law, as recorded on the pillar of the Areopagus Court.*)

You hear, members of the jury, how it is expressly decreed by the Court of the Areopagus itself, which both traditionally and in your own day has been granted the right to try cases of murder, that no person shall be found guilty of murder who catches an adulterer with his wife and inflicts this punishment. The Lawgiver was so strongly convinced of the justice of these provisions in the case of married women, that he applied them also to concubines, who are of less importance. Yet obviously, if he had known of any greater punishment than this for cases where married women are concerned, he would have provided it. But in fact, as it was impossible for him to invent any more severe penalty for corruption of wives, he decided to provide the same punishment as in the case of concubines.

(*To the Clerk of the Court*):

Please read me this Law also.

(*The Clerk reads out further clauses from Solon's laws on rape.*)

You hear, members of the jury, how the Lawgiver ordains that if anyone debauch by force a free man or boy, the fine shall be double that decreed in the case of a slave. If anyone debauch a woman—in which case it is *permitted* to kill him—he shall be liable to the same fine. Thus, members of the jury, the Lawgiver considered violators deserving of a lesser penalty than seducers: for the latter he provided the death-penalty; for the former, the doubled fine. His idea was that those who use force are loathed by the persons violated, whereas those who have got their way by persuasion corrupt women's minds, in such a way as to make other men's wives more attached to themselves than to their husbands, so that the whole house is in their power, and it is uncertain who is the children's father, the husband or the lover. These considerations caused the Lawgiver to affix death as the penalty for seduction.

And so, members of the jury, in my case the laws not only hold me innocent, but actually order me to take this satisfaction; but it depends on you whether they are to be effective or of no moment. The reason, in my opinion, why all States lay down laws is in order that, whenever we are in doubt on any point, we can refer to these laws and find out our duty. And therefore it is the laws which in such cases enjoin upon the injured party to exact this penalty. I exhort you to show yourselves in agreement with them; otherwise you will be granting such impunity to adulterers that you will encourage even burglars to declare themselves adulterers, in the knowledge that if they allege this reason for their action and plead that this was their purpose in entering other men's houses, no one will lay a finger on them. They will all realize that they need not bother about the law on adultery, but need only fear your verdict, since this is the supreme authority in the State.

Consider, members of the jury, their accusation that it was I who on that day told the maid to fetch the young man. In my opinion, gentlemen, I should have been justified in using any means to catch the seducer of my wife. If there had been only words spoken and no actual offence, I should have been doing wrong; but when by that time they had gone to all lengths and he had often gained entry into my house, I consider that I should have been within my rights whatever means I employ to catch him. But observe that this allegation of the prosecution is also false. You can easily convince yourselves by considering the following:

I have already told you how Sostratus, an intimate friend of mine, met me coming in from the country around sunset, and dined with me, and when he felt refreshed, went off. Now in the first place, gentlemen, ask yourselves whether, if on that night I had had designs on Eratosthenes, it would have been better for me that Sostratus should dine elsewhere, or that I should take a guest home with me to dinner. Surely in the latter circumstances Eratosthenes would have been less inclined to venture into the house. Further, does it seem to you probable that I would have let my guest go, and been left alone, without company? Would I not rather have urged him to stay, so that he could help me to punish the adulterer?

Again, gentlemen, does it not seem to you probable that I would have passed the word round among my friends during the daytime, and told them to assemble at the house of one of my friends who lived nearest, rather than have started to run round at night, as soon as I found out, without knowing whom I should find at home and whom away? Actually, I called for Harmodius and certain others who were out of town—I did not know it—and others, I found, were not at home, so I went along taking with me whomever I could. But if I had known beforehand, does it not seem to you probable that I would have arranged for servants and passed the word round to my friends, so that I myself could go in with the maximum of safety—for how did I know whether he too might not have had a dagger or something?—and also in order that I might exact the penalty in the presence of the greatest number of witnesses? But in fact, since I knew nothing of what was going to happen on that night, I took with me whomever I could get.

Witnesses to the preceding, please step up.

(*Further witnesses come forward, and confirm their evidence as read out by the Clerk.*)

You have heard the witnesses, members of the jury. Now consider the case further in your own minds, inquiring whether there had ever existed between Eratosthenes and myself any other enmity but this. You will find none. He never brought any malicious charge against me, nor tried to secure my banishment, nor prosecuted me in any private suit. Neither had he knowledge of any crime of which I feared the revelation, so that I desired to kill him; nor by carrying out this act did I hope to gain money. So far from ever having had any dispute with him, or drunken brawl, or any other quarrel, I had never even set eyes on the man before that night. What possible object could I have had, therefore, in running so great a risk, except that I had suffered the greatest of all injuries at his hands? Again, would I myself have called in witnesses to my crime, when it was possible for me, if I desired to murder him without justification, to have had no confidants?

It is my belief, members of the jury, that this punishment was inflicted not in my own interests, but in those of the whole community. Such villains, seeing the rewards which await their crimes, will be less ready to commit offences against others if they see that you too hold the same opinion of them. Otherwise it would be far better to wipe out the existing laws and make different ones, which will penalise those who keep guard over their own wives, and grant full immunity to those who criminally pursue them. This would be a far more just procedure than to set a trap for citizens by means of the laws, which urge the man who catches an adulterer to do with him whatever he will, and yet allow the injured party to undergo a trial far more perilous than that which faces the law-breaker who seduces other men's wives. Of this, I am an example—I, who now stand in danger of losing life, property, everything, because I have obeyed the laws of the State.

Demosthenes

Demosthenes (ca. 384–322) came from an Athenian family that was neither aristocratic nor politically active but was prosperous during his childhood years. His father died when Demosthenes was seven. The guardians named in the will to administer the estate then took over and bled it dry. Demosthenes girded himself for the counterattack. Under the tutelage of an orator and speech-writer, he studied and exercised to make himself an effective public speaker, and, when he was twenty, he brought his former guardians to trial. He won over the jury, which awarded him generous damages, but in the end he collected practically nothing. From that time on he had to make his living by writing speeches, like Lysias. But, unlike Lysias, he was an Athenian citizen and could apply his talent and increasing renown to politics. In his thirties he began to speak in public debates, joining the succession of assembly orators to which Pericles, Cleon, and Alcibiades had once belonged. For the rest of his life it was his political activity that was most spectacular and most important. Demosthenes took the lead in rallying Athens and the other cities of Greece to resist the empire-builder Philip of Macedon. But the defenders of Greek liberty were defeated by Philip in 338 B.C., defeated again under his son Alexander in 335, and defeated a third time under Alexander's successor in 322. Demosthenes ended his life by poison while on the run.

11. Demosthenes, *The Oration against Eubulides*

The *Oration against Eubulides* is one of the products of Demosthenes' practice as a consultant. It was written, probably about 345, for a man

Translated by Peter White, based on *Against Eubulides* in *Orations of Demosthenes*, vol. 5, pp. 199–216, translated by Charles Rann Kennedy. London: George Bell & Sons, 1897.

167

(Euxitheos) who had been decertified by the deme or neighborhood of Halimus when local assemblies in the Athenian territory were instructed to verify their lists of citizens. The law allowed a trial before a court in Athens for anyone who wished to appeal the local ruling, but frivolous appeals were discouraged by a stiff penalty: Euxitheos would be sold into slavery if he lost. The speech throws some light on relations between the local demes and the central government in Athens, and it shows that the feuds and machinations of Athenian politics went right down to the local level. But above all it provides an account of the attributes that defined citizenship.

Eubulides has made many false charges against me and has laid at my door slanders that are unfounded and indefensible. I will now tell you what is true and right, men of the jury, and will try to demonstrate that I belong to the city and that I do not deserve the treatment I have received from this man. I ask you all, men of the jury, I beg and implore you, to consider the gravity of this proceeding and the shame that goes with the doom of those who are convicted. Hear me, as you have heard my opponent, in silence and with greater sympathy, if possible—you ought to be more sympathetic to those who stand in peril. At all events, hear me with equal sympathy.

I am fully confident of arguing this case successfully, so far as the issue turns on me and my membership in the city. What alarms me, men of the jury, is the current situation, in which the people have felt provoked to strike names off the register. Since many people in all the demes have been expelled with good reason, men like me, who are the victims of political persecution, suffer by this prejudice. We have to deal with the charges brought against them rather than argue our cases independently, and therefore we cannot help being in great alarm.

Nevertheless, I will begin by telling you what I think the right course in this situation is. Persons proved to be aliens, who have taken part in your civic and religious observances by stealth or force, without having obtained or sought your consent, deserve to feel the brunt of your anger. But you ought to aid and protect hapless individuals who can show that they are citizens. Think what a pitiable miscarriage of justice it would be for us to become scapegoats of the general exasperation and to end up under sentence when we would be entitled to sit alongside you passing sentence.

I thought, men of the jury, that it was incumbent on Eubulides, and indeed on all who appear as accusers in support of a vote of exclusion, to state what they know for certain and not to bring up hearsay in a trial of this kind. That has long been considered the height of injustice, so much so that the laws do not allow hearsay testimony even when the charges are most petty. And this is reasonable: when people claiming knowledge of facts have been proved guilty of falsehood, what credence can be given to statements not within the speaker's own knowledge? And when no man is allowed to damage another by evidence he says he has heard, even when he takes personal responsibility for it, how can it be right for you to believe a person who takes no responsibility for what he says? Since my opponent, despite his all too subtle knowledge of the laws, has seized every unfair advantage in the conduct of this prosecution, I must begin by describing to you the outrageous way I was treated in my deme. I ask you, men of Athens, not to interpret my expulsion by the demesmen as proof that I am not a member of the city. If you had assumed that the demesmen would always be able to make the right decision, you would not have allowed appeals to be brought before you. As it is, you supposed that something of this sort might occur, through competition or envy or hatred or some other motive, and therefore you enabled victims of injustice to have recourse to you. By that commendable policy, men of Athens, you have rescued all who have suffered injustice. First, then, I will explain to you how the citizen register was revised at the meeting of demesmen. I am supposed to cover everything that has a bearing on the case, and that means talking about political persecution leading to injuries inflicted in violation of the decree.

This Eubulides, men of Athens, as many of you know, indicted the sister of Lacedaemonius for impiety and did not get 20 percent of the votes. Because in that trial I gave honest testimony, which contradicted him, he became my enemy and is attacking me. And when he gets on the council, men of the jury, and has both authority to administer the oath and control over the list from which he calls up the demesmen, what does he do? In the first place, when the demesmen had assembled, he wasted the day making speeches and offering resolutions. This was not done by accident but as part of his plot against me, so that the vote on my case might take place as late in the day as possible. And he succeeded. There were seventy-three of us who took the oath, and we began to go through the registration list late in the day, so that, by the time my name was called, it was already dark— my name was about the sixtieth on the list, and I was the last to be called on that day. By then the older demesmen had gone home to the country; our deme, men of the jury, is about four miles from the city, and, since most reside there, most had gone home. No more than thirty stayed behind, and they included all the persons Eubulides had recruited. When my name was called, Eubulides jumped up and hurled abuse against me, talking long and fast and in a loud voice, as he did just now. He produced no witness in support of his charges, either from the deme or from the rest of Athens, but urged my demesmen to pass a vote of expulsion. Since it was late and I had no one on my side and was taken by surprise, I asked for an adjournment to the following day. Thus Eubulides would have an opportunity to bring whatever accusations he pleased and to produce any witnesses that he had, while I would be able to make my defense before all the demesmen and produce my relations as witnesses. I offered to abide by whatever decision they should pronounce in my case. Eubulides, however, paid no regard to my proposal but instantly proceeded to take the votes of the demesmen who were present, without allowing me to make either any defense or any rebuttal of his charges. The people in league with him jumped up and gave their votes. It was dark, and they each received two or three ballots from Eubulides and put them into the box. The proof is that, although there were no more than thirty voters, more than sixty ballots were counted, so that we were all astounded.

To show that I am telling the truth—that the votes were not taken when all were present and that there were more votes than voters—I will present witnesses. It so happens that none of my friends or any other Athenians witnessed these proceedings, because it was late and because I did not ask anyone to attend, so I am obliged to resort to the evidence of those who have injured me. I have written down facts, which they will not be able to deny. Read.

[The deposition is read.]

If the Halimusians had managed to review the whole list of demesmen that day, men of the jury, it would have been reasonable to go on balloting to a late hour so that they might comply with your decree and be done with it. But when there were more than twenty demesmen left whose cases had to be reviewed the following day, and when the demesmen were obliged in any case to meet again, what was the difficulty about adjourning to the following day and taking the votes of the demesmen in my case first? The reason, men of the jury, was this: Eubulides well knew that, if a hearing were allowed me, and if all the demesmen were present, and if the vote were honestly conducted, he and his cronies would get nowhere.

What made these people gang up against me, I will tell you, if you like, after I have given an account of my birth. In the meantime what do I consider right, and what have I undertaken to do, men of the jury? To show you that I am an Athenian on both my father's and my mother's side; to furnish witnesses whose veracity you will admit; and to refute the charges and calumnies of my opponents. This is the proper course for me to take. When you have heard my case, it is up to you to rescue me if you think that I am a citizen and have been the target of political persecution. Otherwise, you must act according to your conscience. And now to begin.

They have maliciously asserted that my father spoke with a foreign accent. That he was taken prisoner by the enemy about the time of the Decelean war, that he was shipped as a slave to Leucas, that he came into the possession of Cleander the actor and was ransomed and brought home to his relations after a long time—this they have omitted to mention, but they have reproached him with his foreign accent, as if I should come to grief because of my father's misfortune. In fact, I think I can show you that I am an Athenian with the help of precisely these details. I will call witnesses to testify, first, that my father was taken prisoner and redeemed; second, that after his return home he received from his uncles his share of the estate; and further, that no one, among the people of his deme or brotherhood or anywhere else, ever charged him with being a foreigner, despite his accent. Please read the depositions.

[The depositions are read.]

You have now heard about my father's capture and about the rescue that restored him to Athens. To testify that he was your fellow citizen—that is the actual truth, men of the jury—I will call those relations on my father's side of the family who are still living. Please call first Thucritides and Charisiades: their father, Charisius, was the brother of my grandfather, Thucritides, and of my grandmother, Lysarete (my grandfather married a sister by a different mother), and so was my father's uncle. Then call Niciades: his father, Lysanias, was the brother of Thucritides and Lysarete and was the uncle of my father. Next, Nicostratus: his father, Niciades, was the nephew of my grandfather and my grandmother and was first cousin to my father. Please call all these persons. And you, stop the water clock.

[The witnesses are heard.]

Men of Athens, you have heard my father's relatives on the male side depose and swear that my father was an Athenian and their relative. Surely none of them is risking the curse by which he has bound himself and committing perjury before persons who would recognize false testimony. Now read the depositions of my father's relatives on the female side.

[The depositions are read.]

These persons, the living relatives of my father on the male and on the female side, have testified that he was on both sides an Athenian and a legitimate member of the city. Now please call the members of my brotherhood and, after them, the members of my clan.[1]

[The witnesses are heard.]

---

1. It was not necessary to belong to a brotherhood (*phratry*) or clan (*genos*) in order to be a citizen; these groupings were part of the predemocratic tribal organization of Attica and included only the older families in Athenian society. Euxitheos' argument, both here and later, when he speaks of his candidacy for a priesthood, is that he must surely be a citizen if he can even qualify as a member of one of the old families.

Read now the depositions of the demesmen and those in which my relations testify that the members of the brotherhood elected me their prefect.

[The depositions are read.]

Men of the jury, you have heard testimony from my relations, the members of my brotherhood, my demesmen, and my clansmen, who are the proper persons to give evidence. You are thus in a position to know whether a man with such credentials was a citizen or a foreigner. Now, if I had had recourse to only a couple of people, there would be room for suspicion that I had bribed them. But when it appears that both my father in his lifetime and I myself have been examined and registered in all those groups to which each of you belongs (I mean brotherhood, family, deme, and clan), how is it conceivable or possible that all these persons are phony connections who have been put up to their story? If my father had been a wealthy man and it appeared that, by giving money, he had induced these persons to say that they were his relatives, it would be reasonable to harbor suspicion that he was not a citizen. But if, though he was poor, he could not only point to relatives but could also show that those same individuals had given him a share of their property, is it not perfectly clear that he really was related to them? If he had not been a relative, they would surely not have taken him into the family and given him money besides. He was their relative, as the facts have shown and witnesses have corroborated. Besides that, he was elevated to public offices by lot and served in them after passing his probation. Please read the deposition.

[The deposition is read.]

Does any of you suppose that the demesmen would have permitted that so-called foreigner and noncitizen to hold office among them and would not have prosecuted him for it? Not a single person did prosecute or even lodge an accusation against him. Bear in mind also that there was an emergency that required a vote on the qualifications of all citizens: they sacrificed and gave their oaths when the registration list was lost during the prefecture of Antiphilus, the father of Eubulides. At that time they expelled some of their members, but no one spoke or brought any such charge against my father. To all mankind the end of life is death. It is right that children should always be subject to any challenge that was raised against the parent in his lifetime; but if no objection was made then, is it not monstrous that the children should be open to proceedings by any man? If there was never any inquiry into these matters, let us grant that this claim could have slipped by. But if there was discussion and a thorough review, and if no one ever made any accusation, am I not entitled to count as an Athenian citizen by the same right as my father, who died before his family affiliations were disputed? To prove the truth of my statements, I will call witnesses to these things too.

[The witnesses are heard.]

Besides, he had four children by the same mother as me, and, when they died, he buried them in the ancestral graves that the members of our family all share. And none of these men ever forbade or prevented it or brought suit. But where is the man who would allow persons having no connection with the family to be placed in the ancestral graves? To prove that these statements are true as well, read the deposition.

[The deposition is read.]

These are the arguments I can make to show that my father was an Athenian. I have produced as witnesses persons who have been voted by my opponents themselves to be citizens, and they testify that he was their cousin. It has been shown that, in all the years he lived at Athens, he was never at any point challenged as a foreigner. He appealed to these people as his relations, and they not only received him as one of their own but gave him a share of their property. Furthermore, it is evident that, at the time he was born, he was entitled to be a citizen even if he was Athenian on one side only, since he was born before the archonship of Euclides.[2]

I will now speak about my mother (they have slandered her as well), and I will call witnesses in support of my statements. Note, men of Athens, that Eubulides' attack on us is not only contrary to the decree regulating the market. It is also contrary to the laws that rule that anyone who insults a male or female citizen for carrying on business in the market is liable to an action for malicious talk. We confess that we sell ribbons and do not live in the style we prefer, and if, Eubulides, you take this as a sign that we are not Athenian, I will show you that just the opposite is true and that it is illegal for any foreigner to carry on business in the market. Now please take and read the law of Solon.

[The law is read.]

Now take the law of Aristophon—Solon's law, men of Athens, seemed such such a wise and democratic law that you voted to renew it.

[The law is read.]

So then, men of Athens, if you uphold the laws, you should judge, not that tradesmen are aliens, but that underhanded troublemakers are crooks.

---

2. In 403/402, when a law requiring proof of citizenship on both the father's and the mother's side was reinstated.

And let me point out, Eubulides, that there is another law, one concerning idleness, to which you who denounce tradesmen are liable yourself. But my situation is now so disadvantageous that, while Eubulides can deviate into personal abuse and use every possible means to deprive me of my rights, you will probably rebuke me if I tell you what trade he plies as he makes the rounds of the city. And your rebuke would be reasonable—why tell you what you know? But just consider. It seems to me that our commercial activity is the strongest proof that this man's charges are false. Since my mother, as he says, was a seller of ribbons and notorious to all, there ought surely to have been many who could offer knowledgeable testimony, not just hearsay, about who she was. If she was a foreigner, there should have been witnesses who had inspected the tolls in the market to see whether she had paid the aliens' toll and who could declare her city of origin. If she was a slave, the person who bought her or, failing that, the person who sold her should have come to give evidence, or someone else, to say that she was a slave or that she had been set free. Eubulides, however, has proved none of these things; he has only hurled insults, and apparently every one he could think of. This is what it means to launch a malicious prosecution: to make all kinds of charges and to prove nothing.

And he has also said that my mother was a wet nurse. We do not deny that this occurred in those evil days of our city, when all were badly off. How and why my mother became a nurse I will tell you plainly. Do not let it prejudice you against us, men of Athens: you will find many women of the city who are wet nurses even now. I will name them for you, if you like. Of course, if we were rich, we would not be selling ribbons or be lacking for anything at all. But what does that have to do with my descent? Nothing whatever, in my opinion. Do not scorn the poor, men of the jury (their poverty is trouble enough for them), nor those who choose to work and get their livelihood by honest means. If I show you that my mother has the sort of relatives one would expect of free persons, and that they deny on oath the accusations that Eubulides brings against her, and that they affirm that they know she is Athenian, and if they are witnesses whom you will admit to be credible, then, when you have the evidence, give your just verdict in my favor.

My maternal grandfather, men of Athens, was Damostratus of Melita. He had four children: a daughter and a son, named Amytheon, by his first wife, and my mother and Timocrates by his second wife, Chaerestrata. Amytheon had a son named Damostratus, after his grandfather, and two other sons, Callistratus and Dexitheus. Amytheon, my mother's brother, was one of those who went to the war in Sicily[3] and there lost his life; he is buried in a public monument. (These facts will be proved by testimony.)

---

3. This is the famous Sicilian Expedition of 415–413 that Thucydides describes.

His sister married Diodorus of Halae, and they had a son, Ctesibius; he fell at Abydos in the campaign with Thrasybulus. The only one of these relatives still living is Damostratus, the son of Amytheon, my mother's nephew. The sister of my grandmother, Chaerestrata, was married to Apollodorus of Plothea. They had a son, Olympichus, and Olympichus had a son, Apollodorus, who is still living. Please call them.

[The witnesses are heard.]

You have heard these persons give their sworn testimony. I will also call someone related to me on both sides, together with his sons. Timocrates is my mother's brother by the same father and mother, and he had a son, Euxitheus, who in turn had three sons, who are all living. Please call those who are at Athens.

[The witnesses are heard.]

Now please read the depositions of those belonging to the same brotherhood and deme as my mother's kinsmen and of those who have the same places of burial.

[The depositions are read.]

I have thus laid before you the facts about my mother's parentage, proving that she is Athenian both on the male and on the female side. My mother, men of the jury, was first married to Protomachus by Timocrates, her brother by the same father and mother. By him she had a daughter, and then by my father she had me. You need to hear how she came to marry my father, and I will also clear up the accusations that have been made about Clinias and about my mother's being a nurse, and all that. Protomachus was poor. When he was given an opportunity to marry a rich heiress, he wanted to divorce my mother. He persuaded my father Thucritus, an acquaintance of his, to take her, and Thucritus obtained her hand from her brother, Timocrates of Melita, in the presence of his two uncles and other witnesses. Those who are still living will testify for you. Sometime after this, when she had two children and my father was away on campaign with Thrasybulus, she was compelled by circumstances to begin nursing Clinias, the son of Clidicus. What she did was indeed no help to me, in view of the threat that now hangs over me (all the slander about our family has blown up out of that nursing job), but the poverty in which she lived rendered it perhaps fitting and necessary. To resume, men of Athens, it is clear that my father was not the first man to marry my mother, but Protomachus was, who had children by her, including a daughter, whom he gave in marriage. He is dead, yet even now he testifies by his acts that she is an Athenian and a citizen.

To prove the truth of these statements, please call first the sons of

Protomachus, then the witnesses who were present when my father received my mother in marriage, and the kinsmen from his brotherhood,
to whom he gave the nuptial meal in honor of my mother. After them,
call Eunicus of Cholargus, who received my sister in marriage from
Protomachus, and, next, my sister's son. Call them.

[The witnesses are heard.]

Would it not be the most heartbreaking thing in the world if you decided
that I was a foreigner, men of Athens, when I have all these relations, and
they testify under oath that I am related to them, and there is no question
about their citizen status? Now please take the deposition of Clinias and
that of his relations: they certainly know who my mother was, since she
nursed him. They are obliged in conscience to vouch for, not what I assert
today, but what was thought about my mother, or Clinias' nurse, for all
the time they knew her. Even if a nurse is a lowly creature, I don't shun the
truth. We are guilty not if we were poor but if we were not citizens. The
present trial is not about luck or money but about parentage. Poverty compels free men to do many mean and servile acts, for which, men of Athens,
they deserve rather to be pitied than to be broken on top of everything else.
I am told that many Athenian women became nurses and servants and
grape-pickers owing to the troubles of the city at that period, and many
have now risen from poverty to riches. But more about this in a moment;
now call the witnesses.

[The witnesses are heard.]

From the testimony that has just been given, and from the testimony
given earlier about my father, you know that I can claim citizenship on both
my father's and my mother's side. It remains for me to speak about myself
and to tell you what is surely a self-evident and honest fact: being the son of
two Athenians, and having inherited both property and clan membership, I
am a citizen. Not but what I will present all the appropriate evidence. I will
produce witnesses to prove that I was introduced to the members of my
brotherhood; that I was entered in the register of demesmen; that by these
very persons I was selected, alongside the noblest-born, to draw lots for
the priesthood of Heracles; and that I held offices after passing my probation. Please call them.

[The witnesses are heard.]

If I had won the draw for the priesthood I was proposed for, it would have
been my duty to offer sacrifice on behalf of these people, and Eubulides
would have had to join me in the sacrifice. Is it not outrageous, men of the
jury, that these same persons should not permit me to have even a part in

their sacrifice now? Well, it appears that I have all along been acknowledged as a citizen by every one of those who now accuse me. Surely Eubulides would not have allowed a resident alien and a foreigner, as he now calls me, to hold offices or to be nominated, along with him, for the priestly drawing (he too was one of those nominated and drawing lots). Furthermore, men of Athens, since he was an old enemy of mine, he would not have waited for the present opportunity, which no one could have foreseen, if he had known something like this about me. In fact, he did not know anything. Therefore, the whole rest of the time he continued to take part along with me in the life of the deme and to draw lots for office without seeing any objection. But when the whole city was exasperated and on edge about people who had impudently barged into the deme lists, then he formed his plot against me. The earlier occasion would have suited a man convinced that his charges were true; this one suits an enemy wanting to bring a malicious prosecution. For my part, men of the jury—and by Zeus and the gods, don't let anyone make a disturbance or be annoyed at what I am going to say—I consider myself as good an Athenian as any of you thinks himself to be. From the first I have acknowledged as my mother the same woman I have held up to you; I did not pretend to be her son when I was really someone else's. The same holds for my father. Now, if it is reasonable for you to infer that people who are found to have suppressed their real parents and to have claimed phony ones are foreigners, surely in my case you should regard the opposite as a proof that I am a citizen. I would never have imagined I could get membership in the city by having two foreigners recorded as my parents. If I had known they were foreigners, I would have looked for other persons to claim as my parents. But I knew nothing of the kind, and therefore I always kept to my real parents, assuming that I was a member of the city.

The next point is that I was left an orphan, and yet they say I am wealthy and that some of the witnesses testify to being relatives because I have done them favors. At one and the same time they reproach me with the disgrace of poverty and disparage my family background—and say I am rich enough to buy everything. Which of their stories then are you to believe? Surely, if I were illegitimate or foreign, the witnesses might have claimed to inherit *all* my property. And do they then choose to receive handouts, and to risk prosecution for false testimony, and to perjure themselves, rather than to have it all with no risk and without bringing a curse on their heads? That is absurd. As I see it, they are relations and do what is right by helping one of themselves. And it is not just now that they take action because they are cajoled, but, back when I was a boy, they brought me to the brotherhood, and to the temple of ancestral Apollo, and to the other holy places. Surely, when I was a boy, I did not induce them to do this by giving them money. My father himself in his lifetime swore the customary oath and introduced me to the brotherhood, knowing that I was born a citizen, of a wedded wife who was a citizen—and to this you have heard testimony.

Am I then an alien? Where have I paid the resident alien's tax? Or what member of my family ever paid it? Have I gone to any other deme and, when I could not impose on them there, registered here? When have I done any of the things that persons who are not genuine citizens have been found doing? No, the simple fact is that I am on record as a citizen in the same deme where my great-grandfather, my grandfather, and my father lived. How could anyone, men of Athens, demonstrate to you more plainly that he belongs to the city? I invite each one of you to consider how he could certify his relatives in any other way than I have done, with kinsmen who testify on oath, and who can be traced all the way back to the beginning.

These were the grounds on which I felt confidence in my case and appealed to you. I could see, men of Athens, that the courts were more powerful not only than the Halimusians who expelled me but even than the council and the popular assembly. And that is right, since your verdicts are in every respect most righteous.

And if you belong to one of the larger demes, remember that *you* have not deprived anyone of his right either of accusation or defense. You all deserve commendation for having used this procedure fairly: when someone requests a postponement, you do not refuse him an opportunity to present evidence that will expose the plotting and harassment of personal enemies. And just as you deserve praise, men of Athens, the people who have abused this fair and admirable process deserve censure. In no deme will you find that more outrageous deeds have been perpetrated than among us. Where a set of brothers had exactly the same father and mother, my antagonists have excluded some of them but not the others. They have excluded old men when they were destitute but have kept their sons on the register—I will call witnesses, if you like. But the most outrageous thing this gang has done—by Zeus and the gods, please do not object if I show the wickedness of the people who have wronged me: describing their wickedness is a necessary part of telling what happened to me. Some foreigners, Anaximenes and Nicostratus, wanted to become citizens. Eubulides and his group put them on the list and divvied up a sum amounting to five drachmas each—and they would not be able to swear an oath that they don't know this to be true. In fact, they did not reject these men during the recent revision. What do you think they would balk at doing on the side when they dared to do such a thing officially? For the sake of money, many have been destroyed and many saved, men of Athens, by Eubulides and his group. Even before their time—this bears on my case, men of Athens—

Antiphilus, the father of Eubulides, when he was prefect of the deme, as I mentioned, contrived a scheme to get money from certain persons. He said that the public register was lost and thus induced the Halimusians to vote on everyone's qualifications. By bringing objections he got ten demesmen expelled, all but one of whom were restored by the court. All the older demesmen know about this. It was not very likely they would leave any non-Athenians on the register when they combined to expel even genuine citizens, whom the court restored. And though Antiphilus was the personal enemy of my father at the time, he not only did not voice objections to him but did not even cast a vote that he was not Athenian. How is that shown? Because the vote on my father's citizenship was unanimous.

But why speak of our fathers? Eubulides himself, when I was entered in the register and all the demesmen duly took the oath and cast their votes, neither voiced objection nor voted against me: that time, too, the vote on my citizenship was unanimous. And if they say that I am lying, anyone who wants to give evidence to the contrary is welcome to use my speaking time.

Accordingly, men of Athens, if the fact that my demesmen just disqualified me seems to you a strong point in the argument of my opponents, I point to four previous occasions when the vote was honest and nonpartisan, and they voted that my father and I were citizens like themselves: first, at the examination when my father came of age; second, at my examination; third, in that first revision of the rolls, when these people made away with the register. And last, they voted in my favor when they selected me among the noblest-born to draw lots for the priesthood of Heracles. On all these points you have heard testimony.

I must now speak of my term as deme prefect, which earned me the antagonism of certain people when I crossed a number of them by dunning them for back rents on temple lands or for restitution of other public property they had seized. I would be grateful if you would hear me out, though you may judge this matter irrelevant to the case. But here too I can present proof that they were in league. They struck out of the oath the clause that they would "vote according to their honest judgment, without favor or malice." That became publicly known, as did something else that must be told. These persons from whom I recovered the public money conspired against me, impiously pulling down the shields I had dedicated to Athena and defacing the monument bearing the decree that the demesmen had passed in my honor. And they had the nerve to go round saying that *I* had done these things for the sake of my defense. Could any of you, men of the jury, believe me so insane that, to get this weighty piece of evidence, I would commit an act that deserved the death penalty, and would destroy a public testimonial in my honor? Well, they can hardly claim that I was responsible for the most outrageous episode. No sooner had misfortune struck than some of these people went by night to my cottage in the country and tried to strip it clean—as though I were already a ruined man and an outcast. That shows how little they cared for you and for the laws. If you like, I will call persons who know these facts.

I could point to many other deeds these men have perpetrated and lies that they have told, and I would gladly relate them. But I let them pass, since you consider them extraneous to the case. Remember what I did say, however, and see what a solid case I have brought before you. Let me take myself through the same interrogation to which you subject incoming magistrates. "Who was your father?"—"My father was Thucritus."—"Do you have any relations who bear witness to him?"—"Certainly: first, four cousins; then a cousin's son; then the husbands of the female cousins; then the members of the brotherhood; then the clansmen who worship Ancestral Apollo and Zeus Protector of the Household; then those who use the same place of burial; besides, the demesmen, who voted to put him on the citizen roster, bear witness that he has often passed scrutiny and held offices. What cleaner or more legitimate proof could I present about my father's status? I will call my relations before you, if you desire it."

Now hear my statement about my mother. "My mother is Nicarete, the daughter of Damostratus of Melita."—"Do any of her relations give testimony?"—"First, a nephew; then two sons of her other nephew; then a cousin; then the sons of Protomachus, my mother's first husband; then Eunicus of Cholargus, who married my sister, the daughter of Protomachus; then the son of my sister. Besides them, the members of the brotherhood and deme of my mother's family have borne witness." What more do you require? Testimony has been presented that my father married according to the laws and gave a nuptial meal to the members of his brotherhood. I have shown, further, that I have all those qualifications that belong to free men. A vote in my favor, therefore, would be in every way right and proper and in keeping with the oath you have taken.

One more thing, men of the jury. At the examination of the nine archons you ask whether they behave dutifully to their parents. By my father I was left an orphan. But on behalf of my mother, I beg and beseech you to give back by your verdict the opportunity to bury her in our ancestral graves. Do not prevent me. Do not make me an outcast. Do not cut me off from this great number of relatives I have. Do not absolutely destroy me. If it is impossible for me to be saved by them, I would kill myself sooner than leave them, so that at least I may be buried by them in my own country.

Plato

Plato was born in Athens in 428 B.C., in the fourth year of the Peloponnesian War. He was descended on both sides from the old Attic nobility. It is not surprising that, as we are informed in his *Seventh Letter*, Plato at first intended to take an active part in Athenian politics. (In the ancient world, letters ascribed to famous men frequently prove to be forgeries, but most scholars agree that this letter, if not authentic, was written in the later fourth century by an author well informed about Plato's life. Most of what we know about Plato is derived from this source.)

Plato was dissuaded from active politics in Athens by two events. In 404 B.C. Athens had experienced the final disaster of the Peloponnesian War. The democracy was replaced, nominally by a restricted franchise, in fact by the Thirty. These men, the "best" citizens of Athens, including several close relatives of Plato, displayed a bloodthirsty and lawless greed that evidently appalled Plato. In 399 B.C., under the restored democracy, Socrates was prosecuted by a group of democrats, condemned by a popular jury, and executed. Plato must have been aware of Socrates from early youth, for his relatives, Critias and Charmides, later members of the Thirty, had long been associated with him. Plato's own knowledge of Socrates had convinced him that Socrates was the best and most just of men. As the *Crito* (document 13) shows, Plato's evaluation differed from most Greeks'.

After such experiences, Plato might well have found it difficult to join either faction in politics. With his perceptions of values rendered more acute by hearing Socratic discussions of the most important terms of value, Plato must have realized that the behavior of the Thirty and of Socrates in different ways indicated serious flaws in traditional Greek values. The rehabilitation of Socrates and the development of values conducive to harmony within a polis became his primary concern in ethics and politics.

Having renounced practical politics in Athens, Plato attempted to influence others in three ways: by writing, by founding the Academy, and by giving advice elsewhere.

His writings are copious and mostly in dialogue form. They are usually divided into three periods, early, middle, and late. Of the works included in this volume, the *Apology* and *Crito* are early. They are not, however, characteristic of the early dialogues, which typically portray Socrates asking other participants to define a virtue and attacking their definitions until all, including Socrates himself, admit that they are unable to define it. Socrates equates the inability with ignorance of the virtue. The *Republic*, of which a few pages are printed here, belongs to the middle period, which is marked by the appearance of the theory of Forms, designed to solve some of the problems raised by Socrates' fruitless search for definitions. ("Socrates" should throughout be understood as "Plato's Socrates." None of the dialogues is a transcript of any actual Socratic conversation. Some have a dramatic date before Plato's birth, others in his youth.)

At about the age of forty Plato established the Academy, a novel institution, devoted to research. It was not to be an ivory tower, however. Since Plato by this time believed that poleis could not truly flourish until philosophers became rulers or rulers became philosophers, his goal was to produce enlightened rulers by means of an appropriate education. (His pupils in fact tended to become tyrants.)

Plato made three visits to Sicily. The first probably occurred just before the foundation of the Academy. An important result was Plato's friendship with Dion, the son-in-law of Dionysius I, tyrant of Syracuse. The full effects of the friendship were not felt until Plato was over sixty. In 367 B.C. Dionysius I died and was succeeded by his son, Dionysius II, over whom Dion had great influence. Dion invited Plato to come to Syracuse to take Dionysius II's education in hand. Plato did so, but apparently with much misgiving, which the outcome entirely justified. The final visit was even more disastrous.

Plato's attempt to improve the quality of politicians and of political life had little success in his own lifetime. His fame rests on his written works and on the foundation of the Academy, by which many later institutions were influenced. But his desire to influence the actions of his contemporaries did not wane: at his death, in 348 B.C., he was still putting the finishing touches to his *Laws*, a work in twelve books, which contains detailed regulations for the best polis possible in a world in which philosopher-rulers are not to be found.

12. Plato, The *Apology*

Like the rest of Plato's works, the *Apology* is not a transcript of Socrates' own words, nor does it necessarily contain all the themes, or only the themes, that Socrates employed in defending himself before an Athenian court in 399 B.C. Xenophon also wrote an *Apology of Socrates*, which differs from Plato's in many respects, and there was also a tradition that Socrates stood up in court, mumbled a few words, and sat down without making any coherent defense. Plato's *Apology* presents to us Socrates as Plato would have us view him. His portrait must contain many details drawn from the life, but we cannot be certain which they are.

It is more fruitful to inquire into Plato's motives in presenting us with the portrait he has chosen to draw and to remember the necessity for rehabilitating Socrates. Socrates lost his case. To lose in the courts, or anywhere else, was deemed unworthy of an *agathos*. It is illuminating to observe how Socrates deals with this problem in the *Apology*. Note which kinds of behavior in court he regards as worthy and unworthy of an *agathos*. Note the admired individuals to whom he likens himself, and the admired behavior to which he likens his own, in order to lay claim to excellence (*arete*). Note what reasons he assigns for his unpopularity and for the accusations brought against him, and consider whether any of them are discreditable to Socrates and also what grounds we have for supposing these to be the only reasons for his being accused. Consider, next, Socrates' argument that, if he corrupted the young men, he must have done so unintentionally, since bad (*kakoi*) people would be more likely to harm him than would *agathoi;* then relate this argument to traditional and nontraditional uses of *agathos* and *kakos*, evidence for which is to be found in *Odyssey* 2 (document 1), in the poems of Tyrtaeus and Theognis, and in Plato's *Crito*. When Socrates claims to have spent his life exhorting his fellow citizens to pursue excellence (*arete*), the meaning of *arete* should be carefully evaluated. If the speech is read in this manner, the reader will understand more clearly the means that Plato has employed to transform the defeat of Socrates into a victory.

Men of Athens, how you have been affected by my accusers I do not know; but under their influence I almost forgot who and what I am, so persuasively were they speaking. And yet virtually nothing of what they have

Translated by Arthur W. H. Adkins.

said is true. They uttered many falsehoods, but the one that caused me the most surprise was this: they said that you ought to take precautions against being deceived by me, since I am a formidable speaker. For to feel no shame at being immediately refuted by the facts, when it becomes apparent that I am not a formidable speaker—this, I thought, was the most shameless part of their speeches. Unless, perhaps, they mean by "formidable speaker" the man who speaks the truth. If that is what they mean, I would grant that I am an orator, but not in the same sense as they are. These men, as I am telling you, have uttered hardly one word that is true; but you shall hear the whole truth from me. You will not hear speeches like theirs, men of Athens, tricked out with elegant words and phrases; you will hear sentences spoken artlessly, in the words that chance to come to the tip of my tongue—for I have confidence that what I am saying is just. Let none of you suppose that I shall speak in any other way. It would not be proper, gentlemen, for a man of my age to come into court and fashion clever arguments like a young man. But this, men of Athens, I urgently beg and beseech you: if you hear me defending myself with the same kind of arguments as I have been accustomed to use both at the bankers' tables in the agora—where many of you have heard me—and in other places, do not be surprised, and do not create a disturbance for that reason. This is how the matter stands. This is my first appearance in court, and I am seventy years old. The language used here is literally foreign to me. If I were really a foreigner, you would presumably make allowances for me if I were speaking in the dialect and style that were native to me. So now, in the present circumstances, I make of you this request, which is, I believe, just: set aside the manner in which I speak—it may be worse than another's, it may be better—and consider and pay attention to the justice or injustice of what I say. For this is the mark of a good juryman, whereas the mark of a good orator is to speak the truth.

I may justly claim, men of Athens, to make my defense first against the first false accusations and the first accusers. For I have had many accusers who have been telling you falsehoods about me for a long time—many years now. I fear these accusers far more than I fear Anytus and his followers, though they too are formidable. But more formidable are those men who got hold of the majority of you from childhood onwards and kept on persuading you and making accusations against me of what is nevertheless not true. They said that there is a clever man, called Socrates, who theorizes about the heavens and has researched into things beneath the earth, and who makes the weaker argument prevail over the stronger. Men of Athens, these men, the ones who spread this rumor abroad, are my formidable accusers; for those who hear them suppose that men who search into such matters also do not believe in the gods. These, then, are my accusers. They are many in number. Their accusations have been in existence for a long time now. In addition, they made them to you at a time of life when you would have been especially likely to believe them, since some of you were children and others, young men; and they were accusing in a case that had literally gone by default, since no one was speaking for the defense. The most absurd feature of the case is this: it is not even possible to know or tell you their names, unless there chances to be a comic poet among them. Some were moved by envy to slander; others themselves believed what they were saying. Both groups kept trying to persuade you. All of them are very difficult to deal with, for one cannot even bring them before the court as witnesses and refute any of them; one literally has to shadowbox with them in one's defense and try to refute them, though there is no one to answer one's questions. So you too should accept the fact that I have two groups of accusers, one being those who have recently made their accusations, while the others are those of whom I am telling you, who have been accusing me for a long time; and you should grant that it is necessary for me to defend myself against them first, for you heard their accusations earlier, and their charges were much more prevalent, than the charges of my accusers who are here in court.

Well, then, men of Athens, I must make my defense and try to pluck from your minds this slander, which you have acquired over a long period, in the brief time allowed me in court. I could wish that it would turn out thus, and that I should be successful in making my defense, if it is better so both for you and for me. However, I believe that my task is difficult, and I fully realize what kind of a task it is. But let matters turn out as the god pleases; I must obey the law and make my defense.

Let us take up the question from the beginning and inquire what is the charge from which has sprung the false accusation on which Meletus relied in bringing this case against me. Well, what did the slanderers say when they slandered me? I must read out what would be their affidavit if they were prosecuting me in due form: "Socrates is doing wrong, and meddling with what he should not, in inquiring into the things below the earth and in the heavens, and in making the weaker argument prevail over the stronger, and in teaching these selfsame matters to others." It is something like that. You yourselves saw these things in Aristophanes' comedy—a stage Socrates carried around on the stage machinery, claiming that he walks on air and babbling a great deal more nonsense about matters of which I know nothing. I do not say this to disparage such knowledge, if indeed there is anyone who has wisdom in this field—I hope I shall not have so many accusations laid at my door by Meletus—but I have no part in these concerns, men of Athens. I produce the majority of you as witnesses, and I ask all those of you who have ever heard me in conversation—and many of you have done so—to teach and tell one another whether any one of you ever yet heard me conversing on a small or a great topic of this kind. From this you will learn that the other things that the majority of people say about me have no more basis in fact than these.

In fact, none of these accusations is true. If you have heard anyone claiming that I try to educate people and that I charge a fee, that is not true either. In my opinion it is a fine and honorable thing to be able to educate people as Gorgias of Leontini does, and Prodicus of Ceos and Hippias of Elis. For, gentlemen, each of these men is able to go into any of the poleis and persuade the young men—who could associate, at no expense to themselves, with any of their own citizens that they choose—to give up their former associations and associate with them for a fee, and to give thanks to them as well. And there is another man, a Parian, a wise man, who I am informed is in town; for I happened to meet a man who has spent more money on sophists than everyone else, Callias, the son of Hipponicus. I asked him—he has two sons—"Callias," I said, "if your two sons had been born as foals or calves, we could now find someone to oversee them and hire someone to make them honorable and good in respect of the appropriate excellence, and he would be one of those who are concerned with horses or farming; but as it is, since they are human beings, whom have you in mind to get to oversee them? Who is the expert in that kind of excellence—the human excellence concerned with living in poleis? For I suppose you have considered the matter, since you have sons. Is there anyone of this kind or not?" said I. "There is indeed," said he. "Who?" said I. "Where does he come from? And what does he charge for his instruction?" "Evenus," said he. "From Paros. Five minae." And I thought Evenus must be blessed indeed if he really had such a skill and taught it for such a modest sum. I for my part would put on airs and live in luxury if I understood these matters; but I do not understand them, men of Athens.

One of you might perhaps reply: "But, Socrates, what is this profession of yours? What is the reason for these slanders against you? For I do not suppose that so great a quantity of rumor and gossip is the result of actions of yours that were no stranger than other people's. You must have been doing something different from the majority. Tell us what it is, so that we may not judge you hastily and in ignorance." I think that the person who says that is making a fair request, and I will try to show you what it is that has caused my reputation and the slanders against me. Listen, then. Perhaps some of you will think that I am not being serious, but I assure you that I am telling the whole truth. Men of Athens, the cause of this reputation of mine is nothing other than a kind of wisdom. What kind? The kind that may perhaps be termed the wisdom possible to man; for it looks as if I have that kind of wisdom. Perhaps these men whom I was mentioning just now have a wisdom that is beyond mere mortals. I do not know what I can say about it, for I do not understand it. Anyone who claims that I do is lying and slandering me. Please do not make a disturbance, men of Athens, even if you think I am boasting. For any account I may give is not mine; I shall ascribe it to a speaker who is worthy of your belief. As a witness of the existence and nature of whatever wisdom I may have, I shall introduce the god of Delphi. You know Chaerephon, I suppose. He was both my friend from childhood and also a friend of the democracy. He joined you in your exile and returned with you. You also know what kind of a man he was and how vehemently he behaved in any matter on which he embarked. Well, once he went to Delphi and brought himself to the point of asking the oracle this question—as I was saying, gentlemen, do not create a disturbance—he asked whether there was anyone wiser than myself. The Pythian prophetess replied that no one was wiser. Chaerephon's brother here will testify to the truth of this, since Chaerephon is dead.

Now bear in mind my reason for saying this. I am about to tell you the source of the slanders against me. When I heard this, I thought to myself in this way: "Whatever is the god saying? What is the meaning of his riddle? For I am aware that I am not wise in anything great or small. What then is he saying when he claims that I am the wisest of men? For he is not telling lies; it is not right for him to do so." For a long time I was at a loss to know what he meant. Then I turned very reluctantly to investigating the matter in this way. I went to one of the men who were reputed to be wise, thinking that there, if anywhere, I should refute the prophecy and declare to the oracle that "He is wiser than I am, but you said that I was wiser." Well, I examined this man—I need not mention his name, but it was one of the politicians I was examining when this happened to me, men of Athens— and conversed with him. This man seemed to me to be *thought* wise in the eyes of many other people and especially in his own, but he seemed to me not to *be* wise. Then I tried to show him that, though he thought he was wise, he was not really so. As a result, I made an enemy of him and of many of those who were present. As I was going away, I was thinking to myself that I was wiser than this man; for it looked as if neither of us knew anything fine and good but that he thought that he knew something though he did not, whereas I neither knew anything nor thought that I did. So I seemed to be wiser than this man, at all events, by this tiny margin: I did not suppose myself to know what I did not know. Then I approached another man, one of those who were reputed to be wiser than the first one, and came to the selfsame conclusions and there also made an enemy of him and of many other people.

After that I approached other people, one after the other. I was aware that I was making enemies. I was grieved by this. I was afraid. Nevertheless, I thought it necessary to set a very high value on the god's words. So I had to go to all those who were thought to know anything, in my search for the meaning of the oracle. And, by the dog! men of Athens—for I must tell you the truth—this is the kind of experience I had. As I searched in accordance with the god's wishes, those who had the greatest reputations seemed to me to be almost always the most lacking in wisdom, whereas others, who were thought to be inferior, seemed to be superior in respect of wisdom. I must tell you of my wanderings as I fulfilled my labors to make the oracle absolutely irrefutable. After the politicians I went to the poets— the tragedians, the dithyrambic poets, and the rest—in the expectation of detecting my lack of wisdom in comparison with them. So I would take up those of their poems over which I thought they had taken the most pains, and I would ask them what they meant so that I might, at the same time, learn something from them. I am ashamed to tell you the truth, gentlemen, but it must be spoken. Virtually everyone who is present would give a better account of what the poets themselves had written. I soon came to this conclusion about the poets too, that it was not wisdom that enabled them to compose what they did compose but some kind of natural instinct and divine possession, such as one finds in inspired prophets and soothsayers; for they also say many fine things but understand none of the things they say. It became clear to me that the poets were in a very similar situation; and at the same time I realized that because of their poetry they believed themselves to be the wisest of men also in other respects, in which they were not. So I went away from there, too, thinking that I had the same advantage over the poets as over the politicians.

Last of all I went to the craftsmen. For I was aware that I knew virtually nothing, and I knew that I should find that they at least knew many fine things. In this I was not mistaken. They knew things that I did not know, and they were wiser than I was in this way. But, men of Athens, the good craftsmen seemed to me to make the same mistake as the poets: because he practiced his craft well, each regarded himself as being very wise in everything else—all the most important matters; and this mistake of theirs, I thought, overshadowed the wisdom that they did possess. The result was that I asked myself on behalf of the oracle whether I would rather be as I am—neither wise with their wisdom nor ignorant with their ignorance—or have both things that they have. I answered myself and the oracle that it is better for me to be as I am.

As a result of this program of inquiry, men of Athens, I have acquired much enmity, of the most bitter and burdensome kind, with the consequence that I am much slandered, and I have the reputation of being wise. For the bystanders always suppose that I am myself wise in any subject in which I refute someone else. But, gentlemen, it looks as if it is really the god who is wise and that in this oracle he was saying this: that human wisdom is worth little or nothing. He does not mean Socrates in particular, I believe, but is using my name, treating me as an example, as if he should say, "Mortals, that one of you is wisest who realizes, like Socrates, that he is in truth worth nothing so far as wisdom is concerned." Even now I go around making these searches, and in accordance with the god's wishes I investigate anyone, whether citizen or foreigner, whom I suppose to be wise; and whenever on examination he seems not to be wise, I aid the god by demonstrating that he is not wise. As a result of busying myself in this way, I have had no leisure to take any part worth mentioning in the affairs of the polis or in my own household affairs. As a result of my service to the god, I am in the depths of poverty.

Furthermore, the young men—those who have the most leisure, the sons of the most wealthy—follow me about of their own accord. They are delighted when they hear men being cross-examined, and they themselves often imitate me and try to examine others. And then, I suppose, they find a great abundance of people who think they have some knowledge but really know little or nothing. And then those who are examined by them are angry with me, not with themselves, and say that there is a subversive character called Socrates who corrupts the young; and when anyone asks them what I do and what I teach that corrupts them, they have nothing to say, for they do not know; but so that they may not appear to have no answer, they utter the phrases that lie ready to hand for use against any philosopher, "the things in the heavens and the things under the earth," and "doesn't believe in the gods," and "makes the weaker argument prevail." They wouldn't be willing to tell the truth, I suppose, which is that they have been shown up as people pretending to have knowledge but really knowing nothing. Since they are ambitious and impetuous, and there are many of them, and they speak intensely and persuasively, they have filled your ears with their vehement slanders for a long time. My attackers, Meletus, Anytus, and Lycon, belong to this group. Meletus is angry on the poets' behalf, Anytus on behalf of the craftsmen and the politicians, and Lycon on behalf of the orators. So, as I was saying at the beginning, I should be surprised if, in the short time allowed me, I could pluck from your minds this slander, which has grown so great. This is the truth, men of Athens. In what I am saying I am concealing nothing, great or small; I am dissembling nothing. I know that it is for precisely these reasons that they hate me; and this is a proof that I am speaking the truth, that this is the slander against me and that these are the reasons for it. Whether you inquire into these matters now or at a later time, you will find that the situation is just as I say.

This must serve as my defense against the charges of my first accusers. I will next try to make my defense against Meletus, that excellent and patriotic man, as he styles himself, and the rest of my later accusers. Now again, regarding these men as being a second set of accusers, let us now take up their affidavit. It is something like this: Socrates does wrong in corrupting the young and in worshiping not the gods whom the polis worships but other, new, divinities. Such is the accusation. Let us examine each individual part of it.

He says that I do wrong, for I corrupt the young men. But I say that Meletus does wrong, men of Athens, in that he is frivolous in serious matters. He brings men into court thoughtlessly, pretending that he is serious and in earnest about topics to which he has never yet paid the slightest attention. I will try to show you too that this is the case. Please come here, Meletus, and tell me. Is it not very important to you that the younger men should be as good as possible?

It is.

Well, then, tell these men who makes them better. Clearly you know, since you take an interest in the subject. For now that you have found the man who corrupts them—me, as you say—you are bringing him before the court and accusing him. Come then, tell the jury the person who makes the young better, and identify for them who he is. Do you see, Meletus? You are silent. You have nothing to say. Do you not think it shameful—and a sufficient proof of what I am saying—that the topic has been of no interest to you? But tell me, my good sir, who makes the young better?

The laws.

But that is not what I am asking you, my very good sir. I am asking you what person—the one who starts from knowledge of this very topic, the laws.

The members of the jury here.

What is that, Meletus? Can these men here educate the young men? Do they make them better?

Certainly.

All of them? Or can some do it and not others?

All of them.

By Hera, that is excellent. There is no lack of benefactors. Well, then, do the onlookers here in court make them better or not?

They do so too.

And the members of the Council?

The members of the Council as well.

But surely, Meletus, the members of the Assembly do not corrupt the younger men. Or do they all make them better too?

They do so too.

It seems, then, that all the Athenians except me make the young men honorable and good. I alone corrupt them. Is that what you are saying?

That is what I am saying with all my might.

On your account of the matter, I must be very unlucky. But answer me this. Is the situation the same for horses, in your opinion? Do you suppose that those who make them better are all mankind and that the one who corrupts them is some one person? Or is it quite the opposite? Some one person, or a very few, are able to make them better, namely the horse-trainers, whereas the majority make horses worse if they have to do with them and consort with them. Is not that true, Meletus, of both horses and all other animals? It certainly is, whether Anytus and yourself admit it or deny it. For the young would be very fortunate indeed if there were only one person who corrupted them and everyone else benefited them. But, Meletus, you are giving ample proof that you have never yet thought about the young men and are clearly showing your own lack of interest in the topics that are the subject of your indictment.

Tell us this too, Meletus. Is it better to live among good citizens or bad ones? Answer, my good sir; I am not asking anything difficult. Do not bad men do harm to their neighbors, while good men do good to them?

They do indeed.

Is there anyone who wishes to be harmed by his associates rather than benefited by them? Answer, my good sir. For the law too bids you to answer. Does anyone wish to be harmed?

No indeed.

Well, you are charging me before this court with corrupting the young men and making them worse. Do you claim that I do so intentionally or unintentionally?

Intentionally.

What is that, Meletus? Are you so much wiser at your age than I am at mine that you are aware that bad men always do some harm to their closest associates while good men do some good, whereas I have descended to such depths of ignorance that I am even unaware that, if I make one of my associates bad, I am likely to receive some harm from him, and so I intentionally do this great harm, as you claim? I do not believe this, Meletus, and I do not suppose that anyone else will. No; either I do not corrupt them, or, if I do, I do not do so intentionally. So in either case you are not speaking the truth. If I am corrupting them unintentionally, it is the law or custom not to bring a man before the court for mistakes of this kind but to take him quietly to one side and teach and admonish him. For evidently, if I learn, I shall cease to do what I do unintentionally. But you avoided coming to me and teaching me. You were not willing to do so. Instead, you are bringing me before this court, though the law and custom is to bring here those who need punishment, not instruction.

Men of Athens, it is already apparent that what I was saying is true. Meletus has never yet taken any interest, great or small, in these matters. Nevertheless, tell us, Meletus, how, according to you, I corrupt the young men. Or is it clear from your indictment that I do so by teaching them not to worship the gods that the polis worships but some other, new, divinities? Do you not claim that I corrupt them by teaching them this?

That is what I am saying with all my might.

In the name of those very gods whom we are now discussing, Meletus, tell me, and the jury too, still more clearly what you mean. For I cannot discover whether you are saying that I teach the young men to believe in some gods—in which case I myself believe in gods and am not altogether an atheist, and I am not doing wrong in this way—not, however, the gods in which the polis believes, but different ones. Is your charge that I believe in different gods, or do you claim that I do not believe in gods at all and teach other people not to believe in them?

I claim that you do not believe in gods at all.

My dear Meletus, why do you make this claim? Do I then not believe the sun and moon to be gods, as other people do?

He certainly does not, gentlemen of the jury. He says the sun is a rock and that the moon is made of earth.

Do you think you are accusing Anaxagoras, my dear Meletus? Have you so much contempt for these men here? Do you suppose them so ignorant of the written word as not to know that the books of Anaxagoras of Clazomenae are full of such statements? Do the young men learn these doctrines from me when they could sometimes go to the "dancing-place," [1] buy the books for a drachma at most, and laugh at Socrates if he pretends that the doctrines are his, particularly as they are so odd? But in Zeus's name, is that what you think of me? Do I not believe in any god?

You do not, in Zeus's name. Not in any way at all.

No one believes you, Meletus. I doubt whether you believe yourself. Men of Athens, Meletus here, it seems, is a violent man, lacking in self-

1. "Dancing-place" translates the Greek word *orchestra*. In Greek theaters the chorus sang and danced in the *orchestra;* but many scholars believe that the reference here is to some other location in Athens of which we know nothing.

control, and it is his violence, his lack of self-control, and his youth that have induced him to bring this indictment. He is like someone composing a riddle to test our intelligence: "Will Socrates the wise realize that I am being frivolous and contradicting myself, or will I deceive him and the others who are listening?" For in my opinion Meletus is contradicting himself in the indictment, as if he were to say "Socrates does wrong by not believing in gods but believing in gods." And that is not the behavior of a serious man.

Gentlemen, please join me in looking into his apparent self-contradiction. Answer us, Meletus. And, as I requested of you at the beginning, men of Athens, please remember not to make an uproar if I conduct my arguments in my usual style.

Is there anyone, Meletus, who believes in human activities but does not believe in the existence of human beings? Meletus should answer, gentlemen, and not keep shouting about this and that. Is there anyone who does not believe in horses but believes in equine activities? Or does not believe in flute-players but believes in activities of flute-players? There exists no one of the kind, my very good sir. I will give an answer to you and to the court, if you are not willing to answer yourself. But answer the next question, at least. Is there anyone who believes in divine activities [*daimonia*] but not in divinities [*daimones*]?

There is not.

How obliging of you to bring yourself to reply when the jury insists. Well, then. You say that I believe in *daimonia* and that I teach others to believe in them. They may be new ones or they may be old, but at all events, according to you, I believe in *daimonia*. You even swore to this in your affidavit. Well, if I believe in *daimonia*, I must necessarily believe in *daimones*, must I not? I must. You do not answer, but I take it that you agree. Now, do we not believe that *daimones* are either gods or the children of gods? Do you agree or not?

Certainly I agree.

If, as you say, I believe in *daimones*, and *daimones* are a kind of gods, the result is the frivolous riddle that I am talking about; for you are saying both that I do not believe in gods and that I do believe in them, since I believe in *daimones*. On the other hand, if *daimones* are the bastard children of the gods by nymphs or by some other creatures whose children *daimones* are said to be, what mortal man would suppose that children of gods exist but that gods do not? It would be just as odd as to believe in the children of horses and donkeys—mules—but not to believe in horses and donkeys. In fact, Meletus, you must either have been testing our intelligence when you composed this indictment, or you were despairing of finding a genuine instance of wrongdoing to charge me with. But there is no way of persuading anyone of even moderate intelligence that the same person can believe that there are activities and effects of *daimones* and gods and yet not believe in *daimones* or gods or demigods.

Men of Athens, I do not think it requires much defense to show that I am not guilty as charged in Meletus' indictment. What I have said will suffice. But you know that what I was saying earlier is true. I am bitterly hated by many people. What is assuring my conviction, if it is assured, is not Meletus and Anytus but the slander and envy of the majority of people. Slander and envy have convicted a great many other good men, and they will do so in the future, I suppose. There is no danger of the line's ending with me.

Perhaps someone might say, "Are you not ashamed, Socrates, of a way of life that is now likely to bring your death?" I would give a just answer and say, "You are wrong, fellow, if you suppose that a man who is good for anything at all ought to calculate the chances of life and death rather than consider this, and this alone, whenever he acts: whether he is acting justly or unjustly and whether his actions are those of a good man or a bad one. Poor creatures indeed, by your reckoning, would be the demigods who fell at Troy, especially the son of Thetis, who rated danger so low in comparison with submitting to dishonor that, when he was eager to kill Hector, and his mother, who was a goddess, warned him in some such way as this, I believe: "My son, if you mean to avenge the death of your comrade Patroclus by killing Hector, you yourself will die; for straightway," she said, "after Hector is your death prepared"—on hearing this, he thought little of death and danger but, since he was more afraid of living as a coward and failing to avenge his friends, said: "May I die at once, having punished the wrongdoer, so that I may not remain here by the beaked ships, a laughingstock and a burden on the earth." Surely you don't suppose that he gave any thought to death and danger?

This is the truth of the matter, men of Athens. If a man stations himself anywhere, thinking it the best position for him, or is stationed there by a superior, there, it seems to me, he must stay and face danger, thinking that neither death nor anything else is more important than avoiding what is dishonorable. I should have done something terrible, men of Athens, if, when my superior officers, whom you chose as my commanders, assigned me to my post at Potidaea, at Amphipolis, and at Delium, I then had stood my ground where they posted me and braved death like anyone else, but, when the god was posting me, as I thought and supposed, bidding me pass my life in philosophizing and in examining myself and the rest of mankind, I should be struck with fear of death or anything else and leave my post. It would be terrible; and then in truth someone might justly drag me into court, charging me with not believing in gods, since I do not obey the oracle, and fear death, and think I am wise though I am not. For, gentlemen, to fear death is precisely to think oneself wise though one is not; it is to think that one knows what one does not know. For no one knows whether death is the greatest of all good things for a man; but men fear it as if they knew for certain that it is the greatest of bad things. Surely this is that disgraceful form of ignorance, thinking one knows what one does not. Gentlemen, perhaps in this respect too I do differ from the majority of mankind, and if I were to claim to be wiser than another man in any way it would be in this: that having no adequate knowledge about the world of Hades, I do not think I have any. But I do know that to do wrong and to disobey one's superior, whether god or man, is harmful and dishonorable. I shall never fear or flee things that, for all that I know, may be actually beneficial rather than harmful things that I know are harmful. Suppose you acquit me on this occasion and do not accept the advice of Anytus, who said that maybe I ought not to have been brought into court at all but, now that I had been, there was no possibility of not executing me; for, if I were to be acquitted, your sons would practice what Socrates preaches and would all be utterly corrupted. Suppose you were to tell me, in response to this, "Socrates, on this occasion we will not take Anytus' advice. We will acquit you, but on the understanding that you shall no longer spend your time on this inquiry or engage in philosophy and that, if you are caught doing this any more, you shall die." If you were to acquit me on these terms, I should say, "Men of Athens, I like you and am your friend; but I shall obey the god rather than you, and as long as there is breath in my body and I can do so, I shall not cease from philosophizing and exhorting you and making profession of my beliefs to any one of you that I happen to meet. I shall say what I am accustomed to say: 'My very good sir, you are an Athenian, and your polis is the greatest and most renowned for strength and wisdom. Are you not ashamed that you are making every effort to acquire as much money, honor, and reputation as you can, while you give no effort or thought to wisdom and truth or to making your soul as good as possible?'" And if anyone denies it and claims that he does make an effort, I shall not immediately let him go or go away myself. I shall ask him questions and examine him and try to refute him; and if I think he does not really possess excellence but merely claims to possess it, I shall reproach him and say that he sets a very small value on what is worth most and a greater value on what has less worth. I shall do this to any younger or older man that I meet, be he foreigner or citizen, but more to the citizens, for you are closer in kin to me. For these, I assure you, are the god's commands, and I believe that no greater benefit has yet come upon this polis than my service to the god. For I go around doing nothing else but trying to persuade both the younger and the older men among you not to give greater or prior importance to your bodies or your possessions than to ensuring that your souls are as good as possible. I say, "It is not from possessions that excellence springs. It is from excellence that spring possessions and all other good things for mankind, both in private and in public life." If in saying these things I am corrupting the young men, then what I say is harmful; but if anyone claims that what I say is something different from this, he is talking nonsense. "So," I should say, "men of Athens, either take Anytus' advice or not, and acquit me or not, on the understanding that I shall not behave differently even if I am to die many deaths."

Do not make a disturbance, men of Athens. Please abide by the conditions I asked of you. Listen to what I say; do not make a disturbance. For, I believe, what you hear will benefit you. I am about to tell you other things that will perhaps cause you to shout. But do not do so. I assure you that, if you kill the kind of person that I say that I am, you will not damage me so much as yourselves. For neither Meletus nor Anytus would do me any harm—they could not do so—since I believe it is not permitted that a superior man should be harmed by his inferior. The inferior might kill him, or have him exiled, or deprive him of citizen status. My accuser supposes, and some others perhaps agree, that these things are great evils. I do not think so but rather that the great evil is to do what he is now doing: to try to have a man unjustly executed. So now, men of Athens, it is not for my own benefit that I am speaking in my defense—far from it—but much more for yours, to prevent you from condemning me and so making a terrible mistake about this gift that the gods have given you. For, if you execute me, you will not easily find another man like me, who am literally—laughable though it may be to say it—attached to the polis by the god, as if the polis were a horse, large, and of good pedigree, but sluggish as a result of its size and needing to be roused by a gadfly. In a similar manner the god, I believe, has attached me to this polis as something of the kind: I never cease the whole day long from alighting beside each one of you, waking you up, persuading you, and rebuking you. You will not easily find someone else like me, gentlemen. If you take my advice, you will spare my life. Perhaps in irritation, like drowsing people on being wakened, you may take Anytus' advice, swat me, and easily kill me; but then you would go on sleeping for the rest of your lives, unless the god should show his care for you by sending someone else. That I am the sort of person who might be sent to the polis by the god you might infer from this: that I have neglected my own affairs, and put up with their being neglected for many years now, and have always devoted myself to your interests, approaching each one of you individually, like a father or an elder brother, and persuading you to make excellence your concern. This behavior seems more than human. If I had been getting any benefit from it and was being paid for these exhorta-

tions, the behavior would have been rational; but, as it is, you yourselves
see that, though my accusers have shamelessly put forward all their other
indictments, they were unable to furnish a witness to support the shameless
claim that I ever accepted a fee from anyone or that I asked for one. For, I
suppose, I am providing a good enough witness to the truth of my claims—
my poverty.

Perhaps it may appear odd to you that I go around giving advice and
minding other people's business in private but shun coming before your
whole citizen body and advising you in public. The reason for this is what
you have heard me say at many times and in many places, that I have a kind
of sign from a *daimon* or a god, something that Meletus satirized when he
drew up his indictment. I have had this from childhood onwards, a kind of
voice that comes to me. When it comes, it always dissuades me from whatever it may be that I am about to do; it never urges me to do something. It is
this that opposes my taking part in politics, and I think it does well to oppose it; for I assure you, gentlemen of the jury, that if I had tried, long ago,
to take part in politics, I would have perished long ago and would have
benefited neither you nor myself. Do not be angry when I tell you the truth,
which is that no one can be in safety if he genuinely opposes either you or
any other citizen body and tries to prevent the occurrence of many unjust
and illegal activities in the polis; the person who is really striving on behalf
of justice, if he is to survive even for a short time, must necessarily do so
as a private citizen, not a politician.

I shall furnish you with important proofs of this, not words but what you
value—deeds. Listen while I tell you what happened to me, so that you
may realize that I would not unjustly yield to anyone out of fear of death
but would rather die than yield. What I shall tell you is tiresome and
smacks of the lawcourt, but it is true. Men of Athens, I have never yet held
any other office in the polis, but I have been a member of the Council. It
happened that my tribe, Antiochis, was holding the presidency when you
decided to try, all together, the ten generals who had not picked up the
bodies after the sea battle.[2] Your decision was illegal, as you all agreed
later. At that time I alone among the presiding officers opposed you and
argued that we should do nothing against the laws, and I cast my vote in
opposition. When the orators were ready to impeach me and drag me off,
and you were shouting encouragement to them, I thought I ought rather to
accept danger on the side of the laws and of justice than to join you, when

2. In the battle of Arginusae, fought in 406 B.C., the Athenians were victorious. Seventy
Spartan ships were sunk for a loss of twenty-five Athenian ships; but a strong wind sprang up,
and the Athenian commanders were unable to rescue many Athenian sailors clinging to the
wreckage. The commanders were later prosecuted and condemned to death in the manner
described in the text.

your proposals were unjust, because I feared imprisonment or death. This happened while the polis was still under a democratic government. When the oligarchs came to power, the Thirty summoned me and four others to the rotunda and ordered us to bring Leon the Salaminian from Salamis for execution—the kind of orders they gave often and to many people, wishing to implicate as many as possible in their guilt. But at that time I showed, not by words but by my actions, that I care not one jot for death, if it is not rather vulgar to say so; my care is entirely to avoid doing anything unjust or unholy. For that despotism, powerful as it was, did not terrify me into doing anything unjust: when we left the rotunda, the four of them went off to Salamis and brought back Leon, but I went home. Perhaps I would have been executed as a result had not the oligarchy been put down soon afterwards. I shall produce many witnesses of these events for you.

Now, do you suppose that I would have survived for so many years if I had been taking part in politics and, as a good man should, had been on the side of justice and had been setting the highest value on it, as one should? Far from it, gentlemen of the jury; nor would anyone else. But throughout my life, in all my public actions and in private, too, I shall be patently this kind of person: one who never yet came to an agreement in defiance of justice either with anyone else or with those men whom they slander me by terming my "pupils." I have never yet been anyone's teacher. If anyone, young or old, wished to listen while I was talking and attending to my own business, I never yet grudged that to anyone. I do not converse when I am paid and refuse to converse when I am not paid. I make myself available for questioning to rich and poor alike and also if anyone wishes to answer and hear what I say. If any of these men turns out to be good or bad, it is not right that I should be held responsible. I never yet promised any of them that they would learn anything, and I did not teach them. If anyone claims that he has ever yet learned or heard anything from me in private that none of the others did, I assure you that he is not telling the truth.

But why do some people delight in spending long periods of time with me? You have heard the answer, gentlemen of the jury. I have told you the whole truth. They delight in listening when those who think they are wise, though they are not, are being examined. There is some pleasure in it. On me, as I am telling you, this task has been laid by the god, both through oracles and in dreams and in every way in which any divine power ever commanded any man to do anything whatever. These claims are true, gentlemen of the jury; were they not, they could readily be refuted. For if I am engaged in corrupting some of the young men and have completed my corruption of others, then, if some of them, on growing older, realized that I had ever given some bad advice to them when they were young, they should now, I suppose, be coming forward to accuse me and revenge themselves. If they were not willing to do so themselves, members of their families—fathers, brothers, and other kinsmen—should now remember and take vengeance for any harm their relatives had suffered at my hands. Certainly many of them are here. I see them. First, my contemporary and fellow demesman Crito, the father of Critobulus here; then Lysanias of Sphettus, the father of Aeschines here; next Antiphon of Cephisia, the father of Epigenes; and others whose brothers spent some time in my company: Nicostratus, the son of Theozotides, the brother of Theodotus— Theodotus is dead, so that he could not have entreated Nicostratus not to speak against me—and Paralius here, the son of Demodocus, whose brother was Theages; and here is Adeimantus, the son of Ariston, whose brother Plato is in court, and Aeantodorus, whose brother is Apollodorus here. I can mention many others to you, at least one of whom Meletus ought to have put up as witnesses, preferably in his own speech; but, if he forgot to do it then, let him put them up now—I will step down while he does so—and let him produce any evidence of this kind that he has. But you will find that the opposite is the case, gentlemen: they are all ready to assist me, the corrupter, the man doing harm to their kith and kin, as Meletus and Anytus say. Perhaps those who are themselves corrupted might have some reason for taking my side; but those who are not, men who are already older, the relatives of these men—what reason could they have for taking my side other than the right and just one, that they know that Meletus is telling lies and that I am telling the truth?

Well, gentlemen. These, and perhaps some similar points, are what I have to offer in my defense. Perhaps someone among you may be angry at the remembrance of his own behavior. Possibly he was the accused in a case less serious than this one and begged and supplicated the jurymen and shed many tears. Perhaps he tried to obtain as much pity as he could by bringing his children into court, along with others of his relatives and many of his friends. I shall do none of these things, though I may be thought to be facing the greatest of dangers. Possibly someone may have this in mind and may steel himself against my defense and cast his vote in an anger that is roused by my very different actions. Suppose one of you is in this situation—I do not assert that anyone is, but suppose that it is the case; I think I should be reasonable if I said to him, "My very good sir, I do have relatives of my own. For not even I, in Homer's phrase, sprang 'from an oak tree or a rock.' I am from human stock, so I have relatives and even sons, men of Athens, three of them, one an adolescent and two who are still children. Nevertheless, I shall not bring any of them into court and ask you to acquit me for their sake." Why shall I do none of these things? Not because I have no feelings, men of Athens. Not out of disrespect to you. Because I am courageous in the face of death? That is another matter. But when I consider reputation—mine, yours, that of the whole polis—it does not seem honorable for me to do any of these things at my age and with my reputation. My reputation may or may not be deserved, but the belief that Socrates is not like other people is firmly established. If those of you who are thought to be superior in wisdom or courage or any other excellence are going to behave in this manner, it would be shameful. I mean the kind of people whom I have often seen as defendants in court. They have some reputation, but they behave in an amazing manner, since they think that they will suffer something terrible if they are put to death, as if they will be immortal if you do not execute them. In my opinion, they bring shame to the polis: even a foreigner would suppose that those of the Athenians who are of outstanding excellence, those whom the Athenians themselves elect to positions of power and honor among them, are in fact no better than women. Men of Athens, those of you who have any degree of reputation ought not to do this, and, if we do it, you ought not to allow us to get away with it. You ought to make it quite clear that you will be more certain to condemn the man who stages these plaintive charades and makes the polis a laughingstock than the man who conducts himself in a quiet and orderly manner.

Quite apart from reputation, gentlemen, I do not think it is just to ask a favor from the juryman or to obtain acquittal by doing so; one should rather inform and persuade the jury. For these are not the terms on which the juryman occupies his place. He is not appointed to give away justice as a favor but to judge the justice of the case. He is on oath not to confer favors at his pleasure but to give judgment in accordance with the laws. We ought not to accustom you to break your oaths, and you ought not to become accustomed to breaking them. For neither of us would be pious if we did so. Do not demand of me, gentlemen, behavior that I regard as being neither honorable nor just nor pious, especially, by Zeus! when I am being prosecuted by Meletus here on a charge of impiety. For if I persuaded and forced you by my entreaties when you are on oath, I should evidently be teaching you not to believe in the gods, and in making my defense I should literally be accusing myself of not believing in gods. But the case is far otherwise. I do believe in them, men of Athens, as none of my accusers does, and I leave it to you and to the god to judge my case in the manner that will be best both for me and for you.

*   *   *

For many reasons, men of Athens, I am not distressed by the fact that you voted to condemn me, but principally because I expected you to do so. I am surprised, rather, by the totals of votes on either side. I had not ex-

pected them to be so similar; I was expecting a large majority for my condemnation. In fact, it seems that if a mere thirty of the votes had been cast
differently, I would have been acquitted. As it is, I think, I have been acquitted of Meletus' charges, and not merely acquitted. It is evident to all of
you that, had not Anytus and Lycon come forward to accuse me, Meletus
would not have received the statutory fifth of the votes cast and would have
been fined a thousand drachmas.

The man proposes the penalty of death. Well now, men of Athens, what
shall be my counterproposal?[3] Clearly it should be what I deserve. And
what do I deserve? What punishment or fine do I deserve for not having the
common sense to lead a quiet life, for not having joined in the pursuits of
the majority: making money, caring for my household goods, commanding
armies, speaking in the Assembly, taking my share in the other magistracies, plots, and factions that one finds in the polis? For thinking myself
too honest to ensure my safety by taking such a course? For not going
where I should have been of no use to you or to myself? For going, rather,
where I could confer the greatest benefit on each of you, individually and
in private? For trying to persuade each one of you not to take care of any of
his own possessions before taking care that he himself should be as good
and as wise as possible, and not to take care of the possessions of the polis
before taking care of the polis itself, and to take care of everything else
according to the same order of precedence? What requital does a man like
me deserve to receive? Something good, men of Athens, if I *must* propose
what I really deserve; and something good that would be appropriate for
me. What would be appropriate for a poor man who is your benefactor, a
man who needs leisure so that he may have the time to exhort you? Men of
Athens, for such a man there is no requital more appropriate than free
meals in the council house; he deserves it much more than would any of
you who won an Olympic victory with a horse, a two-horse chariot, or a
four-horse chariot. The one makes you think you are prospering, whereas I
offer you prosperity in the true sense; and he does not need the food,
whereas I do. So if I ought to get my just deserts, I propose, as my requital, free meals in the council house.

Perhaps you may think that in saying this I am simply putting on a bold
front, and you are reminded of what I said about pity and prayers. Not so,
men of Athens. It is more like this: I am convinced that I have not intentionally wronged anyone, but I cannot persuade you to agree. We have had
only a short conversation together. In my opinion, if you had a law, such as
other people in fact have, not to spend one day but many on cases that

3. In some Athenian trials, the prosecutor and the defendant each proposed a penalty, and
the jury chose between them.

carry the death penalty, you would have been persuaded. But it is not easy to destroy powerful slanders in a short time. Convinced as I am that I have wronged no one, I have no intention of wronging myself, accusing myself of deserving some harm and proposing some such requital for myself. What fear could induce me to do so? Am I to fear the requital that Meletus proposes? But, I declare, I do not know whether it is beneficial or harmful. Am I to choose as an alternative one of the things I am certain are harmful? Am I to choose imprisonment? Why should I live in prison, the slave of the magistrates for the time being, the Eleven? Am I to choose a fine—and imprisonment until I have paid it? But that is the same penalty as I was mentioning just now; for I have no money from which to pay the fine. Well, am I to choose exile? For that is a penalty that perhaps you might fix. I must be very fond of life, men of Athens, if I am so irrational as not to be able to reason in the following way. You, my fellow-citizens, could not endure my company and my arguments. They roused disgust and envy in you, and so you are now trying to be rid of them. Will others find them easy to tolerate? Far from it, men of Athens. A fine life it would be if I went into exile at my age, forever being driven out and exchanging one city for another. For I know that, wherever I go, the young men will listen to what I say, just as they do here. If I drive them away, they themselves will persuade their elders to drive me out; and, if I do not drive them away, their fathers and relatives will drive me out to protect them.

Perhaps someone might say, "But Socrates, can you not go into exile, live a quiet life, and say nothing?" My most difficult task is to persuade some of you that I cannot. If I tell you that to behave in this way is to disobey the god and that therefore I cannot live such a life, you will not believe me; for you will assume that I am not being serious. If I tell you that the greatest good for a man is every day to have conversations about human excellence and the other topics on which you hear me conversing and examining myself and other people, and that the unexamined life is not worth living for a man, you will believe me even less. The facts are as I say, gentlemen, but it is not easy to persuade you of them. In addition, I am not accustomed to think that I deserve any harm. If I had money, I would have proposed a fine of the amount I could pay, for I would have suffered no harm from that. But the fact is, I have none, unless you are willing to assess as my penalty the amount I am able to pay. Perhaps I could pay a mina of silver, so I propose that as a penalty.

Gentlemen of the jury, Plato here, and Crito, and Critobulus, and Apollodorus are urging me to propose thirty minae, and they say that they themselves will guarantee the money. So I propose that as a penalty. These men are trustworthy sureties for the sum involved.

* * *

Men of Athens, you will have a bad reputation with those who wish to find fault with this polis. They will say that you are the killers of Socrates, a wise man; for those who wish to abuse you will claim that I am wise, even if I am not. And you will not have gained much time in exchange for your reputation. Had you simply waited for a short time, you would have gained your desire with no effort on your part. You see my age. I am far gone in years and near death. I do not say this to all of you, only to those who voted for the penalty of death. I say this too to those same persons. Perhaps you suppose, men of Athens, that I have been condemned because I lacked the kind of arguments that would have enabled me to persuade you—if, that is, I had thought it appropriate to do or say anything that would have ensured my acquittal. Far from it. I have been condemned because I lacked something, it is true; but not arguments. I lacked effrontery and shamelessness and the willingness to say to you the kind of things that it would have given you the greatest pleasure to hear. You would have liked to hear me wailing and lamenting and doing and saying many things unworthy of me, as I say—the kind of things you are accustomed to hear from others who are accused. I did not think then that I ought to do anything unworthy of a free man in order to escape danger, and I do not now regret having defended myself in this way. I much prefer to make my defense in this way and die rather than do so in the other way and live. For neither in court nor in battle should I or anyone else contrive to escape death at any cost. For in battles, too, it often becomes clear that one might escape death by throwing away one's weapons and begging one's pursuers for mercy; and in each kind of danger there are many other methods of escaping death, provided one has the effrontery to say and do anything that is necessary. Perhaps it is not death that is difficult to escape, gentlemen. Perhaps escape from badness is much more difficult, since it runs more quickly than death. Now I, an old man and slow, have been caught by the slower runner, while my accusers, clever and quick as they are, have been caught by the faster runner, badness. Now I shall go my way, having brought on myself the penalty of death through your agency; and they will go theirs, having brought on themselves badness and injustice through the agency of truth. I abide by my award as they abide by theirs. Perhaps these events were bound to turn out as they did. I think that all is as it should be.

Next, jurymen who voted to condemn me, I wish to prophesy to you, for I am now at that time of life when men are most given to prophecy when they are about to die. I tell you, men who are my killers, that immediately after my death a requital will come upon you much more severe than the one you have inflicted on me by killing me. For now you have done this thinking to escape cross-examination about your lives; but, I assure you, it will turn out quite differently. The number of cross-examiners will increase. I have held them in check till now, though you were not aware of it. They are younger and so will be more severe critics, and you will be more angry. If you think that by killing men you will prevent others from rebuking you for not living as you should, you are mistaken. For this mode of prevention is neither possible nor honorable. There is another, very honorable and very easy: do not harm others, and take the necessary steps to make yourselves as good as possible. This is my prophecy to those who voted for my condemnation. I now take my leave of you.

To those of you who voted for my acquittal I should like to say a few words about what has just happened, while the magistrates are busy and it is not yet time for me to go to the place where I must die. Wait, gentlemen, for just so long. There is no reason why we should not tell each other our fancies while it is still possible. I want to explain to you, my friends, the significance of my present circumstances. Gentlemen who are my judges— for I should be correct in calling you judges—my situation is remarkable. My customary prophetic sign—my *daimonion*—was always a frequent visitor throughout my past life, and it opposed me, even on very unimportant matters, if I was about to behave incorrectly. But now my situation is what you yourselves see it to be, a situation that one might suppose, and is generally thought to be, the most extreme of harmful states of affairs. Yet the sign of the god did not oppose me as I was leaving home this morning. It did not oppose me when I was coming up here to the court. It did not oppose me anywhere in my speech as I was about to say something. In other discourses of mine it often checked me while I was actually speaking, but in the present affair it has not opposed me anywhere, in anything I did or said. What do I suppose to be the reason for this? I will tell you. It looks as if the present situation is beneficial for me and that those of us who regard death as harmful are mistaken. I have a strong proof of this: my accustomed sign would certainly have opposed me if I were not about to do something beneficial to myself.

If we consider the matter in this way too, we shall see that there is strong reason to hope that death is beneficial. Death is one of two things. Either the dead are nothing and have no perception of anything, or, as is said, death is a kind of change and a migration of the soul from this place here to another place. If death is an absence of perception and like a sleep in which the sleeper does not even dream, death would be a wonderful gain. Suppose one chose out the night in which one had a dreamless sleep and compared all the other days and nights of one's life to that night. Now suppose that after due consideration, one had to say how many days and nights in one's life one had lived better and more pleasantly than that night. I suspect that not merely a private citizen but the Great King of Persia himself would have little difficulty in counting them in comparison with the other days and nights. If death is like that, I say it is a benefit. For thus considered, the whole of time seems to be no more than a single night. If, on the other hand, death is like traveling from here to a foreign land, and if it is true that, as is said, all the dead are there, what greater good than that could there be, gentlemen of the jury? Suppose someone, arriving at the house of Hades, freed from the people here who claim to be judges, will find the genuine judges who are said to dispense justice there—Minos and Rhadamanthys and Aeacus and Triptolemus and others of the demigods who were just men in their own lives. That foreign land is not to be despised. Again, what price would not any one of you give to spend his time with Orpheus and Musaeus and Hesiod and Homer? I am willing to die many times if this is true. I myself would find it wonderful to be there and to meet Palamedes and Ajax, son of Telamon, and the rest of the men of old who died because of an unjust judgment and compare my own experiences with theirs. It would not be unpleasant, in my opinion. But the greatest satisfaction of all would be to spend my time examining and testing those who are there as I tested and examined those who are here, to discover which of them is wise and which thinks he is wise though he is not. Gentlemen of the jury, how much would one be willing to pay for the opportunity of questioning the man who led the great expedition to Troy, or Odysseus, or Sisyphus, or countless others whom one could name, men and women alike? To have conversations with them, to spend time with them, and to ask them questions would be a happiness that could not be surpassed. At all events, I do not suppose that the inhabitants of that land put people to death for doing so. Those inhabitants are happier than the inhabitants of this world in other respects, and especially in being now deathless for the future, if what is said of them is true.

You too, gentlemen of the jury, must be of good hope in the face of death. Keep in mind this one truth, that no harm can come to a good man, either in life or in death, and that his acts and experiences are not unobserved by the gods. My present situation is not the result of chance. It is clear to me that it was now better for me to die and be free of my troubles. This is the reason why my sign did not dissuade me at any point. I am hardly angry with those who condemned me or with my accusers. Certainly it was not with this in mind that they condemned me and accused me, but with the intention of harming me; and for this they deserve my blame. But I want to ask of them the following favor. Punish my sons, gentlemen, when they are grown up. Cause them the selfsame troubles as I caused you if they seem to you to care for money or anything else more than they care for excellence; and if they think that they are something when they are really nothing, rebuke them as I once rebuked you, because they are not caring for what they should and think themselves to be something when they are really worth nothing. If you do this, I shall be justly treated by you, I and my sons also. But now it is the time to depart, I to die and you to live. Which of us is going to a better goal, only the god knows.

13. Plato, The *Crito*

The *Crito*, together with the *Phaedo*, constitutes Plato's portrait of Socrates in prison, awaiting execution. Part of the dialogue's effect depends on a series of contrasts and resemblances. Crito and Socrates come from the same neighborhood and are old friends and contemporaries. Crito is wealthy, Socrates poor. In the past (as Socrates reminds him) Crito has accepted the same values as Socrates, but in the present crisis he is prepared to abandon them. Neither a sophist nor a pupil of sophists, Crito is a traditional Greek, one whose first loyalty runs instinctively toward family and friends; loyalty to the city comes second. Having declared his position, he then allows Socrates to lead him through an argument that produces the opposite conclusion, that the city takes precedence over every other human institution. The crucial step comes midway through the dialogue when Socrates asks, "And a good life is equivalent to an honorable and just one—that holds also?" In modern English, words like "just," "good," and "honorable" overlap, and there is no clear distinction between them. But for a Greek of the mid-fifth century, the equation of a "good life" or "living well" with "living justly" was problematic. "Living well" was a self-evident good, since it carried suggestions of success, prosperity, and prominence. It was an altogether different notion from "living justly," which might require the acceptance of merited penalties and certainly required the refusal of unjust gains. Once Crito assents to the equation, he will have to approve of Socrates' refusal to escape, provided that Socrates can demonstrate the justice of not escaping. Socrates then takes a new dialogue partner, the Laws of Athens, whom he introduces in flesh-and-blood form, and who insist that he has made a personal agreement with them, which he is bound to honor.

Socrates. Why have you come at this hour, Crito? it must be quite early?
Crito. Yes, certainly.
Soc. What is the exact time?

From *The Complete Works of Plato*, 3d ed., translated by Benjamin Jowett. Oxford: Clarendon Press, 1892. Translation revised by Peter White.

Cr. The dawn is breaking.

Soc. I wonder that the keeper of the prison would let you in.

Cr. He knows me, because I often come, Socrates; moreover, I have done him a kindness.

Soc. And are you only just arrived?

Cr. No, I came some time ago.

Soc. Then why did you sit and say nothing instead of at once awakening me?

Cr. That I could never have done, Socrates. I only wish I were not so sleepless and distressed myself. I have been looking at you, wondering how you can sleep so comfortably, and I didn't wake you on purpose, so that you could go on sleeping in perfect comfort. All through your life, I have often thought you were favored with a good disposition, but I have never been so impressed as in the present misfortune, seeing how easily and tranquilly you bear it.

Soc. Why, Crito, when a man has reached my age he ought not to be repining at the approach of death.

Cr. And yet other old men find themselves in similar misfortunes, and age does not prevent them from repining.

Soc. That is true. But you have not told me why you come at this early hour.

Cr. I come with a message which is painful—not, I expect, to you, but painful and oppressive for me and all your friends, and I think it weighs most heavily of all on me.

Soc. What? Has the ship come from Delos, on the arrival of which I am to die?[1]

Cr. No, the ship has not actually arrived, but she will probably be here today, as persons who have come from Sunium tell me that they left her there; and therefore tomorrow, Socrates, will be the last day of your life.

Soc. Very well, Crito; if such is the will of the gods, I am willing; but my belief is that there will be a day's delay.

Cr. Why do you think so?

Soc. I will tell you. I am to die on the day after the arrival of the ship.

Cr. Yes; that is what the authorities say.

Soc. But I do not think that the ship will be here until tomorrow; this I infer from a vision which I had last night, or rather only just now, when you fortunately allowed me to sleep.

Cr. And what was the nature of the vision?

---

1. Once every year Athens sent a state ship on a ceremonial pilgrimage to the island of Delos; no executions could be carried out between its departure and return.

Soc. There appeared to me the likeness of a woman, fair and comely, clothed in bright raiment, who called to me and said: O Socrates,

"The third day hence to fertile Phthia shalt thou come." [2]

Cr. What a singular dream, Socrates!

Soc. There can be no doubt about the meaning, Crito, I think.

Cr. Yes; the meaning is only too clear. But, oh! my beloved Socrates, let me entreat you once more to take my advice and escape. For if you die, I shall not only lose a friend who can never be replaced, but there is another evil: people who do not know you and me will believe that I might have saved you if I had been willing to give money but that I did not care. Now, can there be a worse disgrace than this—that I should be thought to value money more than the life of a friend? For the many will not be persuaded that I wanted you to escape and that you refused.

Soc. But why, my dear Crito, should we care about the opinion of the many? Good men, and they are the only persons who are worth considering, will think of these things truly as they occurred.

Cr. But you see, Socrates, that the opinion of the many must be regarded, for what is now happening shows that they can do the greatest evil to anyone who has lost their good opinion.

Soc. I only wish it were so, Crito, and that the many could do the greatest evil; for then they would also be able to do the greatest good—and what a fine thing this would be! But in reality they can do neither; for they cannot make a man either wise or foolish, and whatever result they produce is the result of chance.

Cr. Well, I will not dispute with you; but please tell me, Socrates, whether you are not acting out of regard to me and your other friends: Are you not afraid that, if you escape from prison, we may get into trouble with the informers for having stolen you away and lose either the whole or a great part of our property—or that even a worse evil may happen to us? Now, if you fear on our account, be at ease; for in order to save you, we ought surely to run this or even a greater risk; be persuaded, then, and do as I say.

Soc. Yes, Crito, that is one fear which you mention, but by no means the only one.

Cr. Fear not—there are persons who are willing to get you out of prison at no great cost; and as for the informers, they are far from being exorbitant in their demands—a little money will satisfy them. My means, which are

---

2. The apparition borrows the words in which Achilles contemplated a return from Troy to his home, *Iliad* 9.363.

certainly ample, are at your service; and if, out of solicitude about me, you hesitate to use mine, there are non-Athenians here who will give you the use of theirs; and one of them, Simmias the Theban, has brought a large sum of money for this very purpose; and Cebes and many others are prepared to spend their money in helping you to escape. Therefore do not hesitate to save yourself because you are worried about this, and do not say, as you did in the court, that you will have difficulty in knowing what to do with yourself anywhere else. For men will love you in other places to which you may go, and not in Athens only; there are friends of mine in Thessaly, if you would like to go to them, who will value and protect you, and no Thessalian will give you any trouble. Nor can I think that you are at all justified, Socrates, in betraying your own life when you might be saved. You are only working to bring about what your enemies, who want to destroy you, would and did in fact work to accomplish. And further, I should say that you are deserting your own children; for you might bring them up and educate them, instead of which you go away and leave them, and they will have to take their chances; and if they do not meet with the usual fate of orphans, there will be small thanks to you. No man should bring children into the world who is unwilling to persevere to the end in their nurture and education. But you appear to be choosing the easier part, not the better and manlier, which would have been more becoming in one who has professed a life-long concern for virtue, like yourself. And indeed, I am ashamed not only of you but of us, who are your friends, when I reflect that the whole business will be attributed entirely to our want of courage. The trial need never have come on or might have been managed differently. And now it may seem that we have made a ridiculous bungle of this last chance, thanks to our lack of toughness and courage, since we failed to save you and you failed to save yourself, even though it was possible and practicable if we were good for anything at all. So, Socrates, you must not let this turn into a disgrace as well as a tragedy for yourself and us. Make up your mind then, or rather have your mind already made up; for the time of deliberation is over, and there is only one thing to be done, which must be done this very night, and, if we delay at all, it will be no longer practicable or possible; I beseech you therefore, Socrates, be persuaded by me, and do not be contrary.

Soc. My dear Crito, your solicitude is invaluable if it is rightly directed, but otherwise, the more intense, the more difficult it is to deal with. And so we should consider whether I ought to follow this course or not. You know it has always been true that I paid no heed to any consideration I was aware of except that argument which, on reflection, seemed best to me. I cannot throw over the arguments I used to make in times past just because this situation has arisen: they look the same to me as before, and I respect and honor them as much as ever. You must therefore understand that if, on the present occasion, we cannot make better arguments, I will not yield to you—not even if the power of the people conjures up the bugaboos of imprisonment and death and confiscation, as though we could be scared like little children. What will be the fairest way of considering the question? Shall I return to your old argument about the opinions of men? We were saying that some of them are to be regarded, and others not. Now were we right in maintaining this before I was condemned? And has the argument which was once good now proved to be talk for the sake of talking—mere childish nonsense? That is what I want to consider with your help, Crito: whether, under my present circumstances, the argument will appear to be in any way different or not, and whether we shall subscribe to it or let it go. That argument, which, as I believe, is maintained by many persons of authority, was to the effect, as I was saying, that the opinions of some men are to be regarded, and of other men not to be regarded. Now you, Crito, are not going to die tomorrow—at least, there is no human probability of this—and therefore you are disinterested and not liable to be deceived by the circumstances in which you are placed. Tell me, then, whether I am right in saying that some opinions, and the opinions of some men only, are to be valued and that other opinions, and the opinions of other men, are not to be valued. I ask you whether I was right in maintaining this?

Cr. Certainly.

Soc. The good opinions are to be regarded, and not the bad?

Cr. Yes.

Soc. And the opinions of the wise are good, and the opinions of the unwise are bad?

Cr. Certainly.

Soc. Now what was the argument about this: does the serious athlete attend to the praise and blame and opinion of every man or of one man only—his physician or trainer, whoever he may be?

Cr. Of one man only.

Soc. And he ought to fear the censure and welcome the praise of that one only, and not of the many?

Cr. Clearly so.

Soc. And he ought to act and train and eat and drink in the way which seems good to his single master, who has understanding, rather than according to the opinion of all other men put together?

Cr. True.

Soc. And if he disobeys and disregards the opinion and approval of the one, and regards the opinion of the many who have no understanding, will he not suffer harm?

Cr. Certainly he will.

Soc. And what will the harm be: where will it be localized, and what part of the disobedient person will it affect?

Cr. Clearly, it will affect the body; that is what is destroyed.

Soc. Very good; and is not this true, Crito, of other things, which we need not separately enumerate? In questions of just and unjust, fair and foul, good and evil, which are the subjects of our present consultation, ought we to follow the opinion of the many, and to fear them, or the opinion of the one man who has understanding? Ought we not to fear and reverence him more than all the rest of the world, and, if we desert him, shall we not ruin and mutilate that principle in us which is improved by justice and deteriorated by injustice—there is such a principle?

Cr. Certainly there is, Socrates.

Soc. Take a parallel instance: if, ignoring the advice of those who have understanding, we destroy that which is improved by health and is deteriorated by disease, would life be worth having? and that which has been destroyed is—the body?

Cr. Yes.

Soc. Would life be worth living with an evil and corrupted body?

Cr. Certainly not.

Soc. And will life be worth living if that faculty which injustice damages and justice improves is ruined? Do we suppose that principle—whatever it may be in man which has to do with justice and injustice—to be inferior to the body?

Cr. Certainly not.

Soc. More honorable than the body?

Cr. Far more.

Soc. Then, my friend, we must not regard what the many say of us but what he, the one man who has understanding of just and unjust, will say and what the truth will say. And therefore you begin in error when you advise that we should regard the opinion of the many about just and unjust, good and evil, honorable and dishonorable. "Well," someone will say, "but the many can kill us."

Cr. That is plain, and a person might well say so. You are right, Socrates.

Soc. But dear Crito, the argument which we have gone over still seems as valid as before. And I should like to know whether I may say the same of another proposition—that not life, but a good life, is to be chiefly valued?

Cr. Yes, that also remains unshaken.

Soc. And a good life is equivalent to an honorable and just one—that holds also?

Cr. Yes, it does.

Soc. From these premises I proceed to argue the question whether I am justified in trying to escape without the consent of the Athenians; and if I am clearly right in escaping, then I will make the attempt, but, if not, I will abstain. The other considerations which you mention—of money and loss of character and the duty of educating one's children—are, I fear, only the doctrines of the multitude, who, if they could, would restore people to life as readily as they put them to death—and with as little reason. But since we have been forced this far by the logic of our argument, the only question which remains to be considered is whether we shall do right in giving money and thanks to those who will rescue me, and in taking a direct role in the rescue ourselves, or whether in fact we will be doing wrong. And if it appears that we will be doing wrong, then neither death nor any other calamity that follows from staying and doing nothing must be judged more important than that.

Cr. I think that you are right, Socrates. How then shall we proceed?

Soc. Let us consider the matter together, and you, either refute me if you can, and I will be convinced, or else cease, my dear friend, from repeating to me that I ought to escape against the wishes of the Athenians. It is most important to me that I act with your assent and not against your will. And now please consider whether my starting point is adequately stated, and also try to answer my questions as you think best.

Cr. I will.

Soc. Are we to say that we are never intentionally to do wrong, or that in one way we ought and in another we ought not to do wrong? Or is doing wrong always evil and dishonorable, as we often concluded in times past? Or have all those past conclusions been thrown overboard during the last few days? And have we, at our age, been earnestly discoursing with one another all our life long only to discover that we are no better than children? Or, in spite of the opinion of the many, and in spite of consequences, whether better or worse, shall we insist on the truth of what was then said, that injustice is always an evil and a dishonor to him who acts unjustly? Shall we say so or not?

Cr. Yes.

Soc. Then we must do no wrong?

Cr. Certainly not.

Soc. Nor, when injured, injure in return, as the many imagine; for we must injure no one at all?

Cr. Clearly not.

Soc. Again, Crito, may we do evil?

Cr. Surely not, Socrates.

Soc. And what of doing evil in return for evil, which is the morality of the many—is that just or not?

Cr. Not just.

Soc. For doing evil to another is the same as injuring him?

Cr. Very true.

Soc. Then we ought not to retaliate or render evil for evil to anyone, whatever evil we may have suffered from him. But I would have you consider, Crito, whether you really mean what you are saying. For this opinion has never been held, and never will be held, by any considerable number of persons; and those who are agreed and those who are not agreed upon this point have no common ground and can only despise one another when they see how widely they differ. Tell me, then, whether you agree with and assent to my first principle, that neither injury nor retaliation nor warding off evil by evil is ever right. And shall that be the premise of our argument? Or do you decline and dissent from this? For so I have ever thought, and continue to think; but, if you are of another opinion, let me hear what you have to say. If, however, you remain of the same mind as formerly, I will proceed to the next step.

Cr. You may proceed, for I have not changed my mind.

Soc. The next thing I have to say, or, rather, my next question, is this: Ought a man to do what he admits to be right, or ought he to betray the right?

Cr. He ought to do what he thinks right.

Soc. In light of that, tell me whether or not there is some victim—a particularly undeserving victim—who is hurt if I go away without persuading the city. And do we abide by what we agreed was just or not?

Cr. I cannot answer your question, Socrates, because I do not see what you are getting at.

Soc. Then consider the matter in this way: imagine that I am about to run away (you may call the proceeding by any name which you like), and the laws and the government come and interrogate me: "Tell us, Socrates," they say; "what are you up to? are you not going by an act of yours to destroy us—the laws, and the whole state—as far as in you lies? Do you imagine that a state can subsist and not be overthrown in which the decisions of law have no power but are set aside and trampled upon by individuals?" What will be our answer, Crito, to questions like these? Anyone, and especially a rhetorician, would have a good deal to say against abrogation of the law that requires a sentence to be carried out. He will argue that this law should not be set aside. Or shall we retort, "Yes; but the state has injured us and given an unjust sentence." Suppose I say that?

Cr. Very good, Socrates.

Soc. "And was that our agreement with you?" the laws would answer; "or were you to abide by the sentence of the state?" And if I were to express my astonishment at their talking this way, they would probably add:

"Take control of your astonishment and answer, Socrates—you are in the habit of asking and answering questions. Tell us: What complaint have you to make against us which justifies you in attempting to destroy us and the state? In the first place, did we not bring you into existence? Your father married your mother by our aid and brought you into the world. Say whether you have any objection to urge against those of us who regulate marriage." None, I should reply. "Or against those of us who after birth regulate the nurture and education of children, in which you also were trained? Were not the laws, which have the charge of education, right in commanding your father to train you in music and athletics?" Right, I should reply. "Well then, since you were brought into the world and nurtured and educated by us, can you deny in the first place that you are our child and slave, as your fathers were before you? And if this is true, do you really think you have the same rights as we do and that you are entitled to do to us whatever we do to you? Would you have any right to strike or revile or do any other evil to your father or your master, if you had one, because you had been struck or reviled by him or received some other evil at his hands?—you would not say this? And because we think it right to destroy you, do you think that you have any right to destroy us in return, and your country, as far as in you lies? Will you, o professor of true virtue, pretend that you are justified in this? Has a philosopher like you failed to discover that our country is more to be valued and higher and holier far than mother or father or any ancestor, and more to be regarded in the eyes of the gods and of men of understanding? Also to be soothed and gently and reverently entreated when angry, even more than a father, and either to be persuaded or, if not persuaded, to be obeyed? And when we are punished by her, whether with imprisonment or beatings, the punishment is to be endured in silence; and if she leads us to wounds or death in battle, there we follow as is right; neither may anyone yield or retreat or leave his rank, but whether in battle, or in a court of law, or in any other place, he must do what his city and his country order him, or he must change their view of what is just; and if he may do no violence to his father or mother, much less may he do violence to his country." What answer shall we make to this, Crito? Do the laws speak truly, or do they not?

Cr. I think that they do.

Soc. Then the laws will say, "Consider, Socrates, if we are speaking truly that in your present attempt you are going to do us an injury. For, having brought you into the world, and nurtured and educated you, and given you and every other citizen a share in every good which we had to give, we further proclaim to any Athenian, by the liberty which we allow him, that if he does not like us when he has come of age and has seen the ways of the city and made our acquaintance, he may go where he pleases and take his goods with him. None of us laws will stand in the way if any of you who are dissatisfied with us and the city want to go to a colony or to move anywhere else. None of us forbids anyone to go where he likes, taking his property with him. But he who has experience of the manner in which we order justice and administer the state, and still remains, has entered into an implied contract that he will do as we command him. And he who disobeys us is, as we maintain, thrice wrong: first, because in disobeying us he is disobeying his parents; secondly, because we are the authors of his education; thirdly, because he has made an agreement with us that he will duly obey our commands, but he neither obeys them nor convinces us that our commands are unjust. We show flexibility. We do not brutally demand his compliance but offer him the choice of obeying or persuading us; yet he does neither.

"These are the sorts of accusations to which, as we were saying, you, Socrates, will be exposed if you accomplish your intentions; you, above all other Athenians." Suppose now I ask, why I rather than anybody else? They might reasonably take me to task because I above all other men have acknowledged the agreement. "There is clear proof," they will say, "Socrates, that we and the city were not displeasing to you. Of all Athenians you have been the most constant resident in the city, which, as you never leave it, you may be supposed to love. For you never went out of the city either to see the games, except once, when you went to the Isthmus, or to any other place unless when you were on military service; nor did you travel as other men do. Nor had you any curiosity to know other states or their laws: your affections did not go beyond us and our state; we were your special favorites, and you acquiesced in our government of you; and here in this city you had your children, which is a proof of your satisfaction. Moreover, you might in the course of the trial, if you had liked, have fixed the penalty at banishment, and then you could have done with the city's consent what you now attempt against its will. But you pretended that you preferred death to exile and that you were not unwilling to die. And now you do not blush at the thought of your old arguments and pay no respect to us, the laws, of whom you are the destroyer, and are doing what only a miserable slave would do, running away and turning your back on the compacts and agreements by which you agreed to act as a citizen. And, first of all, answer this very question: Are we right in saying that by your actions if not in words you agreed to our terms of citizenship? Is that true or not?" How shall we answer, Crito? Must we not assent?

Cr. We cannot help it, Socrates.

Soc. Then will they not say: "You, Socrates, are breaking the covenants and agreements which you made with us. You were not compelled to agree, or tricked, or forced to make up your mind in a moment, but had a period of seventy years during which you were free to depart if you were dissatisfied with us and the agreements did not seem fair. You did not pick Sparta or Crete, whose fine government you take every opportunity to praise, or any other state of the Greek or non-Greek world. You spent less time out of Athens than men who are crippled or blind or otherwise handicapped. That shows how much more than other Athenians you valued the city and us too, its laws (for who would value a city without laws?). And will you not now abide by your agreements? You will if you listen to us, Socrates, and you will not make yourself ridiculous by leaving the city.

"For just consider: if you transgress and err in this sort of way, what good will you do either to yourself or to your friends? That your friends will be driven into exile and deprived of citizenship or will lose their property is tolerably certain. And you yourself, if you go to one of the neighboring cities, like Thebes or Megara (both being well-ordered states, of course), will come as an enemy of their government, and all patriotic citizens will eye you suspiciously as a subverter of the laws, and you will confirm in the minds of the judges the justice of their own condemnation of you. For he who is a corrupter of the laws is more than likely to be a corrupter of the young and foolish portion of mankind. Will you then flee from well-ordered cities and law-abiding men? And will life be worth living if you do that? Or will you approach them and discourse unashamedly about—about what, Socrates? Will you discourse as you did here, about how virtue and justice and institutions and laws are the best things among men? Don't you think that such behavior coming from Socrates will seem disgusting? Surely one must think so. But if you go away from well-governed states to Crito's friends in Thessaly, where there is great disorder and license, they will be charmed to hear the tale of your escape from prison, set off with ludicrous particulars of the manner in which you were wrapped in a goatskin or some other disguise and metamorphosed in the usual manner of runaways. But will there be no one to comment that in your old age, when in all probability you had only a little time left to live, you were not ashamed to violate the most sacred laws from the greedy desire of a little more life? Perhaps not, if you keep them in good temper; but if they are out of temper, you will hear many degrading things. You will live as the flatterer and slave of all men, achieving what else but the chance to feast in Thessaly, as though you had gone abroad in order to get a meal? And where will the old arguments be, about justice and virtue? Say that you wish to live for the sake of your children—you want to bring them up and educate them—will you take them into Thessaly and deprive them of

Athenian citizenship? Is this the benefit which you will confer upon them? Or are you under the impression that they will be better cared for and educated here if you are still alive, although absent from them; for your friends will take care of them? Do you fancy that, if you move to Thessaly, they will take care of them but that, if you move into the other world, they will not take care of them? No, if those who call themselves friends are good for anything, they will—to be sure, they will.

"Listen, then, Socrates, to us who have brought you up. Think not of life and children first and of justice afterwards but of justice first, so that you may defend your conduct to the rulers of the world below. For neither will you nor any that belong to you be happier or holier or juster in this life, or happier in another, if you do as Crito bids. Now you depart in innocence, a sufferer and not a doer of evil; a victim, not of the laws but of men. But if you escape, returning evil for evil and injury for injury, breaking the covenants and agreements which you have made with us and wronging those whom you ought least of all to wrong—that is to say, yourself, your friends, your country, and us—we shall be angry with you while you live, and our brethren, the laws in the world below, will receive you in no kindly spirit; for they will know that you have done your best to destroy us. Listen, then, to us and not to Crito."

This, dear Crito, is the voice I seem to hear murmuring in my ears, like the sound of the flute in the ears of the mystic; that voice, I say, is humming in my ears and prevents me from hearing any other. You must realize that you will be wasting your time if you speak against the convictions I hold at the moment. But if you think you will get anywhere, go ahead.

Cr. No, Socrates, I have nothing to say.

Soc. Then be resigned, Crito, and let us follow this course, since this is the way the god points out.

14. Plato, *Protagoras* 320c–328d: Protagoras' Myth

After the Persian Wars the tone of intellectual life in Greece was set by the sophists. These men were at the same time teachers and accomplished and showy performers. They made the circuit of the major cities, giving public lectures and, for sizable fees, individual tuition in what would now be called the disciplines of political theory, law, and rhetoric. Protagoras

From Plato, *"Protagoras" and "Meno,"* translated by W. K. C. Guthrie. Penguin Classics edition, pp. 52–60. © 1956 by W. K. C. Guthrie. Reprinted by permission of Penguin Books Ltd.

was one of the earliest and most dazzling of the sophists, yet not four consecutive lines of anything he said or wrote have been preserved. Almost everything we know of him comes to us at second hand. One of the most informative sources is Plato, who mentioned Protagoras in several dialogues and made him the central character in one.

Written early in the fourth century, the *Protagoras* is an imaginative projection back into the years before the Peloponnesian War. On one of his stopovers in Athens, the great sophist receives a visit from Socrates, who asks him whether virtue can be taught. Protagoras answers by launching into the following discourse. It is not Protagorean in the sense of being a literal report of words actually spoken on one occasion by Protagoras. But one of his lost works did deal with the subject about which he speaks here, and the presentation, with its emphasis on good entertainment, is faithful to the sophistic technique. If the speech is not something that Protagoras really did say, it is at least something he might have said. In any case, it is certainly not Plato's own view of social evolution.

Once upon a time, there existed gods but no mortal creatures. When the appointed time came for these also to be born, the gods formed them within the earth out of a mixture of earth and fire and the substances which are compounded from earth and fire. And when they were ready to bring them to the light, they charged Prometheus and Epimetheus with the task of equipping them and allotting suitable powers to each kind. Now Epimetheus begged Prometheus to allow him to do the distribution himself—"and when I have done it," he said, "you can review it." So he persuaded him and set to work. In his allotment he gave to some creatures strength without speed, and equipped the weaker kinds with speed. Some he armed with weapons, while to the unarmed he gave some other faculty and so contrived means for their preservation. To those that he endowed with smallness, he granted winged flight or a dwelling underground; to those which he increased in stature, their size itself was a protection. Thus he made his whole distribution on a principle of compensation, being careful by these devices that no species should be destroyed.

When he had sufficiently provided means of escape from mutual slaughter, he contrived their comfort against the seasons sent from Zeus, clothing them with thick hair or hard skins sufficient to ward off the winter's cold, and effective also against heat; and he planned that when they went to bed, the same coverings should serve as proper and natural bedclothes for each species. He shod them also, some with hoofs, others with hard and bloodless skin.

Next he appointed different sorts of food for them; to some the grass of the earth, to others the fruit of trees, to others roots. Some he allowed to gain their nourishment by devouring other animals, and these he made less prolific, while he bestowed fertility on their victims, and so preserved the species.

Now Epimetheus was not a particularly clever person, and before he realized it he had used up all the available powers on the brute beasts, and being left with the human race on his hands unprovided for, did not know what to do with them. While he was puzzling about this, Prometheus came to inspect the work, and found the other animals well off for everything, but man naked, unshod, unbedded, and unarmed: and already the appointed day had come, when man too was to emerge from within the earth into the daylight. Prometheus therefore, being at a loss to provide any means of salvation for man, stole from Hephaestus and Athena the gift of skill in the arts, together with fire—for without fire it was impossible for anyone to possess or use this skill—and bestowed it on man. In this way man acquired sufficient resources to keep himself alive, but had no political wisdom. This was in the keeping of Zeus, and Prometheus no longer had the right of entry to the citadel where Zeus dwelt; moreover the sentinels of Zeus were terrible; but into the dwelling shared by Athena and Hephaestus, in which they practised their art, he penetrated by stealth, and carrying off Hephaestus's art of working with fire, and the art of Athena as well, he gave them to man. Through this gift man had the means of life, but Prometheus, so the story says, thanks to Epimetheus, had later on to stand his trial for theft.

Since, then, man had a share in the portion of the gods, in the first place because of his divine kinship he alone among living creatures believed in gods, and set to work to erect altars, and images of them. Secondly, by the art which they possessed, men soon discovered articulate speech and names, and invented houses and clothes and shoes and bedding and got food from the earth.

Thus provided for, they lived at first in scattered groups; there were no cities. Consequently they were devoured by wild beasts, since they were in every respect the weaker, and their technical skill, though a sufficient aid to their nurture, did not extend to making war on the beasts, for they had not the art of politics, of which the art of war is a part. They sought therefore to save themselves by coming together and founding fortified cities, but when they gathered in communities they injured one another for want of political skill, and so scattered again and continued to be devoured. Zeus therefore, fearing the total destruction of our race, sent Hermes to impart to men the qualities of respect for others and a sense of justice, so as to bring order into our cities and create a bond of friendship and union. Hermes asked Zeus in what manner he was to bestow these gifts on men. "Shall I distribute them as the arts were distributed—that is, on the principle that one trained doctor suffices for many laymen, and so with the other experts? Shall I distribute justice and respect for their fellows in this way, or to all alike?" "To all," said Zeus. "Let all have their share. There could never be cities if only a few shared in these virtues, as in the arts. Moreover, you must lay it down as my law that if anyone is incapable of acquiring his share of these two virtues he shall be put to death as a plague to the city."

Thus it is, Socrates, and from this cause, that in a debate involving skill in building, or in any other craft, the Athenians, like other men, believe that few are capable of giving advice, and if someone outside those few volunteers to advise them, then as you say, they do not tolerate it—rightly so, in my submission. But when the subject of their counsel involves political wisdom, which must always follow the path of justice and moderation, they listen to every man's opinion, for they think that everyone must share in this kind of virtue; otherwise the state could not exist. That, Socrates, is the reason for this.

Here is another proof that I am not deceiving you in saying that all men do in fact believe that everyone shares a sense of justice and civic virtue. In specialized skills, as you say, if a man claims to be good at the flute or at some other art when he is not, people either laugh at him or are annoyed, and his family restrain him as if he were crazy. But when it comes to justice and civic virtue as a whole, even if someone is known to be wicked, yet if he publicly tells the truth about himself, his truthfulness, which in the other case was counted a virtue, is here considered madness. Everyone, it is said, ought to say he is good, whether he is or not, and whoever does not make such a claim is out of his mind; for a man cannot be without some share in justice, or he would not be human.

So much then for the point that men rightly take all alike into their counsels concerning virtue of this sort, because they believe that all have a share in it. I shall next try to demonstrate to you that they do not regard it as innate or automatic, but as acquired by instruction and taking thought. No one is angered by the faults which are believed to be due to nature or chance, nor do people rebuke or teach or punish those who exhibit them, in the hope of curing them: they simply pity them. Who would be so foolish as to treat in that way the ugly or dwarfish or weak? Everyone knows that it is nature or chance which gives this kind of characteristics to a man, both the good and the bad. But it is otherwise with the good qualities which are thought to be acquired through care and practise and instruction. It is the

absence of these, surely, and the presence of the corresponding vices, that
call forth indignation and punishment and admonition. Among these faults
are to be put injustice and irreligion and in general everything that is contrary to civic virtue. In this field indignation and admonition are universal,
evidently because of a belief that such virtue can be acquired by taking
thought or by instruction. Just consider the function of punishment, Socrates, in relation to the wrongdoer. That will be enough to show you that
men believe it possible to impart goodness. In punishing wrongdoers, no
one concentrates on the fact that a man has done wrong in the past, or punishes him on that account, unless taking blind vengeance like a beast. No,
punishment is not inflicted by a rational man for the sake of the crime that
has been committed (after all, one cannot undo what is past), but for the
sake of the future, to prevent either the same man or, by the spectacle of his
punishment, someone else, from doing wrong again. But to hold such a
view amounts to holding that virtue can be instilled by education; at
all events the punishment is inflicted as a deterrent. This then is the view
held by all who inflict it whether privately or publicly. And your fellow-
countrymen the Athenians certainly do inflict punishment and correction
on supposed wrongdoers, as do others also. This argument therefore shows
that they too think it possible to impart and teach goodness.

I think that I have now sufficiently demonstrated to you, first that your
countrymen act reasonably in accepting the advice of smith and shoe-
maker on political matters, and secondly, that they do believe goodness to
be something imparted by teaching. There remains the question which
troubles you about good men, why it is that whereas they teach their sons
the subjects that depend on instruction, and make them expert in these
things, yet in their own brand of goodness they do not make them any better than others. On this, Socrates, I will offer you a plain argument rather
than a parable as I did before. Think of it like this. Is there or is there not
some one thing in which all citizens must share, if a state is to exist at all?
In the answer to this question, if anywhere, lies the solution of your difficulty. If there is, and this one essential is not the art of building or forging
or pottery but justice and moderation and holiness of life, or to concentrate
it into a single whole, manly virtue: if, I say, it is this in which all must
share and which must enter into every man's actions whatever other occupation he chooses to learn and practise; if the one who lacks it, man, woman
or child, must be instructed and corrected until by punishment he is re-
formed; and whoever does not respond to punishment and instruction must
be expelled from the state or put to death as incurable: if all this is true, and
in these circumstances our good men teach their sons other accomplish-
ments but not this one thing, then think what extraordinary people good

men must be! We have already shown that they believe it can be taught, both publicly and privately; but although virtue can be taught and culti-vated, yet it seems they have their sons instructed in other arts, ignorance of which is no matter for capital punishment, but although if they are left ignorant of virtue and morally uncultivated they may be punished by death or exile—and not only death but alienation of property and in a word the ruin of their estates—are we to suppose that they neglect this side of their education? Don't they rather bestow every care and attention upon it? Of course they do, Socrates. They teach and admonish them from earliest childhood and throughout their lives. As soon as a child can understand what is said to him, nurse, mother, tutor, and the father himself vie with each other to make him as good as possible, instructing him through every-thing he does or says, pointing out: "this is right and that is wrong, this honourable and that disgraceful, this holy, that impious: do this, don't do that." If he is obedient, well and good. If not, they straighten him with threats and beatings, like a warped and twisted plank.

Later on, when they send the children to school, their instructions to the masters lay much more emphasis on good behaviour than on letters or mu-sic. The teachers take good care of this, and when boys have learned their letters and are ready to understand the written word as formerly the spoken, they set the works of good poets before them on their desks to read and make them learn them by heart, poems containing much admonition and many stories, eulogies, and panegyrics of the good men of old, so that the child may be inspired to imitate them and long to be like them.

The music-masters by analogous methods instill self-control and deter the young from evil-doing; and when they have learned to play the lyre, they teach them the works of good poets of another sort, namely the lyri-cal, which they accompany on the lyre, familiarizing the minds of the chil-dren with the rhythms and melodies. By this means they become more civilised, more balanced, and better adjusted in themselves and so more capable in whatever they say or do; for rhythm and harmonious adjustment are essential to the whole of human life.

Over and above this, they are sent to a trainer, so that a good mind may have a good body to serve it, and no one be forced by physical weakness to play the coward in war and other ordeals.

All this is done by those best able to do it—that is, by the wealthy—and it is their sons who start their education at the earliest age and continue it the longest. When they have finished with teachers, the State compels them to learn the laws and use them as a pattern for their life, lest left to them-selves they should drift aimlessly. You know how, when children are not yet good at writing, the writing-master traces outlines with the pencil before giving them the slate, and makes them follow the lines as a guide in their own writing; well, similarly the State sets up the laws, which are inventions of good lawgivers of ancient times, and compels the citizens to rule and be ruled in accordance with them. Whoever strays outside the lines, it punishes; and the name given to this punishment both among yourselves and in many other places is correction, intimating that the penalty corrects or guides.

Seeing then that all this care is taken over virtue, both individually and by the State, are you surprised that virtue should be teachable, and puzzled to know whether it is? There is nothing to be surprised at. The wonder would be if it were not teachable.

Why then, you ask, do many sons of good men turn out worthless? I will tell you this too. It is nothing surprising, if what I said earlier was true, that this faculty, virtue, is something in which no one may be a layman if a state is to exist at all. If it is as I say—and most assuredly it is—consider the matter with the substitution of any art you like. Suppose a state could not exist unless we were all flute-players to the best of our ability, and everyone taught everyone else that art both privately and publicly, and scolded the bad flute-player, and no one held back on this subject any more than anyone now begrudges information on what is right and lawful or makes a secret of it as of certain other techniques. After all, it is to our advantage that our neighbour should be just and virtuous, and therefore everyone gladly talks about it to everyone else and instructs them in justice and the law. If then, as I say, it were so with flute-playing, and we all showed equal eagerness and willingness to teach one another, do you think, Socrates, that the sons of good players would become good players in their turn any more than the sons of bad ones? Not so, I think, but whoever had a son with the greatest natural talent for the flute, his son would rise to fame, and a son without his talent would remain in obscurity. The son of a good performer would often be a poor one, and vice versa; but at any rate all would be good enough in comparison with someone who knew nothing of flute-playing at all.

Now apply this analogy to our present condition. The man who in a civilised and humane society appears to you the most wicked must be thought just—a practitioner, as one might say, of justice—if no one has to judge him in comparison with men who have neither education nor courts of justice nor laws nor any constraint compelling them to be continually heedful of virtue—savages in fact like those whom the playwright Pherecrates brought on to the stage at last year's Lenaea. If you found yourself among such people—people like the man-haters of his chorus—you would be only too glad to meet a Eurybatus and a Phrynondas, and would bitterly regret the very depravity of our own society. But as it is you are spoilt, Socrates, in that all are teachers of virtue to the best of their ability, and so

you think that no one is. In the same way, if you asked who teaches the
Greek language, you would not find anyone; and again, if you looked for a
teacher of the sons of our artisans in the craft which they have in fact
learned from their father to the best of their ability, and from his friends in
the same trade, there again I don't think it would be easy to point to a master, though in the case of a complete tiro it would be easy enough. Thus it is
with virtue and everything else, so that if we can find someone only a little
better than the others at advancing us on the road to virtue, we must be
content. My claim is that I am one of these, rather better than anyone else
at helping a man to acquire a good and noble character, worthy indeed of
the fee which I charge and even more, as my pupils themselves agree. On
this account I have adopted the following method of assessing my payment.
Anyone who comes to learn from me may either pay the fee I ask for or, if
he prefers, go to a temple, state on oath what he believes to be the worth of
my instruction, and deposit that amount.

There, Socrates, you have both the parable and the argument by which I
have sought to show that virtue is teachable and that the Athenians believe
it to be so, and that at the same time it is quite natural for the sons of good
fathers to turn out good for nothing, and vice versa. Why, even the sons of
Polyclitus, who are contemporaries of Paralus and Xanthippus here, cannot hold a candle to their father, nor can the sons of many other craftsmen.
But it is too early to bring such a charge against these two: they are young,
and there is still promise in them.

15. Plato, *Republic* 5.471c–473e: The Philosopher-Ruler

This brief passage of Plato's *Republic* introduces the philosopher-rulers.
The first four books of the dialogue make no mention of them. The first
book has the form of an early Socratic dialogue: it discusses a virtue, on
this occasion justice, and comes to no definite conclusion. At the beginning of the second book Glaucon and Adeimantus challenge Socrates to
demonstrate that justice is preferable to injustice and that it is preferable
in itself, without regard for any adventitious consequences, good or bad.
In reply, Socrates sketches a polis, on the grounds that it will be easier to
see justice there than in an individual, and duly "finds" justice, self-
control, bravery, and wisdom, first in the polis, then in the individual. In
the polis, each person is to perform only the task for which he is naturally fitted; and, it appears, justice is present when the wise rule the polis,

From Plato, *The Republic*, translated by Desmond Lee. Penguin Classics edition, 2d rev.
ed., pp. 231–33. © 1955, 1974, by H. D. P. Lee. Reprinted by permission of Penguin Books
Ltd.

the brave defend it, and the remainder of the citizens go about their appointed tasks. Nothing so far has suggested that the wise have a wisdom that differs significantly from that of a Solon or a Lycurgus; but Plato now introduces the theory of Forms or Ideas, whose nature and function is later indicated by the allegories of the Sun, the Line, and the Cave. It is the ability to perceive the Forms, the result of arduous education, that defines the philosophers of the *Republic* and also constitutes the basis of Socrates' claim that only poleis ruled by such philosophers will be truly flourishing. Their knowledge of the Forms, the highest of which are objective truths of value, will render the philosophers reliably just themselves and capable of endowing the polis with justice and other desirable excellences. Plato believes that such knowledge is necessary, but he does not believe that it is sufficient: the philosopher-rulers' virtues, in the everyday sense of the word, have been abundantly tested at an earlier stage of their education, and care has been taken to familiarize them with the practical aspects of war and government. In the following passage, the first speaker is Glaucus; the second, Socrates.

"But it seems to me, Socrates, that if we let you go on like this you will forget all about your promise to prove that the state we have described is a practical possibility, and if so how; all you've just been saying has merely been putting the question off. I'll admit that your state would be ideal if it existed, and I'll fill in the gaps in your description myself. I know that the mutual loyalty the citizens would feel because they know they can call each other brothers, fathers, and sons, would make them most formidable enemies; and that the presence of their women on campaign, whether they fought with them or acted as a reserve, would make them altogether invincible, because of the panic it would cause in their enemies and the support it would give in case of need; and I can see how many domestic advantages they would have. I grant all this, and a thousand other things too, *if* our state existed, and I don't want to hear any more details. Let us now concentrate on the job of proving *that* it can exist and *how* it can exist."

"This is a very sudden attack," I countered, "and you've no sympathy with my delays. I've just escaped two waves; but the third, which you are trying to bring on me now, is the biggest and the most difficult of the three, though you may not know it. When you have seen and heard it, you will forgive me for the very natural hesitation which made me afraid to put forward and examine such a paradoxical theory."

"The more of these excuses we hear," he replied, "the less likely we are to let you off explaining how our state can be realised. Get on and don't waste time."

"Well," I said, "perhaps I ought to remind you first of all that we started our discussion by trying to find a definition of justice and injustice."

"Yes—what of it?" he asked.

"I was only going to ask whether, when we find out what justice is, we shall require the just man to answer the description exactly, without any modification? Or shall we be content if he approximates to it pretty closely and has more of it about him than other men?"

"That will content us."

"Then we were looking for an ideal when we tried to define justice and injustice, and to describe what the perfectly just or perfectly unjust man would be like if he ever existed. By looking at these perfect patterns and the measure of happiness or unhappiness they would enjoy, we force ourselves to admit that the nearer we approximate to them the more nearly we share their lot. That was our purpose, rather than to show that they could be realised in practise, was it not?"

"That is quite true."

"If a painter, then, draws an idealized picture of a man, complete to the last detail, is he any the worse painter because he cannot point to a real original?"

"No, certainly not."

"But haven't we been painting a word-picture of an ideal state?"

"True."

"Is our picture any the worse drawn, then, because we can't show how it can be realised in fact?"

"No."

"That, then, is the truth of the matter. But if I'm to go on, to oblige you, and show how and under what conditions we can get nearest our ideal, you must admit that the same principles apply."

"What principles?"

"Does practise ever square with theory? Is it not in the nature of things that, whatever people think, practise should fall short of the precision of theory? What do you think?"

"I agree."

"Then don't insist on my showing that every detail of our description can be realised in practise, but grant that we shall have met your demand that the ideal should be realised, if we are able to find the conditions under which a state can approximate most closely to it. Will you be content with that? I would."

"And so will I."

"The next thing, I suppose, is to try to show what fault it is in the constitutions of existing states that prevents them from being run like ours, and what is the least change that would bring them into conformity with it—a single change if possible, failing that two, or as few and as small as may be."

"Certainly."

"I think we can show that the necessary transformation can be effected by a single change," I said, "but it's hardly a small or easy one, though it is possible."

"Tell us what it is."

"I'm now facing what we called the biggest wave," I replied. "I'll tell you what it is, even if it swamps me in a surge of laughter and I'm drowned in ridicule; so listen to what I'm going to say."

"Go on."

"The society we have described can never grow into a reality or see the light of day, and there will be no end to the troubles of states, or indeed, my dear Glaucon, of humanity itself, till philosophers become kings in this world, or till those we now call kings and rulers really and truly become philosophers, and political power and philosophy thus come into the same hands, while the many natures now content to follow either to the exclusion of the other are forcibly debarred from doing so. This is what I have hesitated to say so long, knowing what a paradox it would sound; for it is not easy to see that there is no other road to happiness, either for society or the individual."

Aristotle

Aristotle was born in Stagira, a small polis in northern Greece, in 384/
383 B.C. His father was court physician at Pella in Macedon, which was
still regarded as backward and barbarous by most Greeks. At the age of
seventeen Aristotle was sent by his guardian, his father being now dead,
to study at Plato's Academy, an institution that had been founded at about
the time of Aristotle's birth. Aristotle's enrollment in the Academy is an
incidental testimony to the prestige that the novel and still relatively
young school had already acquired and also an indication that Athens,
soon to lose permanently any claim to be a significant center of political
power, was on its way to becoming the capital of the Greek philosophical
world.

Aristotle remained in the Academy until the death of Plato. When
Speusippus succeeded Plato as head of the school, Aristotle left Athens
for Assos, a polis near Troy, later moving to Mytilene, on the island
of Lesbos. His study of biology seems to belong to this period. In
343/342 B.C. he was summoned by Philip to the Macedonian court as
tutor to his son, the young Alexander. Returning to Athens, Aristotle
founded the Lyceum in 335 B.C. Three years earlier, the victory of Philip
and Alexander at the battle of Chaeronea had ended the freedom of the
Greeks; the year before, Philip of Macedon had been assassinated; in
335, Alexander was organizing his forces for the expedition against Persia, which began the next year. During the next decade, Alexander con-
quered the whole of the known world to the east. The Athens in which
Aristotle was working at this time was under the sway of the Macedo-
nians, with whom Aristotle was associated: he had been Alexander's tutor, and throughout his eastern campaigns Alexander had zoological and
other specimens sent back to Aristotle. It is not surprising that on the

death of Alexander in 323 B.C. Aristotle found it prudent to leave Athens for Chalcis in Euboea, where he died the following year.

The relationship between the thought of Plato and that of Aristotle and the development of Aristotle's thought while he was a member of the Academy and later are topics too complex and controversial to be discussed here. Those interested are referred to the appropriate works cited in the bibliography.

16. Aristotle, *The Constitution of Athens*

The Constitution of Athens was written by Aristotle or a member of his school between about 335 and 322 B.C. It was rediscovered at the end of the nineteenth century, the only example to survive out of 158 constitutional surveys Aristotle is said to have produced. Ancient lists of his works suggest that the constitutions were arranged by categories—democracies, oligarchies, tyrannies, and aristocracies—and that may be a clue to his purpose in assembling the collection.

In any case, it is clear that the *Constitution of Athens* was conceived as the case study of an evolving democracy. It falls into two parts. Chapters 1–41 are historical, tracing the gradual democratization of the Athenian polity; its growth is analogous to that of a living organism, which develops until it has fulfilled the potential of its biological form. Chapters 42–69 are descriptive, showing how the different parts of the government functioned in the latter half of the fourth century B.C. The beginning of the study, covering the period from the kings of Athens to the late seventh century, is lost. The text picks up with the trial of the Alcmaeonids, who brought a curse on themselves and their city by murdering Cylon and his fellow-conspirators after they had claimed sanctuary (see, in document 7, the second selection from Herodotus' *History*, "The Overthrow of the Pisistratids and the Organization of the Cleisthenic Democracy").

---

1. . . . [They were tried] by a court empanelled from among the noble families, and sworn upon the sacrifices. The part of accuser was taken by

Translated by Frederic G. Kenyon in volume 10 of *The Oxford Translation of Aristotle*, edited by W. D. Ross. Oxford: Oxford University Press, 1921. Reprinted by permission of Oxford University Press.

In this text the volume editors have added the dates in square brackets and have substituted English words in several places where the translator had used transliterated Greek terms. In chapters 63–65 the translation has been corrected on the basis of new archeological information that clarifies the allotment system.

Myron. They were found guilty of the sacrilege, and their bodies were cast out of their graves and their race banished for evermore. In view of this expiation, Epimenides the Cretan performed a purification of the city.

2. After this event there was contention for a long time between the upper classes and the populace. Not only was the constitution at this time oligarchical in every respect, but the poorer classes, men, women, and children, were the serfs of the rich. They were known as clients [Pelatae] and also as Sixth-parters [Hectemori], because they cultivated the lands of the rich at the rent thus indicated. The whole country was in the hands of a few persons, and if the tenants failed to pay their rent they were liable to be haled into slavery, and their children with them. All loans were secured upon the debtor's person, a custom which prevailed until the time of Solon, who was the first to appear as the champion of the people. But the hardest and bitterest part of the constitution in the eyes of the masses was their state of serfdom. Not but what they were also discontented with every other feature of their lot; for, to speak generally, they had no part nor share in anything.

3. Now the ancient constitution, as it existed before the time of Draco, was organized as follows. The magistrates were elected according to qualifications of birth and wealth. At first they governed for life, but subsequently for terms of ten years. The first magistrates, both in date and in importance, were the King, the Polemarch [= war-leader], and the Archon. The earliest of these offices was that of the King, which existed from ancestral antiquity. To this was added, secondly, the office of Polemarch, on account of some of the kings proving feeble in war; for it was on this account that Ion was invited to accept the post on an occasion of pressing need. The last of the three offices was that of the Archon, which most authorities state to have come into existence in the time of Medon. Others assign it to the time of Acastus, and adduce as proof the fact that the nine Archons swear to execute their oaths "as in the days of Acastus," which seems to suggest that it was in his time that the descendants of Codrus retired from the kingship in return for the prerogatives conferred upon the Archon. Whichever way it be, the difference in date is small; but that it was the last of these magistracies to be created is shown by the fact that the Archon has no part in the ancestral sacrifices, as the King and the Polemarch have, but exclusively in those of later origin. So it is only at a comparatively late date that the office of Archon has become of great importance, through the dignity conferred by these later additions. The Regulators [Thesmothetae] were appointed many years afterwards, when these offices had already become annual, with the object that they might publicly record all legal decisions, and act as guardians of them with a view to de-

termining the issues between litigants. Accordingly their office, alone of those which have been mentioned, was never of more than annual duration.

Such, then, is the relative chronological precedence of these offices. At that time the nine Archons did not all live together. The King occupied the building now known as the Bucolium, near the town hall, as may be seen from the fact that even to the present day the marriage of the King's wife to Dionysus takes place there. The Archon lived in the town hall, the Polemarch in the Epilyceum. The latter building was formerly called the Polemarcheum, but after Epilycus, during his term of office as Polemarch, had rebuilt it and fitted it up, it was called the Epilyceum. The Regulators occupied the Thesmotheteum. In the time of Solon, however, they all came together into the Thesmotheteum. They had power to decide cases finally on their own authority, not, as now, merely to hold preliminary hearing. Such then was the arrangement of the magistracies. The Council of Areopagus had as its constitutionally assigned duty the protection of the laws; but in point of fact it administered the greater and most important part of the government of the state, and inflicted personal punishments and fines summarily upon all who misbehaved themselves. This was the natural consequence of the facts that the Archons were elected under qualifications of birth and wealth, and that the Areopagus was composed of those who had served as Archons; for which latter reason the membership of the Areopagus is the only office which has continued to be a life-magistracy to the present day.

4.   Such was, in outline, the first constitution, but not very long after the events above recorded, in the archonship of Aristaichmus [621/620 B.C.], Draco enacted his ordinances. Now his constitution had the following form. The franchise was given to all who could furnish themselves with a military equipment. The nine Archons and the Treasurers were elected by this body from persons possessing an unencumbered property of not less than ten minas, the less important officials from those who could furnish themselves with a military equipment, and the generals [Strategi] and commanders of the cavalry [Hipparchi] from those who could show an unencumbered property of not less than a hundred minas, and had children born in lawful wedlock over ten years of age. These officers were required to hold to bail the Presiders [Prytanes], the Generals, and the Cavalry Commanders of the preceding year until their accounts had been audited, taking four securities of the same class as that to which the Generals and the Cavalry Commanders belonged. There was also to be a Council, consisting of four hundred and one members, elected by lot from among those who possessed the franchise. Both for this and for the other magistracies the lot was cast among those who were over thirty years of age; and no one

might hold office twice until every one else had had his turn, after which they were to cast the lot afresh. If any member of the Council failed to attend when there was a sitting of the Council or of the Assembly, he paid a fine, to the amount of three drachmas if he was a Pentacosiomedimnus, two if he was a Knight, and one if he was a Zeugites.[1] The Council of Areopagus was guardian of the laws, and kept watch over the magistrates to see that they executed their offices in accordance with the laws. Any person who felt himself wronged might lay an information before the Council of Areopagus, on declaring what law was broken by the wrong done to him. But, as has been said before, loans were secured upon the persons of the debtors, and the land was in the hands of a few.

5.   Since such, then, was the organization of the constitution, and the many were in slavery to the few, the people rose against the upper class. The strife was keen, and for a long time the two parties were ranged in hostile camps against one another, till at last, by common consent, they appointed Solon to be mediator and Archon, and committed the whole constitution to his hands. The immediate occasion of his appointment was his poem, which begins with the words:

> I behold, and within my heart deep sadness has claimed its place,
> As I mark the oldest home of the ancient Ionian race
> Slain by the sword.

In this poem he fights and disputes on behalf of each party in turn against the other, and finally he advises them to come to terms and put an end to the quarrel existing between them. By birth and reputation Solon was one of the foremost men of the day, but in wealth and position he was of the middle class, as is generally agreed, and is, indeed, established by his own evidence in these poems, where he exhorts the wealthy not to be grasping.

> But you who have store of good, who are sated and overflow,
> Restrain your swelling soul, and still it and keep it low:
> Let the heart that is great within you be trained a lowlier way;
> You shall not have all at your will, and we will not for ever obey.

Indeed, he constantly fastens the blame of the conflict on the rich; and accordingly at the beginning of the poem he says that he fears "the love of wealth and an overweening mind," evidently meaning that it was through these that the quarrel arose.

6.   As soon as he was at the head of affairs, Solon liberated the people once and for all, by prohibiting all loans on the security of the debtor's per-

---

1. The terms are explained in chapter 7, below.

son: and in addition he made laws by which he cancelled all debts, public and private. This measure is commonly called the Unburdening [Seisachtheia], since thereby the people had their loads removed from them. In connexion with it some persons try to traduce the character of Solon. It so happened that, when he was about to enact the Unburdening, he communicated his intention to some members of the upper class, whereupon, as the partisans of the popular party say, his friends stole a march on him; while those who wish to attack his character maintain that he too had a share in the fraud himself. For these persons borrowed money and bought up a large amount of land, and so when, a short time afterwards, all debts were cancelled, they became wealthy; and this, they say, was the origin of the families which were afterwards looked on as having been wealthy from primeval times. However, the story of the popular party is by far the most probable. A man who was so moderate and public-spirited in all his other actions, that when it was within his power to put his fellow-citizens beneath his feet and establish himself as tyrant, he preferred instead to incur the hostility of both parties by placing his honour and the general welfare above his personal aggrandisement, is not likely to have consented to defile his hands by such a petty and palpable fraud. That he had this absolute power is, in the first place, indicated by the desperate condition of the country; moreover, he mentions it himself repeatedly in his poems, and it is universally admitted. We are therefore bound to consider this accusation to be false.

7.   Next Solon drew up a constitution and enacted new laws; and the ordinances of Draco ceased to be used, with the exception of those relating to murder. The laws were inscribed on the wooden stands, and set up in the King's Porch, and all swore to obey them; and the nine Archons made oath upon the stone, declaring that they would dedicate a golden statue if they should transgress any of them. This is the origin of the oath to that effect which they take to the present day. Solon ratified his laws for a hundred years; and the following was the fashion in which he organized the constitution. He divided the population according to property into four classes, just as it had been divided before, namely, Pentacosiomedimni, Knights, Zeugitae, and Thetes. The various magistracies, namely, the nine Archons, the Treasurers, the Commissioners for Public Contracts [Poletae], the Eleven, and the Exchequer Clerks [Colacretae], he assigned to the Pentacosiomedimni, the Knights, and the Zeugitae, giving offices to each class in proportion to the value of their rateable property.[2] To those who ranked

2. "Rateable property" here, like the expression "rated in the city" in chapter 39, refers to the official valuation placed on every citizen's property. This valuation determined not only the amount of taxes the citizen had to pay but also, in most cities, the level at which he could participate in government.

among the Thetes he gave nothing but a place in the Assembly and in the juries. A man had to rank as a Pentacosiomedimnus if he made, from his own land, five hundred measures, whether liquid or solid. Those ranked as Knights who made three hundred measures, or, as some say, those who were able to maintain a horse. In support of the latter definition they adduce the name of the class, which may be supposed to be derived from this fact, and also some votive offerings of early times; for in the Acropolis there is a votive offering, a statue of Diphilus, bearing this inscription:

> The son Diphilus, Anthemion hight,
> Raised from the Thetes and become a Knight,
> Did to the gods this sculptured charger bring,
> For his promotion a thank-offering.

And a horse stands in evidence beside the man, implying that this was what was meant by belonging to the rank of Knight. At the same time it seems reasonable to suppose that this class, like the Pentacosiomedimni, was defined by the possession of an income of a certain number of measures. Those ranked as Zeugitae who made two hundred measures, liquid or solid; and the rest ranked as Thetes, and were not eligible for any office. Hence it is that even at the present day, when a candidate for any office is asked to what class he belongs, no one would think of saying that he belonged to the Thetes.

8.   The elections to the various offices Solon enacted should be by lot, out of candidates selected by each of the tribes. Each tribe selected ten candidates for the nine archonships, and among these the lot was cast. Hence it is still the custom for each tribe to choose ten candidates by lot, and then the lot is again cast among these. A proof that Solon regulated the elections to office according to the property classes may be found in the law still in force with regard to the Treasurers, which enacts that they shall be chosen from the Pentacosiomedimni. Such was Solon's legislation with respect to the nine Archons; whereas in early times the Council of Areopagus summoned suitable persons according to its own judgement and appointed them for the year to the several offices. There were four tribes, as before, and four tribe-kings. Each tribe was divided into three Trittyes [= Thirds], with twelve Naucraries in each; and the Naucraries had officers of their own, called Naucrari, whose duty it was to superintend the current receipts and expenditure. Hence, among the laws of Solon now obsolete, it is repeatedly written that the Naucrari are to receive and to spend out of the Naucraric fund. Solon also appointed a Council of four hundred, a hundred from each tribe; but he assigned to the Council of the Areopagus the duty of superintending the laws, acting as before as the guardian of the constitution in general. It kept watch over the affairs of the state in most of the

more important matters, and corrected offenders, with full powers to inflict either fines or personal punishment. The money received in fines it brought up into the Acropolis, without assigning the reason for the mulct. It also tried those who conspired for the overthrow of the state, Solon having enacted a process of impeachment to deal with such offenders. Further, since he saw the state often engaged in internal disputes, while many of the citizens from sheer indifference accepted whatever might turn up, he made a law with express reference to such persons, enacting that any one who, in a time of civil factions, did not take up arms with either party, should lose his rights as a citizen and cease to have any part in the state.

9.   Such, then, was his legislation concerning the magistracies. There are three points in the constitution of Solon which appear to be its most democratic features: first and most important, the prohibition of loans on the security of the debtor's person; secondly, the right of every person who so willed to claim redress on behalf of any one to whom wrong was being done; thirdly, the institution of the appeal to the jury-courts; and it is to this last, they say, that the masses have owed their strength most of all, since, when democracy is master of the voting-power, it is master of the constitution. Moreover, since the laws were not drawn up in simple and explicit terms (but like the one concerning inheritances and wards of state), disputes inevitably occurred, and the courts had to decide in every matter, whether public or private. Some persons in fact believe that Solon deliberately made the laws indefinite, in order that the final decision might be in the hands of the people. This, however, is not probable, and the reason no doubt was that it is impossible to attain ideal perfection when framing a law in general terms; for we must judge of his intentions, not from the actual results in the present day, but from the general tenor of the rest of his legislation.

10.   These seem to be the democratic features of his laws; but in addition, before the period of his legislation, he carried through his abolition of debts, and after it his increase in the standards of weights and measures, and of the currency. During his administration the measures were made larger than those of Pheidon, and the mina, which previously had a standard of seventy drachmas, was raised to the full hundred. The standard coin in earlier times was the two-drachma piece. He also made weights corresponding with the coinage, sixty-three minas going to the talent; and the odd three minas were distributed among the staters and the other values.

11.   When he had completed his organization of the constitution in the manner that has been described, he found himself beset by people coming to him and harassing him concerning his laws, criticizing here and questioning there, till, as he wished neither to alter what he had decided on nor

yet to be an object of ill will to everyone by remaining in Athens, he set off on a journey to Egypt, with the combined objects of trade and travel, giving out that he should not return for ten years. He considered that there was no call for him to expound the laws personally, but that every one should obey them just as they were written. Moreover, his position at this time was unpleasant. Many members of the upper class had been estranged from him on account of his abolition of debts, and both parties were alienated through their disappointment at the condition of things which he had created. The mass of the people had expected him to make a complete redistribution of all property, and the upper class hoped he would restore everything to its former position, or, at any rate, make but a small change. Solon, however, had resisted both classes. He might have made himself a despot by attaching himself to whichever party he chose, but he preferred, though at the cost of incurring the enmity of both, to be the saviour of his country and the ideal lawgiver.

12.   The truth of this view of Solon's policy is established alike by common consent, and by the mention he has himself made of the matter in his poems. Thus:

I gave to the mass of the people such rank as befitted their need,
I took not away their honour, and I granted naught to their greed;
While those who were rich in power, who in wealth were glorious and great,
I bethought me that naught should befall them unworthy their splendour and
    state;
So I stood with my shield outstretched, and both were safe in its sight,
And I would not that either should triumph, when the triumph was not with
    right.

Again he declares how the mass of the people ought to be treated:

But thus will the people best the voice of their leaders obey,
When neither too slack is the rein, nor violence holdeth the sway;
For indulgence breedeth a child, the presumption that spurns control,
When riches too great are poured upon men of unbalanced soul.

And again elsewhere he speaks about the persons who wished to redistribute the land:

So they came in search of plunder, and their cravings knew no bound,
Every one among them deeming endless wealth would here be found,
And that I with glozing smoothness hid a cruel mind within.
Fondly then and vainly dreamt they; now they raise an angry din,
And they glare askance in anger, and the light within their eyes
Burns with hostile flames upon me. Yet therein no justice lies.
All I promised, fully wrought I with the gods at hand to cheer,
Naught beyond in folly ventured. Never to my soul was dear

With a tyrant's force to govern, nor to see the good and base
Side by side in equal portion share the rich home of our race.

Once more he speaks of the abolition of debts and of those who before were in servitude, but were released owing to the Unburdening:

Of all the aims for which I summoned forth
The people, was there one I compassed not?
Thou, when slow time brings justice in its train,
O mighty mother of the Olympian gods,
Dark Earth, thou best canst witness, from whose breast
I swept the pillars broadcast planted there,
And made thee free, who hadst been slave of yore.
And many a man whom fraud or law had sold
Far from his god-built land, an outcast slave,
I brought again to Athens; yea, and some,
Exiles from home through debt's oppressive load,
Speaking no more the dear Athenian tongue,
But wandering far and wide, I brought again;
And those that here in vilest slavery
Crouched 'neath a master's frown, I set them free.
Thus might and right were yoked in harmony,
Since by the force of law I won my ends
And kept my promise. Equal laws I gave
To evil and to good, with even hand
Drawing straight justice for the lot of each.
But had another held the goad as I,
One in whose heart was guile and greediness,
He had not kept the people back from strife.
For had I granted, now what pleased the one,
Then what their foes devised in counterpoise,
Of many a man this state had been bereft.
Therefore I showed my might on every side,
Turning at bay like wolf among the hounds.

And again he reviles both parties for their grumblings in the times that followed:

Nay, if one must lay blame where blame is due,
Wer't not for me, the people ne'er had set
Their eyes upon these blessings e'en in dreams:—
While greater men, the men of wealthier life,
Should praise me and should court me as their friend.

For had any other man, he says, received this exalted post,

He had not kept the people back, nor ceased
Till he had robbed the richness of the milk.

But I stood forth a landmark in the midst,
And barred the foes from battle.

13.   Such, then, were Solon's reasons for his departure from the country. After his retirement the city was still torn by divisions. For four years,
indeed, they lived in peace; but in the fifth year after Solon's government
they were unable to elect an Archon on account of their dissensions, and
again four years later they elected no Archon for the same reason. Subsequently, after a similar period had elapsed, Damasias was elected Archon
[for 582/581 B.C.], and he governed for two years and two months, until he
was forcibly expelled from his office. After this it was agreed, as a compro-
mise, to elect ten Archons, five from the Aristocrats, three from the Peasants, and two from the Workers; and they ruled for the year following
Damasias. It is clear from this that the Archon was at the time the magistrate who possessed the greatest power, since it is always in connexion with
this office that conflicts are seen to arise. But altogether they were in a continual state of internal disorder. Some found the cause and justification of
their discontent in the abolition of debts, because thereby they had been
reduced to poverty; others were dissatisfied with the political constitution,
because it had undergone a revolutionary change; while with others the
motive was found in personal rivalries among themselves. The parties at
this time were three in number. First there was the party of the Shore, led
by Megacles the son of Alcmeon, which was considered to aim at a moderate form of government; then there were the men of the Plain, who desired
an oligarchy and were led by Lycurgus; and thirdly there were the men of
the Highlands, at the head of whom was Pisistratus, who was looked on as
an extreme democrat. This latter party was reinforced by those who had
been deprived of the debts due to them, from motives of poverty, and by
those who were not of pure descent, from motives of personal apprehen-
sion. A proof of this is seen in the fact that after the tyranny was overthrown a revision was made of the citizen-roll, on the ground that many
persons were partaking in the franchise without having a right to it. The
names given to the respective parties were derived from the districts in
which they held their lands.
14.   Pisistratus had the reputation of being an extreme democrat, and
he also had distinguished himself greatly in the war with Megara. Taking
advantage of this, he wounded himself, and by representing that his injuries had been inflicted on him by his political rivals, he persuaded the
people, through a motion proposed by Aristion, to grant him a bodyguard.
After he had got these "club-bearers," as they were called, he made an attack with them on the people and seized the Acropolis. This happened in
the archonship of Comeas [561/560 B.C.], thirty-one years after the legisla-

tion of Solon. It is related that, when Pisistratus asked for his bodyguard, Solon opposed the request, and declared that in so doing he proved himself wiser than half the people and braver than the rest,—wiser than those who did not see that Pisistratus designed to make himself tyrant, and braver than those who saw it and kept silence. But when all his words availed nothing he carried forth his armour and set it up in front of his house, saying that he had helped his country so far as lay in his power (he was already a very old man), and that he called on all others to do the same. Solon's exhortations, however, proved fruitless, and Pisistratus assumed the sovereignty. His administration was more like a constitutional government than the rule of a tyrant; but before his power was firmly established, the adherents of Megacles and Lycurgus made a coalition and drove him out. This took place in the archonship of Hegesias [556/555 B.C.], five years after the first establishment of his rule. Eleven years later Megacles, being in difficulties in a party struggle, again opened negotiations with Pisistratus, proposing that the latter should marry his daughter; and on these terms he brought him back to Athens, by a very primitive and simpleminded device. He first spread abroad a rumour that Athena was bringing back Pisistratus, and then, having found a woman of great stature and beauty, named Phye (according to Herodotus, of the deme of Paeania, but as others say a Thracian flower-seller of the deme of Collytus), he dressed her in a garb resembling that of the goddess and brought her into the city with Pisistratus. The latter drove in on a chariot with the woman beside him, and the inhabitants of the city, struck with awe, received him with adoration.

15.   In this manner did his first return take place. He did not, however, hold his power long, for about six years after his return he was again expelled. He refused to treat the daughter of Megacles as his wife, and being afraid, in consequence, of a combination of the two opposing parties, he retired from the country. First he led a colony to a place called Rhaicelus, in the region of the Thermaic gulf; and thence he passed to the country in the neighbourhood of Mt. Pangaeus. Here he acquired wealth and hired mercenaries; and not till ten years had elapsed did he return to Eretria and make an attempt to recover the government by force. In this he had the assistance of many allies, notably the Thebans and Lygdamis of Naxos, and also the Knights who held the supreme power in the constitution of Eretria. After his victory in the battle at Pallene he captured Athens, and when he had disarmed the people he at last had his tyranny securely established, and was able to take Naxos and set up Lygdamis as ruler there. He effected the disarmament of the people in the following manner. He ordered a parade in full armour in the Theseum, and began to make a speech to the people. He spoke for a short time, until the people called out that

they could not hear him, whereupon he bade them come up to the entrance of the Acropolis, in order that his voice might be better heard. Then, while he continued to speak to them at great length, men whom he had appointed for the purpose collected the arms and locked them up in the chambers of the Theseum hard by, and came and made a signal to him that it was done. Pisistratus accordingly, when he had finished the rest of what he had to say, told the people also what had happened to their arms; adding that they were not to be surprised or alarmed, but go home and attend to their private affairs, while he would himself for the future manage all the business of the state.

16.   Such was the origin and such the vicissitudes of the tyranny of Pisistratus. His administration was temperate, as has been said before, and more like constitutional government than a tyranny. Not only was he in every respect humane and mild and ready to forgive those who offended, but, in addition, he advanced money to the poorer people to help them in their labours, so that they might make their living by agriculture. In this he had two objects, first that they might not spend their time in the city but might be scattered over all the face of the country, and secondly that, being moderately well off and occupied with their own business, they might have neither the wish nor the time to attend to public affairs. At the same time his revenues were increased by the thorough cultivation of the country, since he imposed a tax of one tenth on all the produce. For the same reasons he instituted the local justices, and often made expeditions in person into the country to inspect it and to settle disputes between individuals, that they might not come into the city and neglect their farms. It was in one of these progresses that, as the story goes, Pisistratus had his adventure with the man of Hymettus, who was cultivating the spot afterwards known as "Tax-free Farm." He saw a man digging and working at a very stony piece of ground, and being surprised he sent his attendant to ask what he got out of this plot of land. "Aches and pains," said the man; "and that's what Pisistratus ought to have his tenth of." The man spoke without knowing who his questioner was; but Pisistratus was so pleased with his frank speech and his industry that he granted him exemption from all taxes. And so in matters in general he burdened the people as little as possible with his government, but always cultivated peace and kept them in all quietness. Hence the tyranny of Pisistratus was often spoken of proverbially as "the age of gold"; for when his sons succeeded him the government became much harsher. But most important of all in this respect was his popular and kindly disposition. In all things he was accustomed to observe the laws, without giving himself any exceptional privileges. Once he was summoned on a charge of homicide before the Areopagus, and he appeared in person to make his defence; but the prosecutor was afraid to present himself and

abandoned the case. For these reasons he held power long, and whenever he was expelled he regained his position easily. The majority alike of the upper class and of the people were in his favour; the former he won by his social intercourse with them, the latter by the assistance which he gave to their private purses, and his nature fitted him to win the hearts of both. Moreover, the laws in reference to tyrants at that time in force at Athens were very mild, especially the one which applies more particularly to the establishment of a tyranny. The law ran as follows: "These are the ancestral statutes of the Athenians; if any persons shall make an attempt to establish a tyranny, or if any person shall join in setting up a tyranny, he shall lose his civic rights, both himself and his whole house."

17.   Thus did Pisistratus grow old in the possession of power, and he died a natural death in the archonship of Philoneos [528/527 B.C.], three and thirty years from the time at which he first established himself as tyrant, during nineteen of which he was in possession of power; the rest he spent in exile. It is evident from this that the story is mere gossip which states that Pisistratus was the youthful favourite of Solon and commanded in the war against Megara for the recovery of Salamis. It will not harmonize with their respective ages, as any one may see who will reckon up the years of the life of each of them, and the dates at which they died. After the death of Pisistratus his sons took up the government, and conducted it on the same system. He had two sons by his first and legitimate wife, Hippias and Hipparchus, and two by his Argive consort, Iophon and Hegesistratus, who was surnamed Thessalus. For Pisistratus took a wife from Argos, Timonassa, the daughter of a man of Argos, named Gorgilus; she had previously been the wife of Archinus of Ambracia, one of the descendants of Cypselus. This was the origin of his friendship with the Argives, on account of which a thousand of them were brought over by Hegesistratus and fought on his side in the battle of Pallene. Some authorities say that this marriage took place after his first expulsion from Athens, others while he was in possession of the government.

18.   Hippias and Hipparchus assumed the control of affairs on grounds alike of standing and of age; but Hippias, as being also naturally of a statesmanlike and shrewd disposition, was really the head of the government. Hipparchus was youthful in disposition, amorous, and fond of literature (it was he who invited to Athens Anacreon, Simonides, and the other poets), while Thessalus was much junior in age, and was violent and headstrong in his behaviour. It was from his character that all the evils arose which befell the house. He became enamoured of Harmodius, and since he failed to win his affection, he lost all restraint upon his passion, and in addition to other exhibitions of rage he finally prevented the sister of Harmodius from taking the part of a basketbearer in the Panathenaic pro-

cession, alleging as his reason that Harmodius was a person of loose life. Thereupon, in a frenzy of wrath, Harmodius and Aristogeiton did their celebrated deed, in conjunction with a number of confederates. But while they were lying in wait for Hippias in the Acropolis at the time of the Panathenaea (Hippias, at this moment, was awaiting the arrival of the procession, while Hipparchus was organizing its dispatch) they saw one of the persons privy to the plot talking familiarly with him. Thinking that he was betraying them, and desiring to do something before they were arrested, they rushed down and made their attempt without waiting for the rest of their confederates. They succeeded in killing Hipparchus near the Leocoreum while he was engaged in arranging the procession, but ruined the design as a whole; of the two leaders, Harmodius was killed on the spot by the guards, while Aristogeiton was arrested, and perished later after suffering long tortures. While under the torture he accused many persons who belonged by birth to the most distinguished families and were also personal friends of the tyrants. At first the government could find no clue to the conspiracy; for the current story, that Hippias made all who were taking part in the procession leave their arms, and then detected those who were carrying secret daggers, cannot be true, since at that time they did not bear arms in the processions, this being a custom instituted at a later period by the democracy. According to the story of the popular party, Aristogeiton accused the friends of the tyrants with the deliberate intention that the latter might commit an impious act, and at the same time weaken themselves, by putting to death innocent men who were their own friends; others say that he told no falsehood, but was betraying the actual accomplices. At last, when for all his efforts he could not obtain release by death, he promised to give further information against a number of other persons; and, having induced Hippias to give him his hand to confirm his word, as soon as he had hold of it he reviled him for giving his hand to the murderer of his brother, till Hippias, in a frenzy of rage, lost control of himself and snatched out his dagger and dispatched him.

19.   After this event the tyranny became much harsher. In consequence of his vengeance for his brother, and of the execution and banishment of a large number of persons, Hippias became a distrusted and an embittered man. About three years after the death of Hipparchus, finding his position in the city insecure, he set about fortifying Munichia, with the intention of establishing himself there. While he was still engaged on this work, however, he was expelled by Cleomenes, king of Lacedaemon, in consequence of the Spartans being continually incited by oracles to overthrow the tyranny. These oracles were obtained in the following way. The Athenian exiles, headed by the Alcmeonidae, could not by their own power effect their return, but failed continually in their attempts. Among their other

failures, they fortified a post in Attica, Lipsydrium, above Mt. Parnes, and
were there joined by some partisans from the city; but they were besieged
by the tyrants and reduced to surrender. After this disaster the following
became a popular drinking song:

> Ah! Lipsydrium, faithless friend!
> Lo, what heroes to death didst send,
> Nobly born and great in deed!
> Well did they prove themselves at need
> Of noble sires a noble seed.

Having failed, then, in every other method, they took the contract for rebuilding the temple at Delphi, thereby obtaining ample funds, which they
employed to secure the help of the Lacedaemonians. All this time the
Pythia kept continually enjoining on the Lacedaemonians who came to
consult the oracle, that they must free Athens; till finally she succeeded in
impelling the Spartans to that step, although the house of Pisistratus was
connected with them by ties of hospitality. The resolution of the Lacedaemonians was, however, at least equally due to the friendship which had
been formed between the house of Pisistratus and Argos. Accordingly they
first sent Anchimolus by sea at the head of an army; but he was defeated
and killed, through the arrival of Cineas of Thessaly to support the sons of
Pisistratus with a force of a thousand horsemen. Then, being roused to anger by this disaster, they sent their king, Cleomenes, by land at the head of
a larger force; and he, after defeating the Thessalian cavalry when they attempted to intercept his march into Attica, shut up Hippias within what was
known as the Pelargic wall and blockaded him there with the assistance of
the Athenians. While he was sitting down before the place, it so happened
that the sons of the Pisistratidae were captured in an attempt to slip out;
upon which the tyrants capitulated on condition of the safety of their children, and surrendered the Acropolis to the Athenians, five days being first
allowed them to remove their effects. This took place in the archonship of
Harpactides [511/510 B.C.], after they had held the tyranny for about
seventeen years since their father's death, or in all, including the period of
their father's rule, for nine-and-forty years.

20.   After the overthrow of the tyranny, the rival leaders in the state
were Isagoras son of Tisander, a partisan of the tyrants, and Cleisthenes,
who belonged to the family of the Alcmeonidae. Cleisthenes, being beaten
in the political clubs, called in the people by giving the franchise to the
masses. Thereupon Isagoras, finding himself left inferior in power, invited
Cleomenes, who was united to him by ties of hospitality, to return to
Athens, and persuaded him to "drive out the pollution," a plea derived
from the fact that the Alcmeonidae were supposed to be under the curse of

pollution. On this Cleisthenes retired from the country, and Cleomenes, entering Attica with a small force, expelled, as polluted, seven hundred Athenian families. Having effected this, he next attempted to dissolve the Council, and to set up Isagoras and three hundred of his partisans as the supreme power in the state. The Council, however, resisted, the populace flocked together, and Cleomenes and Isagoras, with their adherents, took refuge in the Acropolis. Here the people sat down and besieged them for two days; and on the third they agreed to let Cleomenes and all his followers depart, while they summoned Cleisthenes and the other exiles back to Athens. When the people had thus obtained the command of affairs, Cleisthenes was their chief and popular leader. And this was natural; for the Alcmeonidae were perhaps the chief cause of the expulsion of the tyrants, and for the greater part of their rule were at perpetual war with them. But even earlier than the attempts of the Alcmeonidae, one Cedon made an attack on the tyrants; whence there came another popular drinking song, addressed to him:

> Pour a health yet again, boy, to Cedon; forget not this duty to do,
> If a health is an honour befitting the name of a good man and true.

21.   The people, therefore, had good reason to place confidence in Cleisthenes. Accordingly, now that he was the popular leader, three years after the expulsion of the tyrants, in the archonship of Isagoras [508/507 B.C.], his first step was to distribute the whole population into ten tribes in place of the existing four, with the object of intermixing the members of the different tribes, and so securing that more persons might have a share in the franchise. From this arose the saying "Do not look at the tribes," addressed to those who wished to scrutinize the lists of the old families. Next he made the Council to consist of five hundred members instead of four hundred, each tribe now contributing fifty, whereas formerly each had sent a hundred. The reason why he did not organize the people into twelve tribes was that he might not have to use the existing division into trittyes; for the four tribes had twelve trittyes, so that he would not have achieved his object of redistributing the population in fresh combinations. Further, he divided the country into thirty groups of demes, ten from the districts about the city, ten from the coast, and ten from the interior. These he called trittyes; and he assigned three of them by lot to each tribe, in such a way that each should have one portion in each of these three localities. All who lived in any given deme he declared fellow-demesmen, to the end that the new citizens might not be exposed by the habitual use of family names, but that men might be officially described by the names of their demes; and accordingly it is by the names of their demes that the Athenians speak of one another. He also instituted Demarchs, who had the same duties as the pre-

viously existing Naucrari,—the demes being made to take the place of the naucraries. He gave names to the demes, some from the localities to which they belonged, some from the persons who founded them, since some of the areas no longer corresponded to localities possessing names. On the other hand he allowed every one to retain his family and clan and religious rights according to ancestral custom. The names given to the tribes were the ten which the Pythia appointed out of the hundred selected national heroes.

22.   By these reforms the constitution became much more democratic than that of Solon. The laws of Solon had been obliterated by disuse during the period of the tyranny, while Cleisthenes substituted new ones with the object of securing the goodwill of the masses. Among these was the law concerning ostracism. Seven years after the establishment of this system, in the archonship of Hermocreon [501/500 B.C.], they first imposed upon the Council of Five Hundred the oath which they take to the present day. Next they began to elect the generals by tribes, one from each tribe, while the Polemarch was the commander of the whole army. Then, eleven years later, in the archonship of Phaenippus [490/489 B.C.] they won the battle of Marathon; and two years after this victory, when the people had now gained self-confidence, they for the first time made use of the law of ostracism. This had originally been passed as a precaution against men in high office, because Pisistratus took advantage of his position as a popular leader and general to make himself tyrant; and the first person ostracized was one of his relatives, Hipparchus son of Charmus, of the deme of Collytus, the very person on whose account especially Cleisthenes had enacted the law, as he wished to get rid of him. Hitherto, however, he had escaped; for the Athenians, with the usual leniency of the democracy, allowed all the partisans of the tyrants, who had not joined in their evil deeds in the time of the troubles, to remain in the city; and the chief and leader of these was Hipparchus. Then in the very next year, in the archonship of Telesinus [487/486 B.C.], they for the first time since the tyranny elected, tribe by tribe, the nine Archons by lot out of the five hundred candidates selected by the demes, all the earlier ones having been elected by vote; and in the same year Megacles son of Hippocrates, of the deme of Alopece, was ostracized. Thus for three years they continued to ostracize the friends of the tyrants, on whose account the law had been passed; but in the following year they began to remove others as well, including any one who seemed to be more powerful than was expedient. The first person unconnected with the tyrants who was ostracized was Xanthippus son of Ariphron. Two years later, in the archonship of Nicodemus [483/482 B.C.], the mines of Maroneia were discovered, and the state made a profit of a hundred talents from the working of them. Some persons advised the

people to make a distribution of the money among themselves, but this was prevented by Themistocles. He refused to say on what he proposed to spend the money, but he bade them lend it to the hundred richest men in Athens, one talent to each, and then, if the manner in which it was employed pleased the people, the expenditure should be charged to the state, but otherwise the state should receive the sum back from those to whom it was lent. On these terms he received the money and with it he had a hundred triremes built, each of the hundred individuals building one; and it was with these ships that they fought the battle of Salamis against the barbarians. About this time Aristides the son of Lysimachus was ostracized. Three years later, however, in the archonship of Hypsichides [481/480 B.C.], all the ostracized persons were recalled, on account of the advance of the army of Xerxes; and it was laid down for the future that persons under sentence of ostracism must live between Geraestus and Scyllaeum, on pain of losing their civic rights irrevocably.

23.   So far, then, had the city progressed by this time, growing gradually with the growth of the democracy; but after the Persian wars the Council of Areopagus once more developed strength and assumed the control of the state. It did not acquire this supremacy by virtue of any formal decree, but because it had been the cause of the battle of Salamis being fought. When the generals were utterly at a loss how to meet the crisis and made proclamation that every one should see to his own safety, the Areopagus provided a donation of money, distributing eight drachmas to each member of the ships' crews, and so prevailed on them to go on board. On these grounds people bowed to its prestige; and during this period Athens was well administered. At this time they devoted themselves to the prosecution of the war and were in high repute among the Greeks, so that the command by sea was conferred upon them, in spite of the opposition of the Lacedaemonians. The leaders of the people during this period were Aristides, son of Lysimachus, and Themistocles, son of Neocles, of whom the latter appeared to devote himself to the conduct of war, while the former had the reputation of being a clever statesman and the most upright man of his time. Accordingly the one was usually employed as general, the other as political adviser. The rebuilding of the fortifications they conducted in combination, although they were political opponents; but it was Aristides who, seizing the opportunity afforded by the discredit brought upon the Lacedaemonians by Pausanias, guided the public policy in the matter of the defection of the Ionian states from the alliance with Sparta. It follows that it was he who made the first assessment of tribute from the various allied states, two years after the battle of Salamis, in the archonship of Timosthenes [478/477 B.C.]; and it was he who took the oath of offensive

and defensive alliance with the Ionians, on which occasion they cast the masses of iron into the sea.[3]

24.   After this, seeing the state growing in confidence and much wealth accumulated, he advised the people to lay hold of the leadership of the league, and to quit the country districts and settle in the city. He pointed out to them that all would be able to gain a living there, some by service in the army, others in the garrisons, others by taking a part in public affairs; and in this way they would secure the leadership. This advice was taken; and when the people had assumed the supreme control they proceeded to treat their allies in a more imperious fashion, with the exception of the Chians, Lesbians, and Samians. These they maintained to protect their empire, leaving their constitutions untouched, and allowing them to retain whatever dominion they then possessed. They also secured an ample maintenance for the mass of the population in the way which Aristides had pointed out to them. Out of the proceeds of the tributes and the taxes and the contributions of the allies more than twenty thousand persons were maintained. There were 6,000 jurymen, 1,600 bowmen, 1,200 Knights, 500 members of the Council, 500 guards of the dockyards, besides fifty guards in the Acropolis. There were some 700 magistrates at home, and some 700 abroad. Further, when they subsequently went to war, there were in addition 2,500 heavy-armed troops, twenty guard-ships, and other ships which collected the tributes, with crews amounting to 2,000 men, selected by lot; and besides these there were the persons maintained at the town hall, and orphans, and gaolers, since all these were supported by the state.

25.   Such was the way in which the people earned their livelihood. The supremacy of the Areopagus lasted for about seventeen years after the Persian wars, although gradually declining. But as the strength of the masses increased, Ephialtes, son of Sophonides, a man with a reputation for incorruptibility and public virtue, who had become the leader of the people, made an attack upon that Council. First of all he ruined many of its members by bringing actions against them with reference to their administration. Then, in the archonship of Conon [462/461 B.C.], he stripped the Council of all the acquired prerogatives from which it derived its guardianship of the constitution, and assigned some of them to the Council of Five Hundred, and others to the Assembly and the law-courts. In this revolution he was assisted by Themistocles, who was himself a member of the Areopagus, but was expecting to be tried before it on a charge of treasonable dealings with Persia. This made him anxious that it should be over-

---

3. The act was part of the ritual for sealing the alliance, which was to last until the iron rose from the sea.

thrown, and accordingly he warned Ephialtes that the Council intended to arrest him, while at the same time he informed the Areopagites that he would reveal to them certain persons who were conspiring to subvert the constitution. He then conducted the representatives delegated by the Council to the residence of Ephialtes, promising to show them the conspirators who assembled there, and proceeded to converse with them in an earnest manner. Ephialtes, seeing this, was seized with alarm and took refuge in suppliant guise at the altar. Every one was astounded at the occurrence, and presently, when the Council of Five Hundred met, Ephialtes and Themistocles together proceeded to denounce the Areopagus to them. This they repeated in similar fashion in the Assembly, until they succeeded in depriving it of its power. Not long afterwards, however, Ephialtes was assassinated by Aristodicus of Tanagra. In this way was the Council of Areopagus deprived of its guardianship of the state.

26.   After this revolution the administration of the state became more and more lax, in consequence of the eager rivalry of candidates for popular favour. During this period the moderate party, as it happened, had no real chief, their leader being Cimon son of Miltiades, who was a comparatively young man, and had been late in entering public life; and at the same time the general populace suffered great losses by war. The soldiers for active service were selected at that time from the roll of citizens, and as the generals were men of no military experience, who owed their position solely to their family standing, it continually happened that some two or three thousand of the troops perished on an expedition; and in this way the best men alike of the lower and the upper classes were exhausted. Consequently in most matters of administration less heed was paid to the laws than had formerly been the case. No alteration, however, was made in the method of election of the nine Archons, except that five years after the death of Ephialtes it was decided that the candidates to be submitted to the lot for that office might be selected from the Zeugitae as well as from the higher classes. The first Archon from that class was Mnesitheides. Up to this time all the Archons had been taken from the Pentacosiomedimni and Knights, while the Zeugitae were confined to the ordinary magistracies, save where an evasion of the law was overlooked. Four years later, in the archonship of Lysicrates [453/452 B.C.], the thirty "local justices," as they were called, were re-established; and two years afterwards, in the archonship of Antidotus [451/450 B.C.], in consequence of the great increase in the number of citizens, it was resolved, on the motion of Pericles, that no one should be admitted to the franchise who was not of citizen birth by both parents.

27.   After this Pericles came forward as popular leader, having first distinguished himself while still a young man by prosecuting Cimon on the audit of his official accounts as general. Under his auspices the constitution

became still more democratic. He took away some of the privileges of the Areopagus, and, above all, he turned the policy of the state in the direction of sea power, which caused the masses to acquire confidence in themselves and consequently to take the conduct of affairs more and more into their own hands. Moreover, forty-eight years after the battle of Salamis, in the archonship of Pythodorus [432/431 B.C.], the Peloponnesian war broke out, during which the populace was shut up in the city and became accustomed to gain its livelihood by military service, and so, partly voluntarily and partly involuntarily, determined to assume the administration of the state itself. Pericles was also the first to institute pay for service in the law-courts, as a bid for popular favour to counterbalance the wealth of Cimon. The latter, having private possessions on a regal scale, not only performed the regular public services magnificently, but also maintained a large number of his fellow-demesmen. Any member of the deme of Laciadae could go every day to Cimon's house and there receive a reasonable provision; while his estate was guarded by no fences, so that any one who liked might help himself to the fruit from it. Pericles' private property was quite unequal to this magnificence and accordingly he took the advice of Damonides of Oia (who was commonly supposed to be the person who prompted Pericles in most of his measures, and was therefore subsequently ostracized), which was that, as he was beaten in the matter of private possessions, he should make gifts to the people from their own property; and accordingly he instituted pay for the members of the juries. Some critics accuse him of thereby causing a deterioration in the character of the juries, since it was always the common people who put themselves forward for selection as jurors, rather than the men of better position. Moreover, bribery came into existence after this, the first person to introduce it being Anytus, after his command at Pylos. He was prosecuted by certain individuals on account of his loss of Pylos, but escaped by bribing the jury.

28. So long, however, as Pericles was leader of the people, things went tolerably well with the state; but when he was dead there was a great change for the worse. Then for the first time did the people choose a leader who was of no reputation among men of good standing, whereas up to this time such men had always been found as leaders of the democracy. The first leader of the people, in the very beginning of things, was Solon, and the second was Pisistratus, both of them men of birth and position. After the overthrow of the tyrants there was Cleisthenes, a member of the house of the Alcmeonidae; and he had no rival opposed to him after the expulsion of the party of Isagoras. After this Xanthippus was the leader of the people, and Miltiades of the upper class. Then came Themistocles and Aristides, and after them Ephialtes as leader of the people, and Cimon son of Miltiades of the wealthier class. Pericles followed as leader of the people,

and Thucydides, who was connected by marriage with Cimon, of the opposition. After the death of Pericles, Nicias, who subsequently fell in Sicily, appeared as leader of the aristocracy, and Cleon son of Cleaenetus of the people. The latter seems, more than any one else, to have been the cause of the corruption of the democracy by his wild undertakings; and he was the first to use unseemly shouting and coarse abuse on the platform, and to harangue the people with his cloak girt up short about him, whereas all his predecessors had spoken decently and in order. These were succeeded by Theramenes son of Hagnon as leader of the one party, and the lyre-maker Cleophon of the people. It was Cleophon who first granted the two-obol donation for the theatrical performances, and for some time it continued to be given; but then Callicrates of Paeania ousted him by promising to add a third obol to the sum. Both of these persons were subsequently condemned to death; for the people, even if they are deceived for a long time, in the end generally come to detest those who have beguiled them into any unworthy action. After Cleophon the popular leadership was occupied successively by the men who chose to talk the biggest and pander the most to the tastes of the majority, with their eyes fixed only on the interests of the moment. The best statesmen at Athens, after those of early times, seem to have been Nicias, Thucydides, and Theramenes. As to Nicias and Thucydides, nearly every one agrees that they were not merely men of birth and character, but also statesmen, and that they ruled the state with paternal care. On the merits of Theramenes opinion is divided, because it so happened that in his time public affairs were in a very stormy state. But those who give their opinion deliberately find him, not, as his critics falsely assert, overthrowing every kind of constitution, but supporting every kind so long as it did not transgress the laws; thus showing that he was able, as every good citizen should be, to live under any form of constitution, while he refused to countenance illegality and was its constant enemy.

29. So long as the fortune of the war continued even, the Athenians preserved the democracy; but after the disaster in Sicily, when the Lacedaemonians had gained the upper hand through their alliance with the king of Persia, they were compelled to abolish the democracy and establish in its place the constitution of the Four Hundred. The speech recommending this course before the vote was made by Melobius, and the motion was proposed by Pythodorus of Anaphlystus; but the real argument which persuaded the majority was the belief that the king of Persia was more likely to form an alliance with them if the constitution were on an oligarchical basis. The motion of Pythodorus was to the following effect. The popular Assembly was to elect twenty persons, over forty years of age, who, in conjunction with the existing ten members of the Committee of Public

Safety, after taking an oath that they would frame such measures as they thought best for the state, should then prepare proposals for the public safety. In addition, any other person might make proposals, so that of all the schemes before them the people might choose the best. Cleitophon concurred with the motion of Pythodorus, but moved that the committee should also investigate the ancient laws enacted by Cleisthenes when he created the democracy, in order that they might have these too before them and so be in a position to decide wisely; his suggestion being that the constitution of Cleisthenes was not really democratic, but closely akin to that of Solon. When the committee was elected, their first proposal was that the Presiders should be compelled to put to the vote any motion that was offered on behalf of the public safety. Next they abolished all indictments for illegal proposals, all impeachments and public prosecutions, in order that every Athenian should be free to give his counsel on the situation, if he chose; and they decreed that if any person imposed a fine on any other for his acts in this respect, or prosecuted him or summoned him before the courts, he should, on an information being laid against him, be summarily arrested and brought before the generals, who should deliver him to the Eleven to be put to death. After these preliminary measures, they drew up the constitution in the following manner. The revenues of the state were not to be spent on any purpose except the war. All magistrates should serve without remuneration for the period of the war, except the nine Archons and the Prytanes for the time being, who should each receive three obols a day. The whole of the rest of the administration was to be committed, for the period of the war, to those Athenians who were most capable of serving the state personally or pecuniarily, to the number of not less than five thousand. This body was to have full powers, to the extent even of making treaties with whomsoever they willed; and ten representatives, over forty years of age, were to be elected from each tribe to draw up the list of the Five Thousand, after taking an oath on a full and perfect sacrifice.

30.   These were the recommendations of the committee; and when they had been ratified the Five Thousand elected from their own number a hundred commissioners to draw up the constitution. They, on their appointment, drew up and produced the following recommendations. There should be a Council, holding office for a year, consisting of men over thirty years of age, serving without pay. To this body should belong the Generals, the nine Archons, the Amphictyonic Registrar [Hieromnemon], the Regiment Commanders [Taxiarchs], the Cavalry Commanders, the Tribe Commanders, the commanders of garrisons, the Treasurers of Athena and the other gods, ten in number, the Hellenic Treasurers [Hellenotamiae], the Treasurers of the other non-sacred moneys, to the number of twenty, the ten Commissioners of Sacrifices [Hieropoei], and the ten Superintendents of

the Mysteries. All these were to be appointed by the Council from a larger number of selected candidates, chosen from its members for the time being. The other offices were all to be filled by lot, and not from the members of the Council. The Hellenic Treasurers who actually administered the funds should not sit with the Council. As regards the future, four Councils were to be created, of men of the age already mentioned, and one of these was to be chosen by lot to take office at once, while the others were to receive it in turn, in the order decided by the lot. For this purpose the hundred commissioners were to distribute themselves and all the rest as equally as possible into four parts, and cast lots for precedence, and the selected body should hold office for a year. They were to administer that office as seemed to them best, both with reference to the safe custody and due expenditure of the finances, and generally with regard to all other matters to the best of their ability. If they desired to take a larger number of persons into counsel, each member might call in one assistant of his own choice, subject to the same qualification of age. The Council was to sit once every five days, unless there was any special need for more frequent sittings. The casting of the lot for the Council was to be held by the nine Archons; votes on divisions were to be counted by five tellers chosen by lot from the members of the Council, and of these one was to be selected by lot every day to act as president. These five persons were to cast lots for precedence between the parties wishing to appear before the Council, giving the first place to sacred matters, the second to heralds, the third to embassies, and the fourth to all other subjects; but matters concerning the war might be dealt with, on the motion of the generals, whenever there was need, without balloting. Any member of the Council who did not enter the Council-house at the time named should be fined a drachma for each day, unless he was away on leave of absence from the Council.

31.   Such was the constitution which they drew up for the time to come, but for the immediate present they devised the following scheme. There should be a Council of Four Hundred, as in the ancient constitution, forty from each tribe, chosen out of candidates of more than thirty years of age, selected by the members of the tribes. This Council should appoint the magistrates and draw up the form of oath which they were to take; and in all that concerned the laws, in the examination of official accounts, and in other matters generally, they might act according to their discretion. They must, however, observe the laws that might be enacted with reference to the constitution of the state, and had no power to alter them nor to pass others. The generals should be provisionally elected from the whole body of the Five Thousand, but so soon as the Council came into existence it was to hold an examination of military equipments, and thereon elect ten persons, together with a secretary, and the persons thus elected should hold

office during the coming year with full powers, and should have the right, whenever they desired it, of joining in the deliberations of the Council. The Five Thousand was also to elect a single Cavalry Commander and ten Tribe Commanders; but for the future the Council was to elect these officers according to the regulations above laid down. No office, except those of member of the Council and of general, might be held more than once, either by the first occupants or by their successors. With reference to the future distribution of the Four Hundred into the four successive sections, the hundred commissioners must divide them whenever the time comes for the citizens to join in the Council along with the rest.

32. The hundred commissioners appointed by the Five Thousand drew up the constitution as just stated; and after it had been ratified by the people, under the presidency of Aristomachus, the existing Council, that of the year of Callias [412/411 B.C.], was dissolved before it had completed its term of office. It was dissolved on the fourteenth day of the month Thargelion, and the Four Hundred entered into office on the twenty-first; whereas the regular Council, elected by lot, ought to have entered into office on the fourteenth of Scirophorion. Thus was the oligarchy established, in the archonship of Callias, just about a hundred years after the expulsion of the tyrants. The chief promoters of the revolution were Pisander, Antiphon, and Theramenes, all of them men of good birth and with high reputations for ability and judgement. When, however, this constitution had been established, the Five Thousand were only nominally selected, and the Four Hundred, together with the ten officers on whom full powers had been conferred occupied the Council-house and really administered the government. They began by sending ambassadors to the Lacedaemonians proposing a cessation of the war on the basis of the existing position; but as the Lacedaemonians refused to listen to them unless they would also abandon the command of the sea, they broke off the negotiations.

33. For about four months the constitution of the Four Hundred lasted, and Mnasilochus held office as Archon of their nomination for two months of the year of Theopompus [411/410 B.C.], who was Archon for the remaining ten. On the loss of the naval battle of Eretria, however, and the revolt of the whole of Euboea except Oreum, the indignation of the people was greater than at any of the earlier disasters, since they drew far more supplies at this time from Euboea than from Attica itself. Accordingly they deposed the Four Hundred and committed the management of affairs to the Five Thousand, consisting of persons possessing a military equipment. At the same time they voted that pay should not be given for any public office. The persons chiefly responsible for the revolution were Aristocrates and Theramenes, who disapproved of the action of the Four Hundred in retaining the direction of affairs entirely in their own hands, and referring

nothing to the Five Thousand. During this period the constitution of the state seems to have been admirable, since it was a time of war and the franchise was in the hands of those who possessed a military equipment.

34.   The people, however, in a very short time deprived the Five Thousand of their monopoly of the government. Then, six years after the overthrow of the Four Hundred, in the archonship of Callias of Angele [406/ 405 B.C.], the battle of Arginusae took place, of which the results were, first, that the ten generals who had gained the victory were all condemned by a single decision, owing to the people being led astray by persons who aroused their indignation; though, as a matter of fact, some of the generals had actually taken no part in the battle, and others were themselves picked up by other vessels. Secondly, when the Lacedaemonians proposed to evacuate Decelea and make peace on the basis of the existing position, although some of the Athenians supported this proposal, the majority refused to listen to them. In this they were led astray by Cleophon, who appeared in the Assembly drunk and wearing his breastplate, and prevented peace being made, declaring that he would never accept peace unless the Lacedaemonians abandoned their claims on all cities allied with them. They mismanaged their opportunity then, and in a very short time they learnt their mistake. The next year, in the archonship of Alexias [405/404 B.C.], they suffered the disaster of Aegospotami, the consequence of which was that Lysander became master of the city, and set up the Thirty as its governors. He did so in the following manner. One of the terms of peace stipulated that the state should be governed according to "the ancient constitution." Accordingly the popular party tried to preserve the democracy, while that part of the upper class which belonged to the political clubs, together with the exiles who had returned since the peace, aimed at an oligarchy, and those who were not members of any club, though in other respects they considered themselves as good as any other citizens, were anxious to restore the ancient constitution. The latter class included Archinus, Anytus, Cleitophon, Phormisius, and many others, but their most prominent leader was Theramenes. Lysander, however, threw his influence on the side of the oligarchical party, and the popular Assembly was compelled by sheer intimidation to pass a vote establishing the oligarchy. The motion to this effect was proposed by Dracontides of Aphidna.

35.   In this way were the Thirty established in power, in the archonship of Pythodorus [404/403 B.C.]. As soon, however, as they were masters of the city, they ignored all the resolutions which had been passed relating to the organization of the constitution, but after appointing a Council of Five Hundred and the other magistrates out of a thousand selected candidates,

and associating with themselves ten Archons in Piraeus, eleven superintendents of the prison, and three hundred "lash-bearers" as attendants, with the help of these they kept the city under their own control. At first, indeed, they behaved with moderation towards the citizens and pretended to administer the state according to the ancient constitution. In pursuance of this policy they took down from the hill of Areopagus the laws of Ephialtes and Archestratus relating to the Areopagite Council; they also repealed such of the statutes of Solon as were obscure, and abolished the supreme power of the law-courts. In this they claimed to be restoring the constitution and freeing it from obscurities; as, for instance, by making the testator free once for all to leave his property as he pleased, and abolishing the existing limitations in cases of insanity, old age, and undue female influence, in order that no opening might be left for professional accusers. In other matters also their conduct was similar. At first, then, they acted on these lines and they destroyed the professional accusers and those mischievous and evil-minded persons who, to the great detriment of the democracy, had attached themselves to it in order to curry favour with it. With all of this the city was much pleased, and thought that the Thirty were doing it with the best of motives. But so soon as they had got a firmer hold on the city, they spared no class of citizens, but put to death any persons who were eminent for wealth or birth or character. Herein they aimed at removing all whom they had reason to fear, while they also wished to lay hands on their possessions; and in a short time they put to death not less than fifteen hundred persons.

36. Theramenes, however, seeing the city thus falling into ruin, was displeased with their proceedings, and counselled them to cease such unprincipled conduct and let the better classes have a share in the government. At first they resisted his advice, but when his proposals came to be known abroad, and the masses began to associate themselves with him, they were seized with alarm lest he should make himself the leader of the people and destroy their despotic power. Accordingly they drew up a list of three thousand citizens, to whom they announced that they would give a share in the constitution. Theramenes, however, criticized this scheme also, first on the ground that, while proposing to give all respectable citizens a share in the constitution, they were actually giving it only to three thousand persons, as though all merit were confined within that number; and secondly because they were doing two inconsistent things, since they made the government rest on the basis of force, and yet made the governors inferior in strength to the governed. However, they took no notice of his criticisms, and for a long time put off the publication of the list of the Three Thousand and kept to themselves the names of those who had been

placed upon it; and every time they did decide to publish it they proceeded
to strike out some of those who had been included in it, and insert others
who had been omitted.

37.   Now when winter had set in, Thrasybulus and the exiles occupied
Phyle, and the force which the Thirty led out to attack them met with a
reverse. Thereupon the Thirty decided to disarm the bulk of the population
and to get rid of Theramenes; which they did in the following way. They
introduced two laws into the Council, which they commanded it to pass;
the first of them gave the Thirty absolute power to put to death any citizen
who was not included in the list of the Three Thousand, while the second
disqualified all persons from participation in the franchise who should have
assisted in the demolition of the fort of Eetioneia, or have acted in any way
against the Four Hundred who had organized the previous oligarchy.
Theramenes had done both, and accordingly, when these laws were ratified, he became excluded from the franchise and the Thirty had full power
to put him to death. Theramenes having been thus removed, they disarmed
all the people except the Three Thousand, and in every respect showed a
great advance in cruelty and crime. They also sent ambassadors to Lacedaemon to blacken the character of Theramenes and to ask for help; and
the Lacedaemonians, in answer to their appeal, sent Callibius as military
governor with about seven hundred troops, who came and occupied the
Acropolis.

38.   These events were followed by the occupation of Munichia by the
exiles from Phyle, and their victory over the Thirty and their partisans.
After the fight the party of the city retreated, and next day they held a meeting in the marketplace and deposed the Thirty, and elected ten citizens with
full powers to bring the war to a termination. When, however, the Ten had
taken over the government they did nothing towards the object for which
they were elected, but sent envoys to Lacedaemon to ask for help and to
borrow money. Further, finding that the citizens who possessed the franchise were displeased at their proceedings, they were afraid lest they should
be deposed, and consequently, in order to strike terror into them (in which
design they succeeded), they arrested Demaretus, one of the most eminent
citizens, and put him to death. This gave them a firm hold on the government, and they also had the support of Callibius and his Peloponnesians,
together with several of the Knights; for some of the members of this class
were the most zealous among the citizens to prevent the return of the exiles
from Phyle. When, however, the party in Piraeus and Munichia began to
gain the upper hand in the war, through the defection of the whole populace to them, the party in the city deposed the original Ten, and elected
another Ten, consisting of men of the highest repute. Under their administration, and with their active and zealous co-operation, the treaty of rec-

onciliation was made and the populace returned to the city. The most prominent members of this board were Rhinon of Paeania and Phayllus of Acherdus, who, even before the arrival of Pausanias, opened negotiations with the party in Piraeus, and after his arrival seconded his efforts to bring about the return of the exiles. For it was Pausanias, the king of the Lacedaemonians, who brought the peace and reconciliation to a fulfilment, in conjunction with the ten commissioners of arbitration who arrived later from Lacedaemon, at his own earnest request. Rhinon and his colleagues received a vote of thanks for the goodwill shown by them to the people, and though they received their charge under an oligarchy and handed in their accounts under a democracy, no one, either of the party that had stayed in the city or of the exiles that had returned from the Piraeus, brought any complaint against them. On the contrary, Rhinon was immediately elected general on account of his conduct in this office.

39.   This reconciliation was effected in the archonship of Eucleides [403/402 B.C.], on the following terms. All persons who, having remained in the city during the troubles, were now anxious to leave it, were to be free to settle at Eleusis, retaining their civil rights and possessing full and independent powers of self-government, and with the free enjoyment of their own personal property. The temple at Eleusis should be common ground for both parties, and should be under the superintendence of the Ceryces and the Eumolpidae, according to primitive custom. The settlers at Eleusis should not be allowed to enter Athens, nor the people of Athens to enter Eleusis, except at the season of the mysteries, when both parties should be free from these restrictions. The secessionists should pay their share to the fund for the common defence out of their revenues, just like all the other Athenians. If any of the seceding party wished to take a house in Eleusis, the people would help them to obtain the consent of the owner; but if they could not come to terms, they should appoint three valuers on either side, and the owner should receive whatever price they should appoint. Of the inhabitants of Eleusis, those whom the secessionists wished to remain should be allowed to do so. The list of those who desired to secede should be made up within ten days after the taking of the oaths in the case of persons already in the country, and their actual departure should take place within twenty days; persons at present out of the country should have the same terms allowed to them after their return. No one who settled at Eleusis should be capable of holding any office in Athens until he should again register himself on the roll as a resident in the city. Trials for homicide, including all cases in which one party had either killed or wounded another, should be conducted according to ancestral practice. There should be a general amnesty concerning past events towards all persons except the Thirty, the Ten, the Eleven, and the magistrates in Piraeus; and these too

should be included if they should submit their accounts in the usual way. Such accounts should be given by the magistrates in Piraeus before a court of citizens rated in Piraeus, and by the magistrates in the city before a court of those rated in the city. On these terms those who wished to do so might secede. Each party was to repay separately the money which it had borrowed for the war.

40.   When the reconciliation had taken place on these terms, those who had fought on the side of the Thirty felt considerable apprehensions, and a large number intended to secede. But as they put off entering their names till the last moment, as people will do, Archinus, observing their numbers, and being anxious to retain them as citizens, cut off the remaining days during which the list should have remained open; and in this way many persons were compelled to remain, though they did so very unwillingly until they recovered confidence. This is one point in which Archinus appears to have acted in a most statesmanlike manner, and another was his subsequent prosecution of Thrasybulus on the charge of illegality, for a motion by which he proposed to confer the franchise on all who had taken part in the return from Piraeus, although some of them were notoriously slaves. And yet a third such action was when one of the returned exiles began to violate the amnesty, whereupon Archinus haled him to the Council and persuaded them to execute him without trial, telling them that now they would have to show whether they wished to preserve the democracy and abide by the oaths they had taken; for if they let this man escape they would encourage others to imitate him, while if they executed him they would make an example for all to learn by. And this was exactly what happened; for after this man had been put to death no one ever again broke the amnesty. On the contrary, the Athenians seem, both in public and in private, to have behaved in the most unprecedentedly admirable and public-spirited way with reference to the preceding troubles. Not only did they blot out all memory of former offences, but they even repaid to the Lacedaemonians out of the public purse the money which the Thirty had borrowed for the war, although the treaty required each party, the party of the city and the party of Piraeus, to pay its own debts separately. This they did because they thought it was a necessary first step in the direction of restoring harmony; but in other states, so far from the democratic parties making advances from their own possessions, they are rather in the habit of making a general redistribution of the land. A final reconciliation was made with the secessionists at Eleusis two years after the secession, in the archonship of Xenaenetus [401/400 B.C.].

41.   This, however, took place at a later date; at the time of which we are speaking the people, having secured the control of the state, established the constitution which exists at the present day. Pythodorus was Archon at

the time, but the democracy seems to have assumed the supreme power
with perfect justice, since it had effected its own return by its own exer-
tions. This was the eleventh change which had taken place in the constitution of Athens. The first modification of the primaeval condition of things
was when Ion and his companions brought the people together into a community, for then the people was first divided into the four tribes, and the
tribe-kings were created. Next, and first after this, having now some semblance of a constitution, was that which took place in the reign of Theseus,
consisting in a slight deviation from absolute monarchy. After this came
the constitution formed under Draco, when the first code of laws was
drawn up. The third was that which followed the civil war, in the time of
Solon; from this the democracy took its rise. The fourth was the tyranny of
Pisistratus; the fifth the constitution of Cleisthenes, after the overthrow
of the tyrants, of a more democratic character than that of Solon. The
sixth was that which followed on the Persian wars, when the Council of
Areopagus had the direction of the state. The seventh, succeeding this, was
the constitution which Aristides sketched out, and which Ephialtes brought
to completion by overthrowing the Areopagite Council; under this the nation, misled by the demagogues, made the most serious mistakes in the
interest of its maritime empire. The eighth was the establishment of the
Four Hundred, followed by the ninth, the restored democracy. The tenth
was the tyranny of the Thirty and the Ten. The eleventh was that which
followed the return from Phyle and Piraeus; and this has continued from
that day to this, with continual accretions of power to the masses. The democracy has made itself master of everything and administers everything
by its votes in the Assembly and by the law-courts, in which it holds the
supreme power. Even the jurisdiction of the Council has passed into the
hands of the people at large; and this appears to be a judicious change,
since small bodies are more open to corruption, whether by actual money
or influence, than large ones. At first they refused to allow payment for
attendance at the Assembly; but the result was that people did not attend.
Consequently, after the Presiders had tried many devices in vain in order
to induce the populace to come and ratify the votes, Agyrrhius, in the
first instance, made a provision of one obol a day, which Heracleides of
Clazomenae, nicknamed "the king," increased to two obols, and Agyrrhius
again to three.

42.   The present state of the constitution is as follows. The franchise is
open to all who are of citizen birth by both parents. They are enrolled
among the demesmen at the age of eighteen. On the occasion of their enrollment the demesmen give their votes on oath, first whether the candidates appear to be of the age prescribed by the law (if not, they are dismissed back into the ranks of boys), and secondly whether the candidate is

free born and of such parentage as the laws require. Then if they decide that he is not a free man, he appeals to the law-courts, and the demesmen appoint five of their own number to act as accusers; if the court decides that he has no right to be enrolled, he is sold by the state as a slave, but if he wins his case he has a right to be enrolled among the demesmen without further question. After this the Council examines those who have been enrolled, and if it comes to the conclusion that any of them is less than eighteen years of age, it fines the demesmen who enrolled him. When the youths [Ephebes] have passed this examination, their fathers meet by their tribes, and appoint on oath three of their fellow tribesmen, over forty years of age, who, in their opinion, are the best and most suitable persons to have charge of the youths; and of these the Assembly elects one from each tribe as guardian, together with a director, chosen from the general body of Athenians, to control the whole. Under the charge of these persons the youths first of all make the circuit of the temples; then they proceed to Piraeus, and some of them garrison Munichia and some the south shore. The Assembly also elects two trainers, with subordinate instructors, who teach them to fight in heavy armour, to use the bow and javelin, and to discharge a catapult. The guardians receive from the state a drachma apiece for their keep, and the youths four obols apiece. Each guardian receives the allowance for all the members of his tribe and buys the necessary provisions for the common stock (they mess together by tribes), and generally superintends everything. In this way they spend the first year. The next year, after giving a public display of their military evolutions, on the occasion when the Assembly meets in the theatre, they receive a shield and spear from the state; after which they patrol the country and spend their time in the forts. For these two years they are on garrison duty, and wear the military cloak, and during this time they are exempt from all taxes. They also can neither bring an action at law, nor have one brought against them, in order that they may have no excuse for requiring leave of absence; though exception is made in cases of actions concerning inheritances and wards of state, or of any sacrificial ceremony connected with the family. When the two years have elapsed they thereupon take their position among the other citizens. Such is the manner of the enrollment of the citizens and the training of the youths.

43.   All the magistrates that are concerned with the ordinary routine of administration are elected by lot, except the Military Treasurer, the Commissioners of the Theoric fund, and the Superintendent of Springs. These are elected by vote, and hold office from one Panathenaic festival to the next. All military officers are also elected by vote.

The Council of Five Hundred is elected by lot, fifty from each tribe. Each tribe holds the office of Presiders in turn, the order being determined by lot; the first four serve for thirty-six days each, the last six for thirty-five, since the reckoning is by lunar years. The Presiders for the time being, in the first place, mess together in the Roundhouse, and receive a sum of money from the state for their maintenance; and, secondly, they convene the meetings of the Council and the Assembly. The Council they convene every day, unless it is a holiday, the Assembly four times in each presidency. It is also their duty to draw up the programme of the business of the Council and to decide what subjects are to be dealt with on each particular day, and where the sitting is to be held. They also draw up the programme for the meetings of the Assembly. One of these in each presidency is called the "sovereign" Assembly; in this the people have to ratify the continuance of the magistrates in office, if they are performing their duties properly, and to consider the supply of corn and the defence of the country. On this day, too, impeachments are introduced by those who wish to do so, the lists of property confiscated by the state are read, and also applications for inheritances and wards of state, so that nothing may pass unclaimed without the cognizance of any person concerned. In the sixth presidency, in addition to the business already stated, the question is put to the vote whether it is desirable to hold a vote of ostracism or not; and complaints against professional accusers, whether Athenian or aliens domiciled in Athens, are received, to the number of not more than three of either class, together with cases in which an individual has made some promise to the people and has not performed it. Another Assembly in each presidency is assigned to the hearing of petitions, and at this meeting any one is free, on depositing the petitioner's olive-branch, to speak to the people concerning any matter, public or private. The two remaining meetings are devoted to all other subjects, and the laws require them to deal with three questions connected with religion, three connected with heralds and embassies, and three on secular subjects. Sometimes questions are brought forward without a preliminary vote of the Assembly to take them into consideration.

Heralds and envoys appear first before the Presiders, and the bearers of dispatches also deliver them to the same officials.

44. There is a single Chairman of the Presiders, elected by lot, who presides for a night and a day; he may not hold the office for more than that time, nor may the same individual hold it twice. He keeps the keys of the sanctuaries in which the treasures and public records of the state are preserved, and also the public seal; and he is bound to remain in the Roundhouse, together with one-third of the Presiders, named by himself. Whenever the Presiders convene a meeting of the Council or Assembly, he appoints by lot nine Heads, one from each tribe except that which holds the office of Presiders for the time being; and out of these nine he similarly appoints one as Chairman, and hands over the programme for the meeting

to them. They take it and see to the preservation of order, put forward the various subjects which are to be considered, decide the results of the votings, and direct the proceedings generally. They also have power to dismiss the meeting. No one may act as Chairman more than once in the year, but he may be a Head once in each presidency.

Elections to the offices of General and Cavalry Commander and all other military commands are held in the Assembly, in such manner as the people decide; they are held after the sixth presidency by the first board of Presiders in whose term of office the omens are favourable. There has, however, to be a preliminary consideration by the Council in this case also.

45.   In former times the Council had full power to inflict fines and imprisonment and death; but when it had consigned Lysimachus to the executioner, and he was sitting in the immediate expectation of death, Eumelides of Alopece rescued him from its hands, maintaining that no citizen ought to be put to death except on the decision of a court of law. Accordingly a trial was held in a law-court, and Lysimachus was acquitted, receiving henceforth the nickname of "the man from the drum-head"; and the people deprived the Council thenceforward of the power to inflict death or imprisonment or fine, passing a law that if the Council condemn any person for an offence or inflict a fine, the Regulators shall bring the sentence or fine before the law-court, and the decision of the jurors shall be the final judgement in the matter.

The Council passes judgement on nearly all magistrates, especially those who have the control of money; its judgement, however, is not final, but is subject to an appeal to the law-courts. Private individuals, also, may lay an information against any magistrate they please for not obeying the laws, but here too there is an appeal to the law-courts if the Council declare the charge proved. The Council also examines those who are to be its members for the ensuing year, and likewise the nine Archons. Formerly the Council had full power to reject candidates for office as unsuitable, but now they have an appeal to the law-courts. In all these matters, therefore, the Council has no final jurisdiction. It takes, however, preliminary cognizance of all matters brought before the Assembly, and the Assembly cannot vote on any question unless it has first been considered by the Council and placed on the programme by the Presiders; since a person who carries a motion in the Assembly is liable to an action for illegal proposal on these grounds.

46.   The Council also superintends the triremes that are already in existence, with their tackle and sheds, and builds new triremes or quadriremes, whichever the Assembly votes, with tackle and sheds to match. The Assembly appoints master-builders for the ships by vote; and if they

do not hand them over completed to the next Council, the old Council cannot receive the customary donation—that being normally given to it during its successor's term of office. For the building of the triremes it appoints ten commissioners, chosen from its own members. The Council also inspects all public buildings, and if it is of opinion that the state is being defrauded, it reports the culprit to the Assembly, and on condemnation hands him over to the law-courts.

47.   The Council also co-operates with the other magistrates in most of their duties. First there are the treasurers of Athena, ten in number, elected by lot, one from each tribe. According to the law of Solon—which is still in force—they must be Pentacosiomedimni, but in point of fact the person on whom the lot falls holds the office even though he be quite a poor man. These officers take over charge of the statue of Athena, the figures of Victory, and all the other ornaments of the temple, together with the money, in the presence of the Council. Then there are the Commissioners for Public Contracts [Poletae], ten in number, one chosen by lot from each tribe, who farm out the public contracts. They lease the mines and taxes, in conjunction with the Military Treasurer and the Commissioners of the Theoric fund, in the presence of the Council, and grant, to the persons indicated by the vote of the Council, the mines which are let out by the state, including both the workable ones, which are let for three years, and those which are let under special agreements for [ten?] years. They also sell, in the presence of the Council, the property of those who have gone into exile from the court of the Areopagus, and of others whose goods have been confiscated, and the nine Archons ratify the contracts. They also hand over to the Council lists of the taxes which are farmed out for the year, entering on whitened tablets the name of the lessee and the amount paid. They make separate lists, first of those who have to pay their instalments in each presidency, on ten several tablets, next of those who pay thrice in the year, with a separate tablet for each instalment, and finally of those who pay in the ninth presidency. They also draw up a list of farms and dwellings which have been confiscated and sold by order of the courts; for these too come within their province. In the case of dwellings the value must be paid up in five years, and in that of farms, in ten. The instalments are paid in the ninth presidency. Further, the King-archon brings before the Council the leases of the sacred enclosures, written on whitened tablets. These too are leased for ten years, and the instalments are paid in the [ninth] presidency; consequently it is in this presidency that the greatest amount of money is collected. The tablets containing the lists of the instalments are carried into the Council, and the public clerk takes charge of them. Whenever a payment of instalments is to be made he takes from the pigeon-holes the pre-

cise list of the sums which are to be paid and struck off on that day, and
delivers it to the Receivers-General. The rest are kept apart, in order that
no sum may be struck off before it is paid.

48.   There are ten Receivers-General [Apodectae], elected by lot, one
from each tribe. These officers receive the tablets, and strike off the instalments as they are paid, in the presence of the Council in the Council-
chamber, and give the tablets back to the public clerk. If any one fails to
pay his instalment, a note is made of it on the tablet; and he is bound to pay
double the amount of the deficiency, or, in default, to be imprisoned. The
Council has full power by the laws to exact these payments and to inflict
this imprisonment. They receive all the instalments, therefore, on one day,
and portion the money out among the magistrates; and on the next day they
bring up the report of the apportionment, written on a wooden notice-
board, and read it out in the Council-chamber, after which they ask publicly in the Council whether any one knows of any malpractice in reference
to the apportionment, on the part of either a magistrate or a private individual, and if anyone is charged with malpractice they take a vote on it.

The Council also elects ten Auditors [Logistae] by lot from its own
members, to audit the accounts of the magistrates for each presidency.
They also elect one Examiner of Accounts [Euthunus] by lot from each
tribe, with two assessors [Paredri] for each examiner, whose duty it is to sit
at the ordinary market hours, each opposite the statue of the eponymous
hero of his tribe; and if any one wishes to prefer a charge, on either public
or private grounds, against any magistrate who has passed his audit before
the law-courts, within three days of his having so passed, he enters on a
whitened tablet his own name and that of the magistrate prosecuted, together with the malpractice that is alleged against him. He also appends his
claim for a penalty of such amount as seems to him fitting, and gives in the
record to the Examiner. The latter takes it, and if after reading it he considers it proved he hands it over, if a private case, to the local justices who
introduce cases for the tribe concerned, while if it is a public case he enters
it on the register of the Regulators. Then, if the Regulators accept it, they
bring the accounts of this magistrate once more before the law-court, and
the decision of the jury stands as the final judgement.

49.   The Council also inspects the horses belonging to the state. If a
man who has a good horse is found to keep it in bad condition, he is
mulcted in his allowance of corn; while those which cannot keep up or
which shy and will not stand steady, it brands with a wheel on the jaw, and
the horse so marked is disqualified for service. It also inspects those who
appear to be fit for service as scouts, and any one whom it rejects is deprived of his horse. It also examines the infantry who serve among the cavalry, and any one whom it rejects ceases to receive his pay. The roll of the

cavalry is drawn up by the Commissioners of Enrollment [Catalogeis], ten in number, elected by the Assembly by open vote. They hand over to the Cavalry Commanders and Tribe Commanders the list of those whom they have enrolled, and these officers take it and bring it up before the Council, and there open the sealed tablet containing the names of the cavalry. If any of those who have been on the roll previously make affidavit that they are physically incapable of cavalry service, they strike them out; then they call up the persons newly enrolled, and if any one makes affidavit that he is either physically or pecuniarily incapable of cavalry service they dismiss him, but if no such affidavit is made the Council vote whether the individual in question is suitable for the purpose or not. If they vote in the affirmative his name is entered on the tablet; if not, he is dismissed with the others.

Formerly the Council used to decide on the plans for public buildings and the contract for making the robe of Athena; but now this work is done by a jury in the law-courts appointed by lot, since the Council was considered to have shown favouritism in its decisions. The Council also shares with the Military Treasurer the superintendence of the manufacture of the images of Victory and the prizes at the Panathenaic festival.

The Council also examines infirm paupers; for there is a law which provides that persons possessing less than three minas, who are so crippled as to be unable to do any work, are, after examination by the Council, to receive two obols a day from the state for their support. A treasurer is appointed by lot to attend to them.

The Council also, speaking broadly, co-operates in most of the duties of all the other magistrates; and this ends the list of the functions of that body.

50.   There are ten Commissioners for Repairs of Temples, elected by lot, who receive a sum of thirty minas from the Receivers-General, and therewith carry out the most necessary repairs in the temples.

There are also ten City Commissioners [Astynomi], of whom five hold office in Piraeus and five in the city. Their duty is to see that female flute- and harp- and lute-players are not hired at more than two drachmas, and if more than one person is anxious to hire the same girl, they cast lots and hire her out to the person to whom the lot falls. They also provide that no collector of sewage shall shoot any of his sewage within ten stadia of the walls; they prevent people from blocking up the streets by building, or stretching barriers across them, or making drain-pipes in mid-air with a discharge into the street, or having doors which open outwards; they also remove the corpses of those who die in the streets, for which purpose they have a body of state slaves assigned to them.

51.   Market Commissioners [Agoranomi] are elected by lot, five for

Piraeus, five for the city. Their statutory duty is to see that all articles offered for sale in the market are pure and unadulterated.

Commissioners of Weights and Measures [Metronomi] are elected by lot, five for the city, and five for Piraeus. They see that sellers use fair weights and measures.

Formerly there were ten Corn Commissioners [Sitophylaces], elected by lot, five for Piraeus, and five for the city; but now there are twenty for the city and fifteen for Piraeus. Their duties are, first, to see that the unprepared corn in the market is offered for sale at reasonable prices, and secondly, to see that the millers sell barley meal at a price proportionate to that of barley, and that the bakers sell their loaves at a price proportionate to that of wheat, and of such weight as the Commissioners may appoint; for the law requires them to fix the standard weight.

There are ten Superintendents of the Mart, elected by lot, whose duty is to superintend the Mart, and to compel merchants to bring up into the city two-thirds of the corn which is brought by sea to the Corn Mart.

52.   The Eleven also are appointed by lot to take care of the prisoners in the state gaol. Thieves, kidnappers, and pick-pockets are brought to them, and if they plead guilty they are executed, but if they deny the charge the Eleven bring the case before the law-courts; if the prisoners are acquitted, they release them, but if not, they then execute them. They also bring up before the law-courts the list of farms and houses claimed as state-property; and if it is decided that they are so, they deliver them to the Commissioners for Public Contracts. The Eleven also bring up informations laid against magistrates alleged to be disqualified; this function comes within their province, but some such cases are brought up by the Regulators.

There are also five Introducers of Cases [Eisagogeis], elected by lot, one for each pair of tribes, who bring up the "monthly"[4] cases to the law-courts. "Monthly" cases are these: refusal to pay up a dowry where a party is bound to do so, refusal to pay interest on money borrowed at 12 per cent., or where a man desirous of setting up business in the market has borrowed from another man capital to start with; also cases of slander, cases arising out of friendly loans or partnerships, and cases concerned with slaves, cattle, and the office of trierarch, or with banks. These are brought up as "monthly" cases and are introduced by these officers; but the Receivers-General perform the same function in cases for or against the farmers of taxes. Those in which the sum concerned is not more than ten

4. So named either because these proceedings had to be settled within a month's time or because they could be instituted in any month.

drachmas they can decide summarily, but all above that amount they bring into the law-courts as "monthly" cases.

53.   The Forty are also elected by lot, four from each tribe, before whom suitors bring all other cases. Formerly they were thirty in number, and they went on circuit through the demes to hear causes; but after the oligarchy of the Thirty they were increased to forty. They have full powers to decide cases in which the amount at issue does not exceed ten drachmas, but anything beyond that value they hand over to the Arbitrators. The Arbitrators take up the case, and, if they cannot bring the parties to an agreement, they give a decision. If their decision satisfies both parties, and they abide by it, the case is at an end; but if either of the parties appeals to the law-courts, the Arbitrators enclose the evidence, the pleadings, and the laws quoted in the case in two urns, those of the plaintiff in the one, and those of the defendant in the other. These they seal up and, having attached to them the decision of the arbitrator, written out on a tablet, place them in the custody of the four justices whose function it is to introduce cases on behalf of the tribe of the defendant. These officers take them and bring up the case before the law-court, to a jury of two hundred and one members in cases up to the value of a thousand drachmas, or to one of four hundred and one in cases above that value. No laws or pleadings or evidence may be used except those which were adduced before the Arbitrator, and have been enclosed in the urns.

The Arbitrators are persons in the sixtieth year of their age; this appears from the schedule of the Archons and the Name-Heroes. There are two classes of Name-Heroes, the ten who give their names to the tribes, and the forty-two for the age-classes. The Ephebes, on being enrolled among the citizens, were formerly registered upon whitened tablets, and the names were appended of the Archon in whose year they were enrolled, and of the Name-Hero who had been in course in the preceding year; at the present day they are written on a bronze pillar, which stands in front of the Council-chamber, near the Name-Hero of the tribes. Then the Forty take the last of the Name-Heroes of the age-classes, and assign the arbitrations to the persons belonging to that year, casting lots to determine which arbitrations each shall undertake; and every one is compelled to carry through the arbitrations which the lot assigns to him. The law enacts that any one who does not serve as Arbitrator when he has arrived at the necessary age shall lose his civil rights, unless he happens to be holding some other office during that year, or to be out of the country. These are the only persons who escape the duty. Any one who suffers injustice at the hands of the Arbitrator may appeal to the whole board of Arbitrators, and if they find the magistrate guilty, the law enacts that he shall lose his civil rights.

The persons thus condemned have, however, in their turn an appeal. The Name-Heroes are also used in reference to military expeditions; when the men of military age are despatched on service, a notice is put up stating that the men from such-and-such an Archon and Name-Hero to such-and-such another Archon and Name-Hero are to go on the expedition.

54.   The following magistrates also are elected by lot: Five Commissioners of Roads [Hodopoei], who, with an assigned body of public slaves, are required to keep the roads in order: and ten Auditors, with ten assistants, to whom all persons who have held any office must give in their accounts. These are the only officers who audit the accounts of those who are subject to examination, and who bring them up for examination before the law-courts. If they detect any magistrate in embezzlement, the jury condemn him for theft, and he is obliged to repay tenfold the sum he is declared to have misappropriated. If they charge a magistrate with accepting bribes and the jury convict him, they fine him for corruption, and this sum too is repaid tenfold. Or if they convict him of unfair dealing, he is fined on that charge, and the sum assessed is paid without increase, if payment is made before the ninth presidency, but otherwise it is doubled. A tenfold fine is not doubled.

The Clerk of the Presidency, as he is called, is also elected by lot. He has the charge of all public documents, and keeps the resolutions which are passed by the Assembly, and checks the transcripts of all other official papers and attends at the sessions of the Council. Formerly he was elected by open vote, and the most distinguished and trustworthy persons were elected to the post, as is known from the fact that the name of this officer is appended on the pillars recording treaties of alliance and grants of consulship and citizenship. Now, however, he is elected by lot. There is, in addition, a Clerk of the Laws, elected by lot, who attends at the sessions of the Council; and he too checks the transcript of all the laws. The Assembly also elects by open vote a clerk to read documents to it and to the Council; but he has no other duty except that of reading aloud.

The Assembly also elects by lot the Commissioners of Public Worship [Hieropoei], known as the Commissioners for Sacrifices, who offer the sacrifices appointed by oracle, and, in conjunction with the seers, take the auspices whenever there is occasion. It also elects by lot ten others, known as Annual Commissioners, who offer certain sacrifices and administer all the quadrennial festivals except the Panathenaea. There are the following quadrennial festivals: first that of Delos (where there is also a sexennial festival), secondly the Brauronia, thirdly the Heracleia, fourthly the Eleusinia, and fifthly the Panathenaea; and no two of these are celebrated in the same place. To these the Hephaestia has now been added, in the archonship of Cephisophon [329/328 B.C.].

An Archon is also elected by lot for Salamis, and a Demarch for Piraeus. These officers celebrate the Dionysia in these two places, and appoint Choregi. In Salamis, moreover, the name of the Archon is publicly recorded.

55.   All the foregoing magistrates are elected by lot, and their powers are those which have been stated. To pass on to the nine Archons, as they are called, the manner of their appointment from the earliest times has been described already. At the present day six Regulators are elected by lot, together with their clerk, and in addition to these an Archon, a King, and a Polemarch. One is elected from each tribe. They are examined first of all by the Council of Five Hundred, with the exception of the clerk. The latter is examined only in the law-court, like other magistrates (for all magistrates, whether elected by lot or by open vote, are examined before entering on their offices); but the nine Archons are examined both in the Council and again in the law-court. Formerly no one could hold the office if the Council rejected him, but now there is an appeal to the law-court, which is the final authority in the matter of the examination. When they are examined, they are asked, first, "Who is your father, and of what deme? who is your father's father? who is your mother? who is your mother's father, and of what deme?" Then the candidate is asked whether he possesses an ancestral Apollo and a household Zeus, and where their sanctuaries are; next if he possesses a family tomb, and where; then if he treats his parents well, and pays his taxes, and has served on the required military expeditions. When the examiner has put these questions, he proceeds, "Call the witnesses to these facts"; and when the candidate has produced his witnesses, he next asks, "Does any one wish to make any accusation against this man?" If an accuser appears, he gives the parties an opportunity of making their accusation and defence, and then puts it to the Council to pass the candidate or not, and to the law-court to give the final vote. If no one wishes to make an accusation, he proceeds at once to the vote. Formerly a single individual gave the vote, but now all the members are obliged to vote on the candidates, so that if any unprincipled candidate has managed to get rid of his accusers, it may still be possible for him to be disqualified before the law-court. When the examination has been thus completed, they proceed to the stone on which are the pieces of the victims, and on which the Arbitrators take oath before declaring their decisions, and witnesses swear to their testimony. On this stone the Archons stand, and swear to execute their office uprightly and according to the laws, and not to receive presents in respect of the performance of their duties, or, if they do, to dedicate a golden statue. When they have taken this oath they proceed to the Acropolis, and there they repeat it; after this they enter upon their office.

56.   The Archon, the King, and the Polemarch have each two as-

sessors, nominated by themselves. These officers are examined in the law-courts before they begin to act, and give in accounts on each occasion of their acting.

As soon as the Archon enters office, he begins by issuing a proclamation that whatever any one possessed before he entered into office, that he shall possess and hold until the end of his term. Next he assigns Chorus-sponsors to the tragic poets, choosing three of the richest persons out of the whole body of Athenians. Formerly he used also to assign five Chorus-sponsors to comic poets, but now the tribes provide the Chorus-sponsors for them. Then he receives the Chorus-sponsors who have been appointed by the tribes for the men's and boys' choruses and the comic poets at the Dionysia, and for the men's and boys' choruses at the Thargelia (at the Dionysia there is a chorus for each tribe, but at the Thargelia one between two tribes, each tribe bearing its share in providing it); he transacts the exchanges of properties for them, and reports any excuses that are tendered, if any one says that he has already borne this burden, or that he is exempt because he has borne a similar burden and the period of his exemption has not yet expired, or that he is not of the required age; since the Chorus-sponsor of a boys' chorus must be over forty years of age. He also appoints Chorus-sponsors for the festival at Delos, and a chief of the mission for the thirty-oar boat which conveys the youths thither. He also superintends sacred processions, both that in honour of Asclepius, when the initiated keep house, and that of the great Dionysia—the latter in conjunction with the Superintendents of that festival. These officers, ten in number, were formerly elected by open vote in the Assembly, and used to provide for the expenses of the procession out of their private means; but now one is elected by lot from each tribe, and the state contributes a hundred minas for the expenses. The Archon also superintends the procession at the Thargelia, and that in honour of Zeus the Saviour. He also manages the contests at the Dionysia and the Thargelia.

These, then, are the festivals which he superintends. The suits and indictments which come before him, and which he, after a preliminary inquiry, brings up before the law-courts, are as follows. Injury to parents (for bringing these actions the prosecutor cannot suffer any penalty); injury to orphans (these actions lie against their guardians); injury to a ward of state (these lie against their guardians or their husbands); injury to an orphan's estate (these too lie against the guardians); mental derangement, where a party charges another with destroying his own property through unsoundness of mind; for appointment of liquidators, where a party refuses to divide property in which others have a share; for constituting a wardship; for determining between rival claims to a wardship; for granting inspection of property to which another party lays claim; for appointing oneself as guardian; and for determining disputes as to inheritances and wards of state. The Archon also has the care of orphans and wards of state, and of women who, on the death of their husbands, declare themselves to be with child; and he has power to inflict a fine on those who offend against the persons under his charge, or to bring the case before the law-courts. He also leases the houses of orphans and wards of state until they reach the age of fourteen, and takes mortgages on them; and if the guardians fail to provide the necessary food for the children under their charge, he exacts it from them. Such are the duties of the Archon.

57.   The King in the first place superintends the mysteries, in conjunction with the Superintendents of Mysteries. The latter are elected in the Assembly by open vote, two from the general body of Athenians, one from the Eumolpidae, and one from the Ceryces. Next, he superintends the Lenaean Dionysia, which consists of a procession and a contest. The procession is ordered by the King and the Superintendents in conjunction; but the contest is managed by the King alone. He also manages all the contests of the torch-race; and to speak broadly, he administers all the ancestral sacrifices. Indictments for impiety come before him, or any disputes between parties concerning priestly rites; and he also determines all controversies concerning sacred rites for the ancient families and the priests. All actions for homicide come before him, and it is he that makes the proclamation requiring polluted persons to keep away from sacred ceremonies. Actions for homicide and wounding are heard, if the homicide or wounding be wilful, in the Areopagus; so also in cases of killing by poison, and of arson. These are the only cases heard by that Council. Cases of unintentional homicide, or of intent to kill, or of killing a slave or a resident alien or a foreigner, are heard by the court of Palladium. When the homicide is acknowledged, but legal justification is pleaded, as when a man takes an adulterer in the act, or kills another by mistake in battle, or in an athletic contest, the prisoner is tried in the court of Delphinium. If a man who is in banishment for a homicide which admits of reconciliation incurs a further charge of killing or wounding, he is tried at the precinct of Phreatos, and he makes his defence from a boat moored near the shore. All these cases, except those which are heard in the Areopagus, are tried by the special jurors [Ephetae] on whom the lot falls. The King introduces them, and the hearing is held within sacred precincts and in the open air. Whenever the King hears a case he takes off his crown. The person who is charged with homicide is at all other times excluded from the temples, nor is it even lawful for him to enter the market-place; but on the occasion of his trial he enters the temple and makes his defence. If the actual offender is unknown,

the writ runs against "the doer of the deed." The King and the tribe-kings also hear the cases in which the guilt rests on inanimate objects and the lower animals.

58.   The Polemarch performs the sacrifices to Artemis the huntress and to Enyalius, and arranges the contest at the funeral of those who have fallen in war, and makes offerings to the memory of Harmodius and Aristogeiton. Only private actions come before him, namely those in which resident aliens, both ordinary and privileged, and agents of foreign states are concerned. It is his duty to receive these cases and divide them into ten groups, and assign to each tribe the group which comes to it by lot; after which the magistrates who introduce cases for the tribe hand them over to the Arbitrators. The Polemarch, however, brings up in person cases in which an alien is charged with deserting his patron or neglecting to provide himself with one, and also of inheritances and wards of state where aliens are concerned; and in fact, generally, whatever the Archon does for citizens, the Polemarch does for aliens.

59.   The Regulators [Thesmothetae] in the first place have the power of prescribing on what days the law-courts are to sit, and next of assigning them to the several magistrates; for the latter must follow the arrangement which the Regulators assign. Moreover they introduce impeachments before the Assembly, and bring up all votes for removal from office, challenges of a magistrate's conduct before the Assembly, indictments for illegal proposals, or for proposing a law which is contrary to the interests of the state, complaints against Heads or their Chairmen for their conduct in office, and the accounts presented by the generals. All indictments also come before them in which a deposit has to be made by the prosecutor, namely, indictments for concealment of foreign origin, for corrupt evasion of foreign origin (when a man escapes the disqualification by bribery), for blackmailing accusations, bribery, false entry of another as a state debtor, false testimony to the service of a summons, conspiracy to enter a man as a state debtor, corrupt removal from the list of debtors, and adultery. They also bring up the examinations of all magistrates, and the rejections by the demes and the condemnations by the Council. Moreover they bring up certain private suits in cases of merchandise and mines, or where a slave has slandered a free man. It is they also who cast lots to assign the courts to the various magistrates, whether for private or public cases. They ratify commercial treaties, and bring up the cases which arise out of such treaties; and they also bring up cases of perjury from the Areopagus. The casting of lots for the jurors is conducted by all the nine Archons, with the clerk to the Regulators as the tenth, each performing the duty for his own tribe. Such are the duties of the nine Archons.

60.   There are also ten Commissioners of Games [Athlothetae], elected

by lot, one from each tribe. These officers, after passing an examination, serve for four years; and they manage the Panathenaic procession, the contest in music and that in gymnastic, and the horse-race; they also provide the robe of Athena and, in conjunction with the Council, the vases, and they present the oil to the athletes. This oil is collected from the sacred olives. The Archon requisitions it from the owners of the farms on which the sacred olives grow, at the rate of three-quarters of a pint from each plant. Formerly the state used to sell the fruit itself, and if any one dug up or broke down one of the sacred olives, he was tried by the Council of Areopagus, and if he was condemned, the penalty was death. Since, however, the oil has been paid by the owner of the farm, the procedure has lapsed, though the law remains; and the oil is a state charge upon the property instead of being taken from the individual plants. When, then, the Archon has collected the oil for his year of office, he hands it over to the Treasurers to preserve in the Acropolis, and he may not take his seat in the Areopagus until he has paid over to the Treasurers the full amount. The Treasurers keep it in the Acropolis until the Panathenaea, when they measure it out to the Commissioners of Games, and they again to the victorious competitors. The prizes for the victors in the musical contest consist of silver and gold, for the victors in manly vigour, of shields, and for the victors in the gymnastic contest and the horse-race, of oil.

61. All officers connected with military service are elected by open vote. In the first place, ten Generals [Strategi], who were formerly elected one from each tribe, but now are chosen from the whole mass of citizens. Their duties are assigned to them by open vote; one is appointed to command the heavy infantry, and leads them if they go out to war; one to the defence of the country, who remains on the defensive, and fights if there is war within the borders of the country; two to Piraeus, one of whom is assigned to Munichia, and one to the south shore, and these have charge of the defence of the Piraeus; and one to superintend the symmories,[5] who nominates the trireme-commanders and arranges exchanges of properties for them, and brings up actions to decide on rival claims in connexion with them. The rest are dispatched to whatever business may be on hand at the moment. The appointment of these officers is submitted for confirmation in each presidency, when the question is put whether they are considered to be doing their duty. If any officer is rejected on this vote, he is tried in the law-court, and if he is found guilty the people decide what punishment or fine shall be inflicted on him; but if he is acquitted he resumes his office. The Generals have full power, when on active service, to arrest any one for

5. The symmories were boards to which the city's wealthiest citizens were assigned, and which shared the expenses of maintaining the city's warships.

insubordination, or to cashier him publicly, or to inflict a fine; the latter is, however, unusual.

There are also ten Regiment Commanders [Taxiarchi], one from each tribe, elected by open vote; and each commands his own tribesmen and appoints captains of companies [Lochagi]. There are also two Cavalry Commanders [Hipparchi], elected by open vote from the whole mass of the citizens, who command the cavalry, each taking five tribes. They have the same powers as the Generals have in respect of the infantry, and their appointments are also subject to confirmation. There are also ten Tribe Commanders [Phylarchi], elected by open vote, one from each tribe, to command the cavalry, as the Regiment Commanders do the infantry. There is also a Cavalry Commander for Lemnos, elected by open vote, who has charge of the cavalry in Lemnos. There is also a treasurer of the Paralus, and another of the Ammonias,[6] similarly elected.

62.   Of the magistrates elected by lot, in former times some, including the nine Archons, were elected out of the tribe as a whole, while others, namely those who are now elected in the Theseum, were apportioned among the demes; but since the demes used to sell the elections, these magistrates too are now elected from the whole tribe, except the members of the Council and the guards of the dockyards, who are still left to the demes.

Pay is received for the following services. First the members of the Assembly receive a drachma for the ordinary meetings, and nine obols for the "sovereign" meeting. Then the jurors at the law-courts receive three obols; and the members of the Council five obols. The Presiders receive an allowance of an obol for their maintenance. The nine Archons receive four obols apiece for maintenance, and also keep a herald and a flute-player; and the Archon for Salamis receives a drachma a day. The Commissioners for Games dine in the town hall during the month of Hecatombaeon in which the Panathenaic festival takes place, from the fourteenth day onwards. The Amphictyonic deputies to Delos receive a drachma a day from the exchequer of Delos. Also all magistrates sent to Samos, Scyros, Lemnos, or Imbros receive an allowance for their maintenance. The military offices may be held any number of times, but none of the others more than once, except the membership of the Council, which may be held twice.

63.   The juries for the law-courts are chosen by lot by the nine Archons, each for their own tribe, and by the clerk to the Regulators for the tenth. There are ten entrances into the courts, one for each tribe; twenty allotment-machines, two for each tribe; a hundred chests, ten for each tribe; other chests, in which are placed the tickets of the jurors on whom the lot falls; and two vases. Further, staves, equal in number to the jurors

6. These were the city's two ships for official business.

required, are placed by the side of each entrance; and the counters are put into one vase, equal in number to the staves. These are inscribed with letters of the alphabet beginning with the eleventh (*lambda*), equal in number to the courts which require to be filled. All persons above thirty years of age are qualified to serve as jurors, provided they are not debtors to the state and have not lost their civil rights. If any unqualified person serves as juror, an information is laid against him, and he is brought before the court; and, if he is convicted, the jurors assess the punishment or fine which they consider him to deserve. If he is condemned to a money fine, he must be imprisoned until he has paid up both the original debt, on account of which the information was laid against him, and also the fine which the court has imposed upon him. Each juror has his ticket of box-wood, on which is inscribed his name, with the name of his father and his deme, and one of the letters of the alphabet up to *kappa;* for the jurors in their several tribes are divided into ten sections, with approximately an equal number in each letter. When the Regulator has decided by lot which letters are required to attend at the courts, the servant puts up above each court the letter which has been assigned to it by the lot.

64.   The ten chests above mentioned are placed in front of the entrance used by each tribe, and are inscribed with the letters of the alphabet from *alpha* to *kappa*. The jurors cast in their tickets, each into the chest on which is inscribed the letter which is on his ticket; then the servant shakes them all up, and the Archon draws one ticket from each chest. The individual so selected is called the Inserter [Empectes], and his function is to insert the tickets from his chest in the slotted column [of the allotment-machine] which bears the same letter as that on the chest. He is chosen by lot, lest, if the Inserter were always the same person, he might tamper with the results. There are five of these columns on each of the allotment-machines. Then the Archon casts in the dice and thereby chooses the jurors of each tribe by means of the allotment-machine. The dice are made of brass, coloured black or white; and according to the number of jurors required, so many white dice are put in, one for each five tickets, while the remainder are black, in the same proportion. As the Archon draws out the dice, the crier calls out the names of the individuals chosen. The Inserter is included among those selected. Each juror, as he is chosen and answers to his name, draws a counter from the vase, and holding it out with the letter uppermost shows it first to the presiding Archon; and he, when he has seen it, throws the ticket of the juror into the chest on which is inscribed the letter which is on the counter, so that the juror must go into the court assigned to him by lot, and not into one chosen by himself, and that it may be impossible for any one to collect the jurors of his choice into any particular court. For this purpose chests are placed near the Archon, as many in num-

ber as there are courts to be filled that day, bearing the letters of the courts
on which the lot has fallen.

65. The juror thereupon, after showing his counter again to the attendant, passes through the barrier into the court. The attendant gives him a
staff of the same colour as the court bearing the letter which is on his
counter, so as to ensure his going into the court assigned to him by lot;
since, if he were to go into any other, he would be betrayed by the colour of
his staff. Each court has a certain colour painted on the lintel of the entrance. Accordingly the juror, bearing his staff, enters the court which has
the same colour as his staff, and the same letter as his counter. As he enters, he receives a voucher from the official to whom this duty has been
assigned by lot. So with their counters and their staves the selected jurors
take their seats in the court, having thus completed the process of admission. The unsuccessful candidates receive back their tickets from the In-
serters. The public servants carry the chests from each tribe, one to each
court, containing the names of the members of the tribe who are in that
court, and hand them over to the officials assigned to the duty of giving
back their tickets to the jurors in each court, so that these officials may call
them by name and pay them their fee.

66. When all the courts are full, two ballot boxes are placed in the first
court, and a number of brazen dice, bearing the colours of the several
courts, and other dice inscribed with the names of the presiding magistrates. Then two of the Regulators, selected by lot, severally throw the dice
with the colours into one box, and those with the magistrates' names into
the other. The magistrate whose name is first drawn is thereupon proclaimed by the crier as assigned for duty in the court which is first drawn,
and the second in the second, and similarly with the rest. The object of this
procedure is that no one may know which court he will have, but that each
may take the court assigned to him by lot.

When the jurors have come in, and have been assigned to their respective courts, the presiding magistrate in each court draws one ticket out of
each chest (making ten in all, one out of each tribe), and throws them into
another empty chest. He then draws out five of them, and assigns one to the
superintendence of the water-clock, and the other four to the telling of the
votes. This is to prevent any tampering beforehand with either the superintendent of the clock or the tellers of the votes, and to secure that there is
no malpractice in these respects. The five who have not been selected for
these duties receive from them a statement of the order in which the jurors
shall receive their fees, and of the places where the several tribes shall respectively gather in the court for this purpose when their duties are completed; the object being that the jurors may be broken up into small groups
for the reception of their pay, and not all crowd together and impede one
another.

67.   These preliminaries being concluded, the cases are called on. If it is a day for private cases, the private litigants are called. Four cases are taken in each of the categories defined in the law, and the litigants swear to confine their speeches to the point at issue. If it is a day for public causes, the public litigants are called, and only one case is tried. Water-clocks are provided, having small supply-tubes, into which the water is poured by which the length of the pleadings is regulated. Ten gallons are allowed for a case in which an amount of more than five thousand drachmas is involved, and three for the second speech on each side. When the amount is between one and five thousand drachmas, seven gallons are allowed for the first speech and two for the second; when it is less than one thousand, five and two. Six gallons are allowed for arbitrations between rival claimants, in which there is no second speech. The official chosen by lot to superintend the water-clock places his hand on the supply-tube whenever the clerk is about to read a resolution or law or affidavit or treaty. When, however, a case is conducted according to a set measurement of the day, he does not stop the supply, but each party receives an equal allowance of water. The standard of measurement is the length of the days in the month Poseideon.[7]
. . . The measured day is employed in cases when imprisonment, death, exile, loss of civil rights, or confiscation of goods is assigned as the penalty.

68.   Most of the courts consist of 500 members . . . ; and when it is necessary to bring public cases before a jury of 1,000 members, two courts combine for the purpose, [while the most important cases of all are brought before] 1,500 jurors, or three courts. The ballot balls are made of brass with stems running through the centre, half of them having the stem pierced and the other half solid. When the speeches are concluded, the officials assigned to the taking of the votes give each juror two ballot balls, one pierced and one solid. This is done in full view of the rival litigants, to secure that no one shall receive two pierced or two solid balls. Then the official designated for the purpose takes away the jurors' staves, in return for which each one as he records his vote receives a brass voucher marked with the numeral 3 (because he gets three obols when he gives it up). This is to ensure that all shall vote; since no one can get a voucher unless he votes. Two urns, one of brass and the other of wood, stand in the court, in distinct spots so that no one may surreptitiously insert ballot balls; in these the jurors record their votes. The brazen urn is for effective votes, the wooden for unused votes; and the brazen urn has a lid pierced so as to take only one ballot ball, in order that no one may put in two at a time.

When the jurors are about to vote, the crier demands first whether the litigants enter a protest against any of the evidence; for no protest can be

7. The text, increasingly damaged in the last chapters, is here almost completely deficient.

received after the voting has begun. Then he proclaims again, "The pierced ballot for the plaintiff, the solid for the defendant"; and the juror, taking his two ballot balls from the stand, with his hand closed over the stem so as not to show either the pierced or the solid ballot to the litigants, casts the one which is to count into the brazen urn, and the other into the wooden urn.

69.   When all the jurors have voted, the attendants take the urn containing the effective votes and discharge them on to a reckoning board having as many cavities as there are ballot balls, so that the effective votes, whether pierced or solid, may be plainly displayed and easily counted. Then the officials assigned to the taking of the votes tell them off on the board, the solid in one place and the pierced in another, and the crier announces the numbers of the votes, the pierced ballots being for the prosecutor and the solid for the defendant. Whichever has the majority is victorious; but if the votes are equal the verdict is for the defendant. Then, if damages have to be awarded, they vote again in the same way, first returning their pay-vouchers and receiving back their staves. Half a gallon of water is allowed to each party for the discussion of the damages. Finally, when all has been completed in accordance with the law, the jurors receive their pay in the order assigned by the lot.

17. Aristotle, *Politics* Book 1.1–2 and Books 7 and 8

It is ironic that the author of the *Politics*, who argues that true well-being can be achieved only by the leisured citizens of an autonomous polis, whose autonomy they are well able to preserve by their own efforts in war, should have lived his life as a resident alien in a variety of cities; that after Chaeronea he should have lived, not only in a polis that, like other Greek poleis of the time, was no longer able to maintain its autonomy, but as the protégé of one of the men who, as the events of the next few years made clear, had brought polis-autonomy to an end; and that, despite his years at the Macedonian court, he seems to have made little attempt to understand and analyze the Macedonian phenomenon that was developing before his eyes.

Book 1 translated by Sir Ernest Barker in *The Politics of Aristotle*. Oxford: Oxford University Press, 1946. Reprinted by permission of Oxford University Press. Books 7 and 8 translated by T. A. Sinclair in Aristotle, *The Politics*, Penguin Classics edition, 1962. © 1962 by the Estate of T. A. Sinclair. Reprinted by permission of Penguin Books Ltd.

Book 1.1–2

1.   Observation shows us, first, that every polis [or state][1] is a species of association, and, secondly, that all associations are instituted for the purpose of attaining some good—for all men do all their acts with a view to achieving something which is, in their view, a good. We may therefore hold [on the basis of what we actually observe] that all associations aim at some good; and we may also hold that the particular association which is the most sovereign of all, and includes all the rest, will pursue this aim most, and will thus be directed to the most sovereign of all goods. This most sovereign and inclusive association is the polis, as it is called, or the political association.

It is a mistake to believe that the "statesman" [the *politikos*, who handles the affairs of a political association] is the same as the monarch of a kingdom, or the manager of a household, or the master of a number of slaves. Those who hold this view consider that each of these persons differs from the others not with a difference of kind, but [merely with a difference of degree, and] according to the number, or the paucity, of the persons with whom he deals. On this view a man who is concerned with few persons is a master: one who is concerned with more is the manager of a household: one who is concerned with still more is a "statesman," or a monarch. This view abolishes any real difference between a large household and a small polis; and it also reduces the difference between the "statesman" and the monarch to the one fact that the latter has an uncontrolled and sole authority, while the former exercises his authority in conformity with the rules imposed by the art of statesmanship and as one who rules and is ruled in turn. But this is a view which cannot be accepted as correct.

Our point will be made clear if we proceed to consider the matter according to our normal method of analysis. Just as, in all other fields, a compound should be analysed until we reach its simple and uncompounded elements (or, in other words, the smallest atoms of the whole which it constitutes), so we must also consider analytically the elements of which a polis is composed. We shall then gain a better insight into the difference from one another of the persons and associations just mentioned; and we shall also be in a position to discover whether it is possible to attain a systematic view of the general issues involved.

2.   If, accordingly, we begin at the beginning, and consider things in the process of their growth, we shall best be able, in this as in other fields,

---

1. In this translation of *Politics* 1.1–2, explanatory material enclosed in brackets has been added by the translator, Sir Ernest Barker.

to attain scientific conclusions by the method we employ. First of all, there must necessarily be a union or pairing of those who cannot exist without one another. Male and female must unite for the reproduction of the species—not from deliberate intention, but from the natural impulse, which exists in animals generally as it also exists in plants, to leave behind them something of the same nature as themselves. Next, there must necessarily be a union of the naturally ruling element with the element which is naturally ruled, for the preservation of both. The element which is able, by virtue of its intelligence, to exercise forethought is naturally a ruling and master element; the element which is able, by virtue of its bodily power, to do what the other element plans is a ruled element, which is naturally in a state of slavery; and master and slave have accordingly a common interest. The female and the slave are naturally distinguished from one another. Nature makes nothing in a spirit of stint, as smiths do when they make the Delphic knife to serve a number of purposes: she makes each separate thing for a separate end; and she does so because each instrument has the finest finish when it serves a single purpose and not a variety of purposes. Among the barbarians, however, the female and the slave occupy the same position—the reason being that no naturally ruling element exists among them, and conjugal union thus comes to be a union of a female who is a slave with a male who is also a slave. This is why our poets have said,

> Meet it is that barbarous peoples should be governed by the Greeks

—the assumption being that barbarian and slave are by nature one and the same.

The first result of these two elementary associations [of male and female, and of master and slave] is the household or family. Hesiod spoke truly in the verse,

> First house, and wife, and ox to draw the plough,

for oxen serve the poor in lieu of household slaves. The first form of association naturally instituted for the satisfaction of daily recurrent needs is thus the family; and the members of the family are accordingly termed by Charondas "associates of the breadchest," as they are also termed by Epimenides the Cretan "associates of the manger." The next form of association—which is also the *first* to be formed from more households than one, and for the satisfaction of something more than daily recurrent needs— is the village. The most natural form of the village appears to be that of a colony or offshoot from a family; and some have thus called the members of the village by the name of "sucklings of the same milk," or, again, of "sons and the sons of sons." This, it may be noted, is the reason why each Greek polis was originally ruled—as the peoples of the barbarian world

still are—by kings. They were formed of persons who were already monarchically governed, for households are always monarchically governed
by the eldest of the kin, just as villages, when they are offshoots from the
household, are similarly governed in virtue of the kinship between their
members. This primitive kinship is what Homer describes:

> Each of them ruleth
> Over his children and wives,

a passage which shows that they lived in scattered groups, as indeed men
generally did in ancient times. The fact that men generally were governed
by kings in ancient times, and that some still continue to be governed in
that way, is the reason that leads us all to assert that the gods are also governed by a king. We make the lives of the gods in the likeness of our own—
as we also make their shapes.

When we come to the final and perfect association, formed from a number of villages, we have already reached the polis—an association which
may be said to have reached the height of full self-sufficiency; or rather we
may say that while it *grows* for the sake of mere life, it *exists* for the sake
of a good life.

Because it is the completion of associations existing by nature, every
polis exists by nature, having itself the same quality as the earlier associations from which it grew. It is the end or consummation to which those
associations move, and the "nature" of things consists in their end or consummation; for what each thing is when its growth is completed we call the
nature of that thing, whether it be a man or a horse or a family. Again the
end, or final cause, is the best. Now self-sufficiency is the end, and so
the best.

From these considerations it is evident that the polis belongs to the class
of things that exist by nature, and that man is by nature an animal intended
to live in a polis. He who is without a polis, by reason of his own nature
and not of some accident, is either a poor sort of being, or a being higher
than man: he is like the man of whom Homer wrote in denunciation:

Clanless and lawless and heartless is he.

The man who is such by nature at once plunges into a passion for war; he is
in the position of a solitary advanced piece in a game of draughts.

The reason why man is a being meant for political association, in a
higher degree than bees or other gregarious animals can ever associate, is
evident. Nature, according to our theory, makes nothing in vain; and man
alone of the animals is furnished with the faculty of language. The mere
making of sounds serves to indicate pleasure and pain, and is thus a faculty
that belongs to animals in general: their nature enables them to attain the

point at which they have perceptions of pleasure and pain, and can signify those perceptions to one another. But language serves to declare what is advantageous and what is the reverse, and it therefore serves to declare what is just and what is unjust. It is the peculiarity of man, in comparison with the rest of the animal world, that he alone possesses a perception of good and evil, of the just and the unjust, and of other similar qualities; and it is association in these things which makes a family and a polis.

We may now proceed to add that the polis is prior in the order of nature to the family and the individual. The reason for this is that the whole is necessarily prior to the part. If the whole body be destroyed, there will not be a foot or a hand, except in that ambiguous sense in which one uses the same word to indicate a different thing, as when one speaks of a "hand" made of stone; for a hand, when destroyed, will be no better than a stone "hand." All things derive their essential character from their function and their capacity; and it follows that if they are no longer fit to discharge their function, we ought not to say that they are still the same things, but only that, by an ambiguity, they still have the same names.

We thus see that the polis exists by nature and that it is prior to the individual. Not being self-sufficient when they are isolated, all individuals are so many parts all equally depending on the whole. The man who is isolated—who is unable to share in the benefits of political association, or has no need to share because he is already self-sufficient—is no part of the polis, and must therefore be either a beast or a god. There is therefore an immanent impulse in all men towards an association of this order. But the man who first *constructed* such an association was none the less the greatest of benefactors. Man, when perfected, is the best of animals; but if he be isolated from law and justice he is the worst of all. Injustice is all the graver when it is armed injustice; and man is furnished from birth with arms which are intended to serve the purposes of moral prudence and virtue, but which may be used in preference for opposite ends. That is why, if he be without virtue, he is a most unholy and savage being, and worse than all others in the indulgence of lust and gluttony. Justice belongs to the polis; for justice, which is the determination of what is just, is an ordering of the political association.

Book 7

1. If we wish to discuss the Best State really adequately, we must first decide what is the most desirable life; for if we do not know that, the best constitution, which we seek, will also elude us. Those who live in a well-ordered society on the basis of their own resources may be expected, bar-

ring accidents, to be those whose lives proceed best. We must therefore first come to some agreement as to what is the most desirable life for all men, or nearly all, and then decide whether the same kind of life or some other is best for men, both in the mass and taken individually.

I have written a good deal elsewhere, including my outside writings, on the subject of the best life and I propose to make use of these now. Certainly no one will dispute one thing: that there are three ingredients which must all be present to make a happy life—our bodily existence, our intellectual and moral qualities, and all that is external to these. No one would deem happy a man who is entirely without courage or self-control or honesty or intelligence, who is scared of flies buzzing past, who will stop at nothing to gratify his desire for eating or drinking, who will ruin his closest friends for a paltry profit, and whose mind also is either as witless as a child's or as deluded as a lunatic's. But while there is general agreement about these three, there is much difference of opinion about their relative importance, the extent to which each ought to be present and whether there is a point beyond which any of them becomes excessive. Thus people suppose that it is sufficient to have a certain amount of goodness, ability, character, but that there is no limit set in the pursuit of wealth, power, property, reputation, and the like.

Our answer to such people will be twofold. First, it is easy to arrive at a firm conclusion on these matters by simply observing the facts; it is not by means of external goods that men acquire and keep the virtues but the other way round; and to live happily, whether men suppose it to consist in enjoyment or in qualities of character or in both, does in fact accrue more easily to those who are outstandingly well-equipped in character and intellect, and only moderately so in the possession of material goods, more easily, that is, than to those who have more goods than they need but are deficient in the other qualities. Second, the matter can be viewed theoretically as well as empirically and the same general view will be obtained. External goods, being like a collection of tools each useful for some purpose, have a limit; one can have too many of them, and that is of no benefit or even a positive nuisance to their possessors. It is quite otherwise with the goods of the mind; every single one of the mind's good qualities is needed and the more there is of each the more useful it will be. (I apply to these the term "useful" as well as the more usual "admirable.") So, putting it in general terms, we shall say that the best condition of anything in relation to any other condition of a thing is commensurate with the relations between the things themselves. Hence as the mind is superior (both absolutely and relatively to ourselves) both to possessions and to the body, its best condition will necessarily show a proportionate superiority over each of the others. Moreover it is for the sake of our minds that these qualities are to be desired and all right-minded persons ought to desire them; it would be wrong to reverse this priority.

Let this then be agreed upon at the start: to each man there comes just so much happiness as he has of moral and intellectual goodness and of performance of actions dependent thereon. God himself is an indication of the truth of this. He is blessed and happy not on account of any of the external goods but because of himself and what he is by his own nature. And for the same reason good fortune must be something different from happiness; for the acquisition of goods external to the mind is due either to the cause of events or to fortune, but no man is righteous or moral as a result of fortune or a lucky coincidence. These same arguments apply with equal force to the state: the best and best-faring city is the happy city; it is impossible for those who do not do good actions to do well. And there is no such thing as a man's or a city's good action without virtue and intelligence. The courage of a nation, or its justice, or its wisdom, have exactly the same effect and are manifested in the same way as in the case of an individual, who by virtue of his share in these is called just, wise, intelligent.

These remarks must suffice to introduce the subject; it was impossible to start without saying something, equally impossible to try and say everything relevant, for that would be a task for another occasion. For the present let this be our fundamental basis: that life is best, both for individuals and for cities, which has virtue sufficiently supported by material wealth to enable it to perform the actions that virtue calls for. As for objectors, if there is anyone who does not believe what has been said, we must pass them by for the purposes of our present inquiry and deal with them on some future occasion.

2.   It remains to ask whether or not we are to say that happiness is the same for the individual human being and for the city. The answer again is obvious: all would agree that it is the same. For those who as individuals hold the view that the good life depends on wealth will likewise, if the whole city be wealthy, count it happy; and those who prize most highly the life of a tyrant will deem most happy that city which rules over the most extensive dominions. So too one who accepts or rejects the single individual on the basis of his virtue will also judge the more virtuous city to be the happier. But there are still these two questions needing consideration: (1) which life is one to choose, the life of a citizen, fully participating in the work of the city, or that of a foreign resident, cutting oneself adrift from the political nexus? and (2) what constitution are we to lay down as a desirable, and what is the best internal arrangement of the affairs of the state (whether we assume that full participation in these is desirable for all or only for the majority)? This is the important question: the first question

was a matter of an individual's choice, this one belongs to political theory and principles and we have chosen to deal with it now. The other question was merely individual, this one is the core of our inquiry.

Obviously the best constitution must be one which is so ordered that any person whatsoever may act and live happily; but it is disputed, even by those who admit that the life of virtue is the most desirable, whether the life of an active citizen is preferable to one which is free of all commitments, the contemplative life, which some say is the only philosophical life. Both in ancient and in modern times men striving for virtue seem generally to have picked out these two kinds of life, the political and the philosophical, as the only possible. It makes considerable difference which of the two is right, because we must, if we are right-minded people, direct ourselves to the better of the two aims, whichever it may be; and this equally as individuals and as a community of citizens. Some hold that to dominate other states despotically involves the greatest injustice but to do so in a statesman-like way involves none, though it does mean making inroads on the leisure and comfort of the ruler. Others hold that this is no drawback, since the busy life of active statesmanship is the only one worthy of a man, and virtuous activity springing from any of the virtues is just as much open to those who take part in the affairs of the city as to individual private citizens. That is one view, but there is also a set of people who go so far as to say that the only happy life is one of absolute and despotic domination. And in some cities the avowed purpose of the laws and constitution is to enable that city to dominate neighbouring states.

Hence, even though in most states their legal provisions have for the most part been established on no fixed principle, yet in so far as laws may be said to have a single purpose they all aim at domination. Thus in Sparta and Crete the educational system and most of the laws are directed towards the establishment of military power for the purposes of war; and outside the Greek peoples such nations as are strong enough to enrich themselves, like the Scythians, Persians, Thracians, and Kelts, have always set great store by military power. In some places there are laws designed to foster military courage, as at Carthage where men wear armlets showing the number of campaigns in which they have served. There used to be a rule in Macedonia that a man had to wear a halter until he had slain his first enemy, and at a certain Scythian feast when the cup was passed round only those were allowed to drink from it who had killed an enemy. Among the Iberians, a very warlike race, the tombs of their warriors have iron spikes stuck in them showing the number of enemy slain. There are many other such laws and customs established among different peoples.

Yet surely, if we will but examine carefully, we shall see how completely unreasonable it would be if the work of a statesman were to be reduced to seeing how he could rule and dominate others with or without their consent. How could that be regarded as part of statecraft or lawgiving which is not even lawful in itself? To rule at all costs, not only justly but unjustly, that is simply non-legal, and merely to have the power is not to have the right. One does not find this insistence on power in any of the other professions; it is not the job of a doctor or a ship's captain to persuade or to force patients or passengers. Certainly most people seem to think that domination and government are one and the same thing; they have no compunction about inflicting upon others what as individuals they regard as neither just nor beneficial to themselves. For themselves and among themselves they ask for just government but in the treatment of others they do not worry about what things are just. Of course we may be sure that nature has made some creatures to be treated despotically and others not, and if this is so, we must try to exercise despotic rule not over all creatures but only over those made for such treatment. We do not pursue human beings to hurt or slay them for food, but only such animals as are wild and edible and suitable to be hunted. Surely too a single city could be happy on its own, assuming of course that its internal government is good. It is possible for a city to exist in isolation following its own good laws; the administration of its constitution will not be directed to war or the defeat of enemies, for the non-existence of these is postulated. The conclusion is obvious: we regard every provision made for war as admirable, not as a supreme end but only as serving the needs of defence. It is the task of a good legislator to survey the city, the clan, and every other human association and to see how they can be brought to share in good life and in whatever degree of happiness is possible for them. There will of course be different rules in different places; if there are neighbouring peoples, it will be part of the legislative function to decide what attitude is to be adopted to this one and that one, and how to use towards each the proper method for dealing with each. But this question "With what end in view should the Best Constitution be designed?" will be properly dealt with at a later stage in our inquiry.

3.   We must now deal with those who, while agreeing that the life which is conjoined with virtue is the most desirable, differ as to how it is to be pursued. Some reject altogether any life of public responsibility, regarding the life of a free man as inconsistent with the work of a statesman and as the most desirable of all lives. Others say that an active public life is best, on the grounds that a man who does nothing cannot be doing well, and happiness and faring well are the same thing. To both parties we may say in reply, "You are both of you partly right and partly wrong." Certainly the life of a free man is better than the life of a despotic ruler; there is no worth or dignity in treating a slave as a slave, and issuing instructions to do this or that is no part of virtuous or noble activity. But not all giving of

commands is despotic and those who think it is are mistaken. The differences between ruling over free men and ruling over slaves is as great as the natural differences between freedom and slavery, a distinction which has been sufficiently emphasized in an earlier passage. But we cannot agree that it is right to value inaction more than action, doing nothing more than doing something. For happiness is doing something and the actions of good and wise men have as their aim the production of a variety of excellent results.

But perhaps someone will object that if we define things in this way, it means that absolute sovereignty is best, because it is in a position to perform the noblest actions; and so anyone who is in a position to rule ought not to yield that position to another, but take and keep it for himself without any regard for the claims of friendship or even parenthood or anything else; the best is most to be desired and nothing could be better than to do well. Perhaps there is some truth in this, but only if we suppose that this most desirable condition is going to belong to those who use robbery and violence. But this is most improbable and the supposition is false. For a man who shows no more superiority over his fellows than husband over wife or father over children or master over slave—how can his actions be always good actions? So he that departs from the path of goodness will never be able to do good sufficient to make up entirely for his previous errors. For equals, the right and just thing is to share and take turns, as is fair and equal. Non-equality, superiority, given to equals, unlike positions given to like persons—these are contrary to nature and nothing that is contrary to nature is right. It is only when one man is superior in virtue and in the ability to perform the finest actions that it becomes right to serve him and just to obey him. But it should be remembered that goodness in itself is not enough; there must also be the power to translate it into action.

If all this is true and if happiness is to be equated with doing well, then the active life will be the best both for any state as a whole community and for the individual. But the active life need not, as some suppose, be always concerned with our relations with other people, nor is thinking only effective when it concentrates on the possible outcome of action. On the contrary, thinking and speculation that are their own end and are done for the sake of thinking and speculation—these are more effective because they are themselves the doing well which is their aim, and they are therefore action. Indeed those who build with their thoughts are quite properly spoken of as the creators of external actions also. As for their counterpart among states, cities that are set up away from others and have chosen to live thus in isolation, there is nothing in that to oblige them to lead a life of inaction. Activity may be internal: the parts of a city provide numerous groups or associations that enter into relations with each other. The same is true of any individual person; otherwise God himself and the whole universe would be in a sorry plight, for they have no external activities, only what they can provide for themselves. It is therefore clear that the same life must inevitably be the best for individuals, for states, and for mankind.

4.   Now that our introduction to these matters is finished and since we have earlier discussed the other constitutions, the first part of what remains to be discussed will deal with the question, "What are the fundamental postulates for a state which is to be constructed exactly as one would wish, one provided with all the appropriate material equipment, without which it would not be the best state?" We must therefore postulate everything as we would wish it to be, remembering however that nothing must be outside the bounds of possibility. I am thinking for example of population and territory; these are part of the essential material. A weaver or a boatmaker must have a supply of the materials necessary for the exercise of his craft, and the better the provision for these, the finer will be the result which his skill will produce. So too a statesman or lawgiver must have the proper material in sufficient quantities.

For the making of a state the first essential is a supply of men and we must consider both how many they shall be and of what kind. The second is territory; we shall need to determine both its extent and its quality. Most people think that if a city is to be happy it must needs be great. This may be true, but they do not know how to judge greatness and smallness in a city. They judge greatness by the number of people living in it; but one ought to look not at numbers merely but at power and effectiveness. A city has a function to perform and the city which is most capable of discharging that function must be regarded as greatest, rather in the same way that one might say that Hippocrates was "a bigger man," not as a man but as a physician, than one of great bodily size. However, even granting that we must have regard to size of population, we must not do so without discrimination; we must allow for the presence in the states of many slaves and many foreigners, residents or visitors. Our concern is only with those who form part of the state, with those sections of population of which a state properly consists. Great numbers of these is a mark of a great city, but a city cannot possibly be great which can put into the field only a handful of citizen-soldiers along with a large rabble of inferior persons. A great city and a populous one are not the same. Moreover, experience has shown that it is difficult, if not impossible, for an over-large population to be well and lawfully governed; at any rate I know of no well-constituted city that does not restrict its numbers. The language itself makes this certain. For law is itself a kind of order and to live under good laws is to live in good order. But an excessively large number cannot be orderly; that would require the power of the divine force which holds the universe together, where to be sure we do find order and beauty conjoined with size and multiplicity. Therefore that city will be finest which though large conforms to the limitations just mentioned. But there must also be a proper norm for the size of a city, as there is a normal size for everything else—animals, plants, instruments, and so on. Each of these can only perform its proper function if it is neither too large nor too small; otherwise its true raison d'être will be either entirely lost or seriously impaired. Thus a boat a few inches long will not really be a boat at all, nor one half a mile long. If it reaches a certain size, it may be long enough (or small enough) to be called a boat, but still be too small (or too large) to be navigated. It is just the same with a city; if it has too few people it cannot serve its own needs as a city should; if it has too many it can certainly meet all its essential requirements, but as an ethnic conglomerate not as a city. Such size makes it difficult for any constitution to subsist. For who will be military commander of the excessive population? Who will be their crier unless he has the voice of a Stentor? Therefore, when first the population becomes large enough to be able to provide for itself all that is needed for living the good life after the manner of the city-state community, then we can begin to speak of a city. It is possible to go on from there; a city greater in population than that will be a larger city, but as we have said this process is not unlimited. What the limit of size should be can easily be determined by an examination of the facts. The activities of a city are those of the rulers and those of the ruled, and the functions of the ruler are decision and direction. In order to give decisions on matters of justice and for the purpose of distributing offices in accordance with the work of the applicants, it is necessary that the citizens should know each other and know what kind of people they are. Where this condition does not exist, both elections and decisions at law are bound to suffer; it is not right in either of these matters to vote at haphazard, which is clearly what takes place where the population is excessive. Another drawback is that it becomes easy for non-citizens, foreigners resident in the country to become possessed of citizenship; the great size of the population makes detection difficult. Here then we have ready to hand the best definition of a city: it must have a population large enough to cater for all the needs of a self-sufficient existence, but not so large that it cannot be easily supervised. Let that be our way of defining the size of a city.

5.   The case is similar when we turn our attention to territory. As regards quality of land, everyone would choose the most self-sufficient, that is to say the most universally productive; to have everything to hand and nothing lacking is the height of self-sufficiency. As to size and extent, these should be such that the citizens can live a life that involves no manual labour, a life of a free man but one without extravagance. Whether this definition is good or bad is a question into which we must later go in greater

detail, when we come to discuss property in general and abundance of resources in private hands; what are the right relations between ownership and use of property. It is a complicated question with many points of dispute, because men tend to go to extremes, some tending to extravagance, others to niggardliness. The general configuration of the land is not difficult to state, though there are some points on which we must take the opinion of those who have experience of conducting operations of war; it ought to be hard for a hostile force to invade, easy for an expeditionary force to depart from. Apart from that, just as we remarked that the population ought to be easily supervised, so we say the same of the territory; in a country that can easily be seen it is easy to bring military assistance at any point. Next, the position of the city: if we are to put it exactly where we would like best, it should be conveniently situated for both sea and land. This will give three advantages: first the point mentioned above, it will be equally well-placed for operations in all directions; also it will form an entrepôt for the receipt of incoming foodstuffs; and it will have access to timber and whatever other raw materials the land may be able to produce.

6.   There is a good deal of argument about communication with the sea and whether it is a help or a hindrance in good government of states. Some say that to open one's city to foreigners, brought up in a different code of behaviour, is detrimental to good order and makes for overcrowding. They say that the use of the sea leads to much coming and going of large numbers of traders and that this is inimical to the good life of the citizens. If these evil consequences can be avoided, it is obviously better both for economic and for defensive reasons that the city and its territory should have access to the sea. To facilitate resistance to an enemy a successful defender needs to be in a position to use both sea and land, and even if he cannot strike a blow against invaders on both elements, it will be easier to strike on one, if he has access to both. So too in the economic sphere; people must import the things which they do not themselves produce and export those of which they have a surplus. For when a city becomes a trading city it must do so in its own interest and not in others'. Some throw their city open as a market for all comers for the sake of the money they bring in; but a city which regards this kind of profit-making as illegitimate ought not to possess that kind of open market at all.

Again, we see in modern times many cities and territories in possession of docks and harbours conveniently situated, not too far away but not so near as to encroach upon the town itself, and dominated by walls and other such defence-works. It is therefore clear that if this intercommunication is productive of good, the city will derive advantage from it; if of evil, it is easy to guard against that by laying down regulations and stating who are and who are not to be allowed to enter the area. Then there is this matter of naval forces; clearly it is desirable that there should be a certain amount of these; for it is important that by sea as well as by land a state should be able to make its power felt or to render aid, not only internally but in relation to certain neighbours. The number of ships and the size of the naval force will have to be decided in the light of the circumstances and way of living of the state concerned. If it is to play a big part as a leading state, it will need naval as well as land forces large enough for such activities. The addition to population, which the enlistment of large numbers of seamen will make necessary, need not swell the membership of the cities; there is no reason why they should have a share in the state as if they were soldiers. The troops that are carried on board are free men belonging to the infantry; they are in authority and take precedence over the crews. But the rowers need not be members of the state; and a potential source of manpower for them is sure to exist wherever the outlying dwellers and agricultural labourers are plentiful. We can see examples of this today: at Heraclea, though their city is of modest size, they find crews for many triremes. So much then for territory, harbours, cities, sea, naval forces; we pass now to the citizens and population.

7.   We have already spoken about limiting the number of citizens; we must now ask what kind of natural qualities they should have. We could form a fair notion of the answer if we glanced first at the most famous Greek states and then at the racial divisions of the whole world. The races that live in cold regions and those of Europe are full of courage and passion but somewhat lacking in skill and brain-power; for this reason, while remaining generally independent, they lack political cohesion and the ability to rule over others. On the other hand the Asiatic races have both brains and skill but are lacking in courage and will-power; so they have remained enslaved and subject. The Hellenic race, occupying a mid-position geographically, has a measure of both. Hence it continues to be free, to have the best political institutions, and to be capable of ruling all others, given a single constitution. But we do observe the same differences among the Greeks themselves when we compare one set with another; some are by nature one-sided, in others the qualities of head and of heart are combined. Both are clearly needed if men are to be as we want them—the kind of person who can easily be moulded by a lawgiver and brought to a high degree of excellence. Some say that to feel friendly at the sight of familiar faces and hostile at the approach of strangers is a requirement for guardians of the state. Now friendliness springs from the heart, from that power in our souls whereby we love. We see this from the fact that our feelings are more likely to be aroused if those whom we love neglect us than by the conduct of those whom we do not know. Hence the lines of Archilochus, reproaching his friends but addressed to his own heart, are aptly spoken:

"About your friends you torture yourself." The power to command and the spirit of freedom have their source in this faculty, which is masterful and unsubdued. But what he says about harshness to strangers is, I think, quite wrong; there is no need to behave thus to anyone and fierceness is not a mark of greatness of mind except towards wrongdoers. Rather, as we have said, is indignation aroused by the sight of friends when we believe ourselves to have been wrongly used by them. And this is understandable; where men expect to receive kindness as their due, they are indignant at being deprived of it and at losing the benefit. Hence the proverbial sayings, "Grievous is fraternal strife" and "Excessive love turns to excessive hate."

So much for the members of the state, their number, and their kind, so much for the size and kind of territory; we need say no more because one cannot expect the same attention to detail in theoretical discussions as one would if the case were presented before our eyes.

8.   Just as, in considering any other object that exists in nature, we do not call "parts" all those indispensable things without which the whole would not be itself, so too we must not list as parts of a city the indispensable conditions of its existence, nor would we in relation to any other form of community that made up a single definite kind; to all its members, irrespective of their degree of participation, the community is the community, one single identical whole. Food-supply, an amount of territory, and the like, these are indispensable but they are not the things that give a specific character to any form of human society. Whenever one thing is a means and another an end, there can be no other relation between them than this—that the one acts, the other is acted upon. Take any set of tools and consider it along with its users in relation to the work which they produce; for example a house and its builders. There is no other relation between house and builders, nothing that can be called cooperation, but the builder's skill with his tools is a means towards building a house. So too a state needs to own property, but property is no part of the state, though many parts of the property are living creatures. When we speak of city or state, we mean a community of like persons whose end or aim is the best life possible. The best is happiness and this consists in the exercise of all good qualities and their fullest possible use. Life is such that some can get a share of happiness, while others get little or none. Here then we clearly have a reason for the existence of different kinds of cities and the variety of constitutions. Different sets of people seek their happiness in different ways and by different means; little wonder that their lives are different or that they have different political constitutions.

We must also ask how many are those things without which there can be no city. (We include what we call parts of the state, because their presence too is essential.) Let us therefore make a count of all the things and actions

needed, for that will show the answer. They are (1) food, (2) handicrafts
and their tools, (3) arms. Arms are included because members of the constitution must carry them even among themselves, both for internal government in the event of civil disobedience and to repel external agression.
(4) Wealth too is required both for war and for all the internal needs. Then
(5) the needs of religion (this might have been put first) and (6) (most essential of all) a method of arriving at decisions, both about policy and
about matters of right and wrong as between one person and another. These
then are the essentials; every state, we may say, has need of these. For a
state is not a chance agglomeration but, we repeat, a body of men aiming
at a self-sufficient life; and if any of these six is lacking, it will be impossible for that community to be thoroughly self-sufficing. It is therefore essential in setting up a city to make provision for all these activities. Quite a
number of agricultural workers will be needed to supply food; skilled
craftsmen will be required, and fighting men, and wealthy men, and
priests, and judges of what is right and expedient.

9.   This enumeration of classes being finished, it remains to consider
whether they shall all take part in all these activities, everybody being, as
occasion requires, farmer and craftsman and councillor and judge (for this
is not impossible) or shall we postulate a different set of persons for each
task? Or again, are not some of the jobs necessarily confined to one set of
people, while others may be thrown open to all? The situation is not the
same in every form of constitution; for as we have said it is equally possible for all to share in everything and for some to share in some. These are
what make differences in constitutions; in democracies all share in all, in
oligarchies the reverse is true.

But since our present inquiry is directed towards the best constitution,
that is to say, that by which a city would be most happy, and we have already said that happiness cannot exist apart from virtue, it becomes clear
that in the best state with the best constitution, one that possesses just men
who are just absolutely and not simply relatively to some postulated standard, the citizens must not live a banausic or commercial life. Such a life is
not noble and not conducive to virtue. Nor will those who are to be citizens
live an agricultural life; for they must have leisure to cultivate their virtue
and talents, time for the activities of a citizen. Now both defence and deliberation, whether about policy or about questions of justice, are at the heart
and centre of the state. And when we ask whether these are to be assigned
to different persons or to be kept together in the hands of the same body,
our answer is partly one and partly the other. In so far as the tasks themselves differ in the best time of life for their performance, one requiring
wisdom, the other strength, they should be assigned to different people.
But as it is impossible to secure that those who are strong enough to en-

force their will shall always tolerate being ruled by others, to that extent they must be assigned to the same people. For those who possess and can wield arms are in a position to decide whether the constitution is to continue or not. So we are left with this conclusion: that this constitution, both in its military and its civil functions, should be put into the hands of the same class of persons, but not both simultaneously. Rather we should follow nature, the young have strength, the older have understanding, so it is both right and expedient that the distribution of tasks should be made on this basis; it takes into account fitness for the work. Property too must belong to this class; it is essential that citizens should have ample subsistence, and these are citizens. The lower-class element has no part in the state nor any other class that is not productive of virtue. This is evident from our postulate; being happy must occur in conjunction with virtue, and in pronouncing a city happy we must have regard not to part of it but to all its citizens. It is also clear that property must belong to these; the agricultural workers will be slaves or non-Greeks dwelling in the country roundabout.

Of the list which we made earlier there remains the class of priests. Their position is clear: no agricultural or commercial worker could be made a priest, since it is only right and proper that the gods should be worshipped by citizens. As we have divided citizens and their duties into military and civil, it is also right and proper that citizens who have thus spent themselves in long service should both enjoy their retirement and serve the gods. These then should be appointed to priestly offices.

We have now stated what are the essential requirements of a state and what are its parts. There must be agricultural workers and craftsmen and paid labourers; but as to parts of the state, these are the military and deliberative elements, which may be separated either permanently or successively.

10.   That division into classes is necessary, in particular the separation of the fighting from the agricultural class, is not a recent discovery; it has been well-known to students of politics for a long time. In Egypt something very similar still exists today and in Crete too. Sesostris is said to have introduced laws in this sense for Egypt, Minos for Crete. The practice of communal feeding also appears to be ancient, introduced in Crete in the reign of Minos, but in Italy very much earlier. For the chroniclers tell us of a certain Italus in that land who was king of Oenotria, and after him the people of Oenotria changed their name to Italians, and the name Italy was given to that part of Europe's coast line which lies south of a line drawn between the Scylletic and Lampetic gulfs, where the distance across is half a day's journey. This Italus, they tell us, transformed the Oenotrians from a pastoral people into farmers and instituted many new customs and laws, including the common meals. So even to this day some of his successors

continue this practice as well as some of his other customs. On the Etrurian side were the Opici, called Ausones both in ancient and modern times; on the other side, that of Iapygia and the Ionian Sea, there was the land called Siritis; and the Chones also were by race Oenotrians. Common messing, then, originated thence, and class-distinctions in Egypt; the kingdom of Sesostris goes back very much farther than that of Minos.

We must, I think, regard it as fairly certain that the rest of the customs have been in the course of the ages discovered, lost, and rediscovered many times over. In the first place there are things we cannot do without, and this very necessity naturally teaches us them. Secondly, when once these are established, the process naturally goes on tending towards more comfort and greater abundance. So we should accept it as a fact that the same process takes place in social and political institutions. That these are all ancient is shown by Egyptian history; the Egyptians are reputed to be the most ancient people and they have always had laws and a social and political organization. Thus we ought to make full use of what has already been discovered, while endeavouring to find what has not.

We stated above that the land ought to be possessed by those who have arms and enjoy full participation in the constitution, and why the cultivators should be different from the owners, also the nature and extent of the territory required. We must speak first about the division of the land for the purposes of cultivation and about those who will cultivate it, who and of what type they will be. We do not agree with those who have said that all land should be communally owned, but we do believe that there should be a friendly arrangement for sharing the usufruct and that none of the citizens should be without means of support. Next as to communal feeding, it is generally agreed that this is a very useful institution in a well-ordered society; why we too are of this opinion we will say later. In any case, where communal meals exist, all citizens should partake of them, though it is not easy for those who are badly off to pay the contribution fixed and keep a household going at the same time. Another thing that should be a charge on the whole community is the public worship of the gods. Thus it becomes necessary to divide the land into two parts, one publicly owned, the other privately. Each of these has to be further divided into two. One part of the public land will support the service of the gods, the other the communal feeding. Of the privately owned land one part will be near the frontier, the other near the city, so that every citizen will have two portions, one in each locality. This is not only in accordance with justice and equality but makes also for greater unity in the face of wars with bordering states. Without this dual arrangement some make too little of hostilities on the border, others too much, some underestimate the dangers of frontier quarrels, others take them too seriously, even sacrificing honour in order to avoid them. Hence in some countries it is the custom that when war against a neighbour is under consideration, those who live near to the border should be excluded from the discussion as being too closely involved to be able to give honest advice. It is therefore important that the territory should for the reasons given be divided in the manner stated. As for those who are to till the land, they should, if possible, be slaves (and we are building as we would wish). They should not be all of one stock nor men of spirit; this will ensure that they will be good workers and not prone to revolt. An alternative to slaves is foreigners settled on the countryside, men of the same type as the slaves just mentioned. They fall into two groups according to whether they work privately on the land of individual owners of property, or publicly on the common land. I hope later on to say how slaves ought to be used in agriculture and why it is a good thing that all slaves should have before them the prospect of receiving their freedom as a reward.

11.   We have already noted that a city should have easy access both to the sea and to the interior, and, so far as conditions allow, be equally accessible to the whole of its territory. The land upon which the city itself is to be sited should be sloping. That is something that we must just hope to find, but we should keep four considerations in mind. First and most essential the situation must be a healthy one. A slope facing east, with winds blowing from the direction of sunrise, gives a healthy site, rather better than one on the lee side of north though this gives good weather. Next, it should be well situated for carrying out all its civil and military activities. For the purposes of defence the site should be one from which defenders can easily make a sally but which attackers will find difficult to approach and difficult to surround. Water, and especially spring water, should be abundant and if possible under immediate control in time of war; alternatively a way has been discovered of catching rain water in large quantities in vessels numerous enough to ensure a supply when fighting prevents the defenders from going far afield.

Since consideration must be given to the health of the inhabitants, which is partly a matter of siting in the best place and facing the right way, partly also dependent on a supply of pure water, this too must receive careful attention. I mention situation and water supply in particular because air and water, being just those things that we make most frequent and constant use of have the greatest effect on our bodily condition. Hence, in a state which has welfare at heart, water for human consumption should be separated from water for all other purposes, unless of course all the water is alike and there are plenty of springs that are drinkable.

In the matter of defensive positions it should be remembered that what is best for one type of government is not so good for another. A lofty central citadel suits both oligarchy and monarchy, a level plain democracy;

neither suits an aristocracy, which prefers a series of strongly held points. In laying out areas for private dwelling houses, the modern or Hippoda-mean method has the advantage of regularity; it is also more attractive and for all purposes save one, more practical. For ease of defence, the old-fashioned irregular siting of houses was better, hard for foreign merce-naries to get out of and for attackers to penetrate. It follows that both meth-ods should be used and this is quite possible: arrange the buildings in the same pattern as is used for planting vines, not in rows but in quincunx, and do not lay out the whole city with geometric regularity but only certain parts. This will meet the needs both of safety and good appearance.

As for walls, it is quite out of date to say, as some do, that cities that lay claim to valour have no need of walls; we have only to look at what in fact has happened to cities that made that boast. Doubtless there is something not quite honourable in seeking safety behind solid walls, at any rate against an enemy equal in numbers or only very slightly superior. But it may happen, and does happen, that the numerical superiority of the at-tackers is too much for the courage of the defenders, both of the average man and of a chosen few. If then we are to save our city and avoid the mis-eries of cruelty and oppression, we must concede that the greatest degree of protection that walls can afford is also the best military measure. The truth of this is emphasized by all the modern improvements in missiles and artillery for attacking a besieged town. Deliberately to give cities no walls at all is like choosing an easily attacked position and clearing away the surrounding high ground. It is as if we were to refrain from putting walls round private property for fear of rendering the inhabitants unmanly. An-other thing that should not be lost sight of is that those who have provided their city with a wall are in a position to regard that city in both ways, to treat it either as a fortified or an unfortified city. Those who have no walls have no such choice. And if this is so, then it is a duty not only to build walls but also to maintain them in a manner suitable both for the city's ap-pearance and for its defensive needs, which in these days are very numer-ous. Just as the attacking side is always on the lookout for methods which will give them an advantage, so too the defenders must seek additional means of defence by the aid of scientific inquiry. An enemy will not at-tempt an attack on those who are really well prepared to meet it.

12.   We have seen that the greater number of the citizens should be dis-tributed over a number of feeding-centres and also that the walls should be furnished at suitable intervals with forts each manned by a garrison. Hence it would seem reasonable that some of the feeding-centres should be lo-cated in the same places as the garrisons. For the rest, institutions devoted to the service of the gods and the chief feeding-places of government offices should have a central position on the same site, unless the sacral law

or some pronouncement of Apollo at Delphi requires the sacred building in the case to be erected somewhere apart. Our purpose would be well served by a site which gives a frontage commensurate with our ideas of good siting and is at the same time easily defended in relation to the neighbouring parts of the city. Just below this is a good place to build a square of the kind which in Thessaly is given the name Free Market. Here nothing may be bought or sold and no member of the lower orders or countryman may be admitted unless summoned by the authorities. The amenities of this area would be enhanced if the gymnasia of the older folk were situated there; for in the taking of exercise also there should be separation of age-groups, the younger in one place, the older in another; government personnel should go in with the latter but should also mingle with the younger men, since the presence of authority's watchful eye is the best way to instil a real feeling of deference and of respect for the upper classes. The market proper, where buying and selling are done, must be in quite a separate place, conveniently situated both for goods sent up from the harbour and for people coming in from the country.

The authorities of the state being divided into secular and religious, it is right that the priests too should have their eating-places near the sacred buildings. As for the minor offices of government—those concerned with contracts, with suits-at-law, summonses, and the ordering of such matters generally (also surveillance of markets and what is called "astynomy")— these should all be located near a market and general meeting-place. This will, of course, be the area of the dealers' market, which is intended for the exchange of necessary commodities: the upper area that we mentioned is intended for recreation. A similar arrangement should be followed in country districts; for there too the officials, forest-wardens, or field-wardens, or whatever they may be called, must have eating-places and garrison-posts to enable them to carry out their work of protection; likewise shrines of gods and heroes situated all over the countryside.

But it is really not necessary now to go on mentioning all these things in detail. It is not at all difficult to think what things are needed; it is quite another matter to provide them. Our talk is the mirror of our desires, but the outcome is in fortune's hands. Therefore we will say no more about these matters now and turn to the *politeia* itself.

13.   We must now discuss the constitution itself and ask ourselves what people and what kind of people ought to form the material out of which is to be made a happy and well-governed city. All men's well-being depends on two things; one is the right choice of target, of the end to which actions should tend, the other lies in finding the actions that lead to that end. These two may just as easily conflict with each other as coincide. Sometimes for example the aim is well-chosen, but in action men fail to attain it. At other

times they successfully perform everything that conduces to the end, but the end itself was badly chosen. Or they may fail in and be wrong about both, as sometimes happens in the practice of medicine, when doctors neither rightly discern what kind of condition is a healthy one for the body nor discover the means which will enable their self-set goal to be attained. Wherever professional skill and knowledge come into play, these two must both be mastered—the end and the means to the end.

It is clear then that all men desire to have happiness and the good life, but some men are in a position to get it, others are not. This may be due to fortune or to their natural disposition; both play a part; the good life needs some material goods at any time, but when the natural disposition is good, fortune will need to provide a lesser amount of these, a greater amount when it is bad. Some indeed, who start with excellent opportunities, fail from the very beginning in the pursuit of happiness. But as our object is to find the best constitution, and that means the one whereby a city will be best ordered, and we call that city best ordered in which the possibilities of happiness are greatest; it is clear that we must keep our conception of happiness constantly in mind. We defined this in our *Ethics* and we may be permitted to make use of the definition here: happiness is activity and the complete utilization of all our powers, our goodness, not conditionally but absolutely. By "conditionally" in this connexion I refer to actions necessary in the conditions and by "absolutely" I mean moral or noble. For example actions relating to justice, the just recovery of damages, and the infliction of just punishment spring from the virtue justice, but they are necessary or conditional and whatever good is in them is there by necessity. I would prefer to see a state of affairs in which such action would be unnecessary either for state or individual. But actions directed towards honours and high standards of living are noble actions absolutely. For the former actions are but the removal of evil, the latter are not; they are on the contrary the creation and the begetting of positive good.

A good man will nobly bear ill-health, poverty, and other misfortunes, but happiness requires the opposite of these. This definition too was given in our ethical writings—that a good man is the sort of man for whom things good absolutely are good in his eyes on account of his own virtue, and clearly his attitudes to what befalls must be good and noble absolutely. Hence men imagine that the causes of happiness lie in external goods and not within our minds. This is as if we were to ascribe brilliant lyre-playing to the quality of the instrument rather than to the skill of the player.

From what has been said it is clear that some things must be there from the start, others must be provided by a lawgiver. We wish for our city good fortune in all that Fortune has it in her power to bestow, that is all we can expect of her. It is not in Fortune's power to make a city good; that is a matter of scientific planning and deliberate policy. On the other hand, a city's being good rests on the citizens who share in the constitution. The question then is, How does a man become good? Of course if it is possible for all to be good (and not just the citizens taken individually), then that is better, since all includes each. But in fact men are good and virtuous because of three things. These are nature, habit or training, reason. First, nature: a man must be born, and he must be born a man and not something else; he must have the body and the mind of a man. It may be of no advantage to be born with certain qualities, because habit and training cause changes. There are some qualities which have a dual possibility; subsequent habits may make them either good or bad. The majority of creatures live by nature only; some live by habit also to some extent. Man lives by reason as well, he alone has the faculty of reason. To make a good man requires all three working concertedly. Reason causes men to do many things contrary to habit and to nature, whenever they are convinced that this is the better course. In an earlier chapter we described what nature can do to make men such that they will easily respond to the handling of the legislator. After that it becomes a matter of education. Men learn partly by training, partly by listening.

14.   Since every association of persons forming a state consists of rulers and ruled, we must ask whether those who rule and those who are ruled ought to be different persons or the same for life; for the education which will be needed will depend upon which way we answer that question. If one group of persons were as far superior to all the rest as we deem gods and heroes to be superior to men, having to begin with great physical and bodily excellence and equally great mental and spiritual superiority, so much so that the superiority of the rulers is indisputable and quite evident to those ruled by them, then, I say, it is better that the same set of persons should always rule and the others always be ruled. But since this is not a condition that can easily be obtained, and since kings are not so greatly superior to their subjects as the writer Scylax says they were in India, it follows that, for a variety of causes, all alike must share in the business of ruling and being ruled by turns. For equality means the same not for all indiscriminately but for those who are like; this is fair and the established constitution can hardly be long maintained if it is contrary to justice. Otherwise there will be a large revolutionary element among the ruled all over the country, and it becomes quite impossible for even a strong governing class to withstand such a combination.

Again it cannot be disputed that rulers have to be superior to those who are ruled. It therefore becomes the duty of the lawgiver to consider how this distinction is to be made and how they shall share in government. We noted earlier that nature herself has provided one distinction: that class which in respect of birth is all the same she has divided into older and younger, the former being more fit for ruling, the latter for being ruled. No one really objects to this method of command by seniority or thinks himself too good for it; after all he knows that once he reaches the required age, he will get what he has earned by waiting. There is then a sense in which we must say "the same persons rule and are ruled" and a sense in which we must say that they are different persons. So too their education must be in one sense the same, in another different; for, as is often said, one who is to become a good ruler must first himself be ruled. Rule, as was said earlier, is of two kinds, according as it is exercised for the good of the ruler, which is despotic rule, or for the good of the ruled, which is rule over free men. The same actions may be ordered to be taken under either kind of rule, but the objects are different. Hence many activities generally considered servile may be honourably performed even by free men, by the younger among them. For the question whether an act is noble or not is to be decided not in reference to the actions themselves but in the light of their end and for whose benefit they are undertaken. But since we hold that the same qualities are needed for citizen and for ruler and for the best man, and that the same man should be first ruled and later ruler, it immediately becomes an essential task of the planner of a constitution to ensure that men shall be good men, to consider what practices will make them so, and what is the end or aim of the best life.

Two parts of the soul are distinguished, one possessing reason in itself, the other not so possessing reason but capable of listening to reason. To these belong, we think, the virtues because of which a good man is called good. To those who accept our division of the soul there is no difficulty in answering the question "To which of the parts does the concept of end belong?" For the inferior is always but a means to the superior; and this is no less clear in matters that have to be planned by human skill than it is in those which belong to the sphere of nature; and the superior in this case is that which is possessed of reason. It is our custom to make a distinction between practical reason and theoretical reason, and so we must similarly divide the rational part of the soul. Actions too will follow suit; there will be three kinds in all and those springing from that which is by nature better, that is, from the two rational parts, must be regarded as preferable by all who are in a position to make a choice from among three kinds or even from among two. For each man, that is to be chosen which is the very best that he can attain.

Again, all life can be divided into work and leisure, war and peace, and of things done some belong to the class of actions that have moral worth, while others are necessary but have no such value. In the choice of these the same principle, the lesser for the sake of the greater, must be followed in actions as in parts of the soul; that is to say, we choose war for the sake of peace, work for the sake of leisure, menial and useful acts for the sake of the noble. The statesman therefore in making laws must have an eye to all these things, with reference both to the parts of the soul and to the actions to which these give rise, and an eye even more to better things and to ends in view. In the same way too he must regard men's lives and their choice of what they shall do. For one must be able to work and to fight, but even more to be at peace and lead a life of cultivated leisure, to do the necessary and useful things, but still more those of intrinsic worth. These then are the targets at which education should be aimed, whether children's education or that of those requiring it at a later age.

It appears however that those Greeks who have the best reputation for good government and the lawgivers who drew up their several constitutions did not in fact construct societies with the best possible aim, and did not direct their laws and education towards producing all the virtues; but instead, following the vulgar way of thinking, turned aside to pursue qualities that appeared to be more lucrative and useful. And in a like manner to these some more recent writers have voiced the same opinion: they express their approval of the Lacedaemonians' regime and admire the aim of their lawgiver, because he ordered all things with a view to war and national strength. This is a view which can easily be refuted by the facts. As most men desire to dominate others, because success in this brings abundance of worldly goods, so the writer Thibran is clearly an admirer of the Laconian lawgiver, and all the others too who, writing about the Spartan constitution, have stated that thanks to their being trained to face dangers they came to rule over many others. But since today the Spartan domination is no more, it is clear that they are not a happy and prosperous nation, and their lawgiver was wrong. There is something laughable in the fact that, for all their care to keep within their own constitution and with no one to stop them from using their own laws and customs, they have lost their particular way of a good life.

They are also wrong in supposing that a lawgiver ought openly to approve the acquisition of mastery; for rule over free men is nobler than despotic rule and more in keeping with virtue. To say that a state has trained itself in the acquisition of power with a view to ruling its neighbours—that is no ground for calling a state happy or applauding its lawgivers. Such an argument may have dangerous consequences; its acceptance requires any citizen who can to make it his ambition to be ruler in his own city—the very thing that the Lacedaemonians accused Pausanias of seeking and that too though he was their king. So none of these theories or principles are of any value for a statesman; they are neither good nor true. The same guiding principles that are best for nations are best also for individuals, and it is these that a lawgiver must instil into the minds of men. And as for military training, the object in practising it regularly is not to bring into subjection men not deserving of such treatment. It has three purposes: (1) to save ourselves from becoming subject to others, (2) to win for our own city a position of leadership, exercised for the benefit of others not with a view to dominating all, (3) to exercise the rule of a master over those who deserve to be treated as slaves. The lawgiver should rather make it the aim both of his military preparations and of his legislation in general to establish peace and a cultured life. And facts support this; for the military states generally, while they fight wars, survive, but when once they establish an empire begin to decline. Like steel they lose their fine temper if they are always at peace; and the lawgiver who has not educated them in the right use of leisure is to blame.

15.   Since it is clear that men have the same purpose whether they are acting as individuals or as a state, and that the best man and the best constitution must have the same distinguishing features, it becomes evident that there must be present in the state the virtues that lead to the cultivation of leisure; for, as has often been said, the end of war is peace and the end of work is leisure. Of the virtues useful for the employment of leisure some are exercised in a period of leisure, others in a period of work, because a lot of things need to be provided before leisured activity can become possible. Hence a city must be self-restrained, courageous, steadfast. Without these men are as slaves, since those who cannot bravely face danger are slaves to an invader and, as the proverb says, slaves have no leisure. We need courage and steadfastness for the work, intellectual ability for cultivated leisure, restraint and honesty at all times, but particularly at times of peace and leisure. For war forces men to be obedient and honest, but the enjoyment of prosperity, peace, and leisure is apt rather to make men violent and self-assertive. Therefore much sound morality and much self-restraint are demanded of those who are conspicuously successful and enjoy the blessings of prosperity, men such as might be living, in the poets' phrase, in the isles of the blest. For these especially will need philosophy, moderation, righteousness; and the more abundant their advantages, the greater their need. Clearly then the state too, if it is to be good and happy, must have a good measure of these virtues. For if it is a mark of inferiority not to be able to behave well, it is especially so in a period of leisure—to appear good when working or on military service, but in leisure and peace to be no better than slaves.

Training in virtue therefore should not follow the Lacedaemonian model. The difference between them and other nations lies not in any disagreement about what are the greatest goods but in their view that there is a virtue which will produce them. They value good things and their enjoyment more than the production of virtues, but it is clear from our argument that virtue must be practised for its own sake, and we have to consider how and by what means.

We have already distinguished three essentials—nature, training, and reason. Of these we have already dealt with the first, determining the natural conditions which it is desirable to be born into; next we must ask whether education should proceed by means of reasoning or by the formation of habits. Certainly these must work together in perfect unison; for it is equally possible to make an intellectual error about the best principle and to find oneself led astray by one's own habits and training.

One thing is clear from the start: as in everything else so here, coming into being proceeds from some beginning, and its end proceeds from a beginning which was the end of something else. So for us as human beings reason and the mind are the end to which our growth tends. Thus it is to these that the training of our habits, as well as our coming into being, must be directed. Next, as soul and body are two, so also we note two parts of the soul, the reasoning and the unreasoning; and each of these has its own natural propensity, the former intellectual, the latter appetitive. And just as the body comes into being earlier than the soul, so also the unreasoning is prior to that which possesses reason. This is shown by the fact that, while passion and will as well as appetite are to be found in children from birth, reasoning and intelligence come into being as they grow older. Therefore the care of the body must begin before the care of the mind, then the training of the appetitive element, but always for the sake of the intelligence, as the body's training is for the sake of the soul.

16.   Now as it is a lawgiver's duty to start from the very beginning in looking for ways to secure the best possible physical development of the young, he must consider first the marriage of their parents, what kind of people should get married to each other and when marital intercourse ought to take place. In making regulations about these matters he should have regard both to the couples themselves and to their time of life, in order that they may attain the right ages in each case at the same time. The period of the father's ability to beget and that of the mother's to bear children should coincide. A period when one of the two is capable and the other not leads to mutual recriminations and separations. Next, as regards the timing of successive births of children, there should not be too great a gap in age between father and children; there is little that the young can do for elderly parents and their fathers are of little help to them. Nor should they be too close in age, for this causes relations to be strained; proper respect is not given to fathers who are almost contemporaries, and the nearness in age leads to bickering in household affairs. And further, to go back to the point

we started from, one should ensure that the physical development of the young will be in accordance with the wishes of the founder of the state.

All these purposes can be fulfilled, or nearly so, if we pay sufficient attention to one thing—the relative ages of man and wife. Since, generally speaking, the upper limit of age for the begetting of children is for men seventy years and for women fifty, the beginning of their union should be such that they will arrive at these two points of life at the proper ages. The intercourse of a very young couple is not good for child-bearing. In animals generally the products of very early unions are defective, usually female and diminutive; so the same kind of results are bound to follow in human beings. There is some evidence that this is so: in countries where very early marriages are the rule, the offspring are small and defective. A further objection to very early marriages is that very young women have greater difficulty and there are more deaths. Some say that here we have also the origin of the oracle given to the people of Troezen ("plough not the new land"), that there is no reference to the production of crops, but to the fact that frequent marriages of young girls were causing many deaths. It is also more conducive to faithfulness in marriage that daughters should be rather older when their fathers bestow them in marriage; it seems that women who have sexual intercourse at an early age are more likely to be dissolute. On the male side too it is held that if they have intercourse while the seed is just growing, it interferes with future growth; for in that too there is a fixed limit of time, after which it ceases to be replenished. Accordingly we conclude that the appropriate age for marriage is about the eighteenth year for girls and for men the thirty-seventh plus or minus. Intercourse will then take place when they are both physically in their prime and they will reach the cessation of childbearing at the proper times in each case. And the succession of births, if pregnancy takes place at the expected time, will begin with the first-born at the parents' prime and end as they decline, the father now approaching his seventieth year.

We have spoken now about the time of life when marriage should take place, but not about the periods of the year best suited for sexual intercourse. However, the common practice of choosing the winter season is satisfactory. In addition those contemplating child-bearing should seek the advice of doctors and scientists; the former can give the requisite information about periods in the life of the body, the latter about weather conditions; they recommend a time of northerly winds rather than southerly. On the question of what kind of physical condition is most advantageous for parents, those who want detailed information must seek it in manuals on the rearing of children; for our present purpose the following outline will suffice. Athletic fitness does not provide the best condition either for a citizen or for health in the production of offspring. A condition of much coddling and of unfitness for hard work is equally undesirable. Something between the two is needed; a condition of one inured to hard but not excessively hard toil, directed not all in one direction as an athlete's, but towards the various activities of the free-born. These provisions are applicable to men and women alike. Further, it is important that women should look after their bodily condition during pregnancy. They must not be lazy or go on a meagre diet. It is easy for a legislator to ensure this by making it a rule that they shall each day take a walk, the object of which is to worship the gods who are especially concerned with childbirth. But while the body should be exercised, the mind should not. Mental exertion is better avoided; the unborn infant appears to take good from her who is carrying it, as plants do from the earth.

With regard to the choice between abandoning an infant or rearing it let it be lawful that no cripple child be reared. But since the ordinance of custom forbids the exposure of infants merely in order to reduce numbers, there must be a limit to the production of children. If contrary to these arrangements a copulation takes place and a child is conceived, abortion should be procured before the embryo has acquired life and sensation; the presence of life and sensation will be the mark of division between right and wrong here. Since we have already decided what are the ages of male and female at which co-habitation should begin, we must also decide upon the length of time during which it may properly continue. The offspring of elderly people, like the offspring of the young, are imperfect in mind and body, those of the aged are feeble. We should therefore be guided by the highest point of mental development, and this in most cases is the age mentioned by certain poets who speak of seven periods of seven years, that is to say about the fiftieth year of a man's life. Thus anyone who has passed this limit by four or five years ought no longer to beget and openly acknowledge children. But for the sake of health or other such good reason intercourse may continue without secrecy. Extra-marital intercourse with persons of either sex is not good, and should, if possible, never be resorted to or admitted, so long as one is a husband and so addressed by a wife. If anyone is found to be acting thus during the period of his begetting of children, let him be punished by such measure of disgrace as is appropriate to his misdemeanour.

17.   The period following birth must be regarded as the time when the nourishment given to a child has the greatest effect on the development of the body. It is clear from an examination, both of other animals and of those nations that make a point of rearing their young to be fighting fit, that an abundant milk diet is very suitable for their young bodies, but a diet that includes wine is likely to upset them. Next, it is good for them to make all

the bodily movements that they are capable of at that age. To prevent the still soft limbs from becoming bent some peoples still make use of mechanical devices for keeping them straight. From infancy too they ought to be used to cold; to be thus habituated is most useful for future health and for the activities of warfare. Hence among certain non-Greek peoples it is the custom to dip newly-born infants in cold river-water; others, for example the Kelts, put on them very little clothing. It is a good thing to start very young in accustoming children to such things as it is possible to accustom them to, but the process must be gradual; the warmth of the young body gives it a condition well-suited for training to resist cold. In these and similar ways the training of children in infancy should proceed.

The next stage is up to five years of age. During this period it is not a good plan to try and teach them anything or make them do tasks that would interfere with their development. At the same time they must have exercise, not a state of passivity. They will get exercise in many ways but most of all in play. Their games, like everything else, should be worthy of free men and neither laborious nor unsystematic. The officials known as inspectors of children's welfare ought also to pay attention to deciding what kind of literature and stories children of this age are to hear; for all that they hear now is to be regarded as preparation for the schooling that is to follow. Hence their games ought largely to consist in playing at or rehearsing what they will later be doing in earnest. It is wrong to try and prohibit small children from crying and dilating the lungs, as is suggested in the *Laws;* it is in fact an exercise of the lungs which is beneficial for the growth of the body. In addition to regulating the time spent on play and on exercise and the rest, those in charge should particularly see that very little time is spent in the company of slaves. Children of this age and up to seven must inevitably live at home, and even as young as that they are liable to pick up by eye or by ear "ungentlemanliness."

In general the legislator ought to banish from the state, as he would any other evil, all unseemly talk; the indecent remark lightly dropped results in conduct of a like kind. Especially therefore it must be kept away from youth; let them not hear or see anything of that kind. If any is found doing or saying any of the forbidden things, he shall, if he is of gentle birth but not yet old enough to be allowed to eat at the common tables, be punished by whipping, while a youth who is rather older shall be punished by loss of privileges of the free-born, just because his conduct has been that of a slave. And since we exclude all unseemly talk, we must also forbid looking at pictures or literature of the same kind. Let it therefore be a duty of the rulers to see that there shall be nothing at all, statue or painting, that is a representation of unseemly actions, except those that are in the shrines of those gods to whom the law concedes the privilege of indecency. The law further allows men who have reached a certain age to pay honour to these gods on behalf of their wives, their children, and themselves. But it should be laid down that younger persons shall not be spectators at comedies or recitals of scurrilous iambics, not, that is to say, until they have reached the age at which they become entitled to recline at banquets, and share in the drinking; by this time their upbringing will have rendered them immune to any harm that might come from such spectacles. What we have just been saying has been said only incidentally; we must later go into the question in greater detail and decide whether or not they ought to attend, and, if so, under what conditions. We have only said as much as would serve the present occasion. Theodorus the tragic actor made, I think, a very apt remark in this connexion when he refused to allow any other actor, even quite an inferior one, to appear on the stage before him, because, he said, an audience always takes kindly to the first voice that meets their ears. I think something of the same kind is true in men's relations with each other and the things they see and hear. We tend to love at first sight. Therefore we must keep all that is of inferior quality far away from the young, particularly these things that contain repulsive evil.

When they have passed their fifth birthday they should for the next two years learn, simply by observation, whatever they may be required to learn. Education after that may be divided into two stages—from the seventh year to puberty and from puberty to the completion of twenty-one years. Thus those who divide life into periods of seven years are not far wrong, and we ought to keep to the divisions that nature makes. For all training and education aim at filling the gaps that nature leaves. It therefore becomes our business to inquire whether we ought to lay down a system for the education of boys, then whether it is advisable to have a public authority in charge of it, or leave it in private hands, as is the usual practice in cities at the present time, and thirdly to discuss what the system of education should be.

Book 8

1. No one would dispute the fact that it is a lawgiver's prime duty to arrange for the education of the young. There is no doubt that where this is not done the quality of the constitution suffers every time. Education must be related to the particular constitution in each case, for the character of the constitution is just that which makes it specifically what it is. Its own character made it at the start and continues to maintain it, the democratic character preserves a democracy, the oligarchic an oligarchy. And in all circumstances the best character produces the best constitution. There must also be the preparatory training for all the various crafts and professions

and a process of habituation to the various jobs; so it is obvious that there must also be training for the activities of virtue. But since there is but one aim for the entire city, it follows that education must be one and the same for all and that the oversight of education must be a public concern, not the private affair which it now is, each man separately bringing up his own children and teaching them just what he thinks they ought to learn. In all matters that belong to the whole community the learning to do them must also be the concern of the community as a whole. And it is not right either that any of the citizens should think that he belongs just to himself; all citizens belong to the state, for each is a part of the state; and the care bestowed on each part naturally looks also towards the care of the whole. In this respect the Lacedaemonians earn our approval; the greatest possible attention is given to youth in Sparta and all on a national basis.

2.   It is clear then that there should be laws laid down about education and that education itself must be made a national concern. But we must not forget the question what that education is to be, and how it is to be brought into operation. For in modern times there are opposing views about the practice of education. There is no general agreement about what the young should learn either in relation to virtue or in relation to the best life; nor is it clear whether their education ought to be directed more towards the intellect than towards the character of the soul. The problem has been complicated by what we see happening before our eyes, and it is not certain whether training should be directed at things useful in life, or at those conducive to virtue, or at nonessentials. (All these answers have been given.) And there is no agreement as to what in fact does tend towards virtue. Men do not all prize most highly the same virtue, so naturally they differ also about the proper training for it.

Then as to useful things—there are obviously certain essentials which the young must learn, but they do not have to learn all useful things, since we distinguish those that are proper for a free man from those that are not. The citizen must take part in only those useful occupations which do not degrade the doer. Among degrading activities and vulgar pursuits we must reckon all those which render the body or soul or intellect of free men unserviceable for the demands and activities of virtue. We therefore call degrading those occupations which have a deleterious effect on the body's condition and all work that is paid for. For these make the mind preoccupied and unable to rise above menial things. Even in the liberal subjects there is a limit beyond which their study becomes illiberal. Too great concentration on them, too much mastering of detail—these are liable to cause the same degradation of spirit that we have been speaking of. In this connexion a most important criterion is the purpose for which the action or the study is undertaken. It is proper for a free man to do something for himself or for his friends or on account of its value in itself, but he that does the same action on others' account may on occasion be regarded as doing something paid for or servile.

3.   The subjects nowadays regularly studied serve both virtue and utility, as we have already noted. About four are generally taught to children, (1) Reading and Writing, (2) Physical Training, (3) Music, and (4), not always included, Drawing. Reading and writing and drawing are useful in daily life in a variety of ways, gymnastic because it aims to make men strong and brave. But about music there is a real question. Most men nowadays take part in music for the sake of the pleasure it gives; but some lay it down that music is fundamental in education on the ground that nature herself, as has often been said, aims at producing men not merely able to work properly but fit also for the life of cultivated leisure. And this latter, we repeat, is the basis of the whole business. It is true that we need both; but if not-working is preferable to, and is the end sought by, working, we must ask ourselves what are the proper activities of leisure.

Obviously not play; for that would be to make play the object of living, our end in life, which is unthinkable. Play has its uses, but they belong rather to the sphere of work; for he who works hard needs rest, and play is a way of resting, while work is inseparable from stress and strain. We must therefore for therapeutic reasons admit the necessity of games, while keeping them to their proper times and proper uses; taking exercise in this way is both a relaxation of the mind and, just because we enjoy it, a recreation. But the way of leisure that we are speaking of here is something positive, in itself a pleasant happy existence which the life of work and business cannot be. For he that is working is working for some hitherto unattained end, and happiness is an end, happiness which is universally regarded as concomitant not with toil but with enjoyment. Admittedly men do not agree as to what that enjoyment is; each man decides for himself following his own character and disposition, the finest character choosing the highest kind of enjoyment on the loftiest plane. Thus it becomes clear that preparation for spending time at leisure requires a great deal of learning and education. The educational processes and the subjects studied must have their own intrinsic merit, as distinct from those necessary professional subjects which are studied for reasons outside themselves. Hence, in the past, men laid down music as part of the curriculum of education, not as being necessary, for it is not in that category, nor yet as being useful in the way that a knowledge of reading and writing is useful for business or administration, for study, and for many citizen activities, or as a knowledge of drawing is useful for the better judging of artists' works, nor again as gymnastic is useful for health and strength; for we do not see either of these accruing as a result of playing music. There remains one purpose—to provide an occupation for leisure; and that is clearly the reason why they did introduce music into education, regarding it as an occupation of free men. Thus Homer wrote "to summon him alone to the rich banquet" and after these words he introduces certain others "who summon the bard whose singing shall delight them all." And elsewhere he speaks of Odysseus saying that the best recreation is when men get together and "sit in rows up and down the hall feasting and listening to the singer."

Clearly then there is a form of education which we must provide for our sons, not as being useful or essential but elevated and gentlemanly. We must on a later occasion discuss whether this education is one or many, what subjects it includes and how they are to be taught. But as it turns out, we have made some progress in that direction; music at least must be included. We have the evidence of the ancients derived from the subjects laid down by them.

The case of music makes that clear, but it does not stand alone; there are other subjects which the young must learn, for example their letters, not only because they are useful but because these are often the means to learning yet further subjects. Similarly drawing and a knowledge of design are useful not merely for the avoidance of mistakes in one's private purchases but that one may not be taken in when buying and selling furniture, or rather more especially because it teaches us to be observant of beauty in any physical object. But to be constantly asking "What is the use of?" is unbecoming to those of superior mentality and free birth.

Since it is obvious that education by habit-forming must precede education by reasoned instruction (as that of the body precedes that of the mind), it is clear that we must subject our children to gymnastic and to training in wrestling and fighting; the former produces the condition of the body, the latter its actions.

4. In our own day those cities which have the greatest reputation for looking after their youth either aim at producing an athlete's condition, to the detriment of both the appearance and the development of the child's body, or else like the Spartans who have avoided that particular error, by severity of treatment they render them like animals, under the impression that this is conducive to courage. But, as has often been pointed out, the care of the young must be directed not to producing one quality only and not that more than the rest. And if courage is their aim, they do not even manage to secure it. For neither among animals nor among less civilized peoples do we find courage to be a characteristic of the most fierce, but rather (among animals) of the gentler and feline species; and among human beings there are many tribes that enjoy slaughter and the consumption of human flesh, in Pontus Achaeans and Heniochi and some of the mainland tribes, some better, some worse; raiders they may be, but they are not en-

dowed with courage. And of the Lacedaemonians themselves too we know that so long as they applied themselves to strenuous training, they were superior to the rest, but nowadays they fall short of others both in war and athletics. For their former superiority was not due to their particular way of training the young but merely to the fact that they trained, and their opponents did not. The prime object therefore must be not any animal quality but nobility of character. One cannot imagine a wolf or any other animal engaging in a dangerous struggle because it is the right thing to do; but that is what a brave man will do. Those who put their young to excessive military training, neglecting their education in essentials, are in sober fact rendering them vulgar and uneducated, making them useful for one part only of citizen life and even for that, as our argument shows, less useful than others. We should judge the Spartans by their present-day performance, not by what they used to be like. They now have rivals in the field of education, which formerly they did not have.

There is to be sure a place for gymnastic in education and there is general agreement as to what that place should be: up to puberty the exercises should be light and easy; nothing should be done that would interfere with the body's growth, no heavy dieting or strenuous forced hardships; for these are liable to have just that ill-effect, as is shown by the fact that it is rare for the same men to be successful in the Olympic games both as boys and as men; their severe gymnastic training as boys has caused them to lose their strength. But when for the three years after puberty they have been engaged in learning other things, then the subsequent period may very properly be devoted to strenuous exercise and compulsory heavy dieting. Vigorous exercise of mind and body must not be combined; each naturally works in the opposite direction from the other, bodily toil interfering with the mind, mental with the body.

5.   We have already discussed some of the questions that arose about music, but it would be well to resume the subject and carry it further, because I think that what I have to say will provide a key to any future discussions about music. To begin with, it is not easy to define either what the effect of music is or what our object is in learning it. Is it for our amusement and refreshment, like taking a nap or having a drink? I hardly think so, because these things are not in themselves of prime importance, though they are pleasant and help us to forget our worries, as Euripides says. This is what causes some people to put all three on the same level, sleep, drink, and music, and to use them all in the same way. Dancing is also sometimes added. Must we not rather regard music as a stimulus to goodness, capable of having an effect on the character, in just the same way as gymnastic training produces a body of a certain type, and so capable of forming men

who have the habit of right critical appreciation? Thirdly, it surely has a contribution to make to the intelligent and cultivated pastimes.

It is clear then that we are not to educate the young with a view to amusement. Learning is hard work; while children are learning they are not playing. They are as yet too young for the cultivation of the intellect by means of music as an occupation; the complete life does not belong to the incomplete body. Still one might perhaps say that serious study in childhood may have for its aim the amusement of the complete and adult man. But if this is so, what need is there for themselves to learn music? Why not do as kings of Persians and Medes do, have others to make music for them, so that they may listen and enjoy? For surely those who have perfected their skill in the making and production of music will give better performances than those who have devoted to learning music only such times as will enable them to listen intelligently. If we reject that and say that we must ourselves work hard at producing music, does it follow that we must also learn to produce good meals? Certainly not.

The same question arises when we ask whether music has the power to improve the character. Why learn music oneself and not rather do as the Lacedaemonians do—acquire the art of right judgement and good taste by listening to others? They claim that without learning music they are capable of correctly distinguishing good music from bad. The same argument applies also when we ask whether music ought to be used as a means to making pleasant and cultivated pastimes for gentlefolk. Why must they learn to perform themselves instead of simply enjoying the fruits of others' study? We may in this connexion refer to our conception of the gods; the poets do not depict Zeus as playing and singing in person. In fact we regard professional performers as belonging to the lower classes, though a man may play and sing for his own amusement or at a party when he has had a good deal to drink.

Perhaps this question should be postponed till later; our chief inquiry now is whether or not music is to be put into education and what music can do. Is it an education or an amusement or a pastime? It is reasonable to reply that it is directed towards and participates in all three. Amusement is for the purpose of relaxation and relaxation must necessarily be pleasant, since it is a kind of cure for the ills we suffer in working hard. As to the pastimes of a cultivated life, there must, as is universally agreed, be present an element of pleasure as well as of nobility, for the happiness which belongs to that life consists of both these. We all agree that music is among the most delightful and pleasant things, whether instrumental or accompanied by singing [The poet Musaeus says "singing is man's greatest joy." Hence because it makes men feel happy, it is very properly included in entertainments and in the pastimes of social intercourse.],[2] so that one might from that fact alone infer that the young should be taught it. For things that are pleasant and harmless belong rightly not only to the end in view but also to relaxation by the way. But since it rarely happens that men attain and keep their goal, and they frequently rest and amuse themselves with no other thought than the pleasure of it, there is surely a useful purpose in the pleasure derived from music.

On the other hand, men have been known to make amusement an end in itself. No doubt there is something pleasant about one's own chosen end but it is a very special kind of pleasure, and men in seeking pleasure mistake the one kind for the other. For there is indeed a resemblance; the end is not pursued for the sake of anything that may accrue thereafter but always for its own sake; similarly these recreation-pleasures are not for future but for present benefits; their pleasure arises from what is past—labour and pain finished. This would seem to be a reasonable explanation of why men try to get happiness through these pleasures. But it is certainly not for this reason alone that men take up music; the main reason, it seems, is that it provides relaxation.

Nevertheless we must ask whether, though this is commonly the case, the true nature of music be not something of greater value than filling the need for relaxation. Music certainly has a pleasure of its own; all ages and all types like and enjoy it. But we must do more than merely share in the general pleasure which all men find in it; we must consider whether music has any effect on the character and the mind. We could answer this question if we could say that we become of such and such a disposition through music. And surely it is obvious from many examples that music does indeed have such an effect, not least from the tunes composed by Olympus. These are well known to affect the personality, making men wildly excited—a frenzied excitement which is both a mental and a moral condition. Again, when listening to theatrical performances all men are affected in a manner in keeping with the performance, even apart from the tunes and rhythms employed. Since music belongs to the class of things pleasant, and since it is virtue therein to enjoy rightly, to like and dislike the right things, clearly there is no more important lesson to be learned or habit to be formed than that of right judgement and of taking pleasure in good morals and noble actions.

Now in rhythms and in tunes there is a close resemblance to reality—the realities of anger and gentleness, also of courage and moderation, and of

2. The words enclosed in brackets occur in the Greek as an integral part of the text. The translator, T. A. Sinclair, chose to treat them as a footnote. We have restored them to the text but have not altered Mr. Sinclair's syntax to accommodate the insertion. The same awkwardness will be encountered again in this chapter and also in chapter 7.

the opposites of these, indeed of all moral qualities; and the fact that music heard does indeed cause an emotional change in us is an indication of this. To have the habit of feeling pleasure (or pain) in things that are like to reality is very near to having the same disposition towards reality. I mean if a man enjoys looking at a statue of someone for no other reason than that he likes the look of it, then inevitably he will enjoy looking at the original, whose likeness he is at the moment contemplating. Now it is true that objects perceived by the senses, touched or tasted, do not present any similarity to moral qualities [Perhaps objects seen do, since appearances may have such an effect, but only to a small extent; and not all people share this reaction to such perception. Moreover the shapes and colours that we see are not strictly representations of character but indications rather, and these indications are visible on our bodies when strong emotion is felt. It does, however, make a great deal of difference what it is we look at; the young ought not to contemplate the paintings of Pauson but rather those of Polygnotus and of other painters and sculptors who are truly ethical.], but in music moral qualities are present, represented in the very tunes we hear. This is obvious, for to begin with there is the natural distinction between the modes or harmonies, which cause different reactions in the hearers, who are not all moved in the same way. For example, men are inclined to be mournful or tense when they listen to that which is called Mixo-Lydian, they are more relaxed when they listen to the looser harmonies. An equable feeling, mid-way between these, is produced, I think, only by the Dorian mode, while the Phrygian makes men greatly excited. These are the results of some excellent work which has been done on this aspect of education; the investigators have made practical tests and based their conclusions on them. The same is true also of the different types of rhythm; some have a steadying effect, others an unsettling, and of these latter some give rise to vulgar movements, some to more gentlemanly.

It follows from all this that music has indeed the power to induce certain conditions of mind, and if it can do that, clearly it must be applied to education and the young must be educated in and by it. And the teaching of music is particularly apt for the young; for they because of their youth do not willingly tolerate anything that is not made pleasant for them, and music is one of those things that are by nature made to give pleasure. Moreover there is a certain affinity between us and music's harmonies and rhythms; so that many experts say that the soul is a harmony, others that it has harmony.

6.   We must now return to a question raised earlier—must they learn to sing themselves and play instruments with their own hands? Clearly actual participation in performing is going to make a big difference to the quality of the person that will be produced; it is impossible, or at any rate very

difficult, to produce good judges of musical performance from among those who have never themselves performed. At the same time learning an instrument will provide children with a needed occupation. Archytas's rattle was an excellent invention for keeping children occupied; they cannot be expected to remain still, and playing with this toy keeps them from smashing things about the house. Of course it is only suitable for the very young; for older children education is their rattle. And all that we have been saying makes it clear that musical education must include actual performing; and it is not difficult to decide what is appropriate and what is not for different ages, or to find an answer to those who assert that learning to perform is vulgar and degrading. First, since as we have seen, actual performance is needed to make a good critic, they should while young do much playing and singing, and then, when they are older, give up performing; they will then, thanks to what they have learned in their youth, be able to enjoy music aright and give good judgements. As for the objection, brought by some, that musical performance is degrading to a gentleman, this can easily be answered if we consider to what extent boys, who are being educated to discharge the highest functions in the state, ought to take part in music, what tunes and what rhythms they are to perform, and on what instruments they are to learn to play, for that too will make a difference. In the answers to these questions will be found the answer to the objection; and an answer must be found, for it is very likely that certain kinds of music do have the effect mentioned.

It is clear therefore that learning music must not be allowed to have any adverse effect on later activities, or make the body banausic and ill-fitted for the training of citizen or soldier, the practice in youth, the theory in later years. What is needed is that the pupil shall not struggle to acquire the degree of skill that is needed for professional competitions, or to master those peculiar and sensational pieces of music which have begun to penetrate the competitions and have even affected education. Musical exercises, even if not of this kind, should be pursued only up to the point at which the pupil becomes capable of appreciating good melodies and rhythms, and not just the popular music such as appeals to slaves, children, and even some animals. From these considerations we can see the answer also to the question what kinds of musical instruments are to be employed. We must not permit the introduction of wind-instruments into education or any that requires the skill of a professional, the cithara and such-like, but only such as will make good listeners to musical education and education in general. Furthermore the pipes are not an instrument of ethical but rather of orgiastic effect, so their use should be confined to those occasions on which the effect desired is not intellectual but a way of working off the emotions. We may add to its educational objections the fact that playing on the pipes prevents one from using the faculty of speech. For these reasons our predecessors were right in prohibiting the use of wind-instruments by the young of the upper classes, though at an earlier period it was permitted. This is what took place: as abundance increased, men had more leisure and acquired higher standards both culturally and socially. Just before, and still more after, the Persian wars, in which their success had increased their self-confidence, they fastened eagerly upon learning of all kinds, pursuing all without distinction. Playing on the pipes was introduced into education and at Sparta the chorus-leader himself piped for his chorus to dance to, and round about Athens the pipes took such firm root that many, perhaps the majority, of the gentry learned them. Thrasippus, who, when he acted as chorus-trainer for Ecphantides, dedicated a picture, is an indication of this. But at a later date as a result of actual experience the pipes went out of favour; men became better able to discern what tends to promote high standards of goodness and what does not. Many other older instruments were found to have similar drawbacks as a means of musical education, for example the plucker, the barbitos, and those which merely titillate the ear, the heptagon, triangle, sambuca, and all those that require manual dexterity. There is sound sense too in the story told by the ancients about the use of the pipes—that Athena invented them and then threw them away. It may well be, as the story says, that she did this because she disliked the facial distortion which their playing caused. But a far more likely reason is that learning to play upon the pipes contributes nothing to the education of the mind; after all, Athena, as we believe, was intelligent, as well as nimble with her fingers.

We reject then as education a training in material performance which is professional and competitive. He that takes part in such performances does not do so in order to improve his own character, but to give pleasure to listeners, and vulgar pleasure at that. We do not therefore regard it as a proper occupation for a gentleman; it is rather that of a paid employee. Inevitably the consequences are degrading, since the end towards which it is directed—popular amusement—is a low one. The listener is a common person and influences music accordingly; he has an effect on the professionals who perform for him; the music which he expects of them, and the motions which they have to make to produce it, affect detrimentally their bodies and their minds.

7.   We must investigate a little this matter of harmonies and rhythms and its relation to education. Are we to make use of all the harmonies and rhythms or should we not make distinctions? And will the same basis of classification serve also those who are concerned with education, or must we lay down a third? Certainly music is, as we know, divided into melody-making and rhythm, and we must not omit to consider what bearing each of these has on education, and whether we are to rate higher music with a good tune or music with a good rhythm. I believe that these topics are very

well dealt with both by some modern musicians and by others whose approach is philosophical but who have actual experience of music in relation to education. I would advise those who want detailed treatment of the several questions to seek advice in that quarter. Here let me give a conventional account and simply refer to the usual typology.

We accept the classification of melodies as given by some educationalists—ethical, active, and emotional, and regard the harmonies as being appropriate one here and another there in that scheme. But we say that music ought to be used not as conferring one benefit only but many; for example for education and cathartic purposes [Here I use the term *catharsis* without further qualifications; I will treat of it more fully in my work on *Poetics*.], as an intellectual pastime, as relaxation and for relief after tension. While then we must make use of all the harmonies, we are not to use them all in the same manner, but for education use those which improve the character, for listening to others performing use both the activating and the emotion-stirring or enthusiastic. Any feeling which comes strongly to some exists in all others to a greater or less degree, pity and fear, for example, but also this "enthusiasm." This is a kind of excitement which affects some people very strongly. It may arise out of religious music, and it is noticeable that when they have been listening to melodies that have an orgiastic effect they are, as it were, set on their feet, as if they had undergone a curative and purifying treatment. And those who feel pity or fear or other emotions must be affected in just the same way to the extent that the emotion comes upon each. To them all comes a pleasant feeling of purgation and relief. In the same way cathartic music brings men an elation which is not at all harmful. Hence these are the harmonies and melodies that ought to receive particular attention from those who are concerned with contests in theatrical music.

In the theatre there are two types of audience, the one consisting of well-educated gentlemen, the other of common persons, drawn from the menial occupations, paid workers and such-like. For the relaxation of this latter class also competitions and spectacles must be provided. But as their minds have become distorted, removed from the condition of nature, so also there are deviations from the norm in their harmonies, in the unnatural pitch and tone of the melodies. Each group finds pleasure in that which is akin to its nature. Therefore allowances must be made for theatrical producers when they use the type of music that appeals to this class of audience.

But as to education, as we have said, for its purposes we must use tunes in accordance with their ethical value and the same with harmonies. The Dorian mode, as we mentioned earlier, is in that category, but we must also admit other modes if they have passed the scrutiny of those authorities who combine the teaching of philosophy and musical education. It is to be regretted that Socrates in the *Republic* singled out the Phrygian mode to be added to the Dorian, while rejecting altogether the use of the pipes. Yet among the harmonies the Phrygian has exactly the same effect as the pipes among instruments; both are orgiastic and emotional. Poetical composition illustrates this; the feeling aroused by Dionysiac and other such poetry is that which belongs to the pipes among musical instruments, and such poetry finds its appropriate expression in tunes composed in the Phrygian mode. The dithyramb, for example, is universally regarded as Phrygiamb. Experts in this field point to numerous examples, notably that of Philoxenus, who tried to compose his myths for dithyramb in the Dorian mode, but could not do so; the very nature of his material forced him back into the Phrygian, the proper mode. But about the Dorian mode all are agreed that it is the steadiest and that its ethical quality is that of manliness. Further, since we approve of that which is mid-way between extremes and assert that this is something to be aimed at, and since the Dorian as compared with the other harmonies does possess this merit, it is clear that Dorian tunes are more suitable than the others for the education of the young.

Two things we keep constantly in view—what can be done and what should be done; every set of men must set out to grasp both things possible and things proper. But these two are different for different ages; those who through age have grown weary do not find it easy to sing the high-pitched harmonies, but for such men nature offers a whole range of lower-pitched. Hence once again some of the musical experts rightly take Socrates to task because he rejected as useless in education all the more relaxed harmonies; he regarded them as having the same effect as drink, not the intoxicating but the soporific effect. (Intoxication produces rather a Bacchic frenzy.) So, looking to our later years, a time of life which will come, we must keep hold of harmonies and melodies of this kind. Furthermore, if there is a harmony of this type, which because of its power to combine orderliness with educative influence is suitable for the age of childhood (the Lydian would seem to be a case in point), it is clear that we have three distinct features to look for in education—the happy mean, the possible, and the appropriate.

18. Aristotle, *Economics*, Book 1

The *Economics* found in the Aristotelian corpus seems to be the work of two hands, neither of them Aristotle's. Both, however, are quite early products of the Aristotelian school. The second book contains numerous

Translated by E. S. Foster in volume 10 of *The Oxford Translation of Aristotle*, edited by W. D. Ross. Oxford: Oxford University Press, 1921. Reprinted by permission of Oxford University Press.

examples; the first, printed here, exhibits attitudes to money and the methods of obtaining it that are today rare but that prevailed widely in the ancient world and later.

---

1. The sciences of politics and economics differ not only as widely as a household and a city (the subject-matter with which they severally deal), but also in the fact that the science of politics involves a number of rulers, whereas the sphere of economics is a monarchy.

Now certain of the arts fall into sub-divisions, and it does not pertain to the same art to manufacture and to use the article manufactured, for instance, a lyre or pipes; but the function of political science is both to constitute a city in the beginning and also when it has come into being to make a right use of it. It is clear, therefore, that it must be the function of economic science too both to found a household and also to make use of it.

Now a city is an aggregate made up of households and land and property, possessing in itself the means to a happy life. This is clear from the fact that, if men cannot attain this end, the community is dissolved. Further, it is for this end that they associate together; and that for the sake of which any particular thing exists and has come into being is its essence. It is evident, therefore, that economics is prior in origin to politics; for its function is prior, since a household is part of a city. We must therefore examine economics and see what its function is.

2. The component parts of a household are man and property. But since the nature of any given thing is most quickly seen by taking its smallest parts, this would apply also to a household. So, according to Hesiod, it would be necessary that there should be

First and foremost a house, then a wife . . . ,

for the former is the first condition of subsistence, the latter is the proper possession of all freemen. We should have, therefore, as a part of economics to make proper rules for the association of husband and wife; and this involves providing what sort of a woman she ought to be.

In regard to property the first care is that which comes naturally. Now in the course of nature the art of agriculture is prior, and next come those arts which extract the products of the earth, mining and the like. Agriculture ranks first because of its justice; for it does not take anything away from men, either with their consent, as do retail trading and the mercenary arts, or against their will, as do the warlike arts. Further, agriculture is natural; for by nature all derive their sustenance from their mother, and so men derive it from the earth. In addition to this it also conduces greatly to bravery; for it does not make men's bodies unserviceable, as do the illiberal arts, but it renders them able to lead an open air life and work hard; furthermore it makes them adventurous against the foe, for husbandmen are the only citizens whose property lies outside the fortifications.

3.   As regards the human part of the household, the first care is concerning a wife; for a common life is above all things natural to the female and to the male. For we have elsewhere laid down the principle that nature aims at producing many such forms of association, just as also it produces the various kinds of animals. But it is impossible for the female to accomplish this without the male or the male without the female, so that their common life has necessarily arisen. Now in the other animals this intercourse is not based on reason, but depends on the amount of natural instinct which they possess and is entirely for the purpose of procreation. But in the civilized and more intelligent animals the bond of unity is more perfect (for in them we see more mutual help and goodwill and co-operation), above all in the case of man, because the female and the male co-operate to ensure not merely existence but a good life. And the production of children is not only a way of serving nature but also of securing a real advantage; for the trouble which parents bestow upon their helpless children when they are themselves vigorous is repaid to them in old age when they are helpless by their children, who are then in their full vigour. At the same time also nature thus periodically provides for the perpetuation of mankind as a species, since she cannot do so individually. Thus the nature both of the man and of the woman has been preordained by the will of heaven to live a common life. For they are distinguished in that the powers which they possess are not applicable to purposes in all cases identical, but in some respects their functions are opposed to one another though they all tend to the same end. For nature has made the one sex stronger, the other weaker, that the latter through fear may be the more cautious, while the former by its courage is better able to ward off attacks; and that the one may acquire possessions outside the house, the other preserve those within. In the performance of work, she made one sex able to lead a sedentary life and not strong enough to endure exposure, the other less adapted for quiet pursuits but well constituted for outdoor activities; and in relation to offspring she has made both share in the procreation of children, but each render its peculiar service towards them, the woman by nurturing, the man by educating them.

4.   First, then, there are certain laws to be observed towards a wife, including the avoidance of doing her any wrong; for thus a man is less likely himself to be wronged. This is inculcated by the general law, as the Pythagoreans say, that one least of all should injure a wife as being "a suppliant and seated at the hearth." Now wrong inflicted by a husband is the formation of connexions outside his own house. As regards sexual intercourse, a man ought not to accustom himself not to need it at all nor to be

unable to rest when it is lacking, but so as to be content with or without it. The saying of Hesiod is a good one:

A man should marry a maiden, that habits discreet he may teach her.

For dissimilarity of habits tends more than anything to destroy affection. As regards adornment, husband and wife ought not to approach one another with false affectation in their person any more than in their manners; for if the society of husband and wife requires such embellishment, it is no better than play-acting on the tragic stage.

5.   Of possessions, that which is the best and the worthiest subject of economics comes first and is most essential—I mean, man. It is necessary therefore first to provide oneself with good slaves. Now slaves are of two kinds, the overseer and the worker. And since we see that methods of education produce a certain character in the young, it is necessary when one has procured slaves to bring up carefully those to whom the higher duties are to be entrusted. The intercourse of a master with his slaves should be such as not either to allow them to be insolent or to irritate them. To the higher class of slaves he ought to give some share of honour, and to the workers abundance of nourishment. And since the drinking of wine makes even freemen insolent, and many nations even of freemen abstain therefrom (the Carthaginians, for instance, when they are on military service), it is clear that wine ought never to be given to slaves, or at any rate very seldom. Three things make up the life of a slave, work, punishment, and food. To give them food but no punishment and no work makes them insolent; and that they should have work and punishment but no food is tyrannical and destroys their efficiency. It remains therefore to give them work and sufficient food; for it is impossible to rule over slaves without offering rewards, and a slave's reward is his food. And just as all other men become worse when they get no advantage by being better and there are no rewards for virtue and punishments for vice, so also is it with slaves. Therefore we must take careful notice and bestow or withhold everything, whether food or clothing or leisure or punishments, according to merit, in word and deed following the practice adopted by physicians in the matter of medicine, remembering at the same time that food is not medicine because it must be given continually.

The slave who is best suited for his work is the kind that is neither too cowardly nor too courageous. Slaves who have either of these characteristics are injurious to their owners; those who are too cowardly lack endurance, while the high-spirited are not easy to control. All ought to have a definite end in view; for it is just and beneficial to offer slaves their freedom as a prize, for they are willing to work when a prize is set before them and a limit of time is defined. One ought to bind slaves to one's service by the pledges of wife and children, and not to have many persons of the same race in a household, as is the case in a city. One ought to provide sacrifices and pleasures more for the sake of slaves than for freemen; for in the case of the former there are present more of the reasons why such things have been instituted.

6.   The economist ought to possess four qualities in relation to wealth. He ought to be able to acquire it, and to guard it; otherwise there is no advantage in acquiring it, but it is a case of drawing water with a sieve, or the proverbial jar with a hole in it. Further, he ought to be able to order his possessions aright and make a proper use of them; for it is for these purposes that we require wealth. The various kinds of property ought to be distinguished, and those which are productive ought to be more numerous than the unproductive, and the sources of income ought to be so distributed that they may not run a risk with all their possessions at the same time. For the preservation of wealth it is best to follow both the Persian and the Laconian methods. The Attic system of economy is also useful; for they sell their produce and buy what they want, and thus there is not the need of a storehouse in the smaller establishments. The Persian system was that everything should be organized and that the master should superintend everything personally, as Dio said of Dionysius; for no one looks after the property of others as well as he looks after his own, so that, as far as possible, a man ought to attend to everything himself. The sayings of the Persian and the Libyan may not come amiss; the former of whom, when asked what was the best thing to fatten a horse, replied, "His master's eye," while the Libyan, when asked what was the best manure, answered, "The land-owner's footprints." Some things should be attended to by the master, others by his wife, according to the sphere allotted to each in the economy of the household. Inspections need only be made occasionally in small establishments, but should be frequent where overseers are employed. For perfect imitation is impossible unless a good example is set, especially when trust is delegated to others; for unless the master is careful, it is impossible for his overseers to be careful. And since it is good for the formation of character and useful in the interests of economy, masters ought to rise earlier than their slaves and retire to rest later, and a house should never be left unguarded any more than a city, and when anything needs doing it ought not to be left undone, whether it be day or night. There are occasions when a master should rise while it is still night; for this helps to make a man healthy and wealthy and wise. On small estates the Attic system of disposing of the produce is a useful one; but on large estates, where a distinction is made between yearly and monthly expenditure and likewise between the daily and the occasional use of household appliances, such matters must be entrusted to overseers. Furthermore, a periodical inspec-

tion should be made, in order to ascertain what is still existing and what is lacking.

The house must be arranged both with a view to one's possessions and for the health and well-being of its inhabitants. By possessions I mean the consideration of what is suitable for produce and clothing, and in the case of produce what is suitable for dry and what for moist produce, and amongst other possessions what is suitable for property whether animate or inanimate, for slaves and freeman, women and men, strangers and citizens. With a view to well-being and health, the house ought to be airy in summer and sunny in winter. This would be best secured if it faces north and is not as wide as it is long. In large establishments a man who is no use for other purposes seems to be usefully employed as a doorkeeper to safeguard what is brought into and out of the house. For the ready use of household appliances the Laconian method is a good one; for everything ought to have its own proper place and so be ready for use and not require to be searched for.

Epicurus

Epicurus was born in 341 B.C. (Plato had died six years earlier, and Aristotle, aged about forty-two, was in Pella as Alexander's tutor. The Battle of Chaeronea occurred three years later.) We are informed by Metrodorus, his most distinguished pupil, that he belonged to the old Attic family of the Philaidae. Though an Athenian of good birth, he was born not in Athens but on the island of Samos, where his father had become a kleruch (allotment holder) in 352/351. In contrast with colonists, kleruchs continued to be Athenian citizens; but few Athenian citizens other than the poor are likely to have found the status of a kleruch attractive. That Epicurus' father, Neocles, also taught in an elementary school—an activity not highly esteemed in ancient Greece—is added evidence of the family's poverty.

In 323 B.C. Epicurus traveled to Athens, where Xenocrates was now head of the Academy, Aristotle head of the Lyceum. Epicurus, however, had not come to study philosophy. (The Academy and Lyceum would probably have been too expensive.) He came to perform his military service, as was required of all Athenian citizens on attaining the age of eighteen. 323 B.C. was also the year in which Alexander died. The family of Epicurus was immediately affected: Perdiccas, for the moment not only the most powerful of the generals who were disputing the succession but the closest to Samos, expelled the kleruchs from the island. Neocles moved his family to Colophon on the Asian mainland, where Epicurus soon joined them.

Epicurus, though he claimed to have been self-taught and made only derogatory references to other philosophers, was at some point a pupil of the Democritean (i.e., atomist) Nausiphanes, and he was certainly well acquainted with the philosophies of Plato and Aristotle. In Colophon, however, he seems to have had no teachers at all, and the twelve years that he spent there were crucial to his philosophical development.

In 310 B.C., aged about thirty-two, he attempted to set up his own philosophical school at Mytilene, on the island of Lesbos. At this time, those who taught philosophy in public did so in the gymnasia. (The Academy and Lyceum were gymnasia.) The permission of the appropriate magistrate, the gymnasiarch, was needed. Epicurus successfully applied for permission; but there was already a Peripatetic school, founded by Aristotle himself, on Lesbos, and its members persuaded the gymnasiarch to withdraw his permission. Epicurus moved to Lampsacus, on the Hellespont. There were Platonists in Lampsacus; but since one of them had, for a time, made himself tyrant, they were not popular. Mithras, the Syrian governor, a subordinate of Lysimachus the Macedonian, gave Epicurus admission to the city. Here he prospered and found influential supporters and financial backing, and in 307/306 he was emboldened to move his school to Athens itself.

In Athens he purchased a vegetable garden for eighty minas, or eight thousand drachmas. His prosperous supporters in Lampsacus must have supplied most of the money. Buildings must have been included, for Epicurus and his immediate followers, who included women and slaves, lived there. Epicurus made no attempt to teach in public. He propagated his philosophy by writing, and his works comprised more than three hundred rolls. Little has survived apart from three letters, of which the letter to Menoeceus is printed here, and the *Kuriai Doxai*. All of this material is preserved in the tenth book of Diogenes Laertius' history of philosophy.

Epicurus shunned public life and advised his followers to do so too. Epicureans should try to win the favor of those who had political power but should themselves live in small communities of friends. By the time he established himself as a philosopher in Athens, a generation after Chaeronea, it must have become apparent to most Greeks that the day of the autonomous polis was over. Epicurus himself, three years old when Chaeronea was fought, passed his formative years in a world in which the irresistible Alexander's victories were constantly increasing the size of his empire. The death of Alexander caused a personal disaster to Epicurus' family, and the subsequent wars of Alexander's generals made it clear that the political units of the future, if smaller than Alexander's empire, would be much larger than the polis. The kleruch's son might not have aspired to a political career in Athens; it is hardly surprising that he turned his back on public life in the new and dangerous world of Hellenistic politics.

Many Epicureans must have been of a social and economic status similar to Epicurus' own. From the beginning, however, not all were. His converts in Lampsacus included some prominent and wealthy people. Communities of friends, similar to the one in Athens, developed in other places in the Aegean during Epicurus' lifetime, and he made two or three journeys to visit them.

Epicurus died in 270 B.C., in his seventy-second year.

---

19. Epicurus, Letter to Menoeceus

Epicurus to Menoeceus, greeting.

Let no one be slow to seek wisdom when he is young nor weary in the search thereof when he is grown old. For no age is too early or too late for the health of the soul. And to say that the season for studying philosophy has not yet come, or that it is past and gone, is like saying that the season for happiness is not yet or that it is now no more. Therefore, both old and young ought to seek wisdom, the former in order that, as age comes over him, he may be young in good things because of the grace of what has been, and the latter in order that, while he is young, he may at the same time be old, because he has no fear of the things which are to come. So we must exercise ourselves in the things which bring happiness, since, if that be present, we have everything, and, if that be absent, all our actions are directed toward attaining it.

Those things which without ceasing I have declared unto thee, those do, and exercise thyself therein, holding them to be the elements of right life. First believe that God is a living being immortal and blessed, according to the notion of a god indicated by the common sense of mankind; and so believing, thou shalt not affirm of him aught that is foreign to this immortality or that agrees not with blessedness, but shalt believe about him whatever may uphold both his blessedness and his immortality. For verily there are gods, and the knowledge of them is manifest; but they are not such as the multitude believe, seeing that men do not steadfastly maintain the notions they form respecting them. Not the man who denies the gods worshipped by the multitude, but he who affirms of the gods what the multitude believes about them is truly impious. For the utterances of the multitude about the gods are not true preconceptions but false assumptions; hence it is that the greatest evils happen to the wicked and the greatest blessings happen to the good from the hand of the gods, seeing that they are always favourable to their own good qualities and take pleasure in men like unto themselves, but reject as alien whatever is not of their kind.

Accustom thyself to believe that death is nothing to us, for good and evil

Reprinted by permission of the publishers and the Loeb Classical Library from *Diogenes Laertius: Lives of Eminent Philosophers*, volume 2. Translated by R. D. Hicks. Cambridge, Mass.: Harvard University Press, 1925.

imply sentience, and death is the privation of all sentience; therefore a right understanding that death is nothing to us makes the mortality of life enjoyable, not by adding to life an illimitable time, but by taking away the yearning after immortality. For life has no terrors for him who has thoroughly apprehended that there are no terrors for him in ceasing to live. Foolish, therefore, is the man who says that he fears death, not because it will pain when it comes, but because it pains in the prospect. Whatsoever causes no annoyance when it is present, causes only a groundless pain in the expectation. Death, therefore, the most awful of evils, is nothing to us, seeing that, when we are, death is not come, and, when death is come, we are not. It is nothing, then, either to the living or to the dead, for with the living it is not and the dead exist no longer. But in the world, at one time men shun death as the greatest of all evils, and at another time choose it as a respite from the evils in life. The wise man does not deprecate life nor does he fear the cessation of life. The thought of life is no offence to him, nor is the cessation of life regarded as an evil. And even as men choose of food not merely and simply the larger portion, but the more pleasant, so the wise seek to enjoy the time which is most pleasant and not merely that which is longest. And he who admonishes the young to live well and the old to make a good end speaks foolishly, not merely because of the desirableness of life, but because the same exercise at once teaches to live well and to die well. Much worse is he who says that it were good not to be born, but when once one is born to pass with all speed through the gates of Hades. For if he truly believes this, why does he not depart from life? It were easy for him to do so, if once he were firmly convinced. If he speaks only in mockery, his words are foolishness, for those who hear believe him not.

We must remember that the future is neither wholly ours nor wholly not ours, so that neither must we count upon it as quite certain to come nor despair of it as quite certain not to come.

We must also reflect that of desires some are natural, others are groundless; and that of the natural some are necessary as well as natural, and some natural only. And of the necessary desires some are necessary if we are to be happy, some if the body is to be rid of uneasiness, some if we are even to live. He who has a clear and certain understanding of these things will direct every preference and aversion toward securing health of body and tranquillity of mind, seeing that this is the sum and end of a blessed life. For the end of all our actions is to be free from pain and fear, and, when once we have attained all this, the tempest of the soul is laid; seeing that the living creature has no need to go in search of something that is lacking, nor to look for anything else by which the good of the soul and of the body will be fulfilled. When we are pained because of the absence of pleasure, then, and then only, do we feel the need of pleasure. Wherefore we call pleasure the alpha and omega of a blessed life. Pleasure is our first and kindred good. It is the starting-point of every choice and of every aversion, and to it we come back, inasmuch as we make feeling the rule by which to judge of every good thing. And since pleasure is our first and native good, for that reason we do not choose every pleasure whatsoever, but ofttimes pass over many pleasures when a greater annoyance ensues from them. And ofttimes we consider pains superior to pleasures when submission to the pains for a long time brings us as a consequence a greater pleasure. While therefore all pleasure because it is naturally akin to us is good, not all pleasure is choiceworthy, just as all pain is an evil and yet not all pain is to be shunned. It is, however, by measuring one against another, and by looking at the conveniences and inconveniences, that all these matters must be judged. Sometimes we treat the good as an evil, and the evil, on the contrary, as a good. Again, we regard independence of outward things as a great good, not so as in all cases to use little, but so as to be contented with little if we have not much, being honestly persuaded that they have the sweetest enjoyment of luxury who stand least in need of it, and that whatever is natural is easily procured and only the vain and worthless hard to win. Plain fare gives as much pleasure as a costly diet, when once the pain of want has been removed, while bread and water confer the highest possible pleasure when they are brought to hungry lips. To habituate one's self, therefore, to simple and inexpensive diet supplies all that is needful for health, and enables a man to meet the necessary requirements of life without shrinking, and it places us in a better condition when we approach at intervals a costly fare and renders us fearless of fortune.

When we say, then, that pleasure is the end and aim, we do not mean the pleasure of the prodigal or the pleasures of sensuality, as we are understood to do by some through ignorance, prejudice, or wilful misrepresentation. By pleasure we mean the absence of pain in the body and of trouble in the soul. It is not an unbroken succession of drinking-bouts and of revelry, not sexual love, not the enjoyment of the fish and other delicacies of a luxurious table, which produce a pleasant life; it is sober reasoning, searching out the grounds of every choice and avoidance, and banishing those beliefs through which the greatest tumults take possession of the soul. Of all this the beginning and the greatest good is prudence. Wherefore prudence is a more precious thing even than philosophy; from it spring all the other virtues, for it teaches that we cannot lead a life of pleasure which is not also a life of prudence, honour, and justice; nor lead a life of prudence, honour, and justice, which is not also a life of pleasure. For the virtues have grown into one with a pleasant life, and a pleasant life is inseparable from them.

Who, then, is superior in thy judgement to such a man? He holds a holy belief concerning the gods, and is altogether free from the fear of death. He has diligently considered the end fixed by nature, and understands how easily the limit of good things can be reached and attained, and how either the duration or the intensity of evils is but slight. Destiny, which some introduce as sovereign over all things, he laughs to scorn, affirming rather that some things happen of necessity, others by chance, others through our own agency. For he sees that necessity destroys responsibility and that chance or fortune is inconstant; whereas our own actions are free, and it is to them that praise and blame naturally attach. It were better, indeed, to accept the legends of the gods than to bow beneath that yoke of destiny which the natural philosophers have imposed. The one holds out some faint hope that we may escape if we honour the gods, while the necessity of the naturalists is deaf to all entreaties. Nor does he hold chance to be a god, as the world in general does, for in the acts of a god there is no disorder; nor to be a cause, though an uncertain one, for he believes that no good or evil is dispensed by chance to men so as to make life blessed, though it supplies the starting-point of great good and great evil. He believes that the misfortune of the wise is better than the prosperity of the fool. It is better, in short, that what is well judged in action should not owe its successful issue to the aid of chance.

Exercise thyself in these and kindred precepts day and night, both by thyself and with him who is like unto thee; then never, either in waking or in dream, wilt thou be disturbed, but wilt live as a god among men. For man loses all semblance of mortality by living in the midst of immortal blessings.

Epictetus

The dates of Epictetus' birth and death are unknown, but a reasonable
guess would place his life between approximately 50 and 130 A.D. He
was a slave of Epaphroditus, an influential freedman of the Emperor
Nero. Presumably Epictetus' intelligence impressed his master, who,
for whatever motive, had him educated, sending him to the lectures of
Musonius Rufus, the most celebrated Stoic philosopher of the day. (Nothing that we learn of Epaphroditus suggests that he had any leanings toward Stoicism himself.) At some date unknown to us Epictetus must have
been given his freedom, and he began to teach in Rome. In 89 A.D.
Domitian expelled all philosophers from Rome. Epictetus moved his
school to Nicopolis, a city on the east coast of the Adriatic, founded by
Augustus to commemorate his victory at Actium. He taught there for the
rest of his life.

Epictetus apparently produced no philosophical writings of his own. It
is to his pupil Arrian, who later wrote a history of Alexander the Great,
that we owe the extant *Discourses*, which give a lively presentation not
merely of the matter but also the manner of Epictetus' classroom teaching. The *Encheiridion*—the word means both "handbook" and "dagger"
and might have connotations of defense against the buffets of life—is an
epitome drawn from the *Discourses*. It was written some three hundred
fifty years after the latest of the other documents printed in this volume.
It is placed here for several reasons. Though Stoicism had existed for
about three hundred fifty years, and many Stoics, some of them very
prolific writers, had written works of philosophy during that time, their
treatises have come down to us only in fragments. The works of two
other Stoic thinkers of the Empire, the younger Seneca and the Emperor
Marcus Aurelius, survive; but their writings do not contain as succinct a
presentation of Stoic ethical doctrines as is furnished by the *Encheiridion*.

The question of the relationship between the ethical doctrines of Epictetus and those of Zeno of Citium, the founder of Stoicism, is too large to discuss here. Epictetus is certainly more quietist than Zeno, for he attempts to deter his pupils from taking part in public life, while Zeno is reputed to have taken no part in public life himself but to have encouraged his pupils to do so. However, the values expressed in the *Encheiridion*, particularly in its earlier chapters, can readily be pressed into service by those leading an active public life, and they will suffice to convey an idea of the values and attitudes of politically active Greeks and Romans who, while not themselves creative philosophers, sought in Stoicism a world view that would enable them to withstand the buffets of a dangerous and baffling world.

20. Epictetus, *Encheiridion*

1. Some things are under our control, while others are not under our control. Under our control are conception, choice, desire, aversion, and, in a word, everything that is our own doing; not under our control are our body, our property, reputation, office, and, in a word, everything that is not our own doing. Furthermore, the things under our control are by nature free, unhindered, and unimpeded; while the things not under our control are weak, servile, subject to hindrance, and not our own. Remember, therefore, that if what is naturally slavish you think to be free, and what is not your own to be your own, you will be hampered, will grieve, will be in turmoil, and will blame both gods and men; while if you think only what is your own to be your own, and what is not your own to be, as it really is, not your own, then no one will ever be able to exert compulsion upon you, no one will hinder you, you will blame no one, will find fault with no one, will do absolutely nothing against your will, you will have no personal enemy, no one will harm you, for neither is there any harm that can touch you.

With such high aims, therefore, remember that you must bestir yourself with no slight effort to lay hold of them, but you will have to give up some things entirely, and defer others for the time being. But if you wish for these things also, and at the same time for both office and wealth, it may be that you will not get even these latter, because you aim also at the former, and certainly you will fail to get the former, which alone bring freedom and happiness.

Make it, therefore, your study at the very outset to say to every harsh

Reprinted by permission of the publishers and the Loeb Classical Library from *Epictetus*, volume 2. Translated by W. A. Oldfather. Cambridge, Mass.: Harvard University Press, 1928.

external impression, "You are an external impression and not at all what you appear to be." After that examine it and test it by these rules which you have, the first and most important of which is this: whether the impression has to do with the things which are under our control, or with those which are not under our control, and, if it has to do with some one of the things not under our control, have ready to hand the answer, "It is nothing to me."

2. Remember that the promise of desire is the attainment of what you desire, that of aversion is not to fall into what is avoided, and that he who fails in his desire is unfortunate, while he who falls into what he would avoid experiences misfortune. If, then, you avoid only what is unnatural among those things which are under your control, you will fall into none of the things which you avoid; but if you try to avoid disease, or death, or poverty, you will experience misfortune. Withdraw, therefore, your aversion from all the matters that are not under our control, and transfer it to what is unnatural among those which are under our control. But for the time being[1] remove utterly your desire; for if you desire some one of the things that are not under our control you are bound to be unfortunate; and, at the same time, not one of the things that are under our control, which it would be excellent for you to desire, is within your grasp. But employ only choice and refusal and these too but lightly, and with reservations, and without straining.

3. With everything which entertains you, is useful, or of which you are fond, remember to say to yourself, beginning with the very least things, "What is its nature?" If you are fond of a jug, say, "I am fond of a jug"; for when it is broken you will not be disturbed. If you kiss your own child or wife, say to yourself that you are kissing a human being; for when it dies you will not be disturbed.

4. When you are on the point of putting your hand to some undertaking, remind yourself what the nature of that undertaking is. If you are going out of the house to bathe, put before your mind what happens at a public bath—those who splash you with water, those who jostle against you, those who vilify you and rob you. And thus you will set about your undertaking more securely if at the outset you say to yourself, "I want to take a bath, and, at the same time, to keep my moral purpose in harmony with nature." And so do in every undertaking. For thus, if anything happens to hinder you in your bathing, you will be ready to say, "Oh, well, this was not the only thing that I wanted, but I wanted also to keep my moral purpose in harmony with nature; and I shall not so keep it if I am vexed at what is going on."

---

1. The remark, like many others of the admonitions, is addressed to a student or a beginner.

5.   It is not the things themselves that disturb men, but their judgements about these things. For example, death is nothing dreadful, or else Socrates too would have thought so, but the judgement that death is dreadful, this is the dreadful thing. When, therefore, we are hindered, or disturbed, or grieved, let us never blame anyone but ourselves, that means, our own judgements. It is the part of an uneducated person to blame others where he himself fares ill; to blame himself is the part of one whose education has begun; to blame neither another nor his own self is the part of one whose education is already complete.

6.   Be not elated at any excellence which is not your own. If the horse in his elation were to say, "I am beautiful," it could be endured; but when you say in your elation, "I have a beautiful horse," rest assured that you are elated at something good which belongs to a horse. What, then, is your own? The use of external impressions. Therefore, when you are in harmony with nature in the use of external impressions, then be elated; for then it will be some good of your own at which you will be elated.

7.   Just as on a voyage, when your ship has anchored, if you should go on shore to get fresh water, you may pick up a small shell-fish or little [edible] bulb on the way, but you have to keep your attention fixed on the ship, and turn about frequently for fear lest the captain should call; and if he calls, you must give up all these things if you would escape being thrown on board all tied up like the sheep. So it is also in life: If there be given you, instead of a little bulb and a small shell-fish, a little wife and child, there will be no objection to that; only, if the Captain calls, give up all these things and run to the ship, without even turning around to look back. And if you are an old man, never even get very far away from the ship, for fear that when He calls you may be missing.

8.   Do not seek to have everything that happens happen as you wish, but wish for everything to happen as it actually does happen, and your life will be serene.

9.   Disease is an impediment to the body, but not to the moral purpose, unless that consents. Lameness is an impediment to the leg, but not to the moral purpose. And say this to yourself at each thing that befalls you; for you will find the thing to be an impediment to something else, but not to yourself.

10.   In the case of everything that befalls you, remember to turn to yourself and see what faculty you have to deal with it. If you see a handsome lad or woman, you will find continence the faculty to employ here; if hard labour is laid upon you, you will find endurance; if reviling, you will find patience to bear evil. And if you habituate yourself in this fashion, your external impressions will not run away with you.

11.   Never say about anything, "I have lost it," but only "I have given

it back." Is your child dead? It has been given back. Is your wife dead? She has been given back. "I have had my farm taken away." Very well, this too has been given back. "Yet it was a rascal who took it away." But what concern is it of yours by whose instrumentality the Giver called for its return? So long as He gives it you, take care of it as of a thing that is not your own, as travellers treat their inn.

12. If you wish to make progress, dismiss all reasoning of this sort: "If I neglect my affairs, I shall have nothing to live on." "If I do not punish my slave-boy, he will turn out bad." For it is better to die of hunger, but in a state of freedom from grief and fear, than to live in plenty, but troubled in mind. And it is better for your slave-boy to be bad than for you to be unhappy. Begin, therefore, with the little things. Your paltry oil gets spilled, your miserable wine stolen; say to yourself, "This is the price paid for a calm spirit, this the price for peace of mind." Nothing is got without a price. And when you call your slave-boy, bear in mind that it is possible he may not heed you, and again, that even if he does heed, he may not do what you want done. But he is not in so happy a condition that your peace of mind depends upon him.[2]

13. If you wish to make progress, then be content to appear senseless and foolish in externals, do not make it your wish to give the appearance of knowing anything; and if some people think you to be an important personage, distrust yourself. For be assured that it is no easy matter to keep your moral purpose in a state of conformity with nature, and, at the same time, to keep externals; but the man who devotes his attention to one of these two things must inevitably neglect the other.

14. If you make it your will that your children and your wife and your friends should live for ever, you are silly; for you are making it your will that things not under your control should be under your control and that what is not your own should be your own. In the same way, too, if you make it your will that your slave-boy be free from faults, you are a fool; for you are making it your will that vice be not vice, but something else. If, however, it is your will not to fail in what you desire, this is in your power. Wherefore, exercise yourself in that which is in your power. Each man's master is the person who has the authority over what the man wishes or does not wish, so as to secure it, or take it away. Whoever, therefore, wants to be free, let him neither wish for anything, nor avoid anything, that is under the control of others; or else he is necessarily a slave.

15. Remember that you ought to behave in life as you would at a banquet. As something is being passed around it comes to you; stretch out your

---

2. That is, the slave-boy would be in a remarkable position of advantage if his master's peace of mind depended, not upon the master himself, but upon the actions of his slave-boy.

hand and take a portion of it politely. It passes on; do not detain it. Or it has not come to you yet; do not project your desire, to meet it, but wait until it comes in front of you. So act toward children, so toward a wife, so toward office, so toward wealth; and then some day you will be worthy of the banquets of the gods. But if you do not take these things even when they are set before you but despise them, then you will not only share the banquet of the gods, but share also their rule. For it was by so doing that Diogenes and Heracleitus, and men like them, were deservedly divine and deservedly so called.

16.   When you see someone weeping in sorrow, either because a child has gone on a journey, or because he has lost his property, beware that you be not carried away by the impression that the man is in the midst of external ills, but straightway keep before you this thought: "It is not what has happened that distresses this man (for it does not distress another), but his judgement about it." Do not, however, hesitate to sympathize with him so far as words go, and, if occasion offers, even to groan with him; but be careful not to groan also in the centre of your being.

17.   Remember that you are an actor in a play, the character of which is determined by the Playwright: if He wishes the play to be short, it is short; if long, it is long; if He wishes you to play the part of a beggar, remember to act even this role adroitly; and so if your role be that of a cripple, an official, or a layman. For this is your business, to play admirably the role assigned you; but the selection of that role is Another's.

18.   When a raven croaks inauspiciously, let not the external impression carry you away, but straightway draw a distinction in your own mind, and say, "None of these portents are for me, but either for my paltry body, or my paltry estate, or my paltry opinion, or my children, or my wife. But for me every portent is favourable, if I so wish; for whatever be the outcome, it is within my power to derive benefit from it."

19.   You can be invincible if you never enter a contest in which victory is not under your control. Beware lest, when you see some person preferred to you in honour, or possessing great power, or otherwise enjoying high repute, you are ever carried away by the external impression, and deem him happy. For if the true nature of the good is one of the things that are under our control, there is no place for either envy or jealousy; and you yourself will not wish to be a praetor, or a senator, or a consul, but a free man. Now there is but one way that leads to this, and that is to despise the things that are not under our control.

20.   Bear in mind that it is not the man who reviles or strikes you that insults you, but it is your judgement that these men are insulting you. Therefore, when someone irritates you, be assured that it is your own opinion which has irritated you. And so make it your first endeavour not to be

carried away by the external impression; for if once you gain time and delay, you will more easily become master of yourself.

21.   Keep before your eyes day by day death and exile, and everything that seems terrible, but most of all death; and then you will never have any abject thought, nor will you yearn for anything beyond measure.

22.   If you yearn for philosophy, prepare at once to be met with ridicule, to have many people jeer at you, and say, "Here he is again, turned philosopher all of a sudden," and "Where do you suppose he got that high brow?" But do you not put on a high brow, and do you so hold fast to the things which to you seem best, as a man who has been assigned by God to this post; and remember that if you abide by the same principles, those who formerly used to laugh at you will later come to admire you, but if you are worsted by them, you will get the laugh on yourself twice.

23.   If it should ever happen to you that you turn to externals with a view to pleasing someone, rest assured that you have lost your plan of life. Be content, therefore, in everything to *be* a philosopher, and if you wish also to be taken for one, show to yourself that you are one, and you will be able to accomplish it.

24.   Let not these reflections oppress you: "I shall live without honour, and be nobody anywhere." For, if lack of honour is an evil, you cannot be in evil through the instrumentality of some other person, any more than you can be in shame.[3] It is not your business, is it, to get office, or to be invited to a dinner-party? Certainly not. How, then, can this be any longer a lack of honour? And how is it that you will be "nobody anywhere," when you ought to be somebody only in those things which are under your control, wherein you are privileged to be a man of the very greatest honour? But your friends will be without assistance? What do you mean by being "without assistance"? They will not have paltry coin from you, and you will not make them Roman citizens. Well, who told you that these are some of the matters under our control, and not rather things which others do? And who is able to give another what he does not himself have? "Get money, then," says some friend, "in order that we too may have it." If I can get money and at the same time keep myself self-respecting, and faithful, and high-minded, show me the way and I will get it. But if you require me to lose the good things that belong to me, in order that you may acquire the things that are not good, you can see for yourselves how unfair and inconsiderate you are. And which do you really prefer? Money, or a faithful and

---

3. That is, every man is exclusively responsible for his own good or evil. But honour and the lack of it are things which are obviously not under a man's control, since they depend upon the action of other people. It follows, therefore, that lack of honour cannot be an evil, but must be something indifferent.

self-respecting friend? Help me, therefore, rather to this end, and do not require me to do those things which will make me lose these qualities.

"But my country," says he, "so far as lies in me, will be without assistance." Again I ask, what kind of assistance do you mean? It will not have loggias or baths of your providing. And what does that signify? For neither does it have shoes provided by the blacksmith, nor has it arms provided by the cobbler; but it is sufficient if each man fulfil his own proper function. And if you secured for it another faithful and self-respecting citizen, would you not be doing it any good? "Yes." Very well, and then you also would not be useless to it. "What place, then, shall I have in the State?" says he. Whatever place you can have, and at the same time maintain the man of fidelity and self-respect that is in you. But if, through your desire to help the State, you lose these qualities, of what good would you become to it, when in the end you turned out to be shameless and unfaithful?

25.   Has someone been honoured above you at a dinner-party, or in salutation, or in being called in to give advice? Now if these matters are good, you ought to be happy that he got them; but if evil, be not distressed because you did not get them; and bear in mind that, if you do not act the same way that others do, with a view to getting things which are not under our control, you cannot be considered worthy to receive an equal share with others. Why, how is it possible for a person who does not haunt some man's door, to have equal shares with the man who does? For the man who does not do escort duty, with the man who does? For the man who does not praise, with the man who does? You will be unjust, therefore, and insatiable, if, while refusing to pay the price for which such things are bought, you want to obtain them for nothing. Well, what is the price for heads of lettuce? An obol, perhaps. If, then, somebody gives up his obol and gets his heads of lettuce, while you do not give your obol, and do not get them, do not imagine that you are worse off than the man who gets his lettuce. For as he has his heads of lettuce, so you have your obol, which you have not given away.

Now it is the same way also in life. You have not been invited to somebody's dinner-party? Of course not; for you didn't give the host the price at which he sells his dinner. He sells it for praise; he sells it for personal attention. Give him the price, then, for which it is sold, if it is to your interest. But if you wish both not to give up the one and yet to get the other, you are insatiable and a simpleton. Have you, then, nothing in place of the dinner? Indeed you have; you have not had to praise the man you did not want to praise; you have not had to put up with the insolence of his doorkeepers.

26.   What the will of nature is may be learned from a consideration of the points in which we do not differ from one another. For example, when some other person's slave-boy breaks his drinking-cup, you are instantly ready to say, "That's one of the things which happen." Rest assured, then,

that when your own drinking-cup gets broken, you ought to behave in the same way that you do when the other man's cup is broken. Apply now the same principle to the matters of greater importance. Some other person's child or wife has died; no one but would say, "Such is the fate of man." Yet when a man's own child dies, immediately the cry is, "Alas! Woe is me!" But we ought to remember how we feel when we hear of the same misfortune befalling others.

27.   Just as a mark is not set up in order to be missed, so neither does the nature of evil arise in the universe.[4]

28.   If someone handed over your body to any person who met you, you would be vexed; but that you hand over your mind to any person that comes along, so that, if he reviles you, it is disturbed and troubled—are you not ashamed of that?

29.   In each separate thing that you do, consider the matters which come first and those which follow after, and only then approach the thing itself. Otherwise, at the start you will come to it enthusiastically, because you have never reflected upon any of the subsequent steps, but later on, when some difficulties appear, you will give up disgracefully. Do you wish to win an Olympic victory? So do I, by the gods! for it is a fine thing. But consider the matters which come before that, and those which follow after, and only when you have done that, put your hand to the task. You have to submit to discipline, follow a strict diet, give up sweet cakes, train under compulsion, at a fixed hour, in heat or in cold; you must not drink cold water, nor wine just whenever you feel like it; you must have turned yourself over to your trainer precisely as you would to a physician. Then when the contest comes on, you have to "dig in" beside your opponent, and sometimes dislocate your wrist, sprain your ankle, swallow quantities of sand, sometimes take a scourging, and along with all that get beaten. After you have considered all these points, go on into the games, if you still wish to do so; otherwise, you will be turning back like children. Sometimes they play wrestlers, again gladiators, again they blow trumpets, and then act a play. So you too are now an athlete, now a gladiator, then a rhetorician, then a philosopher, yet with your whole soul nothing; but like an ape you imitate whatever you see, and one thing after another strikes your fancy. For you have never gone out after anything with circumspection, nor after you had examined it all over, but you act at haphazard and half-heartedly.

In the same way, when some people have seen a philosopher and have heard someone speaking like Euphrates (though, indeed, who can speak like him?), they wish to be philosophers themselves. Man, consider first the nature of the business, and then learn your own natural ability, if you

---

4. That is, it is inconceivable that the universe should exist in order that some things may go wrong; hence, nothing natural is evil, and nothing that is by nature evil can arise.

are able to bear it. Do you wish to be a contender in the pentathlon, or a wrestler? Look to your arms, your thighs, see what your loins are like. For one man has a natural talent for one thing, another for another. Do you suppose that you can eat in the same fashion, drink in the same fashion, give way to anger and to irritation, just as you do now? You must keep vigils, work hard, abandon your own people, be despised by a paltry slave, be laughed to scorn by those who meet you, in everything get the worst of it, in honour, in office, in court, in every paltry affair. Look these drawbacks over carefully, if you are willing at the price of these things to secure tranquillity, freedom, and calm. Otherwise, do not approach philosophy; don't act like a child—now a philosopher, later on a tax-gatherer, then a rhetorician, then a procurator of Caesar. These things do not go together. You must be one person, either good or bad; you must labour to improve either your own governing principle or externals; you must work hard either on the inner man, or on things outside; that is, play either the role of a philosopher or else that of a layman.

30.   Our duties are in general measured by our social relationships. He is a father. One is called upon to take care of him, to give way to him in all things, to submit when he reviles or strikes you. "But he is a bad father." Did nature, then, bring you into relationship with a good father? No, but simply with a father. "My brother does me wrong." Very well, then, maintain the relation that you have toward him; and do not consider what he is doing, but what you will have to do, if your moral purpose is to be in harmony with nature. For no one will harm you without your consent; you will have been harmed only when you think you are harmed. In this way, therefore, you will discover what duty to expect of your neighbour, your citizen, your commanding officer, if you acquire the habit of looking at your social relations with them.

31.   In piety towards the gods, I would have you know, the chief element is this, to have right opinions about them—as existing and as administering the universe well and justly—and to have set yourself to obey them and to submit to everything that happens, and to follow it voluntarily, in the belief that it is being fulfilled by the highest intelligence. For if you act in this way, you will never blame the gods, nor find fault with them for neglecting you. But this result cannot be secured in any other way than by withdrawing your idea of the good and the evil from the things which are not under our control, and in those alone. Because, if you think any of those former things to be good or evil, then, when you fail to get what you want and fall into what you do not want, it is altogether inevitable that you will blame and hate those who are responsible for these results. For this is the nature of every living creature, to flee from and to turn aside from the things that appear harmful, and all that produces them, and to pursue after and to admire the things that are helpful, and all that produces them.

Therefore, it is impossible for a man who thinks that he is being hurt to take pleasure in that which he thinks is hurting him, just as it is also impossible for him to take pleasure in the hurt itself. Hence it follows that even a father is reviled by a son when he does not give his child some share in the things that seem to be good; and this it was which made Polyneices and Eteocles enemies of one another, the thought that the royal power was a good thing. That is why the farmer reviles the gods, and so also the sailor, and the merchant, and those who have lost their wives and their children. For where a man's interest lies, there is also his piety. Wherefore, whoever is careful to exercise desire and aversion as he should, is at the same time careful also about piety. But it is always appropriate to make libations, and sacrifices, and to give of the firstfruits after the manner of our fathers, and to do all this with purity, and not in a slovenly or careless fashion, nor, indeed, in a niggardly way, nor yet beyond our means.

32.   When you have recourse to divination, remember that you do not know what the issue is going to be but that you have come in order to find this out from the diviner; yet if you are indeed a philosopher, you know, when you arrive, what the nature of it is. For if it is one of the things which are not under our control, it is altogether necessary that what is going to take place is neither good nor evil. Do not, therefore, bring to the diviner desire or aversion, and do not approach him with trembling, but having first made up your mind that every issue is indifferent and nothing to you, but that, whatever it may be, it will be possible for you to turn it to good use, and that no one will prevent this. Go, then, with confidence to the gods as counsellors; and after that, when some counsel has been given you, remember whom you have taken as counsellors, and whom you will be disregarding if you disobey. But go to divination as Socrates thought that men should go, that is, in cases where the whole inquiry has reference to the outcome and where neither from reason nor from any other technical art are means vouchsafed for discovering the matter in question. Hence, when it is your duty to share the danger of a friend or of your country, do not ask of the diviner whether you ought to share that danger. For if the diviner forewarns you that the omens of sacrifice have been unfavourable, it is clear that death is portended, or the injury of some member of your body, or exile; yet reason requires that even at this risk you are to stand by your friend, and share the danger with your country. Wherefore, give heed to the greater diviner, the Pythian Apollo, who cast out of his temple the man who had not helped his friend when he was being murdered.[5]

5. The point of the story is that a man does not need to go to a diviner in order to learn whether he should defend his country or his friends. That question was long ago settled by the greatest of diviners, Apollo at Delphi, who ordered to be cast out of his temple an inquirer that had once failed to defend his own friend.

33.   Lay down for yourself, at the outset, a certain stamp and type of character for yourself, which you are to maintain whether you are by yourself or are meeting with people. And be silent for the most part, or else make only the most necessary remarks, and express these in few words. But rarely, and when occasion requires you to talk, talk, indeed, but about no ordinary topics. Do not talk about gladiators, or horse races or athletes, or things to eat or drink—topics that arise on all occasions; but above all, do not talk about people, either blaming, or praising, or comparing them. If, then, you can, by your own conversation bring over that of your companions to what is seemly. But if you happen to be left alone in the presence of aliens, keep silence.

Do not laugh much, nor at many things, nor boisterously.

Refuse, if you can, to take an oath at all, but if that is impossible, refuse as far as circumstance allows.

Avoid entertainments given by outsiders and by persons ignorant of philosophy; but if an appropriate occasion arises for you to attend, be on the alert to avoid lapsing into the behaviour of such laymen. For you may rest assured, that, if a man's companion be dirty, the person who keeps close company with him must of necessity get a share of his dirt, even though he himself happens to be clean.

In things that pertain to the body take only as much as your bare need requires, I mean such things as food, drink, clothing, shelter, and household slaves; but cut down everything which is for outward show or luxury.

In your sex-life preserve purity, as far as you can, before marriage, and, if you indulge, take only those privileges which are lawful. However, do not make yourself offensive, or censorious, to those who do indulge, and do not make frequent mention of the fact that you do not yourself indulge.

If someone brings you word that So-and-so is speaking ill of you, do not defend yourself against what has been said, but answer "Yes, indeed, for he did not know the rest of the faults that attach to me; if he had, these would not have been the only ones he mentioned."

It is not necessary, for the most part, to go to the public shows. If, however, a suitable occasion ever arises, show that your principal concern is for none other than yourself, which means, wish only for that to happen which does happen, and for him only to win who does win; for so you will suffer no hindrance. But refrain utterly from shouting, or laughter at anyone, or great excitement. And after you have left, do not talk a great deal about what took place, except in so far as it contributes to your own improvement; for such behaviour indicates that the spectacle has aroused your admiration.

Do not go rashly or readily to people's public readings, but when you do go, maintain your own dignity and gravity, and at the same time be careful not to make yourself disagreeable.

When you are about to meet somebody, in particular when it is one of those men who are held in very high esteem, propose to yourself the question, "What would Socrates or Zeno have done under these circumstances?" and then you will not be at a loss to make proper use of the occasion. When you go to see one of those men who have great power, propose to yourself the thought, that you will not find him at home, that you will be shut out, that the door will be slammed in your face, that he will pay no attention to you. And if, despite all this, it is your duty to go, go and take what comes, and never say to yourself, "It was not worth all the trouble." For this is characteristic of the layman, that is, a man who is vexed at externals.

In your conversation avoid making mention at great length and excessively of your own deeds or dangers, because it is not as pleasant for others to hear about your adventures, as it is for you to call to mind your own dangers.

Avoid also raising a laugh, for this is a kind of behaviour that slips easily into vulgarity, and at the same time is calculated to lessen the respect which your neighbours have of you. It is dangerous also to lapse into foul language. When, therefore, anything of the sort occurs, if the occasion be suitable, go even so far as to reprove the person who has made such a lapse; if, however, the occasion does not arise, at all events show by keeping silence, and blushing, and frowning, that you are displeased by what has been said.

34. When you get an external impression of some pleasure, guard yourself, as with impressions in general, against being carried away by it; nay, let the matter wait upon *your* leisure, and give yourself a little delay. Next think of the two periods of time, first, that in which you will enjoy your pleasure, and second, that in which, after the enjoyment is over, you will later repent and revile your own self; and set over against these two periods of time how much joy and self-satisfaction you will get if you refrain. However, if you feel that a suitable occasion has arisen to do the deed, be careful not to allow its enticement, and sweetness, and attractiveness to overcome you; but set over against all this the thought, how much better is the consciousness of having won a victory over it.

35. When you do a thing which you have made up your mind ought to be done, never try not to be seen doing it, even though most people are likely to think unfavourably about it. If, however, what you are doing is not right, avoid the deed itself altogether; but if it is right, why fear those who are going to rebuke you wrongly?

36. Just as the propositions, "It is day," and "It is night," are full of meaning when separated, but meaningless if united; so also, granted that for you to take the larger share at a dinner is good for your body, still, it is bad for the maintenance of the proper kind of social feeling. When, there-

fore, you are eating with another person, remember to regard, not merely the value for your body of what lies before you, but also to maintain your respect for your host.

37.   If you undertake a role which is beyond your powers, you both disgrace yourself in that one, and at the same time neglect the role which you might have filled with success.

38.   Just as you are careful, in walking about, not to step on a nail or to sprain your ankle, so be careful also not to hurt your governing principle. And if we observe this rule in every action, we shall be more secure in setting about it.

39.   Each man's body is a measure for his property,[6] just as the foot is a measure for his shoe. If, then, you abide by this principle, you will maintain the proper measure, but if you go beyond it, you cannot help but fall headlong over a precipice, as it were, in the end. So also in the case of your shoe; if once you go beyond the foot, you get first a gilded shoe, then a purple one, then an embroidered one. For once you go beyond the measure there is no limit.

40.   Immediately after they are fourteen, women are called "ladies" by men. And so when they see that they have nothing else but only to be the bed-fellows of men, they begin to beautify themselves, and put all their hopes in that. It is worth while for us to take pains, therefore, to make them understand that they are honoured for nothing else but only for appearing modest and self-respecting.

41.   It is a mark of an ungifted man to spend a great deal of time in what concerns his body, as in much exercise, much eating, much drinking, much evacuating of the bowels, much copulating. But these things are to be done in passing; and let your whole attention be devoted to the mind.

42.   When someone treats you ill or speaks ill of you, remember that he acts or speaks thus because he thinks it is incumbent upon him. That being the case, it is impossible for him to follow what appears good to you, but what appears good to himself; whence it follows, that, if he gets a wrong view of things, the man that suffers is the man that has been deceived. For if a person thinks a composite judgement to be false, the composite judgement does not suffer, but the person who has been deceived. If, therefore, you start from this point of view, you will be gentle with the man who reviles you. For you should say on each occasion, "He thought that way about it."

43.   Everything has two handles, by one of which it ought to be carried and by the other not. If your brother wrongs you, do not lay hold of the

6. That is, property, which is of use only for the body, should be adjusted to a man's actual bodily needs, just as a shoe is (or at least should be) adjusted to the actual needs of a man's foot.

matter by the handle of the wrong that he is doing, because this is the handle by which the matter ought not to be carried; but rather by the other handle—that he is your brother, that you were brought up together, and then you will be laying hold of the matter by the handle by which it ought to be carried.

44. The following statements constitute a *non sequitur*: "I am richer than you are, therefore I am superior to you"; or, "I am more eloquent than you are, therefore I am superior to you." But the following conclusions are better: "I am richer than you are, therefore my property is superior to yours"; or, "I am more eloquent than you are, therefore my elocution is superior to yours." But you are neither property nor elocution.

45. Somebody is hasty about bathing; do not say that he bathes badly, but that he is hasty about bathing. Somebody drinks a good deal of wine; do not say that he drinks badly, but that he drinks a good deal. For until you have decided what judgement prompts him, how do you know that what he is doing is bad? And thus the final result will not be that you receive convincing sense-impressions of some things, but give your assent to others.

46. On no occasion call yourself a philosopher, and do not, for the most part, talk among laymen about your philosophic principles, but do what follows from your principles. For example, at a banquet do not say how people ought to eat, but eat as a man ought. For remember how Socrates had so completely eliminated the thought of ostentation, that people came to him when they wanted him to introduce them to philosophers, and he used to bring them along. So well did he submit to being overlooked. And if talk about some philosophic principle arises among laymen, keep silence for the most part, for there is great danger that you will spew up immediately what you have not digested. So when a man tells you that you know nothing, and you, like Socrates, are not hurt, then rest assured that you are making a beginning with the business you have undertaken. For sheep, too, do not bring their fodder to the shepherds and show how much they have eaten, but they digest their food within them, and on the outside produce wool and milk. And so do you, therefore, make no display to the laymen of your philosophical principles, but let them see the results which come from these principles when digested.

47. When you have become adjusted to simple living in regard to your bodily wants, do not preen yourself about the accomplishment; and so likewise, if you are a water-drinker, do not on every occasion say that you are a water-drinker. And if ever you want to train to develop physical endurance, do it by yourself and not for outsiders to behold; do not throw your arms around statues, but on occasion, when you are very thirsty, take cold water into your mouth, and then spit it out, without telling anybody.

48. This is the position and character of a layman: He never looks for either help or harm from himself, but only from externals. This is the posi-

tion and character of the philosopher: He looks for all his help or harm from himself.

Signs of one who is making progress are: He censures no one, praises no one, blames no one, finds fault with no one, says nothing about himself as though he were somebody or knew something. When he is hampered or prevented, he blames himself. And if anyone compliments him, he smiles to himself at the person complimenting; while if anyone censures him, he makes no defence. He goes about like an invalid, being careful not to disturb, before it has grown firm, any part which is getting well. He has put away from himself his every desire, and has transferred his aversion to those things only, of what is under our control, which are contrary to nature. He exercises no pronounced choice in regard to anything. If he gives the appearance of being foolish or ignorant, he does not care. In a word, he keeps guard against himself as though he were his own enemy lying in wait.

49.   When a person gives himself airs because he can understand and interpret the books of Chrysippus, say to yourself, "If Chrysippus had not written obscurely, this man would have nothing about which to give himself airs."

But what is it I want? To learn nature and to follow her. I seek, therefore, someone to interpret her; and having heard that Chrysippus does so, I go to him. But I do not understand what he has written; I seek, therefore, the person who interprets Chrysippus. And down to this point there is nothing to justify pride. But when I find the interpreter, what remains is to put his precepts into practice; this is the only thing to be proud about. If, however, I admire the mere act of interpretation, what have I done but turned into a grammarian instead of a philosopher? The only difference, indeed, is that I interpret Chrysippus instead of Homer. Far from being proud, therefore, when somebody says to me, "Read me Chrysippus," I blush the rather, when I am unable to show him such deeds as match and harmonize with his words.

50.   Whatever principles are set before you, stand fast by these like laws, feeling that it would be impiety for you to transgress them. But pay no attention to what somebody says about you, for this is, at length, not under your control.

51.   How long will you still wait to think yourself worthy of the best things, and in nothing to transgress against the distinctions set up by the reason? You have received the philosophical principles which you ought to accept, and you have accepted them. What sort of a teacher, then, do you still wait for, that you should put off reforming yourself until he arrives? You are no longer a lad, but already a full-grown man. If you are now neglectful and easy-going, and always making one delay after another, and

fixing first one day and then another, after which you will pay attention to yourself, then without realising it you will make no progress, but living and dying, will continue to be a slave throughout. Make up your mind, therefore, before it is too late, that the fitting thing for you to do is to live as a mature man who is making progress, and let everything which seems to you to be best be for you a law that must not be transgressed. And if you meet anything that is laborious, or sweet, or held in high repute, or in no repute, remember that *now* is the contest, and here before you are the Olympic games, and that it is impossible to delay any longer, and that it depends on a single day and a single action, whether progress is lost or saved. This is the way Socrates became what he was, by paying attention to nothing but his reason in everything that he encountered. And even if you are not yet a Socrates, still you ought to live as one who wishes to be a Socrates.

52. The first and most necessary division in philosophy is that which has to do with the application of the principles, as, for example, Do not lie. The second deals with the demonstrations, as, for example, How comes it that we ought not to lie? The third confirms and discriminates between these processes, as, for example, How does it come that this is a proof? For what is a proof, what is logical consequence, what contradiction, what truth, what falsehood? Therefore, the third division is necessary because of the second, and the second because of the first; while the most necessary of all, and the one in which we ought to rest, is the first. But we do the opposite; for we spend our time in the third division, and all our zeal is devoted to it, while we utterly neglect the first. Wherefore, we lie, indeed, but are ready with the arguments which prove that one ought not to lie.

53. Upon every occasion we ought to have the following thoughts at our command:

"Lead thou me on, O Zeus, and Destiny,
To that goal long ago to me assigned.
I'll follow and not falter; if my will
Prove weak and craven, still I'll follow on." [7]

"Whoso has rightly with necessity complied,
We count him wise, and skilled in things divine." [8]

"Well, O Crito, if so it is pleasing to the gods, so let it be." [9]

"Anytus and Meletus can kill me, but they cannot hurt me." [10]

7. From Cleanthes, who succeeded Zeno as head of the Stoic school.
8. Euripides, frag. 965 Nauck.
9. Plato, *Crito*, 43d (slightly modified). See p. 207.
10. Plato, *Apology*, 30c–d (somewhat modified). See p. 196.

Index